A GILDED VAGABOND

A GILDED VAGABOND

Keith Hindell

Book Guild Publishing
Sussex, England

First published in Great Britain in 2012 by
The Book Guild Ltd
Pavilion View
19 New Road
Brighton, BN1 1UF

Typesetting in Garamond by
Keyboard Services, Luton, Bedfordshire

Printed in Great Britain by
CPI Group (UK) Ltd, Croydon, CR0 4YY

A catalogue record for this book is available from
The British Library

ISBN 978 1 84624 692 0

To Jennifer who made much of it possible and Alison and Juliet who joined in much of the fun.

Contents

Acknowledgements

I should like to thank a number of people who have helped in the writing of this memoir:

Two old friends with similar experience, Robert Montgomery and Geoffrey Robinson, read the chapter on Harrow and made helpful comments.

The Harrow Archivist, Rita Gibbs, was very helpful in searching some documents not on general view.

Christopher Tyerman, who also had difficulty finding Harrow documents when writing his *A History of Harrow School*, made some good suggestions that sparked several lines of inquiry.

Dale Vargas, author of *The Timeline History of Harrow School*, kept me from perpetuating a colourful but quite erroneous account of the origins of the Harrow uniform.

Simon Berry, then Housemaster of Moretons, kindly showed me the House Book written each year by the Head of House.

Douglas Stuart, who was at Harrow fifteen years before me, was a good mentor at the BBC, encouraged me to take the correspondent's post at the UN and in his own memoir, *A Very Sheltered Life*, gave me the idea for the title of this one.

Philip Nyman, an Old Boy of Tottenham Grammar School, who maintains a website about this once ancient and proud school (now sadly closed and demolished), gave me some useful leads and corrected an error.

My climbing partner Frank Palmer, with whom I enjoyed some elegant routes, gave me some striking photos from the Lakes and the Valais.

My editor at Book Guild, Joanna Bentley, has been meticulous in her work and has gently guided me away from some of the rocks of publishing.

My photo editor at Book Guild, Kieran Hood, has produced a fine portfolio of plates, some much enhanced from indifferent originals, and has designed a jacket combining Alpinism with international relations, surely a unique first!

But most important of all my wife Jennifer has deployed her expertise in English to improve the style and correct the text all along the way.

Dulwich, January 2012

Prologue

'Happy is he that can look back upon the past with pleasure.'
                                                    Samuel Johnson

On a grey day in July 1947 a fair-haired boy in short trousers walked with his father from Westminster Underground station to the Middlesex County Education Office at 10 Great George Street, opposite the Treasury. They went up the stairs and within a few minutes were shown into a large room to face a selection committee that comprised the Chief Education Officer, T.B. Wheeler and the Headmaster of Harrow, Dr R.W. Moore. After a brief exchange, the headmaster asked a seemingly innocent question.

'Do you play chess?'

'Yes,' said the boy, enthusiastically, 'I belong to the chess club.'

'Well then, can you explain Fool's Mate?'

'Yes,' said the boy with the confidence of one who could understand chess hieroglyphics. 'If your opponent opens in the usual way, Kp to K4, then you put your bishop on one side of the board to cover his King's Bishop's pawn and move your Queen diagonally onto the other side to Q Castle 5. Then on your fourth move you can take his King's Bishop's pawn with your Queen covered by your Bishop. It's check, and if your opponent hasn't taken any precautions, it's checkmate.'

'Indeed it is,' said the headmaster, lugubriously, but with a glint of delight in his eye.

And with that the die was cast. The pale-faced boy, at 4 feet 11 inches, somewhat small for his age, though over age according to the rules, had sparkled in his interview. He was chosen as one of five out of one hundred and forty-two applicants to go to Harrow for five years at the expense of the county. It was intended as an educational and social experiment that would bridge the gap between the private and state school systems. Of course it did nothing so ambitious. But it did change my life.

1

On Thursday 2 November, 2000 my wife Jennifer and I were mugged on our own doorstep, both of us beaten up badly enough to go to hospital by ambulance and I to need a head X-ray. Early next morning as I lay in bed with two black eyes and a pounding headache it occurred to me that I really should begin to write an account of my life before ... whatever. I had mentioned it earlier only to be encouraged by Jennifer. 'Quite right. You've had a very interesting life.' The reader must judge but at the very least my family – my daughters and my grandchildren – will be better informed.

Most of my work as a producer and editor at the BBC was spent bringing people to the microphone to tell their story or express their point of view. Subsequently, as a correspondent I reported on the deliberations, intentions, resolutions and actions of diplomats and statesmen in over 3,000 dispatches from the United Nations. Finally, as a programme presenter I combined the two functions of impresario and reporter, trying to explain new ideas and developments while testing them with probing questions or sceptical remarks. I trust, therefore, it is not too early for me to narrate my own life and explain my own thoughts. I hope that, like the objectives of the BBC itself, my story will inform, educate and sometimes entertain.

Is autobiography simply an exercise in self-assessment and self-regard, what some people call an ego trip? The geneticists reckon that except for identical twins we are all unique, which in theory means that all our histories are in some way singular. In practical terms this stretches the concept of significance quite some way. Most of us in mass societies fit into a number of categories, which we share with many others, sometimes millions of others. I went to a grammar school, a public school and Oxford. None of those categories are rare but I have probably narrowed down my particular envelope very considerably by combining them all in one person. Then if you add the further refinements of having been the youngest boy to climb the Matterhorn, a Colony Champion and an Oxford Blue, the survivor of a lightning strike and chauffeur to an ex-prime minister, not to mention being a director of an abortion charity, it seems unlikely that anyone else has combined all those experiences. That's before I even reveal what my parents were like, what jobs I have done, what other mountains I have climbed and who I have interviewed, all of which must have had some bearing on how I lived my life. Consequently I feel there is sufficient reason to pursue this enterprise beyond the justification of my original excuse of informing my children and grandchildren.

I also feel that having spent over 40 years chronicling other people's lives, deeds and opinions, there is now a need to narrate my own life and contribution to society. I never had a grand position or title but I did influence the way hundreds of thousands of people thought about events as they happened. My influence can be traced through my selection of news to be covered or ideas to be discussed, through the actual people I contacted on several thousand programmes and the questions they were asked, and indeed how thousands of recorded interviews were actually edited. The same kind of selection and editing process went on while I was a correspondent. Some stories were covered specifically at the request of a particular programme but most were covered because I advised the BBC in London that an event or a speech or an idea was 'news'. I did not have a unique job; a few others did similar jobs but none held quite the same views as me. Good or bad, I did make a difference to the world's sum of knowledge, information and opinion of itself.

Then I also subscribe to a dictum of the *New York Times* columnist James (Scotty) Reston who wrote during a printers' strike: 'How do I know what I think until I have written it?' How do I know what my life has been about until I have transcribed much of the experience into written form?

The writing of memoirs in itself applies a balm to past failures and irritations. I've revisited situations and problems that seemed insoluble at the time but now solutions occur to me which could have made a difference. In reliving confrontations with various authority figures such as headmasters, selection boards, editors and personnel managers, it now occurs to me how I should have responded in reply to probing questions or accusations. Not that such musing can make a difference 30, 40 or even 60 years after the event, but at least it's a trifle reassuring to realise that sometimes one had a better case than it appeared at the time.

Most of the chapters in this tale are first-hand accounts drawn from memory and personal documents. The exceptions are those stories which were too big to be described without also drawing on other sources, such as the United Nations and the Falklands War. I have therefore provided endnotes only in the four chapters which I felt needed them.

This is not a 'misery memoir'. On the contrary, my parents gave me a very good start while my teachers in three schools were both capable and conscientious. My book chronicles the first 50 years of a rewarding life and reflects not only on my schools but on the army, the BBC, the

United Nations and the United States, all seen through the prism of my atypical background. I've called my story *A Gilded Vagabond* because that fits the condition of the journalist; he stays in the best hotels but often reports on the underbelly of society and moves on all too quickly because of the restless imperative of 'news'.

1

Before Memory

I went to my birth in a horse-drawn cab from our house in Zermatt Road in Thornton Heath to the local hospital. Thereby I was linked to an earlier, slower-paced, horse-drawn age, even though it was 1933, an era in which Bluebird racing cars reached 301 mph on the Utah Salt Flats and the Vickers Supermarine seaplane won the Schneider Trophy at the same speed.

My mother had such a hard time with my birth and early childhood that she decided never to have another child. In my first weeks of life I had developed pyloric stenosis, a congenital obstruction that prevents milk passing out of the stomach and generates projectile vomiting. It must have been both very unpleasant and very frightening. The body can absorb very little food and I deteriorated rapidly. A few months earlier an older cousin had died of this inherited malfunction. When it became obvious that something radical had to be done my grandmother and my mother took me to Great Ormond Street Hospital for Children near Russell Square. On the way, by tram from the depot at Tramway Avenue, Edmonton, I went blue. So my grandmother decided they had to get there as soon as possible. They got off the tram and took a taxi at a cost that would have made them wince, but I arrived in time. My grandmother claimed that they had secured the last available bed.

By good fortune surgeons had recently figured out how to correct this not uncommon obstruction. I was one of the first few hundred patients who survived. The procedure requires a large incision into the small stomach of the baby. Years later the hospital followed up with research to enquire about my health since the operation. I had survived the crisis contrary to the normal prognosis, although my mother later told me that I had been very poorly for many months. Even when I had recovered as a child I often had severe stomach pains after meals, which again my mother ascribed to my pyloric weakness and the surgical correction. Luckily I grew out of such troubles by the time I reached double figures.

My mother Violet Ethel was 25 when I was born. She had been a telephonist with the Post Office until her marriage in 1930 to Eric Percival Hindell. Violet was the elder daughter of Albert and Alice Hart who lived in Durants Road, Ponders End, a far northern London suburb. Albert was an expert machinist by trade, always very enthusiastic about his work but also a keen trade unionist. During the Second World War he often told me in great detail how he machined various munitions to within a hundredth of an inch at the British Oxygen factory in Edmonton, usually assuming far more knowledge on my part about this kind of work than I had. In 1919 he had been the first Labour councillor to be elected in the Borough of Enfield. He was a very sociable man, visiting the local public houses as often as he could. He also smoked heavily, which gave the house a sour smell, familiar in many houses in those days. Besides work and politics his other interest was gardening. In a long, narrow garden with a greenhouse he grew excellent tomatoes, beetroot, gooseberries, raspberries and an apricot tree.

My grandmother, Alice Bryant Hart, was generally pleasant but sometimes acerbic, especially towards her husband. Her family came from the Kent countryside but she was brought up in Charlton in South London. As a teenager she had been in domestic service. Alice was the disciplined partner who kept her family functioning and ensured that the family purse was never so empty that she could not put food on the table. She was also an enthusiast for the Enfield Highway Co-operative Society, serving for many years on its education committee. Probably she gained much of her own education this way. She believed in self-improvement and imbued her daughter Violet with a lasting interest in evening classes and summer schools. Once married I don't think she ever had a paid job but she worked hard afternoons and evenings for the Co-operative cause. During the war she used to come to our house one day a week to do the cleaning and laundry while my mother was at work full time. One of my duties when I got home from school was to carry her shopping basket back to the bus.

Her other daughter Gladys was about six years younger than my mother, so was born at the beginning of the First World War. When I was first aware of my aunt Gladys she was working as a clerk in the Ediswan lamp factory (Edison & Swan United Electric Light Co.) in Ponders End. She had a very agreeable sunny nature and always treated me very well. For reasons unclear to me my mother developed an enduring resentment towards and jealousy of Gladys. Reminiscing with us once, she said: 'And then Gladys came along and everything changed.' While in her eighties, years after Gladys had died, Violet was still telling us that Gladys was always her mother's favourite and was always given the best things. She even complained that Gladys had been given the piano when my grandmother died. It was a distinct chip on my mother's shoulder, which did her no credit. I assume this jealousy started long before I was born but it may have been exacerbated by Gladys marrying a very handsome man who for a time was very successful at work. Ted Wright was commissioned as an officer during the war and soon after became a manager earning two or three times as much as my father.

That marriage was in 1940 or 41 when Ted was already in the army. I was old enough to join in the reception at home at 99 Durants Road, Ponders End. For a hungry six-year-old nurtured on wartime rations, the wedding feast was wonderful. The two-tier iced wedding cake was especially yummy for my sweet tooth. After everyone had been served a good slice the remainder was taken up to Gladys's room where much of it was cut up in small slices to be sent to absent friends in silver boxes. As the evening jollifications progressed I crept upstairs to help myself to an extra slice. Delicious but, alas, I was discovered when I boldly tried a second run.

This wedding party was held in the front room at Durants Road, which was only used on grand occasions. With heavy lace curtains, brass candlesticks and brass fire-irons, the décor was vintage Edwardian. Along one wall was the good-looking upright piano at which my mother played a fair selection of music hall songs, helped by a lusty chorus.

2

My Parents

My father Eric Percival Hindell was born in Edmonton in 1904, the eldest of five children of an electrical engineer who had helped to build the tunnels under the Thames for the London Underground. The family had moved to London from Yorkshire in the middle of the nineteenth century. Two of my cousins have traced the family back to the Yorkshire village of Brayton in the early eighteenth century. My paternal grandfather, Percival Nicholson Hindell, who was born in Tadcaster in 1874, married Lily Jane Sanderson in Tottenham in 1901. The wedding photograph clearly shows a prosperous lower middle-class family able to afford smart clothes and very flamboyant hats for the women. However, as my grandfather died the year I was born and my grandmother died when I was four, their influence on my life was negligible. I just remember seeing my grandmother as a very old sick woman in bed but she made no impression on me.

Eric was highly intelligent but under-educated. The defining event in his life was that he never learnt to spell. Nowadays we would call him dyslexic. This disability seems to have obscured from his schoolmasters and perhaps from his parents his clear ability to read, to think deeply and to argue logically. Consequently, unlike his younger brother Donald, he was judged unfit for secondary education and sent out to work at the age of 13. At the very least his family should have apprenticed him to a trade but perhaps he showed no aptitude for carpentry or electrical work. However, by the time he was 17 he began to try to make up for his deficiencies by going to evening classes at one of which, aged 21, he met my mother Violet.

Eric's inability to spell gave him a permanent inferiority complex, a feeling that there was a low ceiling to his working life through which he would never be able to rise. Somewhere along the way he acquired the skills of a welder, which he always described as 'semi-skilled' in contrast to the craftsmen such as engineering tool-makers who were paid a higher rate. In his twenties he had had several periods of unemployment and was actually without a job when I was born in 1933. Soon after, fortunately, he took the job of maintenance welder with the Tottenham Gas Company and stayed in it for the rest of his working life. Until the advent of the war, which brought inflation and some overtime, he never earned more than £3 a week. Only once or twice just after the war did he even consider applying for a better-paid job elsewhere. He was very reluctant to risk his security.

Conscious of his lack of education, he spent a good many hours at evening classes, not learning to spell but instead absorbing radical political ideas. He read both Marx and Lenin and for a short time was an idealistic member of the Communist Party. He rejected capitalism because of its obvious shortcomings and in the thirties its seeming incapacity to provide the industrialised world with even modest prosperity. He used the jargon of communism such as 'dictatorship of the proletariat' and 'the inevitable collapse of capitalism' quite freely but by the mid thirties had abandoned any hope that a workers' revolution would or should occur. By the time I was old enough to understand he declared he was a 'democratic socialist' and he rejected the Soviet government as a brutal dictatorship. He wanted to build a more egalitarian society through non-violent parliamentary means.

He was competent at his work repairing the gas-producing ovens and the wagons of the gas company but he never liked his work, unlike my grandfather, Albert Hart. Eric simply tolerated it with no ambition to advance to a managerial post. Although he was certainly not 'an ordinary working man', he saw himself as one of the working class who, under capitalism, got a poor deal from their employers and who needed to fight collectively for improvements in wages and conditions. To achieve this end he put some of his energy into being the shop steward for the Amalgamated Engineering Union (AEU). Soon after the nationalisation of the gas industry he led a campaign to prevent an obnoxious manager taking charge at Tottenham. A well-qualified gas engineer named Deers with a very abrasive manner had been the manager at the company's second plant at Ponders End. Among other things, Deers had fitted a one-way glass window to his office and was constantly upbraiding men in the yard whom he thought were slacking or walking too slowly. When he was appointed to take over at the main plant in Tottenham his reputation had preceded him. In a packed meeting both the production workers and the maintenance shop declared that they wouldn't have 'Deersie' at any price.

When the management wouldn't budge, the workers walked out and our house quite near to the plant became the strike headquarters. The demands of the strikers and the rotas of the pickets were all drafted in our back room. To a teenage boy it was all very exciting. Quite soon the management yielded and suspended Deers who promptly took them to a tribunal claiming they had ruined his reputation. It was a protracted battle during which the trade unionists had to demonstrate periodically that their members were solidly behind them. Eric was part of the union delegation that put its case to the management. In the end the management promoted Deers to some higher post where he did not have to deal with ordinary manual workers.

A later conflict with the management did not have such a benign outcome. The local AEU branch made a claim for higher wages backed up with the threat of a strike. The management responded with an offer, which Eric thought was as much as they could possibly get. As shop steward he recommended that the members accept the offer but the majority rejected his advice and embarked on a short strike, which achieved little. Feeling he was out of step with the majority, Eric resigned, never to stand for a leadership position again.

His other moment of prominence was early in 1940 when the Home Guard was established. By this time he was 36, too old for conscription to the fighting services. As a welder working in an essential service he was also in a reserved occupation. In the beleaguered atmosphere of Britain at the time he became an enthusiastic member of the Home Guard unit which guarded the gas works particularly against air attack. During the war the works were bombed several times and direct hits were made on gasometers. Although coal gas is highly flammable it does not explode easily unless there is the right mixture of gas and air. Luckily that combination never occurred at Tottenham. Several times Eric was involved helping the fire brigade put out the flames.

His earlier principles had led him to be very critical of the military as an arm of the ruling class. Several times he told me the story of the Invergordon naval mutiny in Scotland in 1931 when ratings' pay was cut by ten per cent. This strike, as the participants described it, caused alarm on the Stock Exchange and helped to persuade the government to go off the gold standard. The strike leaders were treated as mutineers and imprisoned while 200 strikers were discharged from the navy. Eric felt that these 'reprisals' were far too harsh. However, by 1939 the Spanish Civil War and the threat from Germany had modified his former Marxist view that all war was simply an instrument of the ruling class.

11

Although he had had no previous military training he was soon promoted to sergeant. During a training exercise in which professional soldiers occupied the works to show the Home Guard recruits how they should defend it should there be an invasion, Eric led a small detachment over the roof undetected to breach the defensive ring. As long as he didn't have to spell he was full of ideas and initiatives.

For most of his life, however, work was simply a five-and-a-half-day week necessity; the less said about it, the better. Real life for him existed in his leisure time. In the evenings he read extensively – philosophy, poetry and, by the time I was conscious of his reading list, travel and mountaineering. None of these interests came from his family background. They had all emerged from his own browsing in public libraries. Walking to the Carnegie Library in Lower Edmonton was a common family expedition into which I was initiated by the time I was five.

On Sundays we invariably went for a walk in Epping Forest, mostly going by bus to Chingford but sometimes by train to Waltham Cross or Cheshunt further up the Lea valley. In part this was a conscious effort to get away from the polluted, smelly atmosphere of the gasworks and to seek out some really fresh air. Soon it became a desire for exacting exercise, which would enable us to tackle the hills and the mountains of Britain. My mother Violet came with us for a while especially in August and September when the main objective was to pick blackberries. From 1940 onwards, when she went back to work as her contribution to the war effort, she found she had neither the energy nor the time for the Sunday walks.

Twenty minutes on the 102 bus brought us to the Bull & Crown in Chingford where we would walk up an alley beside the police station to emerge on the steep slope of Pole Hill. On the top at all of 300 feet there is an obelisk, which once served as an aiming point for the telescopes at the Royal Observatory in Greenwich, marking 'True North'. It is a splendid viewpoint and psychologically a good place to embark on a longer walk, having just made a 'conquest'. Together Eric and I walked almost every weekend in Epping Forest for more than a dozen years. We never used a map but instead gave many of the landmarks and paths our own names – Plum Pudding Hill, Raft Lake, Lake Minihaha, among others. From Pole Hill, the forest stretches north in a wide swathe for about eight miles. With only a little ingenuity one can easily wend one's way through a ten to twelve-mile walk, climbing several hills and crossing only three or four roads. In the first couple of miles through the deep forest north of Chingford one would meet a few walkers and occasionally some riders on the well-marked but deeply rutted rides. Beyond High Beach, however, we usually had the forest and the farmland in between to ourselves.

As a young man Eric had also absorbed a considerable body of poetry, some of which he recited to me on our walks and climbs. One of his favourites was 'Leisure' by W.H. Davies, which aptly summarised his attitude to work and the natural world. It was the second poem I learnt by heart. As I grew older he regaled me with political poems from a slim anthology entitled *Poems of Revolt,** compiled by Joan Beauchamp. Many of them were anti-war poems as well as anti-the-established-order. Among the contributors were several authors whom we would not now regard as revolutionaries such as Osbert Sitwell, Harold Monro, Siegfried Sassoon and G.K. Chesterton.

> Heaven shall forgive you Bridge at dawn,
> The clothes you wear – or do not wear –
> And Ladies' Leap-frog on the lawn
> And dyes and drugs, and *petits verres.*
> Your vicious things shall melt in air...
> ... But for the Virtuous Things you do,
> The Righteous Work, the Public Care,
> It shall not be forgiven you.

'Ballade D'une Grande Dame' is Chesterton's elegant but deadly critique of charity work by toffs. In our house giving to charity was generally derided as a totally inadequate response to national problems such as poverty and ill health, which could only be tackled by government. That sweeping judgement was probably a legacy of Eric's Marxist self-education.

Best of all was 'The Rebel' by Hilaire Belloc, which Eric could recite with much intensity, thus relieving his pent-up feelings about the inequity of British society. The last stanza in particular provides inspirational gunpowder for the most bloodthirsty revolutionary. Belloc was a prolific 'man of letters' who deployed his talent in diverse styles from comic verse to serious biography, travel-writing and polemics in which he rode his own hobby horses. If Leon Trotsky had hired Belloc as his speech writer he might have made greater progress with his worldwide revolution.

When I first went to Tottenham Grammar School age eleven in 1944 my form master told Eric at the first parents' evening that we must have a high wall built around our house. Based on his observations of my behaviour he meant that the Hindells were isolated from their neighbours and different in character. How he came to this conclusion so quickly I don't know but my father agreed it was a shrewd judgement. We were quite different from the Tongues who lived next door, the Batchelors who lived just beyond them and the Chases and Rideouts who lived across the alley.

My parents did not earn any more money than the average in the street, nor did they have a better education or a more refined accent. But they had few of the interests of the man in the street. For a start they had no interest in sport, never did the football pools and never went to a football match, even though the Spurs football ground was within easy walking distance. Moreover, neither of them smoked nor ever went to a public house, unlike my maternal grandfather. They disliked tobacco and were abstemious with alcohol mainly because of the cost but also because of innate puritanism. In fact Eric was a kind of puritan atheist. He followed the path of an upright citizen who paid all his taxes and his bills on time and bought nothing on credit except his house, not because of any religious or political beliefs or because of fear of retribution but because he thought it was the better way to live.

In these days of heightened awareness of religious belief I might underline that my parents were not at all unusual in rejecting Christianity and never going to church. None of my playmates at home ever went to church. None of my schoolfellows in seven years of primary school and three years of grammar school ever mentioned that they had a religious affiliation or that they ever went to any kind of church. Agnosticism was certainly the majority practice in Edmonton N18 and Tottenham N17, even if most people would not have described their lack of belief in that way.

Equally, in an age in which pub culture is warmly portrayed on popular television, back then very few people in our employed, working-class neighbourhood patronised public houses. We had a pub and an off-licence shop within 200 yards but they were not prosperous businesses. Pubs overflowing with customers may now be commonplace all over London, but then they were rarities in suburban North London. The only ones I can recall were The Hotspur outside the Spurs football ground on match days and the Bricklayers Arms at the Angel, Edmonton. The Bricklayers Arms was then a down-at-heel establishment with a tattered sign, peeling paint and sawdust on the floor. On fine days the customers stood around quietly on the cobblestone yard outside, presumably

14

to get away from the stale smell which emanated from a mixture of tobacco smoke and flat beer.

At that time the cinema was a far more popular form of entertainment than the pub. Queues at our nearest local cinema, The Regal, were very common. It showed only the most popular films so consequently my family tended to avoid it. Instead they patronised about once a fortnight another more comfortable cinema in Palmers Green which had higher standards in its choice of film and a better behaved clientele. This necessitated a bus ride and a long walk but we thought it was worth it. For 1s 9d we saw such classics as *Casablanca* and *Double Indemnity*. Until I was in my teens the cinema was the most stimulating part of my cultural education outside home, school and BBC radio.

Before I was born Eric had been an enthusiastic motor cyclist. He owned a Triumph 550 cc side-valve combination with a side-car for my mother. In his well kept log – penned mostly by my mother – he recorded every journey of consequence together with technical details such as mileage and the oil and petrol consumption. In the summer of 1932 they rode almost every weekend to beaches and beauty spots within a 75-mile radius. In July they made a 'Grand Tour' to Devon and Cornwall and Land's End. When he sold the faithful steed in November after 3,684 miles he wrote 'RIP'. Then they gave up motor cycling for a year to cope with the expense of my arrival, which in the event caused so much trouble that they could hardly have gone out on the road much in 1933 even if they had possessed a bike. But by early 1934 they were raring to go again. At Easter he bought a Raleigh 500 cc OHV with a 'Swallow side-car plus a home built saloon', which I take to mean a home-made hard top. That summer they went to North Wales, starting at 3.45 in the morning. The trip took in a train ride to the summit of Snowdon, which was probably Eric's first introduction to the delights of the mountains. The log records that I joined the crew this season aged ten months and also went up Snowdon. The following year, 1935, was similar, marred only for six hours by a broken side-car chassis at Milnthorpe in Lancashire on the return leg from the Lake District.

The next year they took to four wheels. They bought a two-year-old Austin 7 'De Luxe' as Eric always emphasised. Weekend runs became a normal part of family life. For his first two-week paid holiday in 1936 they toured Scotland in August, this time departing at 3 a.m. for the 300 miles to Penrith. I actually have a hazy memory of driving for miles behind a large lorry in the dark. Violet greatly preferred the Austin to being cooped up in a side-car with me on her lap or behind her. But against the popular trend they sold the car next year in order, as the log records, to take 'to hiking and foreign travel'. From then on their ideal holiday was in the Alps. The first two years they parked me with my grandmother without me realising they had even gone away, but come the summer of 1939 I was brought in on the great adventure of going to Chamonix in France.

Towards the end of the war in which private motoring was banned they bought a tandem bicycle, in part because my mother never learnt to ride solo. They made extensive use of it at weekends, sometimes with me in tow on my first full-size bike, but when the tandem was stolen they were sufficiently discouraged that they did not get another. After the war, when I had left home, Eric toyed with going back to motor cycling on a pukka machine called a Brough Superior, but that dream was scuppered by Violet. They never owned either a bike or a car again.

My mother was a tall good-looking woman who had left school at 14 to become a telephonist with the Post Office. Part of the attraction of the job was that it included 'day release' education until she was 16. In those days all telephone connections were done manually, mostly by girls and women operators. At Clerkenwell Exchange the Post Office taught her how to deal politely but firmly with the public as well as how to connect the wires. By the time she left to get married in 1930 at the age of 22 she had acquired a certain poise, which made her stand out among her neighbours. No wonder then that come the mass evacuation of children from London in 1939 she was given a job as an organiser in Essex.

As my father's writing was pretty poor and his spelling intolerably eccentric my mother was the scribe in our house. Eric would dictate grammatical and cadenced sentences while Violet would pen them in an elegant, flowing hand. Over the years Violet must have learnt as much from Eric as she ever did from her schooling. After the war when for a few years she no longer had a job she became a Labour councillor for a term and, coached by Eric, won a prize or two for public speaking. When she retired from paid work in her fifties she became a forceful member of Chingford Townswomen's Guild, being elected chairman and then president for many years. In North Chingford she was a figure to be reckoned with who could not walk down the High Street without meeting members who wanted to talk to her.

Violet was a very loving mother while I was a small boy and a very supportive adult while I was struggling with Latin and French in my teens. She taught me to sew and to knit and how to make pastry and cakes; she imbued in me too much prudence about spending money. She also did her best to make me frightened of blood. One day before the war we went into a butcher's shop on Edmonton High Street and she promptly fainted onto the sawdust floor at the sight of some blood on the slab. They quickly lifted her onto a chair and gave her a cup of tea. For ten minutes while she recovered her colour and her balance I just stood around feeling embarrassed. For some time after that incident she told me that I too would be frightened at the sight of blood and, as I was only five, I think it did make me rather too anxious about going to the dentist and the doctor for some years.

In later life after my father had died Violet tried to be as forthright with me as she was with her guild members with the result that I found her too dogmatic for comfort. In contrast, my father became much less dogmatic with age. From once being bright red he turned slowly into pink and then pale blue, his political progression being reflected in his daily newspaper. Over the 40 years I knew him he changed from the *Daily Worker* to the *News Chronicle* to *The Guardian* and finally to the *Daily Telegraph*. Often as I read my *Guardian* today I know how he must have felt.

One can read into this political progression simply that he learnt from experience, that the dreams and ideals of his youth were impractical or sometimes, perhaps, undesirable. He was still in his *News Chronicle* phase when he decided that I should try for a place at Harrow, even though it was a bastion of all that he had earlier despised. I suspect that six years of war in which British society of right and left had pulled together pretty well must have taken the sting out of his revolutionary fervour, coupled of course with the revelations about the horrors of Stalinism, which were made plain in the Moscow show trials of the late 1930s. The final nail in the coffin of his Communism came with the Molotov–Ribbentrop 'Non-Aggression Pact' of August 1939. Even though I was only six he conveyed the gist of this diplomatic U-turn to me in words I could understand. Democratic socialists, such as Eric, now openly despised their Communist Party friends who supinely followed the Moscow line, making excuses for the pact with the Nazis.

Socially we were isolated from our neighbours. We were on cordial terms but always at arm's length. Neighbours rarely came in for a chat or a cup of tea and never for a meal. Even the children very rarely went into a neighbour's house to play or have a snack. Some writers and novelists have extolled the chumminess of working-class life between the wars but that was not my experience in a North London suburb of modest owner-occupiers. My mother would have loved a busy social life but found none of her women neighbours to be on her wavelength. She also disliked the hard work of entertaining so was reluctant to invite anyone, even our relatives, for a meal. After she went back to work as a telephonist at a cycle factory converted to armaments, she occasionally invited some of her colleagues and their spouses. One of these female friends, with the very fancy name of Cordelia and striking good looks, was a comptometer operator, one of the few high-tech jobs open to women at that time. She was living 'in sin' with an engaging older man named Jimmy whom she was very obviously supporting. Jimmy had a stamp shop in Muswell Hill and encouraged me with my collection. One Christmas he very thoughtfully gave me a large album with many stamps in it, which stimulated my interest enormously. With a much larger Edwardian house, they entertained on a grander scale than us, both in regard to the tastiness of the food and the number of guests. It was Cordelia who taught us how to play 'Murder in the Dark', which can be very exciting when you are twelve.

Apart from Cordelia and one or two other of Vi's work colleagues, almost all our social life was with other branches of the family. We went by bus to Ponders End fairly often to see my maternal grandparents, Albert and Alice, and their other daughter Gladys and her fiancé Ted Wright before he was called up for the army. We also saw Eric's three brothers and his one sister together with their families two or three times a year. They all lived in a cluster in Enfield about an hour away by train or bus.

The most successful member of Eric's family was his younger brother Donald. He had gained scholarships to grammar school and Goldsmith's College in London where he trained as a teacher. Soon after the war he was appointed headmaster of an imposing new school built around a fine country house called Theobald's on the rural edge of Enfield. Temple Bar, an eighteenth-century gate to London, was parked in the grounds; since then it's been moved back into London behind St Paul's Cathedral.

Donald had a fine deep voice, an air of authority and was more socially assured than Eric, although not more clever. Whenever they met they had long civilised discussions, which sometimes developed into heated political arguments. We had more contact with Donald and his family than with Eric's other siblings, Marjorie, Edgar and Raymond, mainly because Eric was much nearer to Donald in age. The other reason was that Donald's elder daughter Carol was only three years younger than me whereas the age gap with all the other cousins was much larger. As I was educated at boys-only schools from the age of six, Carol was almost the only girl near my own age that I knew.

3

A Boyhood in Edmonton

A happy childhood has often spoiled a good autobiography...

What do I genuinely remember? On the first day at Raynham Road Infants School in September 1937 I was escorted to the classroom by my mother but thereafter I always walked to school with other boys or alone. From our estate of owner-occupied two-bedroom houses, Middleham Road, we went through Thornaby Gardens council estate where all the houses were rented. Even to the four-year-old eye the people were distinctly poorer and their gardens more unkempt, some being littered with old prams used for hauling coke. Thornaby Gardens led to a broad paved alley open on one side through a wire mesh fence to the school playing field. An open storm drain beside the alley provided a perfect pitch for a simple game of marbles on the way home from school.

The first afternoon in the Infants reception class I found very strange. We were all given little mats and told to lie down for a short sleep. As I no longer slept during the day at home nor had any memory of doing so I spent most of the time looking around at the other children and being told to go back to sleep. The following three years in the Infants flashed by without making much impression except that I enjoyed them. In my last year, the senior mistress, Miss Pickles, gave me a prize book for geography, something which pleased me immensely as my father was already playing geography games with me at home.

On Coronation Day, 1937 we infants were all given toy Union Jacks to wave about and take home. When my father saw this flag he immediately flew into a temper, seized it from me and broke it in pieces despite my protests and wails. He regarded it as an appalling symbol of the monarchy, which he despised. Although I was only four I could understand what he was talking about so I suppose he must have expressed anti-monarchist views earlier. My mother protested, saying it was unfair to break up what was only a toy. Looking back it now seems an

21

extraordinarily immature bit of rage for an adult to express at the expense of a child.

Apart from that, all I remember is the very lively playground. Against every wall at playtime the girls did handstands to show off their knickers, a Freudian ritual that was common in many schools. The boys who hardly ever played with the infant girls played endless rough chase games, only drawing breath in the autumn to play conkers. One of the more canny boys baked his conker in the oven and was able to crack open all our beautiful shiny brown new conkers as easy as pie. One day, however, I hit this prize conker, then boasting a score of over a hundred, so hard it pulled off its string. Technically this was not a win for me but even so the boy gave me the conker. I took it on to further triumphs before retiring it at 144. It deserved to be buried with a gravestone.

One reason for my inability to recollect much about the Infants School at Raynham Road might be because my time there was interrupted by evacuation. In September 1939, soon after the outbreak of war, our school was evacuated by train to Braintree, a small town 30 miles away in Essex. On arrival we stood in the playground of an infants school waiting our turn to be assigned a billet. Three of us, all from Middleham Road, seemed to wait for ever while most of the other children were linked to foster parents and taken away. Eventually Raymond, Vera and I were led by a friendly young man and his wife to his pleasant Victorian house quite close to the school. We were given a meal, then tucked up in bed with a comic. As comics were banned at No. 10 Middleham Road I warmed to my new surroundings. Alas they didn't last.

The very next day Raymond and I were taken to the young man's mother-in-law who lived in a poky council house quite a walk further out of the town. Vera who was a very pretty little girl stayed behind with the young man and his wife. Were Raymond and I dumped on the mother-in-law or was it the plan all along? As we were never taken back to see Vera in the original house I think we boys were 'dumped'.

No matter, there were some compensations. The council house had a long garden with a chicken coop full of brown and white chickens right at the bottom. It became our favourite place to play. Vera was even left with the mother-in-law several afternoons a week so we played with her down there. The fare was pretty frugal as it was a fairly poor household, which was probably glad of the fees for taking two evacuees. My mother sent me the odd postal order so that I could buy sweets. The last one, for sixpence, was put up on the high mantelpiece where I couldn't get it and I never saw it again.

After a couple of months Raymond and I both got chicken pox. I lay in bed for what seemed an eternity, scratching my spots and feeling sorry for myself. My mother came to visit but not for some weeks because she had taken a short-term job as an organiser for the national evacuation scheme in another part of Essex. For several years she regaled her friends with her adventures so I'm sure she enjoyed it. It must also have played a part in persuading her to go back to work full-time the following year.

I was reasonably happy in this household and at the school where the evacuees formed a whole class, although the only specific lesson I can recall is a nature walk in a local wood where round red haws were distinguished from oval orange rose-hips, and oak acorns were contrasted with horse chestnut conkers. It was an easy option for both teacher and pupils but it stuck in my mind so must rate as effective.

In the first school holidays my mother brought me home by coach for Christmas. The intention was that I should go back in January 1940 but, as there had been no bombing whatsoever and the war on the western front was being described as 'phoney', my parents decided to keep me at home and send me back to Raynham Road School. So I never recovered my sixpenny postal order to spend on toffees, something I resented at the time because I was never given such largesse at home. But I was pleased to be home again and back among my boyhood friends – Teddy Batchelor, Alan Chase, Alec Mathews, Eileen Rideout, Kenny Livermore, plus Vera and Raymond – all of whom lived within a hundred yards of my house. We played hard in the street at every opportunity – football, cricket and snowballs in season, plus hide-and-seek, high cockalorum, cowboys, truth or dare? kerb or wall? at any time of the year. There was virtually no car traffic and no parked cars at all. The whole road – 800 yards straight – was our playground. Just occasionally we had to skip on to the pavement to escape the heavy steam-driven lorries, which carried coke from the gas ovens at no more than 15 miles an hour. The only other regular vehicles were a horse-drawn Hovis bakery cart and the hand-pushed delivery carts for Co-op milk and bread. It was the Co-op milkman who taught me to wink.

From the age of six onwards we often walked the quarter of a mile to the Northumberland Park recreation ground, which backed on to the Willoughby Lane gasworks and on to the Lea Canal, then still busy with horse-drawn barges. There were some swings and roundabouts but as parks go it was inferior even by the standards of the time. The end nearest to the gasworks was blanketed in a smelly and irritating gas given off by the benzine plant, so we usually went further away out of smell range.

Despite its scrubby appearance we liked the 'rec' because there was always plenty of space for football and cricket and for roaming about. One year we used the remains of a large water pumping station to stage an obstacle course in which we ran elaborate races governed by our own rules. We also used to drag the shallow freshwater channel, running beside the canal, with pieces of sacking to catch tiddlers and sticklebacks. Boys only had proper fishing tackle if they came with their fathers.

That first summer back from evacuation in 1940 I was seven, just the right age to collect Dinky-Toy aeroplanes and to absorb from little booklets the names and shapes of the war planes we sometimes saw in the sky. Although we could name up to two dozen British and German planes – from the Spitfire and Messerschmitt 109 to the more exotic Stuka dive bomber – very few enemy planes reached North London in daylight. That said, we saw many British planes. Towards the end of the war on a summer evening it was common to see 40 to 50 Lancasters or Stirlings lumber over at low altitude on their way to a mass raid on Germany. Holding my silver Vickers Supermarine Spitfire in my hand I used to brace myself to jump from the roof of our shed, some six feet off the ground, on to the lawn below in a daredevil leap. I don't suppose it was very good for me. When I was not a pilot or a parachutist I would play on an old wooden mangle in the shed which in my imagination became a steam engine, a pirate ship or anything I made it.

One day when I was about five I announced that I would dig in the garden for Roman pottery. I suppose it was inspired by a junior archaeology lesson in the Infants. After a time I came across a piece of china with orange paint on it. I scraped it out, covered with dirt, calling for Dad to come to see my treasure. When I had scraped the mud off it looked strangely like our breakfast bowls, which we called our 'piggies' plates after the cereal we ate. By the time Eric reached me with a grin on his face I knew I had been set up. It was one of many jokes Eric played on me during my childhood. Another favourite was played at bedtime just as I went upstairs. In the dark or gloaming Eric would tap me on the back. When I looked round to see who had done it he would say, 'Some bloke', pretending that the 'bloke' had run away.

When I was still small I was given a two-wheeler bicycle with 14-inch diameter wheels. One weekend Eric helped me to learn how to ride it and from then on I was highly mobile throughout childhood. Ordered to stick to the pavement, I soon ventured on to the road. One evening riding near the gasworks, I misjudged a car moving in front of me and came off, landing with my knee on a sharp kerb. It took a sizeable chunk out of the fleshy part just above the kneecap. Blood spurted everywhere and I was rushed into the gasworks first-aid centre. Bystanders muttered that 'he'll need a lot of stitches for that one', but actually the nurse bound up the wound so tightly that it all healed with new flesh of its own accord. When the doctor examined it a day or two later he pronounced stitches unnecessary and so it proved.

I was also given some roller-skates when I was small, finding them quite easy to master. We spent hours zooming around on skates, often playing chase and hide-and-seek games without taking them off. The greatest thrill was to skate as a bunch with hands on the shoulders of the one in front and then to bend the knees down almost to floor level as we swayed around a corner. I expect we took our cue from some American film, though I don't remember such an episode.

My contemporaries in the neighbourhood were almost all boys and mostly two or three years older than me. I learnt how to play football and cricket from Teddy Batchelor who lived only two doors away. With his real football we went to the Northumberland Park recreation ground. Usually there were only three or four of us so he taught us how to play 'attack & defence' with sweaters as goalposts. Even in the street we used caps and sweaters as markers because the traffic was both slow and rare. Later on when I was ten I played for the school football team whose star player was Tony Marchi who could out-kick and out-dribble all of us. One time I organised a scratch team from around Middleham Road to challenge Marchi's team from another part of Edmonton. We played hard but were well beaten. Later Marchi played for England and captained Tottenham Hotspur.

For cricket we used a lamppost as the wicket and a tennis ball instead of a hard ball. Most of the time we played an 'over garden out' rule to encourage forward ground-hugging drives and minimise irritating the neighbours. Most householders around us tolerated it if we nipped in carefully to retrieve the ball, but one grumpy woman whose garden was just across an alley from us built an abnormally high fence on all three sides and would not give us back our ball. This tactic kept us well away from her fence until we were twelve or more, by which time we could actually climb its creosoted heights, retrieve the ball and get back to safety before she had realised what was going on.

I've not thought about this before but I now realise that my father never talked about sport or showed me how to play any of the popular games such as football, cricket or tennis. He never read the sports news or, when I became an avid listener to the cricket scores, discussed them with me. Was it because he didn't like them or was he incompetent at them? He was fit, strong and above medium height. I never found out.

The autumn of the Battle of Britain I went up into the 'Big Boys', the senior boys school at Raynham Road, which was a solid three-storey, yellow brick School Board building dating from the 1890s. The senior girls were strictly segregated on the ground and first floors with senior boys on the top floor. We hardly saw the girls for the next four years and certainly never played with them or joined with them in any school activities. The hierarchy among the boys was not decided so much by age or even size but by who you could fight. To claim that you could fight someone meant you could beat him, and playground fights to establish these claims were common.

It was only in the Seniors that school began in earnest with strict discipline maintained with the cane. My teachers who each taught virtually all the subjects except art were, successively, Mr Barnet, Mrs Lyle, Miss Hargreaves and Mr Rubinstein. Barnet, who was quite agile despite a wooden leg, was fierce and stern in his demeanour. He drove us very hard. The other three were gentler and more agreeable and I learnt a great deal from all of them. The transforming moment of my school life at Raynham Road came when Rubinstein read us *Treasure Island*. He had a slow, lugubrious manner, which suited the text and our capacity to absorb it. Soon afterwards when I met a boy with a copy of *Treasure Island* I offered three *Big Books for Boys* in exchange. My mates thought I had gone mad but I suppose I realised that such volumes full of short stories, puzzles and games were childish stuff compared to the delights of a real story.

The art master, the young and handsome Mr Cudworth, used a very long cane to intimidate us. Early on when a few of us were talking out of turn he brought the end down on our table inches from our hands.

I can hear that cane scything through the air and banging on the table 70 years later. It was a very crude form of discipline that kept us quiet from then on, but I doubt that we learnt much art.

In the autumn of 1940 the Germans began to bomb London almost every night and at one point kept up their nightly attack for eight weeks in a row. The noise from the anti-aircraft guns was sometimes deafening, certainly much more noticeable than the actual bombs. Each morning *en route* to school we used to collect large jagged pieces of shrapnel, which had fallen from the anti-aircraft shells. The prize souvenir to be found lying in the road was a bronze nose cone, which often survived unbroken and was thus tradeable for other trophies or toys. I was usually put to bed about nine o'clock but once the siren went I was brought down to the Anderson shelter in the garden. This shelter consisted of a curved corrugated-iron roof embedded over a trench about four-feet deep, which had been dug by my father. It would probably have given adequate protection against the bombs of the time except in the case of a direct hit. Eric built bunks along the side and laid wooden planks on the clay floor to keep our feet dry. In the middle of the war the Anderson was replaced by the Morrison shelter, which was a strong steel table for use inside the house. It was much more cosy than the Anderson and could barely be distinguished from a large double bed except that it was on the floor and there was less headroom.

If the bombing started early we all went straight to the shelter. Fortunately we were not in a major target area like the docks or the major railway junctions but the Tottenham gasworks only a quarter of a mile away was hit a number of times. One house in our street was destroyed by a small, random bomb, though no one was killed. After a few weeks of intensive nightly bombing my parents decided that it would be sensible for Violet and me to go to a safer part of the country. We went by train to Harrogate in Yorkshire where there was an aunt who they thought would take us in for a while. How wrong they were.

We arrived at the aunt's neat bungalow after a long train journey only to be told over tea that she couldn't possibly put us up, even for one night. Instead she had persuaded one of her friends to give us a bedroom for a few days. This kind woman entertained us royally with home-made bread, which I thought delicious, and I wanted to stay but my mother quite rightly did not want to impose on her. So we scouted around some older, less attractive parts of town where we eventually found a bedsitting room with a small gas ring at 15 shillings per week. I was placed at the local school in the youngest class and got on well for the rest of our stay. I can't remember the teacher, the classroom or any of the lessons but I do remember a very pretty girl with whom I had my first love affair aged seven!

Fifteen shillings a week sounds so little now – 75 pence – but then it was a fifth of my father's wages. So when a tenant moved out on the top floor we moved up two floors into an identical room with a double bed and a gas ring at twelve and six a week. That half a crown represented a significant saving. I remember these figures in detail because my mother, with no other adult to confide in, took me into her confidence. What she did during the day while I was at school I don't know but I don't think we had any further contact with the frosty aunt. After about six weeks the night bombing eased in London so we returned home.

During my last summer at Raynham Road in 1944 the German flying bomb raids became so intense that Miss Hargreaves often had to take our senior class of ten-year-olds in an air-raid shelter in the playground. At the end of the day when we had finished lessons and were simply waiting for the 'all clear' siren she got us to play memory games. 'I walked down Piccadilly,' she would say to start us off, 'with Mr Churchill and Charlie Chaplin.' Then each boy in turn would repeat all the names in play and add another. Once we got up to 38 names before the siren went to allow us to go out into the playground. Our memories at that time must have been like sponges.

Raynham Road Boys School was comprised of seven classes of between 40 and 48 each. About half a dozen of the fourth year were entered for the Eleven Plus, usually known among pupils as the 'scholarship exam'. We took this examination at Latymer Grammar School in Lower Edmonton. When we returned in the late afternoon we were questioned by several of our teachers. On the basis of my report of the questions and my answers Mr Rubinstein declared I had failed. Not exactly an encouraging response. Fortunately he was quite wrong. When my parents were notified that I had passed they decided to send me to Tottenham Grammar School which was within walking distance, rather than Latymer, which meant a bus ride to get there at all or two buses to arrive comfortably. I demurred about this choice because Tottenham played rugby about which I knew nothing. However, Tottenham proved to be the better choice. The fact that it was all boys, whereas Latymer was mixed, did not register with me at all.

During the war my mother found it hard going working full-time and running the house. From the age of about eight, therefore, I was persuaded to take on much of the shopping either at the local corner shops or at the chain stores in Edmonton High Street where we were registered for all our rationed foods. I used to ride my bike to shop at the Maypole mid-week and the London Co-op on Saturday, bringing home a heavy basket suspended from the handlebars. I should have walked because the loads made steering the cycle quite tricky but I never did.

At the Maypole I had a little patter, which I trotted out as I put our three ration books on the counter. 'Margarine, Butter and no eggs,' I would say with a chuckle because fresh eggs were very rare. For most of the war we were served dried egg powder instead, which, when mixed with water and a little milk, had a lurid muddy orange colour and a rather musty taste. No doubt it was reasonably nutritious and certainly it was fine when mixed into a cake, but as scrambled eggs it was distinctly unappetising.

At the Co-op, which was a much bigger establishment, we were registered for meat, sugar and jam. I do not remember ever being told there that something on ration was not available. In fact in the middle of the war this shop served delicacies such as peach jam, which I had never seen before. One day in 1945 when things were obviously becoming easier the Co-op shop assistant asked me whether instead of our strawberry jam ration we would like lime marmalade, which had arrived from the Caribbean that day. It was vivid green in colour and as he made it sound like a very special treat I bought it contrary to the usual routine. Alas it put all our teeth on edge and had to be cast aside. The next week I was sent to the Co-op with stricter instructions.

Our family like most had no access to black market or under-the-counter food, nor could we obtain surplus farm products from a friend. Yet I never went hungry. Of course I had lunch at school which though of variable quality certainly supplemented our family rations. Although school food at Raynham Road and Tottenham Grammar School never matched home cooking it was always palatable, despite rationing, and I usually ate everything offered. One memorable pudding was served at Raynham Road during holiday school in August of 1944. Because there were not many children at the time we were all offered seconds of the delicious plum tart. So delicious several of us went back for thirds, fourths and even a fifth helping, and the kitchen staff were delighted to serve us! At the age of eleven you run everywhere and use a prodigious amount of energy.

At home we did notice the shortage of butter because the margarine was only tolerable with a lot of jam. In our house you were not allowed jam at all if you had butter. It made me appreciate butter as a special delicacy. Of course there were hardships, but whenever I see a film version of the home front or read a history or a novel about the war I find that the directors or authors paint a misleading picture as to the extent of our deprivation. Without any privileges or fiddles our family and millions like us were well fed and clothed throughout the war and its aftermath.

Until I went to boarding school in 1947 aged 14 Eric was the dominant influence in my life, far more important than school or friends. In the previous chapter I described him as a 'puritan' because he eschewed all the common vices of alcohol, tobacco and gambling, partly because of the expense but mostly on principle. He was very self-disciplined especially in spending his money, which was targeted at his own priorities, particularly the annual holiday. He was especially insistent that all bills and mortgage payments were made on time. Both my parents prided themselves on being able to do more with their money than their neighbours or mates at work. They walked when others would take a bus; they were persistent in shopping around for the cheapest. Apart from the mortgage on our house in Middleham Road, Edmonton, they never bought anything on hire purchase. The only regular indulgence while I lived at home was a visit to the cinema, but they only went when they thought there was a good film; they never went out of habit. Their staple entertainment throughout the war was provided by the Home Service on BBC radio. We were avid listeners to the news and regular listeners to the comedy programme *It's That Man Again*, the variety show *Monday Night at Eight* and *Saturday Night Theatre*.

We were not only a radio household but news addicts. We listened as a family to the eight o'clock, one o'clock and six o'clock Home Service news broadcasts every day, following the progress of the war closely. One day in 1941 when Italy was attempting to conquer Greece from its base in Albania, the Greeks reported that they had retaken the town of Koritsa. The same day a very pretty ginger kitten insisted on staying with us. When we wondered what we should call him Eric suggested Koritsa, which we did. It was a good example of Eric's way of thinking that he could apply his mind to a mundane matter and come up with an interesting and unconventional answer. Koritsa lived with us for many years until long after the war and always answered to his unique name.

A couple of years before the war my parents discovered foreign holidays. Skilfully parking me with my maternal grandparents they had two memorable holidays in the Swiss Alps. Then in August 1939 despite the gathering storm of war they took me to Chamonix in the French Alps, together with my Aunt Gladys, something which I describe in a later chapter entitled 'Mountains'. During the war Eric's holidays were reduced from a fortnight to a week but that did not prevent us from using every vacation to full advantage, often tacking the week on to the August bank holiday, thus giving us an extra day. We went to the Lake District three times and to the Derbyshire Peak District, Wales and Scotland. All these journeys were made by train, which I found magical. The rhythm of the train going clickety-click over the joints between the rails – continuous welded rail did not come in for another 30 years – only heightened the excitement of travelling far away and being able to spot strange locomotives not seen in London.

By August 1945 when the war in Europe was already won Eric could take two weeks at Fort William in Scotland, in the middle of which we heard the news of the atomic bomb dropped on Hiroshima. All the adults in the hotel were very excited by this news, which they correctly interpreted as being only a short step from total victory. It was the second time in my childhood that dramatic news came through while I was surrounded by adults on holiday, the other being the outbreak of war in 1939.

Despite having a low income, my parents were always able to save and were never embarrassed by having to delay payment on a bill. Such prudent habits were then commonplace. I learnt from an early age how not to be a consumer and to reject the blandishments of commerce. Unlike Gordon Brown's 'family values', our guiding principles had no religious content but were equally effective at keeping our heads well above water without money worries.

When the European war ended in May 1945 some ebullient, public-spirited residents of Middleham Road organised street races and games, followed by a street party. Such events were common all over London and elsewhere. Middleham Road was straight for almost half a mile so they were able to paint lines for the 100 yards on to the tarmac. These children's races and the relatively extravagant party fare that followed seemed a good way to mark the end of the struggle in which we felt we had all pulled together.

4

Grammar School

Tottenham Grammar School was founded as a church grammar school in the sixteenth century, re-endowed by a Duchess of Somerset in 1690, and at the beginning of the twentieth century absorbed into the state system. However, for my first year until the 1944 Education Act came into effect, we still paid small fees each term. At that time it had a well-designed red brick building, finished in 1938, with playing fields at each end of the school on to which teenage exuberance could spill over at breaks and lunchtime. There was a large oak-beamed and panelled hall, a library, a workshop, an excellent gymnasium and what seemed like plenty of classrooms and well-equipped labs for Science. I don't suppose it was a unique design but it was fit for the purpose of fostering a school with a distinct character and high morale. Forty years after I left, philistines in the local council knocked it down over an Easter weekend without giving any public notice. The school, by then converted to Somerset Comprehensive, had been closed for a year. Only some quick thinking and fast footwork by some alert Old Boys saved a few of its artefacts, such as the school badge set in stone above the main door. So after 400 years the school was erased from public consciousness.

The fact that the building was a great improvement on my nineteenth-century Board School signalled to me that this move was a real step up. The next indication was that some of the affairs of the school were run by the sixth formers. At an induction session in July 1944, at the end of the previous academic year, the house captains led a short session in hall, talking up the school and dividing the new intake among the four houses: Somerset, Bruce, Howard and Morley. In those days all grammar school boys wore caps and at Tottenham each black cap had coloured piping delineating your house. My cap had light blue piping showing I was in Howard.

For my first term I was in Form 1A under an odd bird named Mr Wright and everything seemed fairly easy, especially the French and Latin which in later years I found very difficult. At Tottenham we were rated by each subject and in the class as a whole every term. As I came top of the class I was moved in January to the 'Express' class 1E under Mr Mitchell, which was designed for brighter boys who could take the School Certificate in four years rather than five. Working-class culture was such that many families got their sons to leave school to earn their keep, if not at the minimum age of 14 then certainly after the School Certificate. By putting brighter boys through in four years it was hoped that more of them would be persuaded to stay on for two years in the sixth form.

Mr Mitchell was an enthusiast who taught English very well and produced the school plays. In my second year he recruited me to play Fleance, the son of Banquo, in *Macbeth*. A fleeting role indeed but fun. Later he gave me the lead in a play about the Queen of Hearts, the text of which I thought was childish. When lunchtime rehearsals clashed with practice for the under-13 rugby team I voted for rugby. Mitchell was very annoyed and never offered me another part in his annual Shakespeare play. Ironically I was not picked for the rugby team either, the nearest I got being the reserve who served as linesman. I quickly got fed up with being a reserve so opted out of that too, only to find that I would have played because several people failed to turn up to an away game. Actually I was rather small and at that stage probably not very good.

Where I did shine in all three years at Tottenham was in the cross-country race held at Woodford in Epping Forest. We trained hard on the rugby pitch adjacent to the school, encouraged and inspired by a fourth former named Marchant who was clearly a strong athlete. Amazing what a difference a good example can make. Each year on the day of the race we went out to Woodford by trolley-bus and changed in an old British Legion club house, which is still there on Woodford Green. The race had a good start with a straight run along a broad avenue for a quarter of a mile but then dived into the forest along muddy tracks marked only by boys signalling where we should turn. Halfway round we skirted around a lake where the route was clear, but once back in the forest, route finding was quite a problem. In my first year as I came up the slope out of the forest I saw Marchant lying beside the path in agony. 'Run on,' he yelled. He had twisted his ankle within 500 yards of the finish. When I reached the line in fourth place I reported his accident and masters went to his rescue. As the junior race was for those under 14 and I was only 11 I was quite pleased with my performance.

In my second year, when I came third, the importance of knowing the route was underlined when a senior boy named Watson, who was clearly the best in the field, failed to win because a marker boy strayed from his post. Watson had taken a wrong turn and came in well down the field. As a result Eric and I had the idea that we should walk the course the weekend before the next race. When we did I was struck by how difficult it was to remember even at the third look. Come the race I could still not prevail against an older, taller boy and so completed my third race as second. Our names were read out in school assembly. There was fame!

Apart from Mitchell the other masters who made an impression on me were Dr Worden who taught Latin, Dr Nelson who taught maths and music and the headmaster, H.A.T. Simmonds. Worden was tall, moustachioed, correct and austere but he made Latin interesting. He taught the class to greet him as he entered the room each day with a resounding 'Salve Magister', which usually made us laugh. After I left it transpired to everyone's amazement that he had been carrying on a clandestine affair with the school secretary. Nelson, who was another austere senior master, eventually got me to understand Pythagoras and logarithms and to manipulate the sine and cosine tables as easily as a railway timetable. Alas, Nelson had a very bullying style, especially when he taught us the rudiments of musical notation. I have not retained any of that. Gerry Hawtin, the gym master, was the antithesis of both Worden and Nelson. He was quite short, middle-aged, wiry and bubbling with enthusiasm for his trade. He had just the right touch to make us work hard at the pull-ups and the press-ups without being a bully. He insisted that all boys in the first year take boxing and enter a competition, something which I suspect would be frowned on nowadays. At the end of each term he turned the gym into a giant adventure playground in which we played an exciting chase game.

H.A.T. Simmonds, the headmaster, was a large self-satisfied fellow who could barely button his jacket round his tummy. When two of us were pulled up by a sixth form monitor for talking in hall before assembly he gave us an absolutely vicious caning on the hand. I have not forgiven him. The educational authorities evidently thought highly of him for in my second year he went to be head of a new teacher-training college in Trent Park, Hertfordshire.

In my third year I was pulled to the front of the chemistry lab by the teacher, Miss Pickering, while I was amusing my mates by wagging my ears. I was marched straight down to the new headmaster, Dr F.J. Williams, without explanation, and I thought I was in for another caning. But once in his office Miss Pickering simply got me to repeat my trick. She found it hilarious but Dr Williams was not amused. Fingers were wagged but no other punishment ensued.

Each year at Speech Day I was chosen by my form teacher to take part in a verse-speaking competition. As Eric was very keen on poetry and often recited poems while on our weekend walks in Epping Forest he rehearsed me beforehand. In my second year I won the prize with 'Vitai Lampada' by Sir Henry Newbolt.*

> There's a breathless hush in the close tonight –
> Ten to make and the match to win –
> A bumping pitch and a blinding light,
> An hour to play and the last man in.

Stirring stuff, especially in the second verse: 'The sand of the desert is sodden red / Red with the wreck of a square that broke' and so on.

My friends for three years at grammar school were mainly a group of Jewish boys who came from Stamford Hill: Coppleman, Shulkind, Caplan and Goldstein. They were all clever and active in school societies such as the chess club. Their religion was never mentioned by them or anyone else. It was a secular school with the minimum of Christian observance at assembly.

The most dramatic and tragic moment of my time at Tottenham occurred in March 1945 when a German V2 rocket landed on waste ground just across the road from the dining hall. It blew apart a nearby house and inflicted considerable structural damage on the school. The roof of the hall was very badly damaged, 600 windows were broken and 27 doors were blown out. A slight tweak at the rocket's launch could have put it on the hall where second lunch was in progress. Boys and masters inside were shaken but not seriously hurt. Outside in the junior playground and sports field we were protected from the blast by the school building.

---

* Collected Poems 1897–1907.

On hearing the explosion we all lay down in the playing field as we had been trained to do and there were no casualties there. After half a minute when a column of smoke arose behind the school we ran round into the senior playground which was less protected from the blast. There we found that two 14-year-old boys had been killed outright while a third had had his arm taken off at the elbow. He ran around screaming and bleeding profusely until taken in hand by a master who applied a tourniquet, which saved his life. Luckily he made a full recovery but never came back to attend lessons. Altogether six boys and one master needed treatment in hospital. It was a sobering experience only two months before the end of the war in Europe.

5

Harrow

'Writers and artists are writing their autobiographies all the time.'
Havelock Ellis

In a government report entitled 'The Public Schools & the General Education System' the Fleming Committee declared in 1944 that 'all schools should be fully accessible to qualified pupils without regard to means'.[1] It recommended that schools should offer 25 per cent of their annual admissions to pupils from state schools with the expectation that the proportion would rise still further.[2] Together with similar recommendations for the Direct Grant sector, it proposed a national plan 'to associate the Public Schools with the general educational system', which would give them 'an opportunity for new and wider service'.[3] It was concerned that the Public Schools had segregated their pupils 'one class from another in a world where, much more than in the past, they will meet in later life as equals'.[4] The Committee had been conceived as part of planning for a better post-war world and it described its proposal as 'a first step towards a much greater measure of social and educational unity in the nation'.[5]

In the event, these radical proposals (which potentially affected only one half of one per cent of boys aged 13) were overshadowed by the Education Act of 1944 which promised secondary education for all. Nevertheless a few schools and a few councils applied the idea, if not on the scale envisaged by Fleming. Middlesex County Council, which then had the second largest population of any local authority, instituted awards for boys at Mill Hill and girls at Wycombe Abbey from 1946. The next year five places were offered at Harrow, an allocation that was continued for almost 20 years.

The exact reasons why I was chosen above all those others do not appear to have survived. Any notes the Headmaster and the Chief Education Officer made about the selection process have not been kept among the Middlesex County Council archives or in the Harrow School archives. Whether or not my modest competency at chess really did land me the award, as outlined in my prologue, I really don't know. However, I did have some of the more obvious qualifications. In my first two years at Tottenham Grammar School I was placed in an accelerated form and excelled my contemporaries. It's true that in my third year, when I was in the fourth form, some of my weaknesses became apparent, certainly to me. But at the time of that selection in Great George Street, my reports on nine terms registered a very high average. At Tottenham I had been top of the form five times, which probably placed me on the shortlist.

Whatever the reasons that tipped the balance on the day I could only have been selected on the basis of my own talents, not on anyone's recommendation or inside influence. I had no connection with Harrow School or Harrow on the Hill. My own headmaster, Dr Williams, had tried to discourage my parents from applying by pointing out I was a little too old. He only forwarded my application reluctantly. Whatever he wrote about me certainly did not contain any warmth. He had only been at Tottenham two terms and my application to leave was only my second face-to-face contact. 'You won't like it,' he said grumpily. Thank goodness I took no notice.

Looked at with hindsight, it is surprising that I ever reached the interview. My parents had only heard of the scheme by chance and only obtained details from an advertisement in the local paper some time after the deadline had expired. So when they enquired at Edmonton Education Office an official immediately told them they were too late to apply.

My father was a rebel in his intellect but was a timid, obedient citizen by temperament. He would have accepted that kind of finality from the lowliest of clerks and would on no account have made a plea or invented an excuse for special treatment. But as luck would have it a more senior official in the Education Office came upon the papers, already labelled 'reject – too late', and decided to give this unknown boy a helping hand. He came round after work to our house on his bicycle with the application form in his hand. I was but a bystander, but I remember him yet standing at the side gate delivering the form but never taking his clips off.

But for his intervention I would not have been a blip on educational history. I would not have gone to Harrow and almost certainly never have gone to Oxford. Tottenham Grammar would have seen me through to a university all right but I am sure my character and my adult life would have been very different.

Little did I know that even more formidable obstacles had only been removed from the track with some difficulty. When Dr Moore first approached Middlesex County Council in October 1946, he said the governors wanted to carry out 'the ideas suggested in the Fleming Report'. Harrow offered to take five Middlesex boys provided they had 'academic promise' and were not 'problem children'. Although Middlesex already had schemes at three other schools, the Secondary Education Subcommittee did not recommend the Harrow proposal to the main Education Committee.[6] It was only because of the tenacity of the chairman, Mrs Muriel Forbes, that a 'scheme of cooperation' with Harrow was placed before the Education Committee and survived two votes, the second of which was 20 to 14. Muriel Forbes was herself a retired teacher who at the time was considered to be very left wing if not a fellow traveller. Many years later she became the first female Chairman of Middlesex County Council in 1960, five years before it was abolished.

In September 1947 I became a boarder at Moretons House in Harrow. It soon struck me that I had entered a highly structured and regulated society in which everyone, including masters, had a precise place at almost every hour of the day. The day began with the house butler, Mr Thorpe, knocking on every door to call out in what he knew to be cod-French, '*en sevon*', which meant half past seven. Breakfast at 8 a.m. began with a roll-call by the head of house, which was always attended by the housemaster. Chapel was at 9 a.m. followed by two periods of school, then elevenses (in Moretons, always chocolate) and two more periods until about 12.40 p.m. with lunch at 1 p.m. This was the only meal that the housemaster, Oliver Bowlby, and his wife Nell, took with the boys in hall, sitting on the top table with the matron, Mrs Jolliffe, and the house monitors.

After lunch the housemaster acted as banker with the boys' pocket money, taking it in at the beginning of term and doling it out by the half crown as they requested it. I usually came back from the holidays with £2, which lasted most of the term, although it might be topped up with a postal order or if my parents came to visit.

Besides being opening hour for the bank, the post-lunch session served a disciplinary function. Boys who had been given a 'Georgic' by a form master had to report their misdemeanour to the housemaster. In my day masters rarely set naughty boys to copy out the customary 500 lines from Virgil's *Georgics*, but more often gave them extra prep. But the term 'Georgic' was still commonplace among boys.

On the positive side, masters were encouraged to recognise particularly good work, not only by awarding a high mark – alpha minus or double minus – but also by sending the boy to show it to his housemaster. This was known as a 'send-up' – quite different from the meaning in common currency now. The boy showed the work with the mark and the words 'sent-up' to his housemaster who recorded it in his book. Those who achieved eight send-ups in one term, for all subjects combined, were awarded a book prize at the end of term. I have several such prizes still, including two volumes of Arthur Bryant's history of the Napoleonic era, *The Years of Endurance, 1793–1802* and *The Years of Victory, 1802–12*.

This system of encouraging effort among the upper/middle ranks of each class seemed to work well. The housemaster was made aware of your cumulative achievements during the term. Above the 'send-up' system in the rarified air of scholastic excellence were a number of specially endowed competitive prizes, in which I realised I was out of my depth. These prizes, named after their benefactors, were won by particularly brilliant boys, in Harrow parlance, 'groises', such as David Lindsay-Rea and Christopher Arnander in my house, and Trevor Lloyd in Druries.

At 2.30 p.m. on Monday, Tuesday and Thursday every boy was required on the football pitch or the cricket field. For me this was never irksome – quite the contrary – but I suppose there were some who hated it. Almost every twentieth-century novelist and playwright who wrote about public schools expressed contempt for the compulsory games and derided the 'hearties' who not only starred in the field but also enjoyed such endeavour. I recognised soon enough that Harrow was something of an 'academy of ball chasers'. But I loved all the major games – rugby in the autumn term, Harrow Football in the winter and cricket in the summer.

Friday afternoon was allocated to 'small ball games' – squash, racquets, Eton Fives – and later on there was golf and sailing. I enjoyed Fives so much that I played almost every Sunday afternoon as well, autumn and winter. The only part of the compulsory exercise week that I disliked was the Combined Cadet Force (CCF) training on Wednesday afternoons. It was always known as 'The Corps', tracing its origins back to the Harrow Rifle Corps formed before the First World War.

From the age of 15 onwards we had to drill on the parade ground dressed in khaki uniform. This was 1947 so I understood the need for a trained citizen army but I always resented the arrogant and harsh attitude of the drillmasters, both at Harrow and later on in National Service. In the third and fourth year drill was interspersed with field tactics and tackling obstacles so The Corps became more tolerable and sometimes I actually enjoyed Wednesdays.

After games or The Corps we were more than ready for tea at 4.30 p.m. – the one meal of the day to which you could arrive any time in the half hour. We could theoretically eat as many half slices of bread as we liked but in practice our rations of butter, margarine and jam never went far enough to indulge our appetites to that degree. Most boys brought a little extra jam from home but butter and margarine were not so portable or durable. A few boys with families in farming, hotels or business were sent what was obviously black market butter, which they would bring in by the pound wrapped in silver paper.

On the garden side of the hall beside the top table, where once there had been a large open fire, there was then a gas fire at which two boys could make toast at the same time. Like everything else, the toasting slots were allocated strictly by seniority. The monitors toasted their fill before fourth yearers, third yearers and lesser fry were summoned to the fire. In practice therefore it was very rare for any but third yearers to reach the fire before tea was cleared away at five o'clock.

In the winter each room had its own coal fire on which we could make toast with bread brought from hall, but we were not permitted to light our fires until after supper on full school days and after 6 p.m. on half holidays (and then only one between two rooms). So in practice room toast was rarely more than a weekend treat.

At 5.15 p.m. on full school days we began two more lessons which lasted until 6.45 p.m. For most of the year it seemed we came home to the house in the dark. After an afternoon on the football field or the Fives court, evening lessons were always rather an effort. I suspect some of the masters had doubts about their value. Half holidays on three days a week, including Saturday, were so much nicer for everyone. We had the usual four lessons in the morning followed by games with lock-up at six o'clock. There was more time for tea, more time for going to the tuck shop, more time for extra-curricular activities, such as art and music, and there was more time for prep.

On full days there was only one 40-minute session of prep in hall for boys in their first two years. But on Tuesday and Thursday half holidays there was monitored prep in hall from 6 till 7 p.m. and then prep in rooms after supper from 7.45 p.m. until 8.30 p.m. Every night we had at least two subjects for prep at all levels of the school. The result for me was that I never had enough time for prep on full school days, especially in the first two years when I had a hard time keeping up.

Every evening at lock-up we had 'bill' (roll-call) in hall, and then at 8.45 p.m. after prep we had five minutes of house prayers led by the housemaster. Between 9 and 9.20 p.m. all the junior boys had timetabled 'toshes' (baths) two days a week supervised by monitors, although most boys on most days had already had a bath after games. Lights out were at 9.30 p.m. for the younger boys, at 9.45 p.m. for second yearers and ten o'clock for third yearers. Like the routine toshes, lights out was checked by seniors; nothing was left to chance.

Even Sunday began with a rigid framework of compulsory events. Breakfast at nine a.m. was followed by compulsory chapel at eleven for half an hour and again at 6 p.m. for the main service of the week, lasting three quarters of an hour. However, there was no timetabled prep on Sunday so sometimes there seemed oceans of time in which to play Fives or wander round the park lake or, in the summer, go off to the swimming pool known as Ducker, or indeed sometimes to do all three in one day.

Saturday evening was usually part of the working week. Most Saturdays everyone in the school was set a 'Saturday-nighter' – an essay or sustained work of some kind supposed to be written in the designated prep time between six and seven o'clock. In practice my essay took me much longer so I always had to finish it in my own time on Sunday. Two or three weekends a term, however, we had a respite from schoolwork. A feature film in the Speech Room (Speecher) or some other pleasing diversion such as a debate or a Shakespearean play took precedence over the essay.

Looking back on this complicated pattern of work, games, prep and prayers, I can see it had advantages over the regular day school. We had only 30 lessons of 40 minutes each week, even counting Saturday morning, compared to 40 at my grammar school. At Harrow we also had six and three-quarter hours' designated prep time, most of which was monitored for the junior boys. By the fourth year at Tottenham Grammar we had three subjects for homework a night plus a composition at the weekend, very similar to Harrow. Which, I wonder, was making the best use of its pupils' and its masters' time? There were more lessons at Tottenham but a substantial portion of quiet, supervised prep at Harrow.

In the early months I found it hard to keep up with the school bell, which rang before Speecher on Monday morning, before chapel on other days and before and after lessons four or six times a day. I already knew how to keep to a timetable within one school building but Harrow was scattered through more than a dozen buildings, the most distant of which were half a mile apart. Luckily Moretons was near the middle of the gravel ridge, which is Harrow Hill, but even so, for a couple of classes I had to go from the Estate schools at one end to the Copse at the other in the allotted interval of five minutes. Of course I went along with others in my class but in the initial bewilderment I was often a straggler.

For a month or so I was almost dizzy trying to keep up with the timetable for lessons, games, chapel, meals, prep and prayers. I performed dismally at Latin, being entirely mystified by gerunds and gerundives as explained by Mr Greenstock in 'Remove' 1. At Tottenham Grammar, Latin was a minority subject taken by no more than a quarter of the boys. At Harrow, Latin was the yardstick that determined which class you were placed in and where you stood in the school hierarchy – the Bill list. At Tottenham after the first year I had found Latin hard and slipped in class to between fifth and tenth out of twenty-eight. When I arrived at Harrow the headmaster and my housemaster must have judged correctly that the Tottenham standard would be lower than at Harrow. They decided that I still needed two years before taking the School Certificate, whereas if I had stayed at Tottenham I would have taken it the next year. They placed me in R1, which was the second ranked form in the Remove. There I was seventeenth or eighteenth out of eighteen in Latin and obviously floundering. At the end of my first term I was moved down a form. My housemaster, Oliver Bowlby, wrote in a note to himself: 'Weak in languages. Rest promising. Placed a bit too high.'

At the end of three weeks I took a small step to help myself cope with the many demands on my time. Like many other new boys I had been recruited willy-nilly on the first day to be a treble in the choral society. I had no idea what we would sing or how often we would rehearse. I had no inclination for music, no family background in it and a strong antipathy to anything religious. When I found I had to attend two evenings a week to learn the *St Matthew Passion* I was dismayed. After two or three rehearsals in which I thought the music unappealing and the words nonsense ('See him? Who? The bridegroom Christ', etc.) I asked the enthusiastic and kindly director of music, Mr

McCurrach, if I could drop out. He was very reluctant to let me go not understanding how anyone could feel an aversion to Bach. But the choral society was supposed to be voluntary so at the second time of asking he agreed, perhaps realising by then that I had little talent as a singer.

By a stroke of luck the first exercise organised by the house monitors was a three-and-a-half-mile run around Harrow Hill called 'Short Ducker' because it went past the pool. It was intended as training for the rugby season. It was not a race but inevitably stronger runners forged ahead. Despite being a new boy and shorter than most I found that the cross-country races at Tottenham stood me in good stead. I easily kept up with the leading runners who were all three years older. A week or so later the best athlete in the house, Henry Walter, organised a house cross-country run around the two-and-a-half-mile Torpid – under 16s – course. Again I came home in the first group.

These successes were important because they established that I had sporting ability, which counted strongly with my peers. What you could do for the house on the sports field was the first yardstick by which everyone was judged. After the practice cross-country run, Henry Walter predicted to a group of second yearers that I would win the Torpid steeplechase later that term. It raised my status though it turned out to be well wide of the mark – I came thirteenth out of a hundred plus.

During my first term I shared a large corner room on the second floor overlooking the High Street with John Hedley-Whyte and David Jenkins. They were both six months or so younger than me but much bigger. Hedley-Whyte (we always used surnames) had entered the school the previous summer term so knew the ropes. He was clever without being brilliant; good enough at Latin and Greek to be in the Classical Remove (the highest ranking Remove), though he always knew he was going to be a scientist and ended up as a medical professor at Harvard. He was the son of two affluent doctors in Newcastle. The first time I met his father I came across him already in our room so I said, 'Dr Hedley-Whyte, I presume.' Somehow the joke did not go down well.

David Jenkins was less intimidating, in part because he came from Hathersage in Derbyshire, a place I knew something about because I had spent a walking holiday there in 1941. David also had a regional accent, which marked him out slightly from the many strong 'County' accents that fell new upon my ears, all talking excitedly about their relatives and their 'pris', their private or preparatory schools. To almost all of my fellows these schools, with names like Aysgarth, Sunningdale and Ludgrove, were household names. I had never heard of any of them nor dreamt of their existence as feeders to the public school system.

Another strange feature to me was the social cross-referencing that went on with every new encounter. A 13-year-old boy would not only ask about a fellow pupil's prep school, but as soon as he knew where you came from he would say, 'Do you know my uncle, or my cousin or even my second cousin once removed ... who lives in ... or is rector of ... or is Master of Foxhounds for the Pytchley?' ... and so on. I suppose it was similar to what many people now call 'networking' although the emphasis was on social standing rather than economic advancement.

Next door to us in a smaller room were David Nelson and Douglas Macadam, while beyond them were Pat Spence-Thomas and Geoffrey Brocklehurst. They were all ahead of me in seniority in that they had entered either a year or a term before me, though none was as old as me. In a way I was carrying weight. More was expected of me because I was older and because I had been parachuted into the system at a higher point of entry than usual. This feeling was accentuated in me not least because my Latin was poor. I was downgraded after the first term to Remove 2A whose form master was the school chaplain, Philip Bryant, always known as 'Pumph' Bryant. A few weeks into my first term he led a very pleasant walk in the Chilterns for a few boys too young to be on The Corps' field day. The culmination was lunch in a pub garden in Chorleywood where he bought us a scarlet elixir called 'Vimto'. As chaplain, he once asked me if I wanted to be confirmed but never probed further as to my reasons for saying 'No'.

At the start I was aware that my London accent grated on the ear in contrast to the smoother tones of RP articulated by most of the other boys. One particularly odious boy from Elmfield actually called me an 'oik', the slang term for all boys from the lower social classes. Whenever that pejorative term was used I found myself wincing even if it was not actually directed at me. About a month into my school career the geography master, Major J.A.N. Thompson, took the class on an educational trip to the London docks. When we went aboard an old paddlesteamer at Tower Pier the boat was very crowded with schoolboys from many schools. Turning to his class, he remarked in his usual megaphone voice, 'I see we are travelling with the *hoi polloi*.' Everyone laughed, but though it was not aimed at me, it made me cringe and rather spoilt what was actually a good trip through the Albert and King George V Docks. However, in the year that I was 'up to Thompson' (to use the Harrow terminology) I found him a good teacher – straightforward, good-humoured and usually engaging.

During my interview for the award I had mentioned that I went on climbing holidays with my father. When I arrived at Harrow I was able to tell them that I had just climbed the Matterhorn. The headmaster was impressed because when Leo Amery, an Old Harrovian and a governor, visited the school in my first term, the head made a point of introducing me so that we had a very short chat. I had a vague idea as to the importance of Amery because my father had read his climbing autobiography and had also remarked to me when his son John had been hanged as a traitor in 1945. Amery had been an older contemporary of Churchill at Harrow in the 1880s. He went on to serve as a Cabinet minister in three Conservative governments. During the Second World War he had been Secretary of State for India and Burma.

A day or two after our little talk, Amery sent me a signed copy of his climbing book, *Days of Fresh Air*, the title of which is taken from the Harrow School song, 'Forty Years On'. I could appreciate his prowess as a climber and his enthusiasm for the mountains but I knew nothing of his political significance, especially of his forthright speeches in the Commons in 1940, which had helped to get rid of Neville Chamberlain. Years later when I was a BBC producer I met Amery's other son, Julian, then a Tory MP who supported Ian Smith and the white Rhodesian rebels. Unhappily he was still locked into his father's imperialist ways of thought even though they were by now plainly outdated.

Harrow school uniform in the post-war period was extraordinary and still is. At Tottenham we wore a black blazer with the badge and motto of our seventeenth-century benefactor, the Duchess of Somerset. We also wore a black cap with coloured piping, indicating which house we were in. At Harrow one's clothes were regulated in much more detail. Six days a week we wore plain blue blazers, grey flannel trousers, grey socks, black shoes and a detachable white collar on a striped flannel shirt with a plain black tie. Before entering the school boys were sent a long list which specified the type and colour of each garment. None of this was particularly irksome, nor so different from Tottenham.

On Sunday, however, we returned to the nineteenth century; some said we were still in mourning for George III, though the latest history of Harrow does not mention this.[7] For most boys Sunday garb was a black tailcoat, black waistcoat, black striped trousers, a stiff white wing collar, white shirt and black tie. But for small boys such as myself it was a black Eton jacket with a broad, stiff white collar instead of tails and wing collar. The short Eton jacket and the oversized collar I always thought made us look ridiculous. The tails and wing collar I got used to but they were equally absurd and very hot in the summer.

Two years after I arrived straw hats became available for the first time after the war. At first when in short supply, the wearing of them was voluntary but soon, to my dismay, they became compulsory all the year round. The Harrow boater is a broad-brimmed hat with a crown so shallow that it has to be tilted forward to stay on and even then it needs a comical piece of elastic to hold it in place. The early post-war models drooped when they got wet in the rain so adding to their absurdity. Sixty years on this uniform for weekdays and Sundays is unchanged, although it is only compulsory for a smaller proportion of the time. (I'm told that after my time the boys voted substantially in favour of sticking to this traditional dress.)

Uniform also formed part of the seniority and privileges system, which ruled every stage of school life. New boys, for instance, had to fasten all three buttons on their jackets, known as 'bluers'. In the second year they still had to fasten their bluers with one button at all times. Not until you entered the third year could you undo all those blessed buttons. Quite early on when my head was still in a whirl trying to cope with the timetable and the 'privs', one particularly obnoxious two yearer, Johnny Mengers, clipped me round the ear, demanding that I button up. At the time I was not big enough to resist. A year or so later Mengers and one of his acolytes discussed my clothes in loud voices just across the tea table from me as if I did not exist. Then Mengers swung round to demand if my father had paid for my clothes or whether the school had paid for them. In fact my parents paid a small proportion of the total cost while Middlesex County Council paid the rest. The school paid nothing.

Both these boys had very rich parents so the question boiled down to mental bullying. By this time I had realised that these two were the slugs of the house – pretty useless at schoolwork and not much better at games.

They did little more than hog their lavish tuck and prey on vulnerable boys such as Pat Spence-Thomas. I was no longer vulnerable, even to their mental bullying, although I certainly resented this personal slur.

Mengers had been bullying Spence-Thomas for much of their first year before I arrived. It must have been a major factor in Pat's father's decision to remove him from the school after two years. He had done poorly in class, in part because he was in the same class as Mengers. Nor did he make a mark on the games field. However, I found him agreeable and often amusing. He had practical technical ability, such as being able to construct a cat's whisker wireless set. Although he wouldn't or couldn't fight off the bullies, in some ways he was fearless.

On a dark November night he led me out of his window 30 feet above the High Street, up over an overhanging gutter on to the roof. Even by Matterhorn standards this was a bold, ropeless adventure. From there we walked right along the full length of the house across a small gap on to the roof of the bookshop next door and on to the Headmaster's House. The upper floor of the bookshop was still unrepaired after being hit by an incendiary bomb during the war. The roof had a gaping trap door, which led down on to an unoccupied, semi-derelict floor. We thought about dropping down on to it but could not see how we could get back without a rope or a ladder. All this time masters, boys and the general public were walking by in the street below, oblivious to our antics. Just as well.

Moretons' garden had also been hit by incendiary bombs in 1944 but most of them turned out to be deliberate duds. The housemaster, Oliver Bowlby, had been told by bomb disposal experts that they had been made in Czechoslovakia. As the house was built in 1811 with corridors lined with wood panelling it would have burnt fiercely once alight.

Our room had three folding beds, two of which were made of metal and not more than 20 years old. Mine, however, was a much older wooden model in which the mattress lay on a canvas tied to a wooden frame. Every time I turned over in bed it creaked loudly. It was also quite heavy to lift back into place each morning, but once done there was reasonable space in the room for work and play.

Games

As already mentioned, I enjoyed Harrow in large part because I relished all the sports. The abiding ethos of *mens sana in corpore sano* (a healthy mind in a healthy body) has much to be said for it. Schoolwork was certainly not neglected but for most boys, including me, it took second place. Compulsory games four days a week plus voluntary games at weekends meant there was plenty of opportunity to improve one's performance and to try the other options.

To my surprise I was picked to play centre three-quarter for the Junior Colts under-15s rugby team in my first term. We went by coach to Stowe in Buckinghamshire where we were mown down 27–3, their backs being more proficient at passing and running than us. My opposite number certainly scored a try. Four years later I had the pleasure of leading the school 2nd XV to a victory at Stowe. In between, much of my school rugby career was blighted by a bad ankle, although it did not stop me getting a handsome blue cap with a long silver tassle in my first season in the house 1st XV. A year later, when I was 17, Moretons was narrowly defeated in the final by The Grove. In my last season of rugby I dearly wanted to get into the 1st XV but ended up being captain of the 2nd XV, which had a reasonable record of four wins and three defeats. That same term Moretons was cock house at rugby, beating Newlands in the final 8–3 on a pitch, which a correspondent in *The Harrovian* described as 'strikingly like marzipan'.

I always found rugby a thrilling game to play even on Harrow's notoriously muddy pitches. One afternoon I remember playing a friendly against another house in a tremendous downpour and coming off the field feeling we had achieved something even if we were covered in mud. 'Go for the corner flag,' instructed one of my rugby masters early on and I followed his advice on many occasions.

Harrow Football, which we played in the winter term, was supposedly designed as suitable for the local clay. The ball is larger than the normal football and is oddly shaped, being round in one direction but oval on the sides, more like a floor pouffe than a round football. It was devised in the nineteenth century before either rugby or Association Football became dominant or indeed set in their rules. Most of the time you kick and dribble the ball as in soccer but the key move is to flick it with your toe up into a team-mate's hands right in front of the base (goal). Upon catching the oversize ball he shouts, 'Yards!' The game stops and the catcher is given a free punt at the base while the opponents can come no closer than three yards in an effort to stop him. To score, the ball has simply to pass through the posts at any height. Should the opposing team catch a kick which falls short of the goal, then they too can shout 'Yards!' and have a free kick. Compared to both soccer and rugby it seems somewhat unsophisticated.

In my fifth season, when I was house captain of Harrow Football, we had a very good record. We were a team without any great stars, certainly no one in the 1st XI. Yet we reached the final mainly through sheer persistence. Twice we won replays after a draw. In the final, alas, we were beaten 3–1 by The Park.

I expect the school and the games masters must often have asked whether Harrow Football is still worth playing. One obvious disadvantage is that boys cannot play against other schools, only against teams of old boys from each house. In my day there was a full schedule of matches against old boy teams throughout the winter term. But nowadays the number of 1st XI Harrow Football games is much reduced. Soccer has been introduced and is probably played with more enthusiasm.

As I've said my favourite sport was Eton Fives, a game developed between the buttresses of Eton College but actually played by many people with no fixed rules against the walls of churches and halls around the country since medieval times. We even had a simplified version of it at Tottenham Grammar School, although I was not old enough to play it there. The version codified by Eton has three walls with an elegant buttress on the left-hand side covered in slopes and ledges to make the ball bounce unpredictably. The front floor of the court is raised on a step while the front wall has a three-inch wide sloping ledge marking the lower limit of when a ball is in play. The side walls also have sloping ledges which provide extra hazards. The game is always played between teams of two. Eton first played Harrow in 1885 and over the next century it spread to many other schools. It now has a substantial following with many competitions for schools and old boys' clubs.

I was introduced to Fives by Arthur Macadam who was a three yearer when I arrived. He was captain of Fives in a house that had been pretty poor at all sports for some time. One Friday afternoon he took David Jenkins and me down to the courts to show us the rudiments. By chance there was a house match in progress in the adjoining court. Elmfield, who then dominated Harrow sport, were beating another house. One of the players was the captain of boxing and cricket and the hooker of the 1st XV, Garth Hoyer-Millar, one of the real swells in the school, pointed out to new boys like me. In between our instruction we watched the game next door.

In contrast to the patball game we were playing, finding it difficult to hit the ball at all, let alone with any accuracy, this match was fast and furious. The four players cut the ball to start each point like a bullet, then pounded it into the box or leapt high into the air to return a lofty shot. Immediately I could see this was an absorbing game requiring great energy and skill. The gloved hand could place the ball with precision, sometimes right in the hole beside the buttress, thereby making it a winner. The competitive atmosphere was enhanced by the white, leather-covered balls, which remained in use until the 1960s. Every time they hit the wall they made a sharp click which added to the impact of the hard shot. When they were replaced by a rubber composition ball I felt there was a real loss of speed and control. In fact the new ball often bounces out of the hole whereas the old ball usually stayed in.

For the rest of that first year Jenkins and I played many games with Arthur Macadam and Andrew Beamish, becoming quite competent. We also learned much from the Moretons Torpids pair that year – David McLeod and Geoffrey Shakerley – who won the Torpids Cup. In our second winter season Jenkins and I carried on this tradition by winning the cup, somewhat to our surprise.

This was the start of 30 years playing Fives for the house, the school, for Oxford and then for the Old Harrovians. I only retired when osteoarthritis made it painful to make quick turns in the court. With regret I followed my consultant's advice not to pursue it any longer. Along the way David Jenkins and I were school champions twice, and in my last two years I captained a Moretons team, which took all three Fives cups – the one pair, three pair and Torpids. The huge silver plate awarded for the three pair competition still resides in Moretons. Later David and I were on opposite sides in the 1958 Oxford and Cambridge match, which, alas, Cambridge won. David was always the better player.

In our last two years we were both in the school team playing against schools such as Eton, Westminster, Highgate, Charterhouse and Mill Hill, and old boys' clubs such as the Old Harrovians and the Jesters. One attraction was the away matches for which we were allowed to travel under our own steam. Twice we went to Eton, for instance, by bus via Uxbridge. That may not sound exciting but it was a more practicable route than going back to London first. However, after any away match we usually contrived to return via central London where we marked our one day of freedom with a good dinner.

Apart from these very minor authorised forays outside the school we were supposed to keep within the boundaries of a triangle formed by three railway lines, each about a mile from the top of the Hill. Some boys found this restriction irksome and used to swan off to London or at least to Harrow town surreptitiously. In my second year, for instance, three senior boys in Moretons were caught going down to Harrow at night. Two of them were expelled by the headmaster, though it was only four days to the end of term. The third was allowed to stay to complete his exams the next term but he was deprived of all his privileges as a sixth former – a blow to his prestige if nothing else.

Personally, I never had a yearning for London because I found so much of interest on the Hill or in the sports fields down below. For those who liked to stroll or walk there was a park with a lake beside the very extensive football fields and the farm. In my very last week three of us strolled to the western end of the school grounds (still within the bounds) and then climbed a wire fence to walk boldly through the garden of a Catholic institution. The Head of House, John Hedley-Whyte, hearing of this escapade somehow concocted a plausible letter from the School Secretary instructing us to appear before the Head Master for our transgression. We were taken in by it but Hedley-Whyte and his co-conspirators lost their nerve. Just before the appointed hour they told us of their hoax. So laughs all round. In a traditional school story it would have ended disastrously for all concerned.

At the end of the winter term everyone did a fortnight of athletics. We endeavoured to reach predetermined standards thought to be appropriate for each age group. If you ran a hundred yards, for instance, within a certain time you got a 'Standard', which generated one point. If you did somewhat better than the minimum you got a credit or two points. Altogether there were seven track events, four jumps, the discus, javelin and shot. So if you were good at everything you could get a maximum score of 28. Each day each boy's successes were marked up on a chart on the house noticeboard for all to see. In my first two years I performed dismally but later on reached 16 and then 17 points, which topped everyone in the house. Even so I was not sufficiently outstanding in any one event to appear in the school sports except for the house relay (8 × 400 yards), which Moretons won in 1951 and was runner-up in the following year. Both years we were anchored by Hedley-Whyte who was an ungainly but very strong runner, school champion at 100, 220 and 440 yards.

In my last two years someone had the bright idea of organising a house mile in which the whole house took part, each runner handicapped by age. The first year I won but in the second year the handicaps per month of age were increased, enabling Robin Sagar-Musgrave to beat me by 20 yards. In retrospect I can see I should have taken athletics in the summer rather than cricket. Then I might well have made the school team. By Harrow standards I was a second-rate athlete, though when I reached the army my running put me into the medals. But as I never had any encouragement from a master to take athletics and I really liked cricket that is what I chose to do.

The best I could muster at cricket was one appearance for the 3rd XI and a house cap. My best innings began very badly with me missing the ball while out of my crease in a needle house match against Rendalls. I turned round to see my stumps knocked down amid cries of 'howzat!'. The umpire raised his finger and I began walking towards the pavilion with the score at 10 for 3 wickets. Then suddenly I was called back by the Rendalls team. The wicket-keeper, Alex Cockell, had not caught the ball but had inadvertently knocked off the bails with his pad. A less sporting team would not have pointed that out because the umpire did not spot it. I then went on to hit the highest score, 41 not out, at close of play, with two straight drive sixes and several fours. Alas, the next day we could not hold our own against the school's best fast bowlers, Kok and Hulbert, who mowed us down with their in-swingers. Still I never enjoyed a game so much.

My last appearance on a Harrow cricket field came in an end of term game against a team from the Harrow Clubs which the school ran in West London. Playing wicket-keeper, I unwisely stood too close to the wicket when a batsman missed the ball and swung round to strike me a mighty blow above the left eye. I was taken to the school's own sanatorium, known as 'The San', where the school doctor stitched me up. When I was discharged a day or so later the friendly doctor held up a mirror for me to see the result. He had probably stitched up dozens of boys in his time but in the ways of youth I had the gall to say, 'Not bad ... almost professional.' To his credit he did not reprimand me nor even remind me of his qualifications and experience. My left eyebrow conceals the scar but it has stood up vertically ever since as if I am permanently asking a question or doubting the veracity of my interlocutor. Very suitable for a journalist, I suppose.

In the year I left, my House won 19 cups, a prodigious feat. When our generation had entered Moretons, the house was of no account on the sporting field. The house Harrow Football XI, for example, was beaten 14–0 by Elmfield in 1948 and 11–1 by the Headmasters in 1949. By 1951–52 our generation had transformed the standing of the house in all sports.

The significance of sporting achievement was underlined with photographs and with dress privileges. Every school and house team had its photograph taken as a matter of course, regardless of its success. I have a dozen of these dated photos on my walls to this day. Occasionally as I pass them by a line from a stirring Harrow song comes to mind: 'they were wonderful giants of old you know, wonderful giants of old', showing that sporting rituals, though regularly observed, were not always taken too seriously.

Individual sporting success was also reinforced by an elaborate code of dress privileges, something unheard of at my grammar school. Velvet caps with long tassels were awarded to the school rugby 1st XV; pillbox hats, also with tassels, were awarded to the Harrow Football 1st XI, which looked straight out of the Ark; and of course brightly coloured caps for the cricket XI. In addition, all the school first teams had their own blazer, tie and scarf. The blazer for Harrow Football was in vivid blue and white stripes just like a butcher's coat. Even the lesser games had their own silk scarves and ties often in lurid colours, such as mauve and pink for Fives. Boys who qualified for this fancy dress would swagger about in it on half holidays, parading their success about the Hill, in the tuck shops and in the summer at the open-air Bill (roll-call) in the Old School yard. I had never seen such dandyism before but when I made various teams I joined the parade like everyone else.

As mentioned earlier, at my grammar school I had won a prize for reciting Sir Henry Newbolt's patriotic poem 'Vitai Lampada', which begins with 'There's a breathless hush in the Close tonight' and contains the line 'And it's not for the sake of a ribboned coat'. The habit of sporting dandyism was very well established at Harrow and a function, in part, of a well-heeled clientele who could afford these extras. It certainly encouraged those who aspired to success, but perhaps I can hear all the educational psychologists suck in a collective breath of disapproval as I write.

Leisure

Despite the timetable for schoolwork and games, there was quite a bit of time for optional leisure activities. Those with a practical bent went to the well-equipped workshop known as 'Worker' where they could practise wood and metalworking skills. For a couple of terms I tried art in the very attractive art school. Occasionally I took part in debates on

Saturday night in the Speech-room, which, being a semicircle, was a perfect arena. In one debate, which proposed that 'Poets and writers have done more for England than politicians', I spoke apparently with 'sincerity and conviction' which 'made a long speech interesting'. No doubt that was a delicate way of saying that I went on a bit. The report in *The Harrovian* also made clear that everyone was eclipsed by another Moretonian, Mungo Henderson, a year younger than me, who spoke 'wittily, well and often'.

In our rooms we used to play board-games such as Monopoly and Totopoly (about horse-racing), chess and draughts. In the third and fourth years we played quite a lot of bridge on Saturday and Sunday evenings. Our mentor, Hedley-Whyte, tried to teach us some of the well-known bidding conventions but they were too complicated for me. David Nelson and I formed a successful partnership using only a simple points system based on the face cards. In my final year we also had a lively discussion group in the house called the Hot Air Club with two very bright boys, Mungo Henderson and Gervase Duffield, being particularly active.

In my second year I was somehow recruited for the school farm by Maurice Snell, a sixth-former in the neighbouring house, The Park. The 75-acre farm had been started during the war to provide fresh milk and eggs for the school and had been continued afterwards to provide opportunities to learn about farming and land management. A few boys studied agriculture as their specialist subject in the VIth form.

Initially I joined a team of four or five boys at The Park who went down by van once a week at 6 a.m. to milk the school's 32 shorthorn cows. The farm had ultra-modern Alfa Laval milking machines, though we did have to milk each teat by hand to achieve an initial flow before fixing the machine to the whole udder. In 1949 the farm won the Middlesex County Milk Production Competition gaining maximum points for clean milk. The farm also had some pedigree Essex sows whose care may not have matched that of the cows. Feeding the pigs with swill from a local slaughterhouse was a gruesome task. The smell was enough to numb the brain, though if I had had a more inquiring mind I would have asked if there were not risks in such a diet.

Most of the other boys on the milking team had some farming experience or ambition. Snell, who was the son of the chief maths master, intended to become a vet. I persisted with it for the rest of my school career simply because it was so totally different from everything else. One morning I got up at 5.30 a.m. and crept out of the house up to The Park only to find that I had mistaken the day. It wasn't our turn to milk the cows.

So, sleepily, I went back to Moretons, forgetting that I had pulled the door shut behind me and could not get back into the house. Rather than ring the bell, wake the butler and the housemaster and confess my error, I found my way through an alley into the garden. It was a very cold winter morning and I hadn't enough clothes on to stand around, inactive, out of doors. So I squeezed on to a plant shelf in the unheated greenhouse and lay there for a very uncomfortable hour before the house awoke. I realised then that with the excuse of going milking I could swan off early almost any morning without being questioned but I never exploited this loophole.

When Snell left the school the master in charge of the farm, Sidney Patterson, asked me if I could raise a milking team from Moretons once a week. With regular help from Christopher Cooper and Erroll Mews and sporadic help from a few others I organised a five-boy team for the rest of my time, even becoming secretary of the school farm! I now discover, 60 years later, that Her Majesty's Inspectors of Education described the farm in 1951 as an 'unusually successful enterprise', 'making a valuable contribution to the life and work of the school'.[8]

Sidney Patterson was a somewhat raffish Irishman who taught me maths in my second year. In his classroom on the first floor of the Estates Schools the windows were very large and pivoted about the centre. One day a boy larking about leant on the window and tipped backwards to fall straight out 15 feet into the lane below. Somehow he landed on his bottom and was not seriously hurt. These days the Health & Safety Executive would have made a tremendous fuss and the boy's parents would have sued the school for a large sum. Then he just had an afternoon in his house sick bay and has laughed about it ever since.

The Harrow system was unashamedly competitive and elitist. From the moment of entering the school each boy had a place in the hierarchy. Up to the Vth Form each boy was listed in the school register, known as the Bill Book, alphabetically by class with the Classical Fifth at the top and the Fourth form at the bottom. Most new boys were placed in the Shell or the Remove (in effect grades 2 and 3) according to how well they had done in the Common Entrance Exam. To be placed in the Fourth Form usually indicated you needed remedial teaching.

On being promoted to the lower VIth, as almost everybody was, boys were ranked according to their performance in the School Certificate – three points for a distinction, two for a credit and one for a pass – and seated in Speech-room accordingly. For me this system was a spur to greater effort, although it only just enabled me to overcome my weakness in Latin and French. I was never among the outstanding boys intellectually, though I passed all my exams and gained entry to Oxford. What effect the system had on other boys less bright than me I cannot really say. Perhaps they have spoken for themselves.

In the autumn and winter terms the Bill was read aloud in the house before breakfast and supper by the head of house or one of the monitors. The housemaster was always present at breakfast to hear each one of us answer, 'Here, Sir.' Long ago when the school was much smaller the register of pupils or Bill was read each day in the school yard in front of the Old Schools. When I was there this solemn filing past of the whole school in strict seniority was confined to Tuesday and Thursday half holidays in the summer term. A school monitor would read the list of 500 names and each boy would salute the master on duty by raising his finger deferentially to the brim of his straw hat. The master stood on the lowest step of the long flight of steps going up to the Fourth Form room – a dark panelled room dating from the early seventeenth century and covered with carved names of earlier boys such as Lord Byron and Percy Bysshe Shelley.

Open-air Bill was a formal occasion yet also an opportunity to gossip with friends in other houses and other classes. We used to play a game of entering the line to walk past the master at the last possible moment and as casually as possible. It was a ploy not without risks because you had to pass between two monitors strategically placed ten yards before the master. If you were not in the right Bill order then you were pulled out of the line and made to wait until the end. Infringements of petty rules such as this were always remarked upon by someone in authority and usually punished.

It was still a pretty stern system, although most of the discipline was applied in the house by the house monitors rather than by masters. The head of house was authorised to beat boys with the housemaster's permission. A beating had its own blood-curdling ritual conducted just at lights out. The head of house would shout for his fag with the yell of 'Boy-Up', dragging out the words as long as possible to gain maximum effect. The fag was told to fetch a boy in his pyjamas to the head's room where he was confronted by the four or five house monitors. The head of house would then accuse the boy of some dreadful crime, such as being persistently late for lock-up or cutting house games or worst of all being 'lippy' to a monitor, that is being cheeky. The boy was given a chance to answer the charge but the verdict had usually been decided upon by the court of monitors beforehand.

In Moretons this ritual, sometimes known as a 'haul-up', occurred about three or four times a year. In my first term I was summoned by the military-minded head of house, Tony Teague, who was known as the Iron Duke because of his demeanour. I have forgotten my trans-gression but luckily escaped a beating. Instead I was given a stern warning coupled with other punishment such as extra fagging. Those who were beaten suffered horribly. The cane was very thick and Teague in particular brought it down on the pyjama-clad bottom with great force. When a victim took a tosh the day after, the black bruises were horrible to behold. The weals lasted more than a fortnight and were very painful.

This brutal system should have been abolished long before, although it must be said that corporal punishment was still prevalent in all types of school. Masters at my primary school and my grammar school had used the cane, sometimes quite frequently. I was caned on the hand in both schools and never forgave those masters. I suspect Harrow boys felt much the same about the house monitors who beat them. In our house two strapping boys, too clever for their own good it would seem, were always getting into scrapes. They were beaten several times apiece, for what I do not remember, but I bet they do. One of them rose to become head of house, yet later wasted his life as a petty criminal engaging in property fraud and car scams for which he was imprisoned. Could he have been nudged in that direction by too brutal punishment for schoolboy offences when he was fifteen?

When I was promoted to house monitor in my last year, Hedley-Whyte was head of house. One night he followed the 'Boy-Up' ritual to summon the other monitors to hear charges against two boys who were already third yearers. They had broken some rule, though the transgression did not seem very serious to me. I was shocked when Hedley-Whyte insisted on beating these two boys, both low achievers, and one of whom was small and physically handicapped. I argued against the beating but was overruled. At that point I walked out and thus did not witness the beating being administered. As far as I know that was the only time Hedley-Whyte summoned any boy for a beating. I was accused of not taking responsibility for discipline in the house but no reprisal was brought to bear. I remained a house monitor.

Masters

A number of masters made a real difference to my life at Harrow: Oliver Bowlby, my housemaster; 'Bush' Harris, my English master for the first two years to School Certificate; Willie Stevenson, form master in the lower VIth; Charles Lillingston, who took me in the upper VIth and helped me get into Oxford; Tim Warr, who was in charge of rugby and appointed me captain of the 2nd XV; Major Thompson who took me for geography my first year; and R.W. Moore, the headmaster, who introduced me to Plato and political philosophy as well as trampling on my fundamental rights.

Of all my masters, Bowlby was the most significant because in his class (V2b) he taught Latin at a level I could understand. After a term of bewilderment in Remove 1 and then two terms marking time in R2a with 'Pumph' Bryant, I began in my second year to grasp some of the grammatical concepts essential to a pass the School Certificate. Somehow I had not picked them up at Tottenham and had floundered in the first year at Harrow, feeling I would never be the least bit competent. With Bowlby's skilled and straightforward manner I managed a pass in 1949 and a credit two terms later, which meant I could qualify for the History School at Oxford.

On passing my School Certificate in 1949 I tossed up between taking geography or history as my main subject for the VIth form. I was inclined more towards geography until, by chance, I had a conversation with Bryant. He urged me strongly to go for history on the grounds that the calibre of the Geography Sixth was, he said, so poor. Geography had for years been the domain of E.D. Laborde who had written many books on the subject and whom I knew to be quite a hard taskmaster. But he had just retired to be succeeded by his son, Charles Laborde, who very plainly was not an intellectual. His chief claim to fame and probably the reason for his appointment was that he had captained the school rugby XV for a very successful season in the 1920s. Indeed a stirring school song had been written to commemorate this feat, which was still sung with great gusto. It begins:

The threes may stand in a graceful alignment,
the backs may be shivering cold,
But forwards know none of this dainty refinement,
eternally rolling and rolled.

For some time upper school geography had attracted mostly low achievers, some of whom had not even passed the School Certificate but were over 16 and had to be put somewhere. Most of them had come up from the lowest School Certificate form Vii(d), which in an elitist system was the haven of the non-achievers. Mr Bryant assured me that I would do much better to take history and he was right. Two years later the Ministry of Education Inspectors commented that 'few of the best brains are found on the Geography side'. They went on to say that 'the master in charge of Sixth-Form Geography was without degree qualifications', one of their few critical comments in a highly favourable report.[9]

Charles Lillingston was my teacher in the History VIth for four terms. He had a large room with its own library right at the top of the Estates schools. He was very short-sighted, rather fat, certainly unathletic and slurred his words from some slight speech defect even before sherry; he was an Old Etonian with social pretensions, a bachelor and a prodigious gossip. Despite all this he was a good teacher, caring about the subject and able to enthuse sixth formers into working hard on their own. With only the slightest hint from him I read two volumes of Gibbon's *Decline and Fall of the Roman Empire* just for one essay. He used to loll back in his chair, peering over his thick glasses at the start of a lesson to tease us in various ways before getting down to solid work.[10]

Charlie Lil, as he was known to boys and 'beaks' alike, had a wide range of contacts at Oxford, which he used to place his pupils to good advantage. Without referring to my social background directly he advised that University College, Oxford would suit me better than the other more socially pretentious colleges, which were the choice of most Harrovians. One December I went off to Oxford with Geoffrey Shakerley, also in Moretons but a year ahead of me. Geoffrey was applying to Christ Church as befitted the elder son of a baronet. We stayed in the Mitre Hotel in the High Street, a small seventeenth-century establishment, which oozed deference to the clientele.

After taking papers in History, English, Latin and French, I was accepted on condition I passed A levels and with a strong warning that I had to improve my Latin or I would not get through the first exams called 'Prelims'. Because of National Service we were given places two years in advance, in my case for 1954. I did not resent this interruption to my education at the time and, on reflection, I can see that I was socially immature when I left school in 1952 aged 18. I might not have spent my time at Oxford so profitably or so enjoyably had I gone there straight from school.

Overall the teaching was better at Harrow than at Tottenham. The masters were by and large better qualified but their main advantage was smaller classes. My first class had 21 pupils and the next had 26, but all the rest had fewer. In the History VIth there were only 14; in other subjects, such as modern languages, maths and geography, the numbers were smaller still. At the time the overall teacher to pupil ratio was 1 to 12.

Because the school was so structured in its domestic life, discipline was rarely a problem in the classroom. Once my housemaster pumped me about a new teacher of French who did not maintain order very well. He was an engaging young man but he did not last long. Actually I found him a better teacher than two other masters who taught me French, both of whom kept good or firm order. Their trouble was they were so fluent at French themselves they found it nearly impossible to see our difficulties. They insisted on reading aloud long paragraphs from classical texts, which were too difficult for most of us to understand.

Chapel

Before I went to Harrow my father advised me to put myself down as Church of England and to attend religious services with everyone else. 'Paris,' he said, quoting King Henri IV, 'is worth a mass.' So when I arrived I went through the motions of attending compulsory chapel two mornings a week and twice on Sundays. On weekdays there were house prayers in hall at 8.45 p.m. We also had one or two periods each week of Religious Instruction aimed at the School Certificate in which, incidentally, I got a Pass. I fended off suggestions from the chaplain and my housemaster that I should be confirmed in the Church of England as most of my contemporaries were.

During the second year when compulsory chapel was increased, the long evening service on Sunday became very tedious. It meant nothing to me. It might as well have been mumbo-jumbo. Moreover, the service itself was repetitive: a hymn, a lesson, a psalm, a lesson, the creed (something I had never encountered before), the sermon and a final hymn. Just occasionally the hymns had good tunes which I could sing with gusto but always their words were to me nonsensical. The sermons were heavily laden with scriptural quotations and references which did not resonate with me. Of the 120 or so sermons I must have endured over four and a half years, I only remember one. In the winter of 1948 an Anglican monk just returned from India gave a first-hand account of the communal riots and religious killings in India just after Independence. It was vivid stuff. He laid most of the blame on the Labour government, something which went down well in an overwhelmingly Tory school. Perhaps, like Churchill, he thought Britain should have retained the jewel in its imperial crown for many more years? I had not the experience to challenge his argument but even then I knew it was Indian people of the Hindu and Islamic communities who had done the killing and that they were the same people who for years had screamed at us to leave. I am a democrat but I don't subscribe to the politicians' public creed that only individuals are malign and wicked, that 'the people' are pure, must never be criticised and that the 'will of the people' is always the right answer. 'The people' may be sovereign but in my view they can also be ignorant, stupid and cruel.

In the summer term of my second year I simply got fed up with going to chapel so one Sunday I cut the evening service. Nothing happened so I cut about three more in a row, to my great relief. Who knows how long this might have continued but for a creaky floorboard in my room? By this time I was sharing a room on the first floor with Michael Harper, an Irish Catholic who went with a few others of that persuasion to a Catholic service during chapel.

The house was all quiet when I stepped on the tell-tale floorboard. Unluckily, just at that moment the head of house, Henry Walter, was walking past in the corridor, heard the creak and came in. He himself didn't go to chapel because he was a 'Christian Scientist' but he was quite ready to report me for my absence.

That evening I had to see the housemaster in his cosy upstairs study where his wife Nell Bowlby, was also present. When he asked why I wasn't in chapel I simply told him I was an atheist and found the whole thing silly and meaningless. 'An atheist?' said Bowlby, opening his large blue eyes in wonder, 'an atheist; I've never met an atheist.' Indeed, having spent his whole life in the rarefied atmosphere of Eton as a boy and of Harrow as a master, he may well not have done. Bowlby and his wife were so smitten with this revelation that we had a quiet, civilised conversation concerning my beliefs. I explained that my father was an eloquent, committed atheist and I had never been to a church service, although I had taken part in Christian assemblies in primary and secondary school. Bowlby uttered not a word of reproach or criticism but ended the session by saying I would have to see the headmaster.

R.W. Moore was a doctor of Divinity and a minor theologian, very much in the tradition of public school headmasters in an earlier age. He had a very large jaw and a very pale complexion as if he spent little time in the open air. He was in his forties at the time with a mat of black hair perched on his head. Was it a wig? On the bookcase behind his chair he kept a black bust of himself which we thought rather self-important. In four and a half years this was the second and last time I went to his study or talked to him outside a classroom. Luckily I did not know that he had resumed the practice of beating naughty or rebellious boys after his predecessor had abandoned it.

During a short interview he seemed most concerned that I had been able to cut chapel so many times without being detected. Masters were seated individually every few rows throughout the chapel in part to keep a register and report absentees. Sidney Patterson told me later that he got into hot water for not reporting me. I never found out if it was because he had been absent himself or because he had been idle or simply indulgent.

After a short discussion of my reason for cutting chapel Moore confronted me with a choice. 'Either you go to chapel,' he said in his lugubrious voice, 'or I will have to ask your father to withdraw you from the school.' In retrospect I should have asked for the same tolerance accorded to Catholics, Jews and other denominations. At no time did Moore suggest that I might qualify for a similar exemption. Instead he put it bluntly: conform, go to chapel or be expelled. He did not even suggest that I ought to think more deeply about Christianity with a view to accepting its creed, nor did he attempt to dispute or ridicule my atheism.

Perhaps like Bowlby he had never come across an atheist before? Clearly he thought atheists did not rank with other varieties of Christianity or even other faiths. The school had accepted a few Muslims for many years and indeed King Faisal II of Iraq was in our house. Full religious toleration itself had been accepted in law 70 years before, yet it had not fully sunk in with Dr Moore.

Nor was the idea of human rights then common currency. The

Universal Declaration of Human Rights, of which religious toleration is a key plank, had been agreed in Paris the year before. Article 18 states: 'Everyone has the right to freedom of thought, conscience and religion.' Knowing nothing of such things or indeed about trying to negotiate a compromise or appealing to a higher authority, such as the Middlesex Education Officer, I felt I was cornered. I made an instant decision. Harrow was worth chapel.

With hindsight I see I ought to have appealed to Middlesex County Council whose policy with regard to these awards was that 'no pupil otherwise eligible shall be excluded on religious grounds'.[11] I could also have drawn support from the Fleming Report itself. It commended boarding schools for 'the opportunities of healthy religious development', saying it was one of their great advantages.[12] However, in its suggestions for the selection of bursars under its scheme, the Committee indicated that pupils should have a 'right of withdrawal' from religious services.[13] Harrow had such a right but Moore did not apply it to atheists.

From then on I conformed, switching off my brain during the six sessions, totalling two hours in chapel each week, not to mention house prayers. I yielded to *force majeure*. Neither Bowlby nor Moore ever mentioned the matter again. Two years later when I had reached the History VIth Moore took us once a week for one term for a lesson on Plato's *Republic*. He was an excellent teacher, awakening my interest in Plato with Cornford's lucid translation. Unfortunately Plato does not discuss religious toleration but assigns all authority to Delphi. Like many headmasters who try to continue teaching, Moore missed some of the lessons because of other commitments.

A year later, soon after I had started my National Service, I had to request a reference from my headmaster in order to apply for officer training. In my letter to Moore I described my daily routine in the barrack room, comparing the army's obsession with polishing brass buckles and black boots to the Spartans preparing for battle before Thermopylae by polishing their shields and helmets. His reply, which was very warm, said how rare it was to receive a 'composed letter'. 'I can well understand how much your training must go against the grain, but I am glad to gather that you are contriving to take it good-humouredly.'

In his confidential report to the War Office Selection Board he wrote a very supportive paragraph, which ended: 'he is somewhat of an individualist but I consider that with training he should prove to have qualities of a useful regimental officer'.[14] I couldn't complain about that. Only a few months later Moore died aged 46. If he had lived I might have had some more mature conversations with him on more equal terms.

One premise of the Middlesex Awards was that bright boys would be lifted out of social circumstances that might hold them back and placed in a milieu where they would thrive on greater stimulus from their peers. It was assumed that the school would absorb the five boys a year without difficulty, which in our case certainly proved to be true. I assimilated fast. Going home after my first term I met on a bus Mr Rubinstein, one of my favourite masters at primary school. He remarked that I had already acquired a public school accent – something I had not noticed myself but which was certainly true. I did become a Harrovian with a fondness for the life and a recognition that it was better in many respects than Tottenham Grammar. As I adapted to pretty well everything except chapel one could say I practised 'muscular secularity' rather than 'muscular Christianity'.[15]

However, when I left in 1952 my verdict was that I would never send a child of mine to a boarding school, especially a single-sex school. A great gap had emerged between me and my parents. There were many things at Harrow that I could never describe to them, still less explain. School was more important to me than home. In the holidays I looked forward to going back to school rather than the other way round. In arguments against divorce it's often said that children need their parents as well as a school if they are to grow up as well-balanced human beings. In a boarding school the teachers are substitute parents for much of the year. They try to set standards of behaviour and provide a moral horizon for their pupils to aim at.

My feeling is that no matter how caring and talented they are neither a good teacher nor good support staff, such as a house matron, can do this as well as two good parents. Even in a well-staffed school like Harrow, teachers can never give as much time to each child as parents can give in the home. Over four and a half years I had perhaps three deep personal conversations with my housemaster, three intellectual conversations with Charlie Lil and the odd social non-classroom exchange with a few other masters. Whereas in a good home I would expect intellectual, artistic, social and sporting observations to be part of the fabric of everyday life. In a boarding school the moral milieu and non-classroom exchange is provided almost entirely by the other pupils. Valuable experience though that may be it seems decidedly inferior to a good home.

Single-sex boarding schools seem particularly undesirable. Teenage boys are bursting with testosterone with sport the only outlet. Among ourselves we talked mainly about sport and sex. Homosexual feelings were strong and pretty common; homosexual practice was not uncommon among a small minority. Of course it was thought to be a sacking offence; certainly in my time a handful of boys were sent home when they were caught, including one from Moretons. I suspect that most housemasters did not apply this 'capital punishment' at the first offence but some undoubtedly did. Despite setting up this hothouse the school gave almost no general guidance on what sexual relations were all about, nor even set out specific prohibitions. Perhaps Christians in the school were told at the time of confirmation that homosexual activity was a sin against God? At the time homosexual relations between males of any age were a criminal offence. Without any knowledge of the law most boys knew instinctively that it was simply not allowed.

Sixty years later acquaintance with sex and knowledge about it are more widespread and available from many sources at an early age. Boarding schools can provide no barrier to the heightened awareness and interest in the early teens. Their situation seems even more untenable than it was in 1947. To me it seems that living at home and going to a mixed school provides the best milieu in which to socialise with the opposite sex and to discover the wonders and perils of sex. The Fleming Committee in 1944 and the Newsome Committee in 1965 maintained there was a strong case for boarding education. The Newsome Committee argued that the state should take up half the places at girls' and boys' public schools (then almost all single sex) on educational grounds as well as being a means of diminishing their dominance of British public life. Although I was a beneficiary of Fleming's proposals I think both committees were mistaken in believing that single-sex boarding education was desirable, indeed admirable, in itself.

My view on this matter, which had been maturing for some years, came quickly to fruition in my last few months at Harrow. I had spotted an advert in the *New Statesman* for volunteer staff at Forest School Camps – an outfit I had never heard of. After a curious interview with an eccentric elder statesman of Forest School in London I went to two staff training courses at Whitwell Hall in Norfolk at Christmas 1951 and Easter 1952. Forest School had been a 'progressive' school pre-war;

its unique idea was education through camping, walking and self-reliance. The Hall had been requisitioned during the war and the school had never reopened. However, some enthusiastic former staff and students had rekindled the spirit of the school in the form of summer camps for children aged 5 to 16.

Whitwell Hall was very sparsely furnished and the food was plain to say the least, heavily loaded with raw, coarse-cut vegetables. But the atmosphere engendered by half a dozen youngish adults and another dozen would-be volunteer staff was so different from Harrow that it enabled me to see more clearly what I had known must be the case. Hierarchy, deference, strict rules, harsh punishments, uniforms, dress codes and segregation of the sexes were plainly not fundamental to education. There were other more important principles to follow.

The folk singing and folk dancing at Forest School were a delight to a novice like me, though I already had some proficiency at Scottish reels. Not surprisingly, I found my first girlfriend there, a Cambridge undergraduate whom I remember to this day with great affection. These two brief episodes with Forest School Camps convinced me that co-education was a far healthier system than single-sex schools whether boarding or day schools. I left Harrow in March 1952 feeling it wasn't a moment too soon.

There is another strong argument against boarding education as a principle, not against Harrow in particular. Parents need their children around them almost as much as children need the protection, guidance and example of their parents. The nurturing of children does put extra pressure on a couple but it also gives them a common purpose outside of their individual needs for companionship, sociability and sexual relations. This common purpose, which lasts at least until the children leave home and often for a lifetime, is the most powerful cement that holds couples together. Even when the initial bonds between a couple loosen, their common interest in their children's welfare prolongs a willingness to work together and to compromise. If boarding school were the rule rather than the exception we would have a higher rate of divorce.

The County's Reckoning

In October 1952, six months after I had left, the Schools Subcommittee of Middlesex County Council recommended to the Education Committee that the awards to Mill Hill, Wycombe Abbey and Westonbirt be continued but that the Harrow scheme should be terminated.[16] The Subcommittee had considered a confidential report written by the chief education officer, C.E. Gurr, although this had not made any suggestion for ending the scheme. In fact Gurr's review of the Harrow scheme from the beginning to 1952 was very complimentary.

> The Housemasters speak very highly of these boys ... All have done exceptionally well and have more than held their own in the school. The same can be said of other Middlesex scholars at present in the school. Their record of achievement is very good and the names of Middlesex scholars figure prominently in the award of prizes for good work, etc.

In another paragraph the achievements of the first five who by then had all left were detailed without names but in what is clearly a pecking order as perceived by the school. I am listed as:

> Reached the History Sixth and gained Form prize December 1951. Accepted for University College Oxford. Represented the school at Fives. House Monitor.[17]

One reason for disquiet about the awards in 1952 was that the number of applications for all the schools had declined sharply. For two years running there had been only 32 applications for Harrow awards, the numbers having fallen steadily from the peak of 142 in 1947. That particular summer the numbers of applicants had risen somewhat to 44 applicants for Harrow and 5 awards were given as usual. Curiously the parents of one of those boys then declined the offer of a place.

Why the Schools Subcommittee decided that the Harrow scheme should be discontinued but not the others is not clear from the records. At the next meeting of the full Education Committee, the chairman, still Muriel Forbes, withdrew the item from the agenda before it could be decided. Clearly she had misgivings about the Subcommittee's recommendation.

Neither the cost of Harrow (compared with Mill Hill) nor the small numbers involved seem to have been the issue because the fees at the two girls' schools, Wycombe Abbey and Westonbirt, were almost as high as Harrow and the numbers at Westonbirt were identical; yet the Subcommittee did not recommend terminating either of those schemes.

The minute books for the County Council and its committees are strange documents because they record almost none of the arguments about particular policies and rarely register dissent in the form of a vote. Gurr's report did show that the net annual cost to the County Council of the 292 pupils at the five main schools (Mill Hill, Christ's Hospital, Westonbirt, Wycombe Abbey and Harrow) was £68,000, at an average cost per pupil of £233 per year. Another £39,050 was spent on another 301 pupils at various fee-paying schools where the average cost was £130. The cost of the major schemes at the more expensive schools probably lay at the heart of the disquiet but it was not recorded as such. 'The Committee was of the opinion', wrote Gurr to a county councillor who objected to the proposal, 'that it would be better to discontinue the Harrow scheme and if possible arrange a bigger take-up at Christ's Hospital'.

However, at its meeting in November the full County Council referred back the proposal concerning Harrow. 'As the Education Committee was not prepared to make alternative proposals,' wrote Gurr to the same persistent critic, 'therefore the scheme will continue.'[18] In July of 1953 Gurr reported again to the Schools Subcommittee about Harrow. Further analysis of the statistics showed that the number of applicants had recovered somewhat but that the number of pupils applying from maintained schools had declined sharply. In 1953 there were 85 applicants for Harrow of whom only 7 came from Secondary Modern Schools, 48 from Grammar Schools and 30 from Independent and Direct Grant Schools. Gurr offered three possible explanations: (1) lack of knowledge of the scheme among parents; (2) anxiety about the level of parental contributions in view of the rise in prices at that time; (3) a fear on the part of some parents that their children might become dissatisfied with their own homes.[19]

A year later the Schools Subcommittee considered the scale of aid to parents at Harrow and the other boarding schools, comparing the Middlesex scales with those of other counties such as Buckinghamshire, Hertfordshire and Surrey. As a result the maximum parental contribution was reduced from 40 per cent of net income (gross income less certain allowable expenses such as rent or mortgage payments) to 33 per cent.

The scheme seems to have continued at Harrow until Middlesex was wound up as a county on 1st April, 1965. However, some of the new Greater London Boroughs continued to support individual pupils at some schools even beyond that date.[20]

*　　*　　*

I went to Harrow as a direct result of the Fleming Report which in turn had arisen from an intense debate concerning the public schools in the early years of the war. Fleming's proposals were part of post-war reconstruction and a yearning for a new beginning for British society. It was an argument that was conducted with passion in many books and articles by many eminent academics, headmasters and politicians, including Professors R.H. Tawney and Harold Laski, and the Labour MP Aneurin Bevan. Almost all the arguments centred around the supposed divisiveness of a system that only benefited the well off. Most but not all accepted that the pupils got a much better education than in the state system. Hardly anyone really examined the fact that boarding underpinned most of the leading schools.

These schools had grown up over centuries, before the coming of cheap and fast travel, when to board with the schoolmaster was a practical solution. In the nineteenth century they spawned many similar institutions and their continued popularity with the monied classes was certainly consolidated by social snobbery as much as a desire to give children the best education available. With the great improvements in travel most of these boarding schools could have given way to day schools still charging high fees and still in effect being socially exclusive. In practice the leading boarding schools have grown more popular except during the inter-war period when numbers fell, in some schools such as Harrow, alarmingly. After the second war, however, most of these boarding schools have prospered.

Advocates of boarding education assert that it establishes a community whose benefits go far beyond academic training. In the build-up to the Fleming Committee, Sir Frank Fletcher, a former headmaster of Charterhouse, argued in the *Journal of Education* that the public school 'is essentially a community, not merely a teaching shop'. He went on to write, 'It aims at teaching individual self-respect by means of corporate membership.'[21]

To many of their critics, however, it was the very community created in our class-based, Christian, hierarchical, muscular public schools that was repellent.[22] On the whole I think it a fair claim that boarding schools create a community. For me Harrow was largely a benign community but the reader can see it was one which at times pinched me hard. The template of rules, sport, discipline, punishment and privileges devised or evolved over the years to improve character and physique could have felt like a strait-jacket and could have done a lot of harm. One of the other first five Middlesex bursars of 1947 told me that his experience at Harrow in a different house was 'pretty unpleasant' although in Gurr's report of 1952 he was listed as a considerable success.

Few educational experts have really examined boarding as a principle independent of it being integral to the public school system. Royston Lambert, a Cambridge don who was a research consultant to the Public Schools Commission in the late 1960s, was one of the few people who attempted to disentangle boarding from private education. Most parents, he concluded, after conducting a sample survey, 'do not consider boarding on grounds of educational merit ... but rather because it confers social attributes and increased life chances or because family situation or pattern of life necessitates it'. After five years as headmaster of Dartington Hall he conceded that 'boarding has inherently damaging effects (as well as beneficial ones) which can be mitigated by various schemes'.[23] He also admitted that his attempts to relax Dartington's already unique regime were largely unsuccessful. Overall he was pessimistic as to whether boarding could be used to greater advantage by society at large.

Some people still want to abolish the public schools or requisition their facilities for the state system. It's certainly true that money can buy advantage in many but not all fee-paying schools and that this is demonstrated in the high proportion of their pupils who progress via the top universities to the top jobs in government, academia and commerce. If these schools were abolished you might have a fairer society but you would also have a less free society. It's a classic case of the clash of two principles, both of which we cherish – fairness and freedom.

Whatever one thinks of the schools as a social or educational system, their buildings, libraries and sports fields are impressive. Even a revolutionary government would be foolish to dismantle them like old workhouses. Although I am no champion of these schools I would strongly oppose any move to close them down. Freedom to set up and maintain one's own school independent of the state seems to me fundamental. In a free society citizens are able to spend their money and their time in many different ways even though some of them are very detrimental to society itself. To stop sections of society banding together to support or set up schools to their own design, curriculum and taste would to me be quite unacceptable.

Notes

[1] Board of Education, 'The Public Schools & the General Education System', London, HMSO, 1944, p.62

[2] Ibid., p.66

[3] Ibid., pp.67 & 69

[4] Ibid., p.30

[5] Ibid., p.56

[6] Middlesex County Council, Secondary Education Subcommittee (28.10.46)

[7] Christopher Tyerman, *A History of Harrow School*, Oxford University Press (2000)

[8] 'Report by HM Inspectors on Harrow School, Middlesex' (Ministry of Education, 1951)

[9] Ibid., p.15

[10] Ibid., p.14. The HMI report contained both praise and criticism of Lillingston

[11] MCC Education Committee (8.11.48)

[12] Board of Education op.cit.

[13] Ibid., p.75. The Education Act 1944 also had a right of withdrawal from religious services but it did not apply to independent schools

[14] When I was retired from the Army Reserve in 1957 I was sent a copy of the headmaster's confidential report dated 26.6.52

[15] Benjamin Disraeli, *Endymion*, London, Longmans (1880), Bk. 1, Chap. 14

[16] MCC Schools Subcommittee (13.10.52)

[17] 'Private & Confidential Report by the Chief Education Officer to the Schools Subcommittee'. Unpublished (23.9.52)

[18] Councillor P.W. Tilleard-Haines to C.E. Gurr (30.10.52); Gurr's reply (13.1.53). A small red file at the London Metropolitan Archives entitled 'Awards at Public Schools' (MCC/EO/FIN/5) contains this rare example of retained correspondence.

[19] CEO's Report to the Schools Subcommittee (2.7.53)

[20] At Wycombe Abbey the scheme did not end until 1976; see Lorna Flint, *Wycombe Abbey School 1896–1986* (privately printed, 1989)

[21] Frank Fletcher, 'The Future of the Public Schools', *Journal of Education* (September 1940)

[22] See T.C. Worsley, *The End of the Old School Tie*, London, Secker-Warburg (1941) and Giles Playfair, *My Father's Son*, London, Bles (1937), pp.64–80

[23] Royston Lambert, *Chance of a Lifetime*, London, Weidenfeld & Nicolson (1975), pp.348–352

6

Mountains

Why do we climb mountains? In particular why do we want to climb the highest mountains, the difficult and dangerous mountains and, to refine it even further, the difficult and dangerous routes on mountains? The most clichéd answer is to quote George Mallory who, when asked why he wanted to climb Everest answered, 'because it is there'. It's quoted so often because he achieved heroic status by dying in his attempt on the summit in 1924 along with his companion Andrew Irvine.

Mallory and many other mountaineers have tried to answer the question with more thoughtful essays or asides woven into accounts of actual climbs. The answers are variously poetic or romantic or philosophical or sometimes almost religious. Some mountains are regarded as sacred by those who live around them and some of their names reflect this reverence. The Tibetan name for Everest, for instance, is Chomolungma ('Goddess of the Snows') and Annapurna means 'Goddess of Fertility', while Chimborazo in Ecuador is thought to mean 'the ice throne of God' in Quechua. Almost all climbers cite aesthetic as well as athletic reasons to justify their sport.

Individual climbers of course have their own mixture of motives. The most obvious common thread that links them all, from the hill walkers to the north face tigers, is a desire for fresh air and exercise. Another less remarked on motive is the pleasure derived from the successful practising of a skill. The simplest grassy mountain requires stamina. In bad weather it also demands good navigation. At the other end of the spectrum are climbers who seek fame and a living, sometimes even a fortune, from climbing where no one has been before. The desire to be first is very strong, sometimes to the point of foolhardiness, in those who make the first ascents. Deaths and casualties among leading climbers are regrettably high, yet death is often regarded not as a failure but as an heroic or pioneering effort, displaying 'man's indomitable will'. I suppose the supreme example of such a man is Captain Scott who died in the Antarctic rather than on a mountain and left in his journal a most moving account of the last days of his expedition. The worst examples are those few climbers who may have tried to prove the ascendancy of their country or their race by scaling what to others was impossible. The evidence is inconclusive about most of the accused, but pretty clear for the two Germans and two Austrians who first climbed the Eiger Nordwand in 1937. Those who proclaim they are 'climbing for Britain' are tainted with a touch of this misplaced nationalism. I am no admirer of such spirit.

The best mountaineers climb within the limits of their skill and their strength. They are prudent about the weather and the so-called 'objective risks' such as avalanche, rockfall or hidden crevasse. In recent years, however, the high altitude climbers have insisted on climbing without oxygen, which means they take on a risk that impairs their judgement. Lack of oxygen impairs the functioning of the brain as well as the heart and the limbs. With acclimatisation quite a few people can still climb adequately at the highest altitudes but none of them, even the best, can be said to be running in top gear, able to use all their strength, skills and judgement as they would do at much lower altitudes.

Fortunately perhaps I have always been afflicted with headaches at Alpine altitudes and have never been higher than 17,000 feet. No doubt I could have acclimatised to go higher. My heart had the power but my lungs were probably not efficient enough to take me much higher. So high altitude climbers may resent my criticism as being born of envy.

The first time I climbed in the Alps was 1947 when I was 14. After a 33-hour journey by train from London we arrived at Zermatt about teatime. As we shouldered our rucksacks we enquired about our hotel – the Hotel Sonne or Sun Hotel. The uniformed, frock-coated coachmen waiting beside their landaus waved us up the High Street. We weren't surprised there was no coach grandly marked Hotel Sonne and no mule to trot us there in nineteenth-century style. We walked slowly up the main street through groups of early evening strollers. In those far-off days of 1947 there were no cars at all in Zermatt and even now it's only residents who can bring them up to a car park. In Zermatt everyone walks everywhere, except between the station and their hotel.

At the far end of the village, past the bench of guides outside the Monte Rosa Hotel and past the fountain decorated with bronze marmots, we turned up a dusty alley. We came to a substantial house, long ago painted white with a peeling green sign upon which you could just read 'Hotel Sonne'. We mounted the stone steps and knocked at a neglected door. Already we were somewhat disappointed. We knew that we had booked the cheapest hotel but this place looked miserable. We knocked again. Still no reply. We then went round the back to find nothing but a grass patch. After a few minutes a man came out of a back door to talk to us in German. I replied in schoolboy French. More German in response but the meaning seemed obvious. The house was no longer a hotel; he knew nothing about us and didn't offer to help us. Dazed, we shouldered our rucksacks once again and went back to the main street. It was eight o'clock and almost dark.

We stood in the main square to take stock of our predicament. Did we understand the man correctly? Was there perhaps another house somewhere in the village, which was the real Hotel Sonne? After some dithering I suggested we return to the Hotel Dom, which I had seen on our way up and remembered from the Hotel Plan brochure. At the Dom, the manager told us immediately that the Sonne had closed down two years before and was amazed that we could have paid and been given a booking receipt. This was the high season and the Dom was full so he could not take us himself. However, he phoned the head office in Zurich to find somebody who could take responsibility for this lapse in efficiency and could made a decision. After more phone calls we were sent on our way to the other side of the river to the Beau Site, the only five-star hotel linked to Hotel Plan. There we were greeted with more apologies and given two rooms in the attic, which were normally maids' rooms. We felt a little out of place because there were no climbers and no children and certainly no climbing children. Nevertheless we then enjoyed a fortnight in a luxury hotel rather than the modest one-star establishment which we had booked. Coming from Britain still locked into frugal food rationing, we ate our fill in the dining-room without reserve, though we could only afford apple juice rather than wine. I particularly remember the lavish, elegantly-wrapped packed lunches. When Jennifer and I returned to Zermatt in 2004 for a wedding, the Hotel Sonne had been enlarged and refitted.

If you have ever been to the Swiss Alpine village of Zermatt in high summer you will know that it has a heady atmosphere. The staggering magnificence of the scenery and the barely suppressed nervous hysteria of the climbers combine perfectly with the holiday smiles of visitors, villagers, hoteliers and shopkeepers under a self-assured sun. In such an atmosphere your legs feel twice as long and your nerve twice as strong. In such an atmosphere it is practically impossible for a climber to admit that he is not going to climb the Matterhorn, which Ruskin compared to a rearing horse. 'Just to see the Matterhorn is to feel its challenge,' said Eric.

Looking back on it, I can see now that when the manager of our hotel asked my father if he would like a guide for the Matterhorn, Eric had little choice but to say, 'Yes ... of course.' The only possible counter-ploy would have been to say, 'No thanks ... we're climbing without a guide.' As that was well beyond our competence as well as being foolhardy Eric agreed we needed a guide. We weren't yet in training or acclimatised to the altitude and we didn't know if we were up to it. We should at least have climbed some lesser peaks first. But we couldn't be climbers who didn't climb.

The normal route from Zermatt is up the Hornli ridge – if you remember the pyramid-like shape, that's the corner facing the village. Together with our guide, a sunburnt, leather-skinned giant with a white cloth cap named Peter Biner, we left Zermatt after lunch for the 5,000 foot climb to the Hörnli Hut. Soon after we left the village we were overtaken by a train of mules carrying beer and supplies for the hut. So with a wink and tip to the muleteer Peter offloaded our rucksacks on to the mules, saving us a lot of hard toil.

At the hut I felt small and inadequate surrounded by men and women who looked like climbers. Their equipment was so much more professional than ours. It turned out later that most of them went no further than the hut. I drank gallons of hot lemon and sunk deeper and deeper into my first pair of long trousers. After a fitful night we left at four in the morning just as it was getting light. I no longer have a step-by-step memory of the ascent. What remains in my consciousness is a blurred impression with a few incidents.

Soon after we left the hut an absurd incident occurred, which did not improve my confidence. Climbing a short wall, I jammed my foot in a crack only to find I could not get it out. I struggled with it; my father tried; our guide tried. A massive guide leading the following party impatiently gave it an enormous heave, which nearly parted my leg from my foot but still it did not budge. I felt an utter fool, holding up not only our rope but the party behind. A torrent of advice in unintelligible German merely increased my confusion. Finally the boot seemed to come out of its own accord.

All the way up I had a bad headache because of the altitude. Halfway up at the Solvay Refuge I would gladly have stopped, letting my father complete the climb. But the guide would have none of it, to my everlasting satisfaction. So I continued.

The upper part of the climb comes out over the north face. This is the section where Edward Whymper's party had their accident on the first ascent in 1865. When you are on the climb it feels like coming up under the eaves of a house. There is no actual overhang on the route but it is so steep you cannot see the summit until you are almost there. The summit snow slope is actually described in the guidebooks as 'the roof'.

On reaching the summit (14,780 feet) we sank into the snow to gaze somewhat groggily over the magnificent peaks of the Valais, the most prominent being the Monte Rosa and the Dom, both higher than the Matterhorn. Other climbers were taking photographs, identifying peaks and eating hard sticks of salami they called 'gendarmes'. All I could manage beyond some cold tea from the guide was to release the tension of thinking that I might not have been strong enough or agile enough to reach the summit.

The descent was notable for tension of another kind. A little above the Solvay my father, on the rope in front of me, slipped and fell a few feet. No injury, but it was a little disturbing. The reason was that he was wearing a new type of nail on his boots called BPs or British Pattern nails. These have long since been superceded by rubber-soled boots but at the time they were an interesting experiment intended to replace conventional European nails. One of the snags seemed to be that they were made of a hard steel, which did not always grip the rock as well as the softer continental nails. During the descent to the Hornli Hut my father slipped on the rock several times evoking some strong criticism of these nails from the guide.

We reached the hut at 2 p.m., which was a reasonable time for such an inexperienced pair. However, it was now clear that Eric was much more affected by the altitude than me and needed a good rest. The guide left us at the hut to race down to the valley and up to another client at another hut for another peak the next morning. After an hour's rest Eric and I went on down the path back to Zermatt but I had to wait for him much of the way. In a short note penned back at home Eric wrote that the climb was 'the hardest day's work I ever did, but well worth it, a great experience and an imperishable memory'.

The rest of the holiday was an anticlimax. We climbed some minor peaks from the valley including the Ober Rothorn (11,100 feet). As this involved 5,870 feet of climbing in one day I suppose we were very fit. But we had to decline Peter Biner's repeated suggestions that we tackle something more exciting. It was a time of serious currency restrictions and we simply hadn't enough Swiss francs to pay for another guided climb. In any case we were quite content to gaze at our conquest and to get one up on the hotel manager. With great ceremony he produced what he called 'The Golden Book' wherein were inscribed all the hotel's visitors who had climbed the Matterhorn. Thomas Jefferson signing the Declaration of Independence could not have felt more pleased with himself than I did signing this book, which had indeed a gold silk cover. 'You've climbed it too?' said my father to the manager. But he hadn't and he treated us with great respect for the rest of our stay.

About a month after the Matterhorn I began my first term at Harrow. To a closed community like a boarding school outside experience is pretty irrelevant. Among the boys I'm sure I got less kudos out of my climb than I did for getting into the under-15s rugby XV.

Although the Matterhorn was my first Alpine peak I had had eight years preparation and training mostly in Britain. When we went to Chamonix in the French Savoy Alps in 1939 I was lifted up to a high window in our bedroom just as I was put to bed so that I could admire the alpenglow, the sunset on the snows. When I discovered that Eric was going to climb Mont Blanc with a guide I was most upset that I was excluded. After all, I could keep up with Eric in Epping Forest, and already on walks across the Mer de Glace glacier and up to La Flégère, a view point opposite Mont Blanc, I had kept well ahead of the grownups. I was convinced I would be able to climb to the summit of Mont Blanc despite its height of 15,782 feet. Being only six I expressed my dissent with floods of tears. While Eric climbed Mont Blanc, my mother and my aunt Gladys took me on a bus tour to Geneva though even then I knew I was being bought off.

In the second week of that holiday came the Molotov–Ribbentrop Pact. The guests in the Albert & Milan Hotel gathered each evening in the lounge and all the way up the stairs to listen anxiously to the news on the radio. One evening we heard that the Soviet Union had signed this non-aggression pact with Germany. My father who had once been an admirer of the Soviet Union explained that it seemed to deny all that the socialist state had stood for. The next evening all Americans were advised to leave Europe as war seemed inevitable. By Wednesday all the English guests, including us, were preparing to leave. Most of the French men had already been called back to their units. Alpine troops, with their rakish felt hats, streamed past the hotel which was near the station. All the cars, lorries, carts, horses and petrol were commandeered by the army.

On Thursday morning we were helped to the train by a kindly hotel proprietor, his staff having left already. He told us that he would be leaving himself for his unit later that day. On the station platform there were many sad farewells. When we left the mountain train at St Gervais we clambered on to a very crowded express for Paris. Pushing our way down the corridor full of boy scouts my mother and I were offered a seat in a compartment. Eric and Gladys had to stand. That night as we steamed on towards Paris I had my first experience of sleeping on the luggage rack. Very comfortable it was too. The compartment, however, was so full that few could sleep, so the boys sang songs, ate sausage and drank wine from a leather bottle to keep up their spirits. One senior scout showed me his arm where it had been bitten by an adder while he was climbing a steep rockface. It seemed the height of manliness to be able to survive that ordeal. Every now and again their priest looked in with a smile and a few words of encouragement.

On reaching the Gare de Lyon we found a sea of people rushing hither and thither, many of them very agitated. How my parents and my Aunt Gladys managed to cross the city to the Gare du Nord I cannot remember but it must have been by public transport. Even in an emergency it would have gone too far against the grain to have spent money on a taxi. I am able to relate all these details so long after the event because at Tottenham Grammar School I wrote a three-page composition entitled 'I Was There'. My English master, Mr Mitchell, in Form 3R, marked it '9/10 v.good'. As that was only six years later it would have been fresh in my memory.

During the war we never missed a week's holiday in the mountains, going to the Lakes three times, the Peak District, Snowdonia and Fort William. Each time we climbed hard day after day. Skiddaw near Keswick was my first 3,000 foot peak, aged seven. The next year I did the 21-mile circuit of Kinder Scout in the Peak District. In 1942, besides reaching the summit of ten peaks over 2,000 feet, we also tackled Broad Stand on the flank of Scafell in Cumbria. This has one hard pitch where the holds require a much longer reach than a boy of 4 feet 3 inches could possibly possess. Eric had to lie on a rock platform and lean down to haul me up arm to arm. It was hair-raising and certainly foolhardy, but we did it. When I was ten we walked right round the Snowdon Horseshoe including the scramble along the ridge of Crib Goch.

The first year after the war we booked to go to Macgillycuddy's Reeks in County Kerry, Ireland, but at the last moment had to change our plans because we couldn't get sailing tickets. So instead we carried our tent, food and gear over the highest mountains in the Cairngorms, spending three nights in the wonderful Shelter Stone below Ben MacDhui. The Shelter Stone is a huge block as big as a house, which makes a simple cave by lying across other large boulders. The sides have been filled in with rocks and heather so that it is both watertight and windproof. It was certainly much snugger than our very leaky army surplus tent. Long ago the Stone, along with many others, had fallen from the east face of Ben MacDhui, the highest peak in the group. Just below it lies Loch Avon, as fine and as lonely a loch as one can find in Scotland. In mostly wet weather the distances seemed huge but we still managed to climb three of the five main peaks plus half a dozen others. It must have been good training.

There are so many peaks in this beautiful wilderness that I went back twice more, once with Eric after being rained out of Skye and once in winter with Margaret Atwell, a girlfriend from Forest School Camps. On this second return at New Year, 1954, we arrived at Aviemore early in the morning after an overnight train from London. We then had a very long day with rucksacks loaded for a week walking over the Lairig Ghru pass (2,700 feet) and down the stripling Dee to the Corrour Bothy, once a shelter for deer stalkers but then an unmanned climbers' hut. On the two previous occasions I had been there with Eric we had had to wade across the river. But that was in summer. In winter it was a quite different proposition. I led the way in waist-deep icy water but the current was so strong I was nearly swept away but for a crucial hand from Margaret who may well have saved my life. Together we struggled across 30 foot of river and clambered out soaking wet, in my case from the chest down. We stumbled on to the hut and lit a fire to dry our clothes as soon as we could. The next day we discovered that a climbing club had strung two steel wires across the river some 50 yards below where we crossed but which we didn't see in the dusk.

A day or so later when we had recovered from this chilly start we climbed the highest mountain in the range, Ben MacDhui, and descended to the Shelter Stone where we met another couple – a university lecturer and one of his women students who was obviously new to the mountains. While they were unpacking their sleeping bags on to the heather-covered floor she brought out four large books, which made us all gasp. 'What on earth have you brought all that weight up here for?' the man exclaimed.

'No wonder you said you had no room for the food!' Their partnership went cold before our eyes. Inside the Shelter Stone ours remained warm and close for some time.

Many years later my wife and daughter, Jennifer and Juliet, met a young man way off the beaten track on the lower slopes of Cader Idris in Wales. He was looking for his rucksack, which he said 'was beside a round rock'. As the hillside is littered with rocks they had difficulty hiding their giggles. Three months later Jennifer and I found a large rucksack on a rocky promontory a quarter of a mile from where they had met him the Easter before. It contained camping and cooking gear, half a dozen large library books and a handbook on Survival! Clearly he hadn't read it.

Alas we had to dump the books because they were sodden beyond rescue. However, we salvaged the rucksack and most of the gear. We even found the student's name and address on a student bus card. On reaching home we sent a letter to the address offering to forward the rucksack with contents if he would make contact. We never had a response so were left wondering whether he had just disappeared in the mountains. Or was he so shamed by losing the library books and by not being able to find his own rucksack that he couldn't even acknowledge it to us?

Looking back on my apprenticeship with my father I wonder why he never joined a club. We might have learnt some techniques sooner or become acquainted with more modern gear than we used (especially the tents with which we should have used a flysheet). Most important of all, Eric might have found someone to climb with when I left home. One year when I was in Switzerland as the guest of a Swiss friend, Eric went off to northern Scotland on his own. He found the mountains to be very fine but he carried too much gear so made slow progress. He never reached Cape Wrath in the far north-west as intended. He also sent home a number of letters to my mother indicating he was lonely and missed me terribly. When I got home Violet pleaded with me that I go with him next time. Which I did.

The last time Eric and I climbed together was in 1950 when I was 17 and he was 46. We went to Skye intending to make our own route to the Cuillins from the village of Elgol. The evening we arrived we walked along the seashore camping on the beach underneath a 3,000 feet mountain called Blaven. There was driftwood in abundance so we cooked and toasted ourselves by a large fire. During the night it rained very hard, leaking into another of our tents, this time a US army surplus. From then on the weather was appalling. It rained all the way up Blaven and continued as we hauled our sacks over a pass to the eastern shore of Loch Coruisk. Search as we might we could not find one patch of dryish soil on which to pitch our tent.

On the other side of the loch we could see some climbers seated in the dry under an overhanging rock. We were very envious. The outflow from the loch was so high we could not possibly wade across to the western side in order to go to Glenbrittle as intended. The next morning when we put on our trousers it was just as if we had taken them straight out of the loch. It seemed the right time to change our plans so we abandoned the Cuillins and went east by train to the Cairngorms, by which time we hoped the bout of bad weather would have passed over. Essentially that judgement proved correct and we climbed a number of high peaks we had not climbed on our first visit.

But of course our partnership could not go on. By 1951, when I was 18, I was ready to go off to the Pyrenees with David Nelson, a contemporary who was just leaving Moretons. For the last time I used one of our army surplus tents, again without a flysheet! Obviously it took some time to learn that lesson. From the village of Cauterets we climbed over two passes *en route* to a refuge. We camped at 8,000 feet where we had a good view of the east ridge of the Vignemale (10,700 feet) which we hoped to climb. In the night a thunderstorm crashed around us with so much power we had to hold on to the poles for fear of losing our tent. The next morning it rained even harder so we went on to the Refuge au Vignemale, arriving thoroughly soaked. When I put my rucksack on the floor of the bunkroom the water ran out all over the place. At this hut we met two amiable Frenchmen who left a large melon on the doorstep to keep it fresh, although it was so cold in the hut we wore blankets around our shoulders all the time to keep warm. In the morning one of them insisted that we share his fruity breakfast, describing it with whoops of delight as 'melon glacé'.

The Frenchmen were well equipped and offered us a place on their rope for the climb the next day. Unfortunately snow and low cloud in the morning prevented any serious climbing so we descended to the valley. By which time the sun came out so we charged off up a nearby peak, named, quite rightly, the Pic Pointu (7,620 feet). There David found the quite mild exposure difficult to cope with. Perhaps it was just as well we didn't attempt the Vignemale. After another night in the tent we went on to the magnificent Cirque de Gavarnie where we stayed in a pension for a few days. Even then the village seemed very full of coach tours disgorging people on to horses and mules, which took them up into the Cirque. Gavarnie makes a useful diversion for the thousands who go to Lourdes each year in search of medical miracles.

A couple of days later we passed two people on a zigzag track while climbing an elegant mountain called the Pic Mene (9,100 feet), merely saying, '*Bonjour, monsieur et madame.*' A little while later, having lost the track in misty weather, we heard them talking below us in English so we joined forces. Ronald Hamilton was a housemaster and a language master at Winchester. We felt quite chuffed that he had not rumbled our accent when we first greeted them.

When the sun came out they offered to share their huge packed lunch. Hungry as two 18-year-olds can be, we still didn't finish all the lunch provided by their hotel. The climb was easy until the top which was rather sharp. Whereas I could walk along the summit ridge without turning a hair, I looked back to find all three of them astride the knife edge. I saw then that I had a better head for heights than most and that vertigo was a common handicap not easy to overcome.

We both had a jolly holiday enjoying the scenery, the quite deserted mountains and the independence, but it didn't make David a mountaineer. We ended up in the luxury hotel, Edward VII, in St Jean de Luz on the Atlantic coast for a few days with David's mother, Lady Nelson. It was the first time I had ever spent a holiday lazing on a beach.

After that apprenticeship I rarely missed an Alpine season of some kind for the next 25 years, climbing many good routes and summits, enduring bad weather too often and occasionally surviving the odd epic. Besides the Alps and Pyrenees, Jennifer and I climbed in the Cascades and the Olympics in Washington State and the Andes in Peru. With the Canadian Alpine Club I pioneered some new routes in the Selkirk range in Canada and also made a long trek to Annapurna in Nepal where we climbed an easy 17,000 feet peak. Almost all these seasons tested our skill and physique and brought great personal satisfaction that one was pushing oneself near to the limit. It must be said, however, that two episodes ended in disaster and four of my climbing partners were killed on mountains, though only one when with me. These deaths underlined the inherent risk involved in mountaineering.

My personal *annus mirabilis* was 1956 when I spent three weeks in the Valais with the Oxford University Mountaineering Club (OUMC). With Clive Harris, I climbed seven 4,000-metre peaks including the Weissmies, the Rimpfischhorn, Allalinhorn, Zinal Rothorn, Weisshorn and Monte Rosa, at 15,200 feet the second highest summit in the Alps. For this last climb I roped up with Peter Nelson, a strong climber who had been at Oxford three or four years earlier and was already a fast track civil servant. He led three of us up the Cresta Rey, a steep rock rib high on the Swiss side of Monte Rosa, named after a famous Italian guide, Guido Rey. From the main summit we traversed over a couple more peaks to reach the Margherita Hut which is perched above the very long and impressive Italian face at almost 15,000 feet. It's the highest building in Europe.

The jolly Italian warden supplied us with aspirins and six blankets each. In the unheated dormitory we needed them all. The aspirins may have relieved the headaches and certainly thinned our blood, which can become too viscous at altitude because of the natural dehydration. The next morning we had intended to traverse the Lyskamm and the twin peaks of Castor and Pollux but a heavy snowfall kept us in the hut. On the third day we descended slowly to Zermatt down the glacier in deep snow.

Four members of that OUMC party in Saas and Zermatt in 1956 were later killed climbing. Peter Nelson died on an ice slope in the Himalayas when he was unroped. Derek Hill (with whom I had a hitch-hiking adventure on the way home) died descending an easy ridge of Ben Nevis, having just completed a hard climb. Bernard Jillott and John Emery were the leading spirits on an expedition in 1957 to climb Haramosh (24,000 feet) in the Karakoram, which came to grief on a slope of loose snow. Despite an epic rescue Jillott died on the descent while Emery suffered severe frostbite, involving horrible amputations of his fingers. One of the rescuers, Rae Culbert, also died because his crampons broke so he could not, despite several desperate attempts, climb out of the snow bowl into which Jillott and Emery had fallen. To his great chagrin, the leader, Tony Streather, abandoned Culbert although he was still alive. He was the boyfriend of one of Jennifer's close friends at Somerville so we actually knew him better than the other two. Several years later when Emery had recovered, he had an accident on the Weisshorn in which both he and his more able-bodied partner were killed. Whatever thrill or glory climbers get from their sport should always be tempered by the cost in human lives.

* * *

Jennifer, though an experienced hill walker, was not a climber when we met but gamely learnt to enjoy the high mountains with me for more than 20 years. Among her notable climbs was the Aiguille Dibona in the Dauphiné region of the Alps. Dibona was a famous French guide and his eponymous mountain is shaped just like the blade of a knife, very steep from all sides and barely room for four at the top. The whole climb was very exposed, liable to make you suck in air and grit your teeth if, like Jennifer, you were susceptible to vertigo. Despite that she came up after me in fine form. However, just as I was taking in the rope on the summit, preparing to bring Jennifer up the last pitch, a tubby French guide overtook her and leapt up beside me. He had probably climbed this route 50 times a year and, as it was close to the hut, sometimes twice a day. So without so much as a by your leave he began to bring up his client, crossing our rope, something which he knew was bad practice and for which he apologised. He was in a hurry but his client, a good-looking young woman, was not as agile as him. She took her time while Jennifer gave way. From the top the guide and I both looked straight down on the woman because the rock-face was almost vertical. As she gingerly stretched her arms out to grasp the holds she revealed in her loose blouse some of her classical assets. 'Ha, ha,' said the guide, relishing the scene and giving me a nudge, '*La vue dans la vallée c'est magnifique.*' It was truly a boys' own moment.

On that same excellent holiday with some members of the lively Tuesday Climbing Club, three of us, all men, traversed the premier peak of the district, La Meije (12,800 feet). The French climbing guide of 1951 described it as one of the most difficult of the grand Alpine peaks with no easy routes. It is a fine classic climb, which ascends a rock ridge at the western end of the mountain, crosses a small snowfield and then traverses from one summit to another along a high, airy ridge before descending to a glacier on the north face. Despite having the French guidebook or perhaps because we took it too literally we were rather slow. The route up to the first summit was described in animal images – *Dos d'Ane, Pas du Chat* and *Cheval Rouge* – followed as you might expect by a *Chapeau du Capucin*. We couldn't recognise any of these features but they made us laugh.

Having started before first light we lunched at the shoulder, climbed the crux to the first summit a little slowly and then traversed over two more summits to reach a brèche at the far end of the ridge where we knew we had to descend. The sky was overcast and the light was fading. While the south face of the Meije is rocky, the north face is all snow and ice. Belayed by my two friends, I descended a steep snow slope to the edge of a huge *bergschrund* – in effect a yawning gap between the mountain and the glacier. The warden of the French Alpine Club hut in La Bérarde had told us that early in each season the local guides planted a stake in the snow from which you could rope down across the *bergschrund*. I cast around for some time in the murky light but failed to find a stake. Did it really exist? Was our guidebook still up to date? Nowadays a party would carry its own ice screw for such a move. Without an ice screw I had to climb back to the ridge where we agreed we should bivouac and try again in the morning.

From our perch on the ridge we could look down into the valleys at the twinkling lights and imagine the delicious meals and comfortable warm beds which Jennifer and two other members of the club were certainly enjoying. They had set out with us but instead of climbing the Meije had circumvented it by going over a high pass. After a cold, dry night dozing on hard, sharp rocks without room to stretch out we awoke to a brilliant day. This time I found the stake straightaway. We all abseiled across the *bergschrund* with ease and descended a large glacier to a very high hut called the Eagle's Nest. As we arrived another party left in such a hurry they wouldn't stop to share their knowledge of the descent. Climbers are grumpy, bad-tempered and selfish from time to time like everyone else. Luckily they did leave a large bowl of water melted from the snow. We were very parched, not having carried our own stove. Like elephants at the trough we drank deeply from this very heavy bowl which was made of cast iron so that it could be placed on the top of the wood stove.

It seemed a very long way down from the Eagle's Nest into the valley and, as is normal, we lost the route a couple of times and had to make awkward traverses across boulder fields to get back to the barely visible path. As we reached the forests and then the meadows we could feel the air getting warmer and thicker. It's one of the delights of descending from the cold odourless Alpine heights that the warmth of the lower altitude brings out all the scents of the forest for you to relish once again.

We reached the main road at La Grave at about 1 p.m. to find that a bus was due. When it arrived, to our great surprise Jennifer, Valerie and Tony were already on it, having boarded at the previous village. So the six of us were able to make a jolly party, taking two long bus rides right round the mountain and back to our tents at La Bérarde. A memorable expedition. Incidentally, Leo Amery described his traverse of the Meije with a guide in 1930 in his second volume of climbing adventures, *In the Rain and the Sun* as follows: 'All in all for interest and variety and for the beauty of its setting, the Meije traverse is the most delightful of all the great rock climbs in the Alps.' By 1962 it was no longer classified as a 'great rock climb' but I would certainly endorse the rest of his comment.

In 1967 I went to Chamonix and Zermatt to make a documentary programme called *British Tigers in the Alps*, 'tigers' being the current nickname given to those who ventured on the hardest routes. No sooner had I arrived in Chamonix than I encountered a tragedy involving someone I knew. John Harris had climbed the steep and arduous Pear route on the Italian face of Mont Blanc with John Allen and two others. Harris's party gained the crest after a twelve-hour climb in reasonable time but before they reached the summit of Mont Blanc it began to snow heavily. Harris was already looking very tired. As they descended what is normally an easy snow route the weather turned to a 'white-out'; there was no horizon and they could not see where they were heading. Harris now began to fall behind and became a drag on the party until he finally flopped in the snow.

The basic ethos of climbing is that you are a party, safer because roped together, pooling your strength, expertise, shelter and food. If you can't help a straggler to descend then one fit member of the party should stay with him while the others descend to fetch help. On this occasion in a horrible storm at 15,000 feet self-preservation won the day. The three fit members made Harris comfortable and then pressed on, promising to return as soon as they reached the Vallot Refuge at 14,000 feet. But very soon they decided they were off the route and, rather than risk going over a cliff or falling through a cornice, they bedded down in a primitive snow hole to let the storm pass. After an uncomfortable night the visibility was clear enough the next morning to press on to the unmanned hut. Once arrived, however, they were so tired themselves they could not return to rescue Harris, which was probably beyond their strength anyway. Even in good conditions at low altitude it takes a lot of manpower to carry someone on a mountain. Eventually the party reached a manned hut with a phone and the Chamonix mountain rescue team were alerted. However, a party couldn't be landed from a helicopter high on the mountain until two days later. They found John Harris but he had not survived.

While John Allen and his party were struggling to stay alive in this storm another English party was attempting to retreat down the north ridge of Mont Blanc de Tacul. It is much more difficult than the normal descent of Mont Blanc and the weather conditions trumped their skill. Several of them died on the descent and were left behind. My programme included interviews with survivors of both tragedies. In fact these deaths made the BBC television news in Britain. In the cemetery at Chamonix where many famous climbers are buried, including Edward Whymper, I met a Frenchwoman refreshing the flowers on a grave. She cried as she told me her son had been climbing a hard route earlier in the year and had also died in a storm. Mountains are beautiful goddesses in the sunshine but in bad weather they are unforgiving witches who have no pity.

The other tragedy which brushed me closely was the death of my dear friend and climbing partner Peter Dean who was a railway engineer by profession. We had climbed together in the Alps, Wales and the Lakes. Once on Scafell I made a slip while leading a moderate rock climb. The rope from my waist went through a protective belay so I only fell about ten feet before Peter held me. I bruised my knee, but with him leading we still climbed the route to the summit. The walk home was painful. Our most successful exploits were in 1967 when we climbed the highest mountain all in Switzerland, the Dom (14,900 feet), by the elegant Festigrat ridge on one day, and then traversed the Nadelhorn/Lenzspitze ridge the next. It was sparkling sunshine along most of the ridge during which I took one of my best mountain photos of the Dom and the distant Breithorn. Enlarged, it still has pride of place in our dining-room. But soon after we left the summit of the Lenzspitze it began to snow. We descended via a steep gully until we finally reached a large *bergschrund*. We prospected along the top edge of the *bergschrund* before we found a place where it narrowed. We couldn't jump across because both the upper and lower edges of the crevasse were too steep. Peter immediately screwed in an ice screw as an anchor about ten feet above the gap. From there we roped down across the chasm on to very steep ice. Peter was always a cool, skilled and cautious mountaineer.

Three years later we went with our families to the Savoy Alps to stay in a small chalet at Les Houches below Chamonix. After warming up with a traverse of the Aiguille du Chardonnet we set out before it was light from the Tête Rousse Hut to attempt our first north face. In the Alps the north faces have the worst weather and the most snow and ice. We were trying the north face of the Aiguille de Bionnassay (13,294 feet), a beautiful satellite of Mont Blanc, much painted by John Ruskin and others. On the morning we climbed it the face itself was about three and a half thousand feet of hard snow with some ice. Climbing in crampons, we made good progress and were just reaching the ridge very near the summit when we saw a huge storm approaching from the west. The Bionnassay is the most westerly of the big Alpine peaks so it always catches the bad weather first.

We thought we had time to reach the summit and descend a little way down the ridge towards Mont Blanc before the storm reached us. But just as we reached the western end of the narrow summit the lightning struck, knocking us both to the ground. We staggered to our feet and almost ran along the ridge 20 yards to the far end when the lightning hit us a second time, knocking us over and twisting my knee. As we sat up in the snow I found that the back of my wool balaclava had been singed by the lightning. It was a very close shave. As soon as I stood up I knew it would be a long way to the Gouter Hut on another flank of Mont Blanc. Not surprisingly we did not linger to take any photos but a fine impression of the ridge can be gained from the photo of Frank Smythe printed on the dust jacket of his book *Adventures of a Mountaineer*.

Down the knife-edge ridge we went and then up over a shoulder of Mont Blanc before descending to the Gouter Hut in poor, misty weather. As we reached the entrance about three in the afternoon a young Austrian climber came out, his eyes exclaiming that he had endured a horrible event. He told us that his guide had been killed instantly by a lightning strike on the summit of Mont Blanc, probably a few minutes after our brush with the elements. It was a sobering reminder of what might have happened to us. Being in the news business I rang *The World Tonight*, the BBC radio programme I worked for in London. I offered them a dramatic offbeat story of two lightning strikes perhaps including an interview with the Austrian. Not a chance, the producer said. The PLO had just destroyed two airliners on the ground in Amman and all their attention was on that.

The next morning my knee had swollen so much I could not get my trousers on, let alone descend as we had intended. Mid-morning in good weather Peter decided to descend to our families over a route that we had both been up and down in earlier years. The route from the Gouter

Hut at 12,400 feet to the Tête Rousse Hut, 2,000 feet below, is easy and obvious, needing no more than a little care. But near the bottom it crosses a snow couloir, down which there are frequent stone falls. Climbers normally wait for a burst and then cross in the interval. Somehow Peter fell from this point, slid down the long snow slope and died. Although no cause of death was ever established definitely, the most likely was that he was hit by a stone, which may have knocked him out or at least knocked him over so that he slid off the route two or three hundred feet. The snow slope here is not very steep so I feel sure he must have been knocked unconscious. Otherwise he would have stopped his slide by rolling on his front and sticking his ice axe in the snow, a method we had both used from time to time to arrest a minor slip.

Very late that evening the mayor of the village of Les Houches came round to our chalet to tell Shirley Dean that her husband had been found badly injured on the glacier above the Tête Rousse Hut. He said he knew no more but as Jennifer walked with him along the track back to his house he let slip: 'il est déjà à la morgue'. When she returned to the chalet Jennifer agonised for an hour before being able to tell Shirley, who had been married barely a year and had a young baby girl. Jennifer and Shirley then spent a sleepless night together grieving for Peter and wondering if I was dead too. Come the morning, the mayor's office confirmed Peter's death but also told them that I was alive and still up at the Gouter Hut. At the refuge the warden told me that he had just heard about the accident by phone. I was appalled but couldn't move until the next morning which coincided with the complete closure of the hut at the end of the season.

As if to emphasise that the descent was normally quite obvious and quite easy I was able to limp down it unaided and alone despite a lot of pain in the knee. I called in at the Tête Rousse Hut whose warden had recovered Peter's body. He could not give me an explanation as to the cause of the fall. Two hours below the hut at Bellevue I took the téléphérique straight down to the village and plodded slowly back to our chalet where both Shirley and Jennifer were very upset. Two days later we buried Peter, not in Chamonix but at the cemetery at Les Contamines above St Gervais. It was the worst end to a holiday one could possibly imagine and Jennifer announced on our way home she was no longer going to come as a 'camp follower' with the children on a serious climbing holiday as it was too stressful. I could see her point.

Despite that vow Jennifer and our daughters did come with me to camp and climb as a family in the Jotunheim in Norway and the Enchanted Mountains in the Pyrenees. The last 4,000-metre peak Jennifer and I climbed together was Gran Paradiso in the Italian Alps in 1979.

I trust it is clear that my view of mountaineering is quite ambivalent. The reckoning between pleasure, triumph and exhilaration on the one hand and the risk of injury and death on the other is difficult to make, especially in the case of high altitude climbing where the lack of oxygen impairs your judgement as well as weakening your limbs and sometimes destroys your most vital bodily functions without you being aware that it's happening. High altitude sickness can make you blind, inflict deadly blood clots or even send you mad. It is an uncontrollable risk. Yet climbing without using supplementary oxygen has become *de rigueur* for top-flight climbers. When such a mountaineer dies on a difficult peak his friends are too inclined to say, 'He died doing what he loved best.' Which may be true but is also trite. Those who die are treated as heroes when more often they are really failures – they fail to judge the weather or the snow conditions or they don't turn back when that is really the rational choice. For a very thoughtful discussion of the effect of such deaths on their families and friends I commend *Where the Mountain Casts its Shadow: The Dark Side of Extreme Adventure* by Maria Coffey, an American non-climber. She was a girlfriend to Joe Tasker, an English climber who disappeared in 1982 pioneering a new route on Everest. It's a good antidote to the heroics and the imperative of conquering the natural world at all costs that one will find in most books written by the 'tigers' – the celebrity mountaineers – and their acolytes.

Let Edward Whymper have the last word:

There have been joys too great to be described in words, and there have been griefs upon which I have not dared to dwell; and with these in mind I say:

Climb if you will, but remember that courage and strength are nought without prudence, and that a momentary negligence may destroy the happiness of a lifetime. Do nothing in haste; look well to each step; and from the beginning think what may be the end.

From *Scrambles Amongst the Alps*

7

Army 1952–1954

When I received my call-up papers for National Service in May 1952 I immediately gave up my temporary teaching post and hitch-hiked to North Wales. After a week's climbing I reported direct to the Royal Artillery (RA) training camp in Oswestry. In the 6th Regiment RA we were trained to be field gunners using 25-pounders such as had been massed at El Alamein in 1942 with great effect. We were also trained in how to lay any field gun correctly using some basic mathematics to calculate the angles of direction and elevation. Some of the squad went on to become clerks, serving gun position officers. To memorise the sequence for laying the gun we were taught a catchy mnemonic: 'In Italy Mussolini Always Interferes.' What those initials mean now I have no idea!

To practise with live ammunition we went to a range at Trawsfynydd in Snowdonia where we fired a few rounds uphill at obvious targets. It proved much harder to hit them than we had thought from our previous 'paper' exercises. A year later when I was in Hong Kong my troop commander, Brian Peckham, had been a gunnery instructor at the RA's chief gunnery school at Larkhill. During the Italian campaign, he told us, his battery had tried to destroy a house occupied by German troops in sight perhaps two miles away. They shelled it, he said, virtually every day for three months but never hit it. Well-tried weapons, even when manned by battle-hardened gunners, don't always live up to specification.

To round off our 12 weeks training our troop of about 30 had a pleasant interlude of a weekend camp beside Pistyll Rhaeadr, the highest waterfall in Wales. On a baking hot July day we climbed the Berwyns and picked bilberries. For the first time since our induction no one complained about anything. For a finale the four large training regiments at Oswestry competed in an afternoon of athletics. I was entered for the half-mile relay, much against his better judgement, by a physical training instructor (PTI) with whom I had had several run-ins. He thought I was lazy. I knew he was a bully and a bit of a sadist, insisting on press-ups and backlifts, which were well beyond our capacity. I ran the third leg of two laps. I started 20 yards behind but gained steadily on the leading runner to pass him in the second back straight, enabling me to pass the baton for the anchor leg with yards to spare. Our PTI was so surprised that I had saved the day that he actually congratulated me.

Towards the end of our training at Oswestry half a dozen from our squad were sent off to the War Office Selection Board (WOSB) for officers at Barton Stacey in Hampshire. We spent a couple of days doing written and practical tests, making a presentation and having an interview. One of the written tests was to devise a plan for a boys' club based on an old house, which had a 'garage (two cars)'. In my response I proposed selling the cars in order to provide money for expeditions but afterwards it dawned on me that the examiners only intended the '(two cars)' to indicate the size of the garage! I still passed.

By chance one of my contemporaries from Harrow was also at the WOSB, arriving in a beautiful, light blue 1930s Morris 10. One evening four of us would-be officer cadets zoomed off to nearby Winchester, enjoying the exhilaration of riding in an open-top car at 50 mph, no less. I had hoped to call on Ronald Hamilton, a housemaster at Winchester, whom David Nelson and I had met in the Pyrenees the previous summer, but alas he was on holiday. A week or so after we returned to Oswestry we were all given leave and told to report to our new postings – in my case Mons Officer Cadet School in Aldershot. I sewed the white flashes on my lapels before travelling home happy that I had made the grade.

At Mons I felt I had taken a step back in time to an earlier age of harsh army discipline with too much parade-ground drill. Regimental Sergeant-Major (RSM) Ronald Brittain and a group of Guards' company sergeant-majors set the tone, seeming to dominate all the public parts of the course. Every two weeks there was a passing-out parade for each batch of 30 newly-minted officers. The whole school spent hours on the parade-ground preparing for these grand occasions on one of which we were 'inspected' by Princess Margaret who wore scarlet lipstick inches thick and very high heels. After the whole school had marched past in quick time to the tune of the 'British Grenadiers', the new officers marched up the steps in imitation of the protocol at Sandhurst to the stirring chords of the 'Royal Artillery Slow March', which still reverberate in my mind 60 years later. I still loathed drill and despised this fat, bull-necked giant in his ancient uniform, RSM Brittain, who by then was an institution whom no one crossed, certainly not the officers running the school. Incidentally, the adjutant of the school was Guards Major Robin Leigh Pemberton who later became Governor of the Bank of England. At one of these passing-out parades Brittain somehow bellowed out the wrong step. Our company had just begun to swing into line so our company sergeant-major overrode Brittain's call with an even stronger voice, insisting several times to 'Take the time from me! Left, Right, Left, Right! Take the time from me,' which we did, so that he prevailed and Brittain was left shouting to himself.

The first six weeks at Mons were infantry training under the guidance of a glider pilot who had survived Arnhem. Eight years later he was still only a captain, which I suppose showed that a surfeit of young officers had opted to become regulars at the end of the war. My troop commander in Hong Kong, Brian Peckham, was even more experienced and qualified, yet when I arrived in February 1953 he too was still only a captain. On a night exercise from Mons my three-man patrol found an old mobile cattle feeder, which, with a great deal of effort, we upended over our freezing trench to give more warmth. We were roundly bawled out by the glider pilot at about two o'clock in the morning for our pains. Quite right too, as once it was in position we couldn't see out and therefore could not have defended ourselves.

The second ten weeks we were trained to fire and deploy the Bofors 40 mm mobile anti-aircraft gun, another veteran of the war. During this period we were upgraded from an ordinary 20-bed barrack room to a three-man billet, which afforded some comfort and privacy. One of my fellows was David McCardle, a very agreeable Scotsman who could not read music but could play any tune by ear. I met him again at Oxford where he was in great demand in the Union cellar night-club.

In this artillery period at Mons much of the course was in the classroom as anti-aircraft gunnery was a highly technical affair requiring some knowledge and considerable application. The climax was three days shooting practice on the range at Tonfanau, a couple of miles north of Tywyn on the coast of Cardigan Bay. A two-engined Dakota trundled past at about 150 mph, towing a long sleeve as a target, 200 yards behind. It could not have been a popular assignment for the pilots to fly back and forth in front of some very green anti-aircraft gunners firing 40 mm shells. Of course there was a safety officer standing behind each gun to ensure none locked on to the plane rather than the sleeve but you never know. No one scored a direct hit, though this was just about the easiest target an ack-ack gunner would ever have faced. On the last evening we had a very well conducted revision session in which we had to ask questions of other members of the class. I remember I asked a routine question of the man on my left which he couldn't answer. As he was one of only two who failed the course I still wince as I wonder whether indirectly I was responsible. From Tonfanau we were allowed home for Christmas leave, part of which I spent with my parents at a hotel in Haslemere. The guests organised a dance, which included one very welcome and energetic eightsome reel, which I had learnt in the last year at Moretons, at that time my only social accomplishment! I also spent some time revising my artillery theory, something that bore fruit in the exam, which took place as soon as we returned to Aldershot.

The keenest member of our artillery squad was a tall and earnest man named Clarkson. He was obviously the best at drill and probably the best all-round soldier. As a result he was promoted towards the end of the course to the spurious rank of junior under-officer with an impressive flash on his right sleeve. I say spurious because it carried no pay and only lasted until the end of the course. Even so he commanded us as we marched around the barracks and up the steps on that final day. In contrast, I was regarded as part of the awkward squad, having had several eyeball confrontations with Brittain and others in charge. I hated the atmosphere so much it showed, but because of that I was determined not to fail, hence the homework at the Haslemere hotel over Christmas. Much to the surprise of the CSM and the chagrin of some of my fellows I achieved the highest marks in the exam with the result that I was given first choice in postings. Clarkson was second. There were only three overseas postings – Far East, Egypt and Rhine Army. I put Far Eastern Land Forces in all three boxes only to be told off yet again for not reacting more respectfully as expected. I still got Hong Kong. In contrast, another member of our squad chose to be posted to Woolwich Artillery Depot because it was just across the river from his home in Essex. He reckoned that the best way to serve out his two years' army service would be to go home every weekend. I realised that much of our service might be routine military exercises, but along with several others, I also thought here was an opportunity to be seized.

Playing rugby at Mons I injured my back, which meant I was sent for physiotherapy in the next barracks. Luckily it couldn't have been too bad because I used to go there on my bicycle. It proved to be a delightful introduction to the art of physiotherapy. The therapists were two beautiful young women – one tall and dark and the other short, with flame-coloured hair. While I waited my turn the tall one worked on the leg of a paratroop captain who had had a parachute accident that ripped a great slice out of his leg. When I saw him it was all healed up but it still looked frightful. The tall woman treated him with very tender, loving care, which I felt sure would lead to a permanent liaison. Sometimes I would contemplate this affair from an adjoining bed while the flame-haired woman gave me soothing and eventually curative massage. I hadn't the nerve to take her out to dinner but I should have done!

After two weeks of embarkation leave I joined the Royal Mail liner *Asturias* in Southampton at the end of January 1953 complete with my tropical kit. The *Asturias* was a large, fast ship, despite having had a hard war in which she had been sunk in Freetown harbour. We carried several hundred troops in bunks on the lower decks most of whom were bound for Singapore, Hong Kong and Korea. On the upper decks was a large group of families also *en route* to Singapore and Hong Kong. At first I was assigned to supervise a group of paratroops who were housed in very close quarters, three bunks high, which I could see would get hot and unpleasant when we reached warmer climes. After a couple of days, however, some senior officer took me off that job but gave me no regular duties. I never found out why but I had little to do for 26 days except look at the sea, play deck quoits and chat to some of the families. For meals in the officers' dining-room I was seated with a major and his wife and their two small children under five. The wife confided in me that they had had a most romantic encounter at Philippeville on the coast of Algeria during the war. She was still only in her twenties while he looked ten years older. He was a major in the Pay Corps with considerable ability. For the duration of the voyage they were very agreeable companions, although towards the end she became rather too affectionate for her own good. Although I would certainly have enjoyed having a girlfriend I had the sense to see that on this boat I had to keep the major's wife at arm's length. Once in Hong Kong our friendship soon ended rather dramatically. After a dinner in their very nice apartment he asked me if I had taken part in the Queen's Birthday parade in June 1953. In fact I had ignored the parade to climb Tai Mo Shan, the highest peak in the colony. Unwisely I also expressed my anti-royalist feelings, which clearly grated on all his sentiments. 'If that's how you feel you had better go home,' he said, insisting on driving me the five miles back to my mess. It was the last time I saw him, though I did meet her at the yacht club one day by chance where she seemed to be enjoying life.

The most dramatic incident on the voyage occurred in Singapore where I drew the short straw as Orderly Officer for the day we were in port. Everyone else went ashore. Late that afternoon a navy Leading Seaman came up the gangplank with a torn white shirt and bleeding profusely from his head and arm. He had been leading a naval military police patrol when he and a couple of other NCOs were set upon by Scottish troops who had had more than enough to drink. Whether or not he had been rather too officious with high-spirited young men afflicted with a touch of cabin fever I could not determine. We were about 20 days out from England and 5 days from our last short stop at Colombo. After I got the surgery to patch him up I stationed him at the top of the gangplank to identify his assailants as they came back. I also summoned help from a couple of military police we had on board. As the deadline approached several hundred of our lads straggled back, some obviously too well oiled for their own good, but for a long time our naval man identified none. The deadline passed but we knew without counting that there were still some to come. Finally about an hour after the ship was supposed to leave a half dozen 'jocks' from the Black Watch rolled to the bottom of the gangplank singing and swearing no doubt in the way to which they were accustomed back home. We barely needed the naval patrolman to identify them. It was obvious they had been on a rampage, probably causing a lot more havoc with Singaporeans than with the naval patrol. They too had torn uniforms and flecks of blood on their arms and faces. As they came up the gangplank the military policemen grabbed them and, after quite a tough struggle, got them all down to the brig. After three weeks of civilised, almost bourgeois, cruising it was a rude awakening to the real world of other ranks and lower decks. I had not been able to put more than one foot ashore on the dock.

Hong Kong

When I arrived in Hong Kong in February 1953 I was driven to the headquarters of the 27th Heavy Anti-Aircraft Regiment in Stanley, situated on a rocky peninsula on the south-east corner of the island. The atmosphere in this unit deployed in the field was far more friendly and relaxed than in the training regiment or the cadet school. Within days

I was posted on from the spacious officers' mess at Stanley to become the third officer in charge of a troop of four 3.7-inch heavy anti-aircraft guns perched on Sai Wan hill overlooking the entrance to Hong Kong harbour. It was a most dramatic gun position, staring straight out to sea with a long arm of mainland China forming our easterly horizon five miles away. Below was the narrow Lei Yue Mun gap, through which hundreds of ships and junks passed each day. At eye level dozens of planes would glide down to make a tricky landing at Kai Tak airport on the north shore of the magnificent harbour. We used both the aircraft and the ships as target practice for our drills.

The gunners and their NCOs lived in bare, corrugated-iron barrack rooms in the fort but our two sergeants and the three officers lived in quite congenial brick messes halfway down the hill in Lei Yue Mun barracks. The officers' mess was a pleasant, airy two-storey building with large rooms for everyone, a terrace overlooking the bay and its own squash court. The 2nd lieutenant I was replacing, Jock Burns, was a very smart regimental type who had an enormous repertoire of filthy songs. Soon after I arrived he sailed off home supposedly to become a Church of England parson! I wonder if he ever went through with it? My other junior colleague was Tony Veitch, a very cultured regular lieutenant who was agreeable and relaxed. The commander of Easy Troop was Captain Brian Peckham whom I've mentioned earlier. He was very efficient and generally courteous but sometimes he could be frightful even with his own wife. He had a fine moustache, yellowed by chain-smoking. A month or two before I left in June 1954 Peter Sterwin, my replacement, arrived after four years in Oxford reading classics. We got on well and have remained friends ever since.

The gun position was a three-level concrete fort built in the 1930s. It even contained a secret tunnel, seemingly for escape. On the lowest level was a small parade-ground-cum-vehicle-park, plus a few small rooms for offices and stores and the corrugated-iron barrack huts. Thirty feet above were the four guns set on concrete gun emplacements with all-round traction. Then up a 1 in 3 slope was the radar set, control room and predictor, an early computer for translating the electronic information achieved by radar detection into gun angles and elevations necessary to shoot down the planes. It was all technology left over from the Second World War. During the siege of Hong Kong in December 1941 Japanese troops had crossed the Lei Yue Mun Straits at night and caught the Sai Wan garrison off guard, killing many of them in the barracks. Those that were captured had to endure three and a half years of imprisonment in one of the ghastly prison camps. All the prisoners of war who survived emerged as near skeletons.

For 16 months I 'defended the far-flung frontier' against the threat from the 'Chinese hordes' or at least their planes. I was an imperialist fending off Communism in a colonial enclave into which millions of Chinese had fled. Pre-war, the population had been about 800,000, but following the Communist victory in 1949 the number rose quickly to two and a half million while in later years it more than doubled again, mostly immigrants and/or refugees from the mainland. Maybe we had no business taking over a slice of the Chinese empire in the first place but from 1949 to 1997 the colony afforded millions of Chinese protection from the rigours and persecution of their own government. Because of the autonomous status negotiated by the British government in 1997 Hong Kong remains a haven to this day.

Besides routine gun maintenance, training and exercises, I also led two patrols into the remote eastern part of the New Territories, which were inhabited mainly by fishermen and their families. Accompanied by a Hong Kong police sergeant who acted as liaison and interpreter, a small patrol of a dozen would make a three-day march to visit some of the remote villages, in part to pick up the latest intelligence but also to show the flag and deal with the most obvious medical problems. Our medical orderlies always had a dozen urgent patients in every village we passed through. The Chinese authorities were still in a hostile frame of mind towards the colony and towards Britain as one of their main adversaries in Korea. Soon after I arrived they seized a Hong Kong yacht sailing in the South China Sea only a little way up the coast from where we patrolled. The half dozen British crew were detained for months.

One of my best friends in Hong Kong was Chris Gardner, another National Service officer stationed on a similar isolated gun position on the north side of the harbour. Our two troops were part of the same battery. One of our joint tasks each week was to collect the cash for pay day from a bank right next door to the Peninsula Hotel in Kowloon. Our regular drill was to put our money – about 15,000 Hong Kong dollars each – in a small case and then retire to a café for a coffee before returning to our units. After some jolly chat we would get back into our 15-hundredweight trucks and drive back to pay the troops. One day Chris reached his barracks some eight miles from Kowloon when he realised he had left his case of money under his chair. Panic.

He raced back to find it still there! Later we were both at Oxford together and he came to my wedding.

My other main duty was organising sport for the troop, something that Tony Veitch shied away from for obvious reasons as he did not have the build of an athlete. To begin with I was able to take the troop swimming once a week at the beautiful Sheko Bay but our three-ton truck showed signs of wear so restrictions were placed on 'recce transport', that is recreational transport, and we never went again. I found out the next year that one could actually walk to Big Wave Bay near Sheko by climbing a steep mountain and finding a path through the bush. On a summer evening there was just time to walk there and back to enjoy a delicious swim before dark.

In the winter I refereed the troop playing football, only to find that the referee's decision is frequently challenged. The players complained that I did not apply the offside rule; I thought they simply wanted a partial referee. I note from a full-page advertisement in *The Guardian* that the Football Association's own referees are being challenged or ignored so often that a third of amateur games are now played without a referee. Whatever their expertise, it seems many players do not accept the referee's decision. In the spring and summer we also did a lot of athletics on a pitch at Lei Yue Mun just below our officers' mess. As it happened, our troop contained several good runners who performed well in the regimental sports. In the spring of 1954 I organised a competition between our troop, the independent mortar battery and personnel from a nearby RAAF electronic surveillance station, which went off well.

That spring my own athletics career came to a peak. I won cups and medals galore in the regimental sports which brought invitations to compete at higher levels, such as the Land Forces Championships and the Colony Championships. I usually ran only in the quarter- and half-mile races but on one occasion came second in an invitation mile. In the Colony Championships held at the Happy Valley racecourse I came second in the half mile and was a member of the army team that won the 440-yard relay for which we were awarded genuine silver medals. In stark contrast to today's sportsmen, we did not parade as heroes before fans, nor did we even celebrate together. We were Colony Champions yet we simply went back to our separate regiments as if it was just another day's sport.

On a neighbouring hill, just across the parade-ground from the Lei Yue Mun mess was the headquarters of the Hong Kong Regiment – locally recruited non-commissioned soldiers who took up roles as drivers, orderlies, etc. They had their own NCOs but I was never aware of any Chinese officers. The unit was headed by a genial major who should have been assisted by a captain from an Irish infantry regiment whose nickname was 'Bones'. In reality he was an alcoholic with whom the army did not know how to deal. He couldn't do his job yet they could neither cure him nor retire him. Instead they left him in our mess all alone with nothing to do for several months during which he simply got worse. Eventually he was sent home but I felt sure the story would end tragically.

To begin with the three junior officers from Easy Troop shared the mess with half a dozen officers of the Royal Australian Air Force (RAAF) who were operating the wireless monitoring station near Lei Yue Mun. For a few pleasant weeks I was the mess officer charged with supervising the cook and his staff. But very soon the RAAF moved out to be replaced by an independent mortar battery equipped with 4.2-inch mortars. The battery commander was an austere bachelor whose whole life was the army. His junior officers likened him to Captain Queeg in the novel *The Caine Mutiny*, which was current at the time. He kept one hand in a jacket pocket just as if he was fingering those ball bearings that the fictional Queeg so loved to play with. We messed together for over a year yet I don't think I ever had a sustained conversation with 'Queeg' whose real name I cannot now remember.

The army was not exactly a nine-to-five job because there were numerous calls on our time at night and at weekends, the most notable being overnight orderly officer one week in three. For that chore we had to sleep in a cold concrete cell on the gun position and turn out the guard sometime in the middle of the night. Nevertheless I did have much free time which I used for sailing, walking, country dancing and visiting friends of my Uncle Ted. He had been an artillery major at the end of the war in Hong Kong in charge of rehabilitating civilian prisoners and reuniting them with their families. He had been of particular help to a man named Will Carr and his Chinese wife. Carr had been a clerk in the Hong Kong government pre-war and suffered badly in Sham Shui Po prison camp. After Ted left Hong Kong he remained friends with Will Carr and when I was posted there put me in touch. The Carrs were very hospitable inviting me to their home in Kowloon and including me in many social occasions, the invitations for which usually came from Chinese businessmen seeking government contracts. It was at one of these that I discovered the delights of fresh lychees. The custom at these dinners was for most of the guests to play fast and furious games of mahjong as soon as the main course was finished. One evening I was chatting with a Eurasian man about my own age, away from the games table in the restaurant, when he pointed to a huge meat plate stacked with lychees, which had been forgotten or ignored. His nudge was an invitation to a memorable piece of gluttony, for lychees are surely close to ambrosia, the legendary food of the gods. Not very slowly, we ate our way through most of them and lived to tell the tale.

Will Carr also had a friend who was the chief nurse on the small island of Cheung Chau, which then had a large fishing fleet. The market there was full of the most extraordinary fish, some of which made me shudder rather than slaver. The nurse's boyfriend was a civil servant in the government who told me his hair-raising war story. Along with hundreds of other prisoners of war he was being transported to Japan in 1945 to work in the armaments factories. Suddenly they were torpedoed by an allied submarine; the ship listed and was obviously soon going to sink. The Japanese troops then escaped in the lifeboats, leaving a skeleton guard to keep the prisoners in the holds under locked hatches. Somehow the prisoners suborned a guard and forced their way out to find that they could just see a strip of shore a long way off. All the lifeboats had gone so the swimmers took their chance. Luckily the sea was calm but my storyteller said it took him five hours to reach a beach on a small island. Not many others made it.

The first spring Tony Veitch took me to the yacht club on an island just off shore in Victoria, the nerve centre of the colony. On a cool afternoon with a very fresh wind, he taught me how to sail a small gaff-rigged dinghy. The rest I remembered from Arthur Ransome's yarns about the Swallows and Amazons. During the next year I sailed at weekends as often as possible becoming proficient enough to win the club's annual dinghy race. During the second summer I booked to take leave in Japan by travelling on a troop ship but when it fell through I opted to stay at the Royal Artillery mess on Stonecutters Island. Again I spent most of my time sailing. One day I sailed out of the western end of the harbour to the large island of Lantao, much of which is today used for the airport. It was a long way for a dinghy but with a strong wind I made the crossing in good time to find a deserted little beach just right for a swim. All went well on the return leg until I reached the western point of Hong Kong Island when the tide changed. Finding I could make no headway against the tide I tied up to a huge buoy of which there were many in the harbour designed to hold large ships. I had been there two hours or more before a police launch came by. Seeing my plight the crew threw me a rope and towed me back to the yacht club at high speed in the dark. I arrived just in time to get the last ferry back to Stonecutters. I found out afterwards that the fee for tying up to one of those buoys was enormous!

One afternoon out sailing in a dinghy with a friend I noticed the Army Sailing Association's yacht, the *Elinor*, tied up on a quay. The *Elinor* was a 70-ton, gaff-rigged ketch, which originally must have been built as a trader some 50 years earlier. We tied up and climbed aboard, hoping to browse around this interesting craft – how did it ever get to Hong Kong? – and learn about its history. Instead we found four men reclining in the saloon drinking G & Ts. We introduced ourselves as from 27th Heavy Anti-Aircraft Regiment, but before we could even indicate our interest in having a look round were interrupted by a supercilious question: 'Come to do some work on the old girl, have you?' Well not exactly, we replied, not knowing much about the ship or what work might be required. We asked if we could look over the vessel but the man with the drawling voice barely gave us a nod and no one offered to show us anything. We had a brief walk round and left feeling decidedly unwelcome. The drinkers made it sound as if the *Elinor* was their own private yacht instead of being owned by the Army Sailing Association, which, in a sense made us joint owners, at least as much as them.

Many months later I was asked at the yacht club if I would like to crew the *Elinor* from a remote berth in the north-east of the New Territories back to Victoria. I made my own way there by bus from Kowloon and then a long walk of five or six miles just to reach the vessel. To my relief none of that original 'crew' were there. Somewhat late in the day we chugged out of the small harbour and down a long bay out into the South China Sea. There we hoisted sail and for a couple of hours tried to sail to Victoria. She was not a sleek, modern vessel but pottered along in a reasonable offshore wind. Soon, however, it was clear we would never make it by sail so we hauled down the sails – mainsail, jib and staysail – and motored the rest of the way round the eastern headlands of the New Territories and back through the Lei Yue Mun gap to Victoria, arriving just before midnight. For much of the way I at least had the satisfaction of taking the wheel. It was hardly *Two Years Before the Mast*, the book by R.H. Dana which my father often told me about, but it was such a contrast to the first time I stepped on to the *Elinor* that the experience of handling this substantial vessel has stayed with me. For a time I even climbed into the rigging below the bowsprit, just above the rolling, breaking waves.

Our mess in Lei Yue Mun barracks was halfway up the steep Sai Wan hill. Taxis were thought to be the only appropriate transport for officers but I always went to Victoria on foot down a steep zigzag path and then by tram. The trams were distinctly decrepit but the service was frequent and cheap. I was able to get to the centre of Victoria in about half an hour. I joined a Scottish dance club at the Union Church run by an enthusiastic Scottish minister. The members were a mixture of civilians and service personnel; apart from me there were no officers. I thoroughly enjoyed the dancing, acquiring a reasonable repertoire. This modest expertise proved a useful social skill as it led directly to meeting Jennifer in my first term at Oxford in a similar club. About two years after I left Hong Kong I met one of my dancing partners, Sheila Smith, on an overnight ferry from Dunkirk to Dover, one of the few encounters I have had with my Hong Kong acquaintances in more than 50 years. The hilarious circumstances of how I came to be travelling on that ferry I relate in the chapter on Oxford.

Soon after I arrived in Hong Kong I decided that I would take the opportunity to sail home across the Pacific. I booked a passage from Sydney to Marseilles on a French cargo boat belonging to Messageries Maritimes. The route went via Tahiti through the Panama Canal, Martinique and Guadeloupe to Marseilles. It would have taken about six weeks but I had the time after demob to make the trip before going up to Oxford in October. I saved enough money to travel steerage. Alas the shipping line cancelled my booking without explanation about a month before I was due to sail for Sydney. To make my normal discharge date in Britain I should have embarked on a troop ship home several weeks earlier. Instead I was quickly put on a troop ship to Singapore then flown home in one of the early flights for families. It took four days flying with nights at Calcutta, Karachi and Nicosia and refuelling *en route* at Bangkok, Bahrain (where it was like a furnace) and Naples.

Flying was then still a novel and comfortable way to travel in stark contrast to the journey I might have had. If I hadn't asked for local demob I might well have sailed home on the *Empire Windrush* troopship with, among others, our regimental quartermaster. While serving in Hong Kong for several years he had collected some fine sandalwood chests and dragon carpets. Chugging through the Mediterranean, however, the old ship suffered an explosion in the engine room, which developed into a fire so intense it had to be abandoned. As the power had failed many of the lifeboats couldn't be lowered. The quartermaster, I am told, gave a good example of leadership by being the first to jump into the water from where all the passengers were rescued by passing ships. He must have gritted his teeth over the lost chests.

I was discharged from the army – demobbed was the popular term – in the middle of June 1954 with an obligation of part-time service in the territorial army for three years, during which I had to attend a minimum number of training sessions including one summer camp. By the luck of the draw I was assigned to the 7th Battalion of the Argyll and Sutherland Highlanders, which had the 40-mm Bofors light anti-aircraft guns that I was trained on at Mons. As I had the time I decided to go to their camp in August at Bude on the north coast of Cornwall. It was a pleasant interlude, not too regimental and there was more pay at a decent rate. I was issued with a splendid beret but no kilt or trews! Three months later when I had already arranged to attend a weekend camp in Scotland I was informed by the War Ministry that the reserve obligations of my intake of national servicemen had just been cancelled and that all we had to do was maintain our uniform for another three years for which we actually received a small grant. With the Korean War definitely over and the Suez conflict beyond the horizon the government was winding down National Service and moving towards an all-professional army.

8

Oxford 1954–1958

After two years in the army I went up to Oxford with three aims – to get a first, to achieve a Blue and to find a wife. By the time I left I had scored two and a half. I had taken the entrance exam at University College in 1951, when most of the other candidates at Univ, all young men, were applying to start two years later after National Service. At the time I thought I wanted more time at school so applied for 1954. Looking back on it this seems like a mistake. I should have left as soon as I could once I had achieved entrance to Oxford.

I did quite well in the exams except in Latin where I was sternly warned that I had some way to catch up if I was to pass the Preliminary Examinations for History taken after the first two terms. In the event I did have a hard time with the Venerable Bede's *Ecclesiastical History of the English People* in Latin but somehow scraped through.

My first tutor at University College (always known as Univ) was Giles Alington, a tall, imposing bachelor with a splendid set of rooms in the Radcliffe Quad. He was the son of a celebrity cleric who had been Headmaster of Eton and Dean of Durham and who also wrote more than 50 books. Giles was himself dean and senior tutor at Univ. I think he was probably a good teacher but unfortunately, after about three tutorials, he fell ill and soon died. From then on my history course was supervised by David Cox who himself taught Anglo-Saxon history. He was a very pleasant man who, among other things, was a distinguished climber. While I was at Univ he and Wilfrid Noyce made the first ascent of Machupachare or the Fishtail, a very elegant peak of 22,000 feet next door to Annapurna in western Nepal. Officially they did not tread right on the summit in deference to local religious belief but he once confided that 'of course we went to the top, we couldn't climb all that way and not do so'. Despite having climbing in common, somehow I didn't relate to him; for my taste he was too diffident in his comments and made little attempt to push us towards extra study or extra effort. In fact he did not seem to have pushed himself because he never wrote a book other than a climbing guide!

My other Univ tutor was the chaplain, the Reverend Tom Parker, who was a rotund clerical bachelor straight out of Anthony Trollope. His study was so full of books there was barely room to sit down. He taught us medieval history, a time in which clerics like himself had been far more prominent in society. He was more outgoing than Cox but to me not much more inspiring. To his credit he never asked me to go to chapel. As far as I was concerned these Univ dons did not give me either rigorous or inspiring tutorials. In theory tutorials are Oxbridge's unique selling point. I was fairly diligent in preparing my essays and going to the recommended lectures but reading out one's essay to the tutors in Univ never seemed satisfactory either for me or for them. Perhaps it's much better now that everyone has a computer and essays can be sent electronically in advance. If used properly the tutor can now make more thoughtful and accurate criticism than previously.

My very agreeable colleague sharing all my Univ tutorials was Graham Greene, a nephew of the novelist and the son of Hugh Carleton Greene, later Director General of the BBC. Graham did not seem to give his full attention to his studies, in part because, unlike me, he did not have any academic ambition. I thought I would be a schoolmaster whereas Graham knew he would join the family bank. In fact, after a short spell in finance, he moved into publishing, eventually becoming chairman of Jonathan Cape and a member of the great and good serving on a number of quangos.

Although I was loosely supervised by University College for the three years of my History course, the tutors I responded to the most were all from other colleges. In fact the two best were both newly-minted Doctors of Philosophy (D.Phil) – Keith Thomas and David Adams. Thomas was already numbered among the scholarly elite, being a Fellow of All Souls. I remember one particularly warm afternoon when he held my tutorial in the quadrangle, sitting on the lawn in deck-chairs. At the end of which I admired this beautiful space flanked by the Codrington Library – one of the most elegant in Oxford – and then remarked flippantly that it would make a splendid place for a cricket match. He pretended to be shocked by my irreverence for this hallowed place. Keith Thomas took me for seventeenth-century European history in which I did well in finals.

For my special subject, the build-up to the American Civil War, I had tutorials from David Adams, then a Research Fellow at Nuffield

College. He was a very tall, handsome man who had won a fancy scholarship to Yale. He probably did not know nearly as much about this subject as Cox and Parker knew about theirs but his approach was so affable and encouraging, spiked with anecdotes from his own experience in America, that I worked harder for him than for anybody. Again my results on the two Civil War papers were good. Later he became Professor of American History at Keele University while Keith Thomas became Master of St John's College in Oxford. Clearly I was lucky to have them as tutors.

During the first year my rooms in Univ were in the High Street above the Co-op and opposite Queen's and St Edmund Hall. They were spacious but cold, heated only by a two-bar electric fire. I hung a large yachting picture on the wall and placed my ice axe on the mantelpiece but it must have been pretty bare. Still my sitting room had a comfortable sofa and a large table just right for assembling all one's notes prior to writing an essay. It was also right above one of my fellow history students, David Geekie, with the aid of whose fire escape rope I let myself down some 20 feet to the High Street early one May morning in 1955. Alas, the miserable scout reported me and I was fined.

In the second year, I moved to a large, well-furnished bedsit in an Edwardian building called Kybald at the other end of the college. Kybald was next to the library and very near hall unlike my High Street rooms, which were quite a hike. Another advantage of Kybald was that it overlooked a low wall leading to Merton Street over which I occasionally climbed back into college when the main gate was closed. In those days undergraduates were still treated like schoolboys even though most of them were in their twenties because they had done National Service.

One of my neighbours in Kybald was Geoffrey Robinson who had been a contemporary of mine with a Middlesex Award at Harrow. For his National Service he had flown jet fighters, having previously learnt to fly while at school with a scholarship to a flying school in Canada. His worst experience in the RAF was when his jet engine conked out at 600 mph somewhere in the skies. Luckily he was near his base and was talked down by a controller on the ground. He continued as a reservist pilot in the University Air Squadron and many years later, after a career in industry, became a flying instructor.

While I was reasonably diligent with my studies I could, as I have indicated, have done much more work if all my tutors had been as good as Keith Thomas and David Adams. However, if I had spent more time in the Radcliffe and Rhodes House libraries I might not have come away from Oxford with such golden memories. From the start I rejected both rugby and athletics as being too time-consuming. In any case I had some troubling tonsils, which had to be taken out in the Radcliffe Infirmary during the first Christmas holiday. I took a long time to recover from this relatively minor operation. While I was in an ear, nose and throat ward for a week a middle-aged man who looked as if he had just come out of Belsen was parked for a day or two on a spare bed near me. He was horribly emaciated and was being fed intravenously and through his nose. The nurses professed not to know what was wrong with him but it was clearly something very serious. It was a timely reminder that though I found it very difficult to swallow for two or three months and my throat seemed lined with coarse sandpaper it was nothing compared to the pain suffered by this apparition. He was literally ghostly.

My sport at Oxford was Eton Fives. The university owned a Fives court built in the garden of a small shop in a side street off the Abingdon Road. How and why it came to be built in such an unlikely and inconvenient place must be a story in itself. You needed a bicycle to get there. Luckily I found a good partner at Univ, John Kay-Mouat, so that in my second year we won several rounds of the college competition. In my third and fourth years I played often for the university team including some hard away matches. On the way to Shrewsbury School in a two-seater sports car I remember we took the wrong turning out of Worcester and so arrived late when the rest had finished lunch. Starting on the wrong foot as it were, we were pressed very hard by a couple of schoolboys who beat us 3–2. In my fourth year while a graduate student I was chosen for the varsity match against Cambridge, which was held at Eton. In the first Cambridge pair was my partner at Harrow, David Jenkins.* I played in the Oxford third pair and, regrettably, lost.

I dabbled in a few societies such as the Labour Club and the Union and also worked on the weekly magazine, *Isis*. In the Labour Club the leading lights were Anthony Howard, Brian Walden, David Marquand and Bill McCarthy, all of whom went on to become national figures. They were also prominent in the Union Debating Society along with Michael Heseltine and Jeremy Isaacs. In fact the best debaters at that time were undoubtedly Isaacs, later Head of Channel 4 and the Royal Opera house, and McCarthy who became a don at Nuffield College. Of these, McCarthy was the more interesting. He had worked at the

---

*After Cambridge David became a parson, rising to Canon Prebendary.

bench in industry and rose through trade union scholarships and Ruskin College to become one of the foremost experts on labour relations. Harold Wilson's government made him a Life Peer in 1976 but should have made him a minister. During the 18 years of continuous Conservative government from 1979 to 1997 he was an acerbic critic as Opposition spokesman for employment. His was a neglected talent.

In my second year I tried my hand at being a journalist on *Isis*. My contributions were of little consequence and at this stage I confess I felt no desire to become a journalist in stark contrast to the editor, Jeremy Wolfenden, who had already done stints at *The Times* and had his future mapped out. Wolfenden was the very picture of the gilded clever youth – a mop of dyed blond hair over his forehead, a cigarette hanging from his mouth, and a habit of firing off hip remarks all too frequently. He got a First without seeming to do any work and was soon elected a Fellow of All Souls, the very pinnacle of academic success. But he spurned Oxford to take up a career in journalism, being appointed a foreign correspondent before he was 30. While in Moscow some thought he was also a spy. Unhappily, he destroyed his health with drink and drugs and died in harness in Moscow in his early thirties. He could have come straight out of a novel by Evelyn Waugh. A short, frank, but sympathetic account of his life can be seen in *The Fatal Englishman* by Sebastian Faulks.

Beyond the hard work, the sport and the earnest societies was a social life such as I had never had at Harrow and had had too little of even in the army. At that time there were only four colleges for women and the ratio to men was one to seven. In my first term I met Jennifer Thomas at the Scottish Dance Club held in a somewhat dingy gymnasium in Alfred Street just off the High Street. Jennifer was a very good dancer, part of the club's demonstration team who gave little shows around the county. Although she is nine months younger than me she was two years ahead of me in her final year, reading English at Somerville College. By February 1955 we were a couple and have remained so ever since. Together we danced, punted on the Cherwell, went to many plays and films, and climbed quite a few mountains even before we left Oxford. What clinched our partnership was seeing *The Male Animal* by James Thurber, which is both very funny and deadly serious at the same time. Its portrayal of right-wing paranoia on a university campus also proved a useful preparation for our two years in America from 1958 to 1960.

Oxford had many enterprising and innovatory drama clubs at that time eager to produce new plays or revive old ones well outside the popular canon. In the summer many of them were set in college gardens where, weather permitting, they could be magical. Although the actors and directors were all amateurs, they often played with such *joie de vivre* and in such idyllic settings as Worcester College gardens that they have left a smile in the mind 50 years later. When our elder daughter Alison had just been accepted at Somerville we went *en famille* to a garden party for old members. As soon as we arrived on the lawn a Somervillean who had been at school with Alison whipped her and Juliet, then aged 15, away to gossip and giggle about what the university was really like. That evening after tea on the Somerville lawn we went to a Shakespearean romance in Oriel Quad, which was done with considerable *élan* and style. Until then Juliet had not talked about university at all, but going home that night she announced, 'I'm going to Oxford.' The magic had worked; we never had to persuade her that it would be worth all the hard work necessary to get a place.

While drama was one part of the magic for us, the other half was punting on the Cherwell. Somerville had half a dozen punts up river at Bardwell Road from where we made many trips. In 1955 Jennifer was studying for her finals so used to justify her time out of the library by bringing a few books. Punting is very relaxing and, perhaps in the right, disciplined or puritanical company, could provide a suitable environment in which to work. But on a warm afternoon the erotic coefficient of the Oxbridge punt is very high so I doubt that she retained much from her books of value in the exams. Once or twice we also took a canoe in order to go north, way beyond the Oxford bypass. One day we disembarked on a grassy bank in the shade of a willow tree and Jennifer took out her books. As it was my first summer term and I had cleared my immediate hurdle of Prelims I thought I would paddle upstream in the quite narrow river to give Jennifer time to study. I had no sooner pushed off from the bank than I turned the canoe over and disappeared from sight. In the muddy water Jennifer couldn't see me and feared the worst. Of course I surfaced none the worse for wear except that I had to dry my clothes in the sun before we could return. Nothing was learnt about *Beowulf* that day but our relationship made great progress.

Despite many hours in a punt during her last term Jennifer got a good 2nd in English (nothing after 1830 in those days!) and might have gone higher but for the fact that she was quite ill during the finals exam week. She was determined not to teach so took a secretarial course in Oxford in order to equip herself for a job. After rejecting an offer from

The Spectator to be the editor's assistant, because the pay was too low, she gained an administrative post with the Oxfordshire Rural Community Council. That meant that we spent three years together enjoying all the fun of Oxford before we got married in Univ in January 1958.

One of my favourite aphorisms is 'Youth is wasted on the young', indicating that an older generation shakes its head over the follies of youth. When David Cameron became leader of the Conservative party he was soon shown to have been a member of the Bullingdon Club at Oxford, famed for its excesses, and in effect he admitted that he had smoked cannabis because, when pressed by the media, he would not deny it. These follies, though minor, will undoubtedly dog him for all his political life. As perhaps they should because they do tell us a little about his character, his lifestyle and his affluent background. However, young adults the world over indulge in many kinds of foolishness, the most obvious being excessive drinking, smoking, gambling and drug-taking. In fact some supporters of Cameron argued that we shouldn't worry about his record because 'everyone did it as an undergraduate at university'.

That assertion might be true today, although I doubt it, but it certainly was not the norm in the 1950s. No one ever suggested I try cannabis in my four years at Oxford and I was not aware that any of my contemporaries even experimented with drugs of any kind other than tobacco and alcohol. University College had its own small bar in the basement of the hall but had few regular patrons. It was not an era of excess.

My folly was my beard. When you climb in the Alps the cold winds and intense sunshine reflected off the snow cut deep into the face. So in the summer of 1956, when I spent three weeks climbing in Switzerland with the Oxford University Mountaineering Club, I let my beard grow for self-protection, and at the end of the holiday fancied my appearance enough not to shave it off. It was a mixture of vanity and bravado. At the first meeting that October of the Univ historians with David Cox our supervisor, he asked each one of us how we had spent the summer. When he came to me he remarked that he knew what I had been up to: 'growing your beard'. I should have taken the hint from that mild mockery but stubbornly kept my rather unimpressive bristles for the next two years. Only when we decided in November 1957 to get married did I admit to myself that my beard was absurd and better disposed of.

Hitch-hiking

In those days undergraduates had little cash but were rich in time. Many spent their long vacations earning money, sometimes gaining useful work experience. Although I did a few short jobs at Christmas and Easter I spent the long vacations in more exciting endeavours. I found that my grant from Middlesex County Council was adequate to cover my expenses, especially as I could supplement it with money saved from my army salary in Hong Kong. The fare from Hong Kong to Marseilles via Sydney, which I would have spent but for the incompetence of Messageries Maritimes, went a long way round Europe.

Throughout our time in Oxford hitch-hiking was our usual mode of travel in Britain, Ireland, France, Switzerland, Germany, Austria, Yugoslavia and Italy. It proved to be reasonably efficient, often interesting, sometimes exciting and always challenging.

Jennifer and I must have had several thousand miles of free transport. I say 'reasonably efficient' because you always had to work at it to gain a lift, it was always slower than travelling by train or bus (plane was rarely an option because of cost) and sometimes it left one well short of one's objective. *En route* to the Alps in 1956 Clive Harris and I had an excellent lift the first day up the Rhine from Dusseldorf to Heidelberg with two American medical students from Chicago. But then made so little progress that we took trains most of the way from Freiburg to Brig in the Rhone Valley. Coming back from that same Oxford University Mountaineering Club meet, Clive and I made a bet at the village of Randa. We had just climbed the Weisshorn, one of the most beautiful of Alpine peaks. Clive had all his gear with him but I had to go back to Zermatt to collect mine. So, who could get back to London first solely by hitch-hiking?

About a week later Clive wrote to claim his prize. He had been very lucky on his second day just leaving Switzerland. He was picked up by an Englishman with a vintage Rolls-Royce and travelled in style all the way home. Unluckily, the beautiful car broke down in the middle of France and, as it could not be repaired, had to be towed all the way to London. Nevertheless, he only took four and a half days.

In contrast there was little stylishness about my trip. I set off the day after Clive in heavy rain. Finding little success outside Visp in the Rhone Valley I sheltered under a road bridge. Soon a Vespa scooter stopped beside me, the driver dripping with water. We exchanged rueful remarks about the weather but when it eased he said to my great surprise, 'Hop

116

on', and he took me some 50 miles to Martigny where we both stayed overnight in the youth hostel. The second day I made fitful progress with several short lifts along the north shore of Lake Geneva to the French frontier. On the other side I was picked up by a nice Frenchman in a fast Peugeot. A hundred yards further on we passed another Oxford mountaineer from our party named Derek Hill. 'Stop,' I cried and the driver immediately agreed that my friend could climb in.

I had no idea where the Frenchman was going but it turned out that he was in a terrific hurry. He drove at speeds I never encountered on any other hitch, touching 80 miles per hour, which was exceedingly fast for an ordinary *route nationale*, not stopping till he kindly delivered us to the campsite in the Bois de Boulogne. Come the third day we took a bus to the northern edge of Paris and then separated as it was usually much easier for one to gain a lift than two, especially two bearded climbers carrying ice axes and heavy packs. Again I made only fitful progress for most of the day. Around eight o'clock in the twilight I was eyeing a corn field wondering whether I could get a dry night under some stooks when another couple of American students – David and Harry – stopped their Citroen 2CV and invited me aboard. The back seat was so small and covered with their luggage that I had difficulty fitting myself and my rucksack inside.

As we trundled along, never at more than 30 mph David turned to me to say that Harry was a very good driver but really he was reassuring himself. David also announced that they were going to catch the midnight ferry from Dunkirk, which was then about 70 miles away. As I had no ticket Dunkirk was as good as anywhere. There clearly was no time to lose. David also explained why he prompted Harry, the driver, from time to time. It was because Harry couldn't tell his left from right. All three of us took this as a joke and laughed heartily but in fact it was true. David, who was a non-driver but the unchallenged leader of their trip, also expressed anxiety that they might run out of petrol. This austerity model had no petrol gauge. You had to stop and use a dipstick. They had already run out earlier in the day many miles back. As we failed to spot an all-night petrol station on this particular *route nationale* – long before the days of motorways – he soon grew very anxious that we might actually run out again.

We motored along for about three hours until, on the outskirts of Dunkirk, we could see the ships and the cranes all lit up on the dockside. At that point we ran dry. It was about 15 minutes to midnight. Two of us leapt out and began to push. The car was so light we could soon get up some speed and ran with the car for over a mile right into the port where the car park was completely empty. Our ferry was still there so we rushed into the ticket office crying, 'Wait for us, we've tickets for the midnight ferry.' 'Bravo,' said a smiling ferryman, 'it doesn't go until half past two.'

After a very sound sleep on the deck we were approaching Dover in the early morning when (as mentioned in the previous chapter) I bumped into an old dancing partner of mine from Hong Kong travelling on the same boat. We had a pleasant exchange of gossip about mutual acquaintances. On arrival, David, Harry and I went down to the car deck and drove slowly down the ramp off the boat. 'Remember they drive on the left,' said David, the front-seat passenger, for the third or fourth time. Harry nodded but then, just as we reached the main road in front of a huge sign saying, 'Drive on the Left', he drove straight into the right-hand lane. This time we didn't laugh but yelled at him. He swerved and we survived. My American friends then drove me all the way to London. My journey time, including the 18-hour delayed start, was three and a half days. The kindness of strangers had served me very well and I beat Clive by more than a day.

Chance meetings happen frequently in fiction. In John Buchan's thrillers for instance, they so often save the day for our hero that one has to gulp hard to suspend disbelief. Yet this was the second time I bumped into a friend on a cross-Channel ferry and my second accidental meeting with Sheila Smith, the woman on the Dunkirk ferry. Two years earlier I had met her by chance in a restaurant and was just beginning to have a promising conversation when the commanding officer of the Hong Kong Regiment, whose HQ was next door to us in Lei Yue Mun, came with his wife and sat down at our table uninvited. He was a nice enough man but I could have wished him further. From then on he dominated the conversation and blotted out all our personal chat.

In real life such chance meetings ought to be rare. The odds against seeing someone far from home are very long. A few minutes' difference and they would be travelling on a different plane, train or boat or at least in a different section where one would never see them. Yet I now recall six such unlikely chance meetings of which two were on cross-Channel ferries, two were with David Geekie, a friend from Univ, and two with Miss Smith. I first met David by chance, outside a factory gate in Birmingham when I was making a programme about industrial relations and he was working for Cadbury. The second time Jennifer and I met him on a plane to Geneva with his family about 20 years after Oxford. He was going summer skiing while we were going to Courmayeur in Italy to climb. A more bizarre accidental meeting was with two officers from the mess in Hong Kong, Lieutenants Carter and Lacey, while riding my bike in North Oxford in 1958. They came out of a side turning in a car and asked me for directions. Five seconds either way and we would never have seen each other. Our exchange lasted 15 seconds before they were on their way, never to be seen by me again.

Jennifer and I also had a bit of luck, comparable to my 2CV lark, when hitch-hiking in Ireland one Easter. Returning from Killarney, we were given a lift by a very smart moustachioed salesman all the way from Cork to Dublin (some 150 miles), which took all of one afternoon. Some Irishmen were a bit surly towards the English at that time but this man had served as a volunteer in the British Army in the Second World War. He kept referring to us with a smile on his face as 'You PRO testants', not that we were, but we could see what he meant. He insisted on taking us to the door of our youth hostel. Thanks very much to him and his company.

Our longest 'hitch' together was our grand tour from Geneva to Yugoslavia and Italy and back in 1955. Going east from Basel towards Austria, Jennifer and I were picked up by a middle-aged couple in a luxurious Mercedes, a car we had never ridden in before. We cruised along for an hour when they suddenly stopped outside a baroque church. 'Want to see inside? It's very special.' So we had a guided tour to an eighteenth-century church full of madonnas and saints with everything gilded up to the eyeballs. It wasn't to our taste but it was a pleasant cultural interlude in a hard day's hitching.

A couple of days later when we were trying to get over the Brenner Pass into the Tyrol a robed priest stopped his car in response to our thumbs held plaintively in the air. We ran up to the car and took our sacks off. The priest got out but instead of opening the boot explained at length why he couldn't take us. He didn't think his car was strong enough and with that he jumped back in and sped off leaving us open-mouthed. About two days later – after an interesting night in Innsbruck where the landlady of a bed and breakfast gave us a double room without our asking because she took us for brother and sister! – we hitched over another pass to Kitzbühl. On this occasion a small truck loaded with a heavy diesel engine stopped for us on a steep bend. The driver, who was some kind of mechanic, had a passenger but he offered us the open back. Hitch-hikers should not be choosers so we climbed in beside the diesel engine. Then began a very slow, painful climb through steep gradients and many hairpins, never going more than walking pace until we reached the top of the pass. In the circumstances it was very thoughtful of him to take us on board.

Our first destination after Austria was Bled in Slovenia in northern Yugoslavia where we stayed with the Vovk family. The father had once been a figure of consequence in this Alpine town set beside a beautiful lake but had been displaced and to some extent dispossessed by the communist regime after the war. My mother had made friends with the elder daughter, Melita, while on holiday in Bled a few years earlier. On this occasion we were looked after by the younger daughter, Dudi, who was our age and studying to be an architect. She took us on a fine three-day expedition through the Julian Alps, during which we climbed the highest mountain, the Triglav. We have been friends with the family ever since.

From Bled we walked over a mountain pass, climbing another peak on the way, and descended to a youth hostel on our way towards Italy. Beside the rough road we found a patch of tiny wild strawberries with such delicious flavour that we dawdled an hour to pick a large mug full. This delightful interlude was in stark contrast to the austerity found in the hostel where the main meal was plain cooked maize. We had already found the shops in Bled pretty bare, being unable to buy butter and being fobbed off with some lip-curling margarine. The next day we got a long hitch in a huge Italian wood lorry all the way to the frontier at Solkan. Because we had found little to buy in Yugoslavia we still had a tidy sum in our wallets. At the frontier post we were told sternly that we could not take any Yugoslav money out of the country. Annoyed by this we sat on the veranda of the frontier post wondering what to do when along came a donkey cart. Bestride the road at right angles almost exactly on the border was a railway bridge. Just as the cart approached the bridge a train rattled over. It was too much for the donkey who raced on as fast as he could out of control of his master. Donkey and cart broke through the one arm barrier to flee into Italy from this grating noise. To us it seemed one in the eye for restrictive bureaucracy and it gave us a good laugh. At least someone could get the better of the system. Forthwith we stopped gnashing our teeth and walked back into the town determined to spend all our Yugoslav money on a hotel.

Coming home from the same holiday we were given a lift at the foot of the St Gothard Pass by a South African. He didn't really know how to drive in the mountains and kept flooding the engine. Twice we had to hop out and push him round to face downhill so that he could restart the engine and return uphill for us. We crossed this famous Alpine pass with him to Andermatt but it was a great effort. On another leg from Lucerne to Basel we were offered another open back of a small pick-up truck where we sat with our backs to the driver's cabin. In the early evening with the sun setting on a panorama of snowy Alpine peaks we had an absolutely delightful journey. In fact I decided that it was far better to travel facing backwards in a car because you were not distracted by the traffic or the road ahead. Instead one can devote one's whole attention to the view. Unfortunately I have never been able to repeat this experience except on a train. Despite many unproductive hours with thumbs raised on the roadside, hitch-hiking was fun and I cordially thank once again all those drivers who gave us a lift.

Graduate Student

I graduated in Modern History in the summer of 1957, gaining a good second-class degree, which must have impressed someone in the Ministry of Education because they awarded me one of the new Graduate Scholarships for Arts subjects. Earlier that summer term during a session with the director of the Oxford University Careers Service I had rejected a job at a grammar school in Middlesex and instead opted to do a one year teacher-training course at Exeter University. Now I withdrew from that to embark on historical research. After a little reflection and some discussion with Henry Pelling, one of the few Labour historians in Oxford, I embarked on a research degree known as a BLitt. I felt I should know more about the struggles of the working man and his trade unions, struggles in which my father Eric had played a part. However, as I also had a strong interest in America I asked myself why was it that their trade unions had not sponsored a political party or at least one that had survived into the mid-twentieth century? Such a subject would obviously necessitate study in the United States. When I got an offer for an assistantship at the University of Illinois I narrowed down my subject to manageable proportions: 'Labour Politics in Illinois'. It proved to be quite a good choice. I spent two years at the Institute of Labor & Industrial Relations in Urbana working halftime for the Institute and the rest of the time on my thesis.

In my first term as a graduate student Jennifer and I decided to get married. It was the best decision either of us made in our entire lives.

We decided that we did not want anything white or too elaborate, nor did we want to involve our parents in the arrangements. Instead we set up a modest affair in Oxford with our own resources. Jennifer had a beautiful dress made to her specifications, wool for the January weather and coral in colour to suit my passion for orange. Her mother made the wedding cake but a local caterer created a mountain of icing sugar suspiciously like the Matterhorn to adorn its top. The ceremony was held in the Registrar's Office in St Giles on a Saturday. This office we were informed only opened Monday to Friday. We explained that all our guests were coming from far afield and couldn't possibly be there during the working week. With some reluctance the Registrar agreed to a Saturday. Both our families turned out in strength. My best man was Robert Montgomery who by chance had done his teacher training in Oxford after graduating in Maths at Cambridge. He had been in the same class at Tottenham Grammar School and had gained a Middlesex Award to Mill Hill public school the year before I went to Harrow. As usual he gave a very funny speech.

We held the reception in an elegant, oak-panelled room in Univ recently refurbished and named in memory of my first tutor, Giles Alington. Although I had booked the room well in advance there was almost a mix-up because the college servant who looked after the room had not been told. When the caterers arrived with the food and drink they couldn't get into the room. The keeper was only found with some difficulty and thought he was hard done by having to open 'his room'! As we left the college *en route* to a honeymoon in Granada it was snowing.

That proved to be an auspicious start because after we had explored the courtyards of the Alhambra and the gardens of the Generalife in Granada we went off to climb in the Sierra Nevada, for which we had gone prepared with ice axes and crampons. Rather than just walk up the dirt road to the hotel-cum-hut, which was the springboard for the highest peaks in the range, we thought we would climb there by a path faintly marked on the map. We trundled out on a tram and could see there would be a snow field to cross near the top of our climb some 2,000 feet above us. The snow proved to be up to our knees so over the last two hours we made slow progress and for a time thought we might be benighted. We kept thinking we ought to be able to see the hotel but it never came into sight. Instead, just as it was getting dark we spotted a decrepit building. As we arrived we were greeted by four Spanish soldiers, looking cold and bored but pleased to see us as a diversion. What they were guarding we never discovered, but they insisted on sharing their very thin soup before pointing us in the direction of the hotel only a few hundred yards away but just out of sight.

This establishment, which functioned as a poorly appointed ski lodge, was managed by a woman in her forties who insisted on wearing suggestive, skin-tight clothes quite out of keeping with the cold Alpine surroundings. It was at 8,000 feet. The food was little better than the military soup while the bedroom was chilly. At least as newlyweds we were certainly in the best frame of mind to cope with that. The next day was clear, cold and windy – just right for our climb to the summit of the Veleta (11,305 feet), which was near to Mulhacen, the highest peak in the range. The wind lashed into our faces all the way, coating our cheeks with ice, but we were rewarded with some wonderful views including the Atlas Mountains in Morocco, 200 miles away across the Mediterranean.

From January to September 1958 we lived in a cosy flat in Linton Road, which had originally been designed for the cook on one end of a classic North Oxford Edwardian residence. The owner of the house was a very nice scatty woman named Mrs Daniel who couldn't really face up to the fact that her clever academic husband had left her.

She was always very hospitable to us, among other things encouraging us to play on her grass tennis court. She used to play herself in short wellington boots. I regret that we saw her only once after our return from America.

When we packed up the morning we were going to join the *Queen Mary* in Southampton *en route* to Illinois we covered our luggage with handsome Fulbright and Cunard labels but found we had miscalculated how much space we needed for a two-year stay. Despite having been given a luxury double-sided trunk by my Uncle Ted, one of his trophies from Hong Kong, we had to rush out to buy a second-hand trunk. It was a very hurried departure from Linton Road.

9

An American Adventure – Illinois 1958–1960

Our two years in America were among the most invigorating and enjoyable of our whole lives. To pursue my study of American trade unions for my BLitt I applied to labour relations institutes at Cornell and Illinois. Both made good offers but only Illinois invited me to start an assistantship at the more convenient time of September 1958. As it turned out I could not have chosen a more congenial place. The director, the staff and my fellow students were all very friendly and helpful. Equally, Jennifer found a very untaxing but reasonably paid job right away and then switched into a much more stimulating appointment in the second year. We embarked wondering whether we would be able to last financially, but in the event always had more than enough for our needs. Much of our 'adventure' was very well chronicled by Jennifer in her letters home, especially during the first year when she had plenty of spare time at work. Altogether she wrote about a hundred thousand words, which even now evoke the novelty, fun and energetic activity of the experience.

After a little hassle with the US Educational Commission in the UK I was awarded one of the famous Fulbright travel scholarships, which paid for my passage each way. The Master of University College exerted a little extra pressure, much appreciated by me, which overcame some bureaucratic blockage at the last moment. A.L. Goodhart was a very distinguished American academic lawyer so I suspect a seemingly routine letter from him ensured that someone took notice in time. It was one of the rare occasions in my life when I summoned help from on high.

Once on board the *Queen Mary* in Southampton dock we were struck by the plush 1930s décor, newly restored after war service. Although we travelled Tourist we had an excellent outside cabin on A deck. Despite the obvious gap between the three classes – First, Cabin and Tourist – we were still bemused by the rituals such as the procedure for taking a bath. First we summoned the steward who informed the bath attendant, who in turn came to say that the tub was ready. ' Bath run, bathmat arranged, bath towel hung ready, salt water soap in the dish,' as Jennifer described it. We felt the whole vessel was much overstaffed but then they did have 1900 passengers to look after. Apart from the essential members of the crew whom we never saw, there were stewards, pursers, baggage officers, tourist office staff, nurses, doctors, musicians, cinema technicians, hairdressers and of course deckchair attendants. And this was all in Tourist Class. One morning for a dare we went through the empty dog kennels to the First Class section and walked right round to see what we were missing. We found the luxury and the wood panelling even more '*de trop*'. These liners clearly took their cue from the elegant country houses of the Edwardian era in which the guests were pampered beyond belief.

After a smooth crossing lasting a week we sailed into New York harbour early in the morning when the tops of the skyscrapers and the Statue of Liberty were all shrouded in mist. Steaming slowly round the Battery at the lower end of Manhattan Island and then more slowly up the East River to the Cunard Pier was an impressive way to enter the country. But once docked we encountered not brisk efficiency but incompetent bureaucracy, which took hours to clear our papers and our bags. A customs officer spent a long time turning over the mundane contents of our bags until he put his hand on a sponge bag. 'What's in this?' he demanded. With admirable sang-froid Jennifer replied: 'Contraceptives.' Blushing, the officer quickly concluded his examination and stamped our papers. It had taken four hours.

Waiting on the dock was my great-uncle, Ted Bryant, my grandmother's brother who had emigrated in the 1920s. He whisked us off by bus from the Port Authority bus station to his well-appointed house in Elizabeth, New Jersey. He was a craftsman who had always found work even in the Depression. By 1958 he was comfortably retired with his wife Enid. They were very hospitable but made us uncomfortable with too many racist remarks. During our time in America they twice invited us to stay without ever consulting us as to the practicality of travelling from Illinois or the suitability of the dates. They were also strict Episcopalians, which would have made a Christmas visit very awkward. On our very last journey to the east coast prior to departure we did visit them again. They were still generous hosts primed with interesting anecdotes but so antipathetic to our views that we even considered doing a bunk from their house in the middle of the night! Fortunately we suppressed this very foolish urge, which would have caused an awful family row. However, we were glad to leave them after a very short stay.

After one night with the Bryants we boarded the Pullman train, the Broadway Limited, at Newark station for an overnight journey to Chicago. In the club car we met the principal of a meat-packing business who told us proudly he had moved his whole operation to New Orleans to escape from oppressive union control. It was a timely introduction to the world of American unionism, which unhappily too often was corrupt. At Chicago we had a long wait between trains so were able to stroll along the lakeside park beside Michigan Avenue and even dip into the museum. Finally the Illinois Central took us 120 miles south to Champaign–Urbana, two small towns which had been joined together by the growth of the large university.

To our great good fortune we had met through Jennifer's work Fred and Virginia Sargent who had had a sabbatical in Oxford during the previous academic year. In those first few months Virginia looked after us as if we were her own family. She met us at the station and drove us to our student apartment which she had already equipped with utensils, furniture and other essentials for living. Within a month they had invited us twice to dinner with friends, shown us the ropes at a large reception for visiting students and faculty and taken us to see the Lincoln museums at Salem and Springfield miles away in the western part of the state. When the weather got cold Virginia took me to a charity shop because she saw my own overcoat was quite inadequate for Illinois' winter weather. How right she was and how suitable my purchase was. She was a very warm-hearted woman who craved children of her own. During that first year she adopted a small baby after some ups and downs with the adoption society. From then on of course we saw less of them, in part because by then we had established our own social circle.

Fred Sargent was a very genial pipe-smoking professor of physiology who was then moving into the new field of human ecology. In fact he was far more eminent than we realised. He was the first president of the International Society of Biometeorology. We continued to see the Sargents occasionally until we left two years later. When I visited Illinois on an American lecture tour in 1965 I went to see Virginia and her little girl. Unhappily, all was not well. A few years later when Fred replied to our Christmas card from Texas it emerged that he had left Virginia. From that time onwards neither of them replied to our enquiries. What had happened we do not know but suspect a very sad story, especially for Virginia.

*   *   *

It had been very hot and sticky when we arrived in New York and was absolutely sweltering by the time we reached the Midwest. Our one room 'efficiency apartment' faced west, catching a strong afternoon sun. It was far too hot throughout September and most of October so the first purchase we made was a large fan. In Britain the weather men give 'severe weather warnings' so often that one feels they are simply doing so to protect their own reputations. The weather in Illinois, however, really can be severe. For much of the year it is too hot and too humid for comfort, so even back then air-conditioning was the norm in the office and the home. During the summer tornadoes are a common and deadly occurrence, especially in the southern part of the state. Then from November until March it is either cold or very cold, going down to 40 degrees of frost or −10°F while we were there. That first winter an ice storm coated all the campus elms with ice an inch thick. The day after, the branches looked magnificent, clad in a silver sleeve, which sparkled in the sun. But very soon those elms could take it no longer. The weight of ice made them groan and then crack in spectacular fashion as if a gun was fired. The campus and the whole town were strewn with massive limbs, which had split apart from the mature trees. The damage was so bad that most of the elms and other large trees had to be felled. They were replaced with puny honey locusts which I trust have been less susceptible to such exceptional weather.

On the whole we preferred the cold weather to the hot and humid. Both of us did a lot of skating on a rink in the Urbana park, on a large lake just out of Champaign, and best of all, one day on an old drift mine, what we would call an open-cast mine, which we came across by accident on a trip to Kickapoo State Park in Indiana. Rough or wild skating we felt was always much nicer than on the rink but it usually suffered from an uneven surface, the bumps being caused by snow or by a strong wind blowing as the ice was freezing. In this case the ice had frozen six inches thick on a day without any snow, producing a surface as smooth as glass. The old mine was dead straight for about a hundred yards with high banks on both sides sheltering it from the wind. The result was the most beautiful skating you can imagine. The ice was so clear you could see the weeds many feet below the surface. We went there again the second year but alas the conditions were not nearly so favourable.

The Institute of Labor & Industrial Relations (ILIR) was housed on the first floor of an old post office overlooking the main shopping street in the centre of the university. This street, on the boundary between the towns of Champaign and Urbana, was known as 'Chambana'. The Director of the Institute, Martin Wagner, was very friendly and helpful throughout my stay and I felt more at home there than at Oxford. Wagner and several of the staff were former employees of the National Labor Relations Board, the problem-solving board set up under the New Deal. Their mission was to study, devise and teach good practice. It was axiomatic that good labour relations required strong, competent unions to represent the employees and to negotiate decent contracts. American private enterprise was prosperous; it was in its own interest to pay good wages and provide good conditions. That was the way to achieve maximum productivity and healthy profits over the long term. The Institute's task was to educate employers, employees, union and state officials so that collective bargaining resolved disputes without either side resorting to conflict and helped to produce rising prosperity for all. Most of my fellow students were doing an MA in this relatively new field with a view to becoming labour managers, labour lawyers, union business agents or policy advisers. One of my colleagues later became the director of labour relations for the whole university which had several thousand employees at all levels. Another became a senior official in the US Department of Labor.

My role as a part-time research assistant at $1,800 a year was to do the field work for Milton Derber and W. Ellison Chalmers who were attempting to describe and analyse labour relations in this state. Bill Chalmers was a very affable, pipe-smoking fellow who always had a twinkle in his eye and a slightly raffish air about him. His colleague, Milton Derber, was younger and much more serious. They had devised a standard questionnaire, which the research assistants conducted with two managers and two union officials in thirty-seven plants around the state. As the questionnaire had 152 questions, the process in each plant took most of a day.

My work was mainly in Decatur and East St Louis. I used to pick up a smart new car from the university car pool (Chevrolets with ridiculous wings were the fashion in 1959) and drive off across the flat prairie. In Decatur, almost in the centre of the state, the main industry was corn processing from which they made cooking oil and corn syrup. Everyone was very cooperative and I was easily able to go there and back in a day having done four interviews in a particular plant.

East St Louis was a different proposition. It was an unattractive, gritty neighbour of St Louis just across the Mississippi with a history of very bad race relations. The plants were varied in output and character but the labour force could not be described as docile. Some of the local politicians had strong connections with union business agents for their mutual benefit. As I had to drive 150 miles each way I used to stay either in the only hotel in East St Louis, which was convenient, or in one of the many swish hotels in St Louis. From a personal point of view this was nicer because I was sometimes able to sample one of the few theatres in St Louis. One day I noticed in the excellent local newspaper, the *St Louis Post-Dispatch*, that a famous British yachtswoman was in town for a day or two. Just after the war Ann Davison had been involved in a tragic yachting accident on the coast of Dorset. She and her husband Frank had set out in an old ketch to sail to Cuba to throw off their creditors but were caught in a very bad storm and ran aground near Portland Bill. Frank Davison had been a daring stunt pilot in the 1930s but now had a nervous breakdown and died in the sea. Ann was washed up on a rocky cove and somehow climbed the cliffs to safety. Undaunted, a few years later she became the first woman to sail the Atlantic single-handed. Ten years on she had remarried and was living in Florida. Now she was making a very long trip around eastern America in a small motor yacht using the rivers and canals.

My father, who never did any sailing himself, nevertheless read many accounts by intrepid single-handed sailors from Joshua Slocum onwards. He had drawn Davison's autobiography to my attention and I had read it. Chancing my arm, I drove down to the dock and took her out to a jazz and comedy club called The Crystal Palace where, fortunately, the humour did not put our teeth on edge. Her book of this voyage published two years later is called *By Gemini or Marshmallows in the Salad – A Coast-wise Cruise from Miami to Miami.*

That was a nice diversion from the serious work of the day. On the east bank of the Mississippi I stayed several times in a large but run-down hotel, which looked like part of the set for a gangster film. In fact, when one of my fellow graduate students was staying there a man hobbled into the lobby having just been shot on the sidewalk outside. My colleague did not go out again that evening.

Five years after I left Illinois, Derber and Chalmers published their second study, *Plant Union-Management Relations; From Practice to Theory.* I have no doubt that it provided a great deal of factual information concerning the practice but even the authors did not lay claim to a theory. Instead they deduced 'a wide variety of hypotheses ... for further exploration in the unending search for understanding'. In the half century since I was a student at Illinois the influence of unions has greatly declined. ILIR has renamed itself as The School of Labor & Employment Relations. It now grants PhDs as well as MAs and has twice the number of students.

At the Institute labour studies were regarded as a practical branch of economics, sociology and psychology. Political ideology was rarely mentioned save in the context of history. Nevertheless, two bizarre incidents reminded Jennifer and me that antipathy to unions and left of centre politics could easily burst on to the surface. Just before Christmas in 1958 students of 40 different nationalities displayed their crafts and culture in a large international fair. The displays, which included costumes, dancing, cooking and goods for sale, induced in us a feeling of benign goodwill and mutual understanding towards our brothers and sisters around the globe.

By the time we reached the British stand we were positively exuding solidarity with humankind whatever their colour or political persuasion. I introduced myself to the graduate student behind a display of tartans by saying that I was studying labour relations. Those few simple words provoked an instant, bare-toothed reaction from a Scotsman. 'I hate trade unions' were his first words of reply, 'they ought to be abolished.' He went on to claim all trade unions were communist organisations just seeking more money for undeserving workers. Several times I made him speechless by showing the utter absurdity of his view. We slugged it out verbally for several minutes, finally parting without any pleasantries, he grinding his teeth and me laughing my head off. So much for international understanding; even two people from the same country had little common ground.

The other incident took place at a garden wedding reception for two friends given by a professor at the Institute in the summer before we left. I was explaining to someone about my job and my research when a professor of agriculture butted in to ask who was paying for all this. When I told him I had an assistantship and a Fulbright scholarship he spat out the comment: 'Communist spongers.' Once again I was reduced to laughter but actually that antipathy to any political view other than right-wing American orthodoxy was common then and has persisted to this day. Europe was regarded by many as being a feeble, subversive continent dominated by obnoxious ideas such as socialism. Joe McCarthy was still in the Senate though his star had faded. Only the previous year the Illinois State Legislature had outlawed the Communist Party with penalties of ten years in prison and/or a $10,000 fine. So much for those amendments to the US constitution which safeguarded the rights of free speech and free association.

Looking back on these two years, I can see they were filled with more sociability than any other time in our lives. We had both had a fine time at Oxford with numerous clubs, plays, films, a few parties and, of course, punting. But we surpassed that at Illinois. Through a contact at the Speech Research Laboratory, where Jennifer worked, we fell in with a group of friends who liked hiking and folk singing. One of these was Tom Farrar, then finishing off his doctorate in chemistry before going on to Cambridge for further high level research. He had a very laid-back manner. Later he became a very distinguished physical chemist. Now in his retirement he is trying to find a way to convert ammonia into nitrogen and hydrogen in order to power a fuel cell for a car!

Through Tom we met Ivan Scheier, a psychologist who made his living devising tests for personnel selection boards. He was spare and lean and an exceptionally good dancer. At Illinois you could study dance as a full-time course. We saw Ivan dance as one of a troupe who performed someone's MA in dance where the 'music' was supplied entirely by the rhythmic beats of the dancers themselves. Years later I climbed with Ivan in Colorado.

Beside the skating and hiking we did with our outdoor friends, we took part in and produced readings both for live performance and for the university's broadcasting station, WILL. One highlight of our efforts with the Illini Readers was a production of *The Little Prince* by Antoine de Saint-Exupéry in which Jennifer appeared in her coral wedding dress as the Rose, to much admiration. Another was a production of *The Secret Life of Walter Mitty* by James Thurber for which we drew some life-size backdrops from cartoons in his book. In the second year we danced frequently with an international folk dancing club, which had a far more varied repertoire than either of the clubs in Oxford. This was both stimulating and refreshing. We particularly enjoyed the Greek and Israeli dances which had haunting tunes with strong rhythms. Occasionally we were able to demonstrate how the Scottish dances should be performed. In the last summer we even had a Scottish dance party for friends in our garden. They entered fully into the spirit of this, arriving in highland dress with cakes encased in tartan icing, and telling Scottish stories. Our very last party, entitled 'Columbus went too far', engendered a great deal of hilarity and proved a fitting send-off.

132

On the strength of our radio readings we were invited to represent Illinois at the Apple Blossom Festival of Oral Interpretation at Michigan State University in East Lansing. 'Oral Interpretation' we discovered meant reading aloud, with feeling. That in itself was a good illustration of how the American culture over-dramatised and over-sold almost everything compared to 'normal' usage in Britain. Now we call it 'hyped', which, alas, has become standard practice here as well. The festival was very well run by an eccentric American woman with a taste for the 'over-the-top' in all things. Her name was Marie Compere, which seemed appropriate. We did hear some excellent readings from other contributors and we were widely complimented for our articulation and accents, something we had also experienced often in Illinois.

I wanted to read an excerpt from the speech made by Aneurin Bevan when he introduced the National Health Service Bill in 1948 because 'socialised medicine' was so commonly despised and still is in the US. Unfortunately the library, huge and usually excellent though it was, couldn't get the text. Instead I read poems of protest by Hilaire Belloc, G.K. Chesterton and Wilfred Owen. I also read an excerpt from *The Lady's Not For Burning* by Christopher Fry and another from an engaging new book about American family culture entitled *Where Did You Go? Out. What Did You Do? Nothing.* For this I was gently chided because I had made no attempt at the right accent. Quite right, I knew I couldn't do it.

The first evening in Lansing we went to a faculty party at Miss Compere's exotic house, decorated in many styles from Chinese to primitive African and even to the latest in contemporary American. It was non-stop talk. At midnight we were discussing the aesthetic principles of oral interpretation versus the technical attributes on which we felt there was rather too much emphasis. The second evening we watched a reading of a new experimental play about the Civil War produced in a full-size auditorium, which far excelled any university theatre in Oxford. Afterwards we had drinks with a group who called themselves radicals. They proceeded to tell us what was so wrong with America, just in case we should have the misapprehension that all Americans believed it was 'God's Own Country'. As an aside, we ran across little evidence of religion in our two years other than seeing plenty of locals go to church on Sunday. No one of our age whom we knew went to church or ever talked about religion. In the intervening half century there has been quite a change. In fact one of our closest climbing and folk-singing friends has since become a 'born-again Christian'.

Although we worked reasonably hard we both enjoyed long academic vacations during which we travelled extensively. We went to the south for the first Christmas, to the West and north-west in the summer of 1959, to Washington DC and Virginia at Christmas 1959 and finally to New England on our homeward swing to New York in August 1960. Each trip had its own adventures and mishaps; each trip introduced us to a broad cross-section of Americans. Most were helpful and pleasant but often the cultural divide was pretty wide. In the museum in Montgomery, Alabama, we were taken aside by an elderly attendant. In hushed tones she pointed out of the window to some black men sweeping the square. 'They're all murderers you know,' she confided. 'Never go in an elevator with one on your own,' she cautioned. It seemed pathetic at the time but actually I wondered afterwards if they might have been trusties let out from gaol for useful gardening. The famous bus boycott initiated by Rosa Parks and led by Martin Luther King had occurred three years before. The freedom rides and major civil rights marches in this, the most racist of states, were all in the future.

Another astounding episode on that trip occurred on the bridge across Lake Pontchartrain leading into New Orleans. We were driving along at 50 miles an hour when a tyre bounced past us. We looked further ahead to see sparks flying from the car in front as it ran along lopsided on the rim of its near-side front wheel. The tyre had just disintegrated but drivers were forbidden to stop on the narrow 19-mile bridge on pain of a large fine. This driver plainly thought it was better to ruin a wheel than to risk being picked up by the state police.

When our friend Tom Farrar left for Cambridge in the spring of 1959 he very kindly gave us his twelve-year-old Chevrolet with 89,000 miles on the clock. By American standards that was pretty old. At the Institute there was a resident labour bard named Archie Green who occasionally entertained us with the folklore of the American labour movement, including some of their songs evoking the struggles against the owners of mines and factories. One of these songs parodied a cowboy ditty of the 1940s called 'Old Paint'. Archie's 'Old Paint – a finer horse there ain't' was a 'horse with a union label'. Consequently we named our Chevrolet 'Old Paint' as indeed it had a few scrapes and nicks in the paintwork and a dent on its sun visor, which made it look as if it was winking at you.

In the summer of 1959 we took a seven-week holiday in the west.

Despite a worn steering gear we drove across the plains, through New Mexico, Arizona and California and on to climb in Washington State. From New Mexico onwards the scenery was spectacular, much of which is described in our diary of the trip. We tried as much as possible to use minor roads and, in one case, certainly drove a section that can't now be repeated. In northern Arizona we bumped across 50 miles of the dirt road through Monument Valley past those sandstone towers so often used as a backdrop in old cowboy films. The earth is absolutely barren, for the most part deep red and orange. This landscape is the scarcely cooled crust of the earth, the stripes of geological formation in reds and greys standing out quite clearly. While we had lunch at the entrance to the valley there was a huge thunderstorm accompanied by a fierce wind. We sat in the car watching the lightning forking its way along the centre of the storm. What had promised to be an excessively hot day very soon cooled off to a pleasant temperature. There was so much rain that at one point we had to stop to drain the road with an improvised shovel. The dirt road from Kayenta to Tonalea was by turns sandy, bumpy, marshy and muddy.

There were signs saying the road was about to be improved and you could certainly see why. We travelled at less than 20 miles an hour and it took the whole of our attention to avoid the hazards. We saw no other vehicles except one car towing a caravan, which overtook us at what seemed high speed. We kept our steady pace only to come across it broken down ten miles later. Not many Good Samaritans passed this way so we stopped to see if we could help. A few hundred yards previously we had edged our way across a wide hole two feet deep, which had snapped the axle on their caravan. A Presbyterian minister was stranded with his wife and two children. We could now see Tonalea so I drove the minister to the village to get some help. Two cheerful 'can-do' mechanics who were working on an impressive new school came out on the asking but soon saw it was a welding job so took the parts off to their workshop.

Meanwhile we settled down to a convivial supper on camp tables in the ditch. We were just discussing the vicissitudes of western travel in earlier times when out of the darkness on silent hoofs rode a Navajo Indian who was lost and hopelessly drunk. He asked for more drink, but we gave him water, and we suggested that he let his horse take him home. We were certainly relieved when he rode off because 'drunken Indians' to quote the mechanics or 'inebriated Navajos' to quote our minister were notoriously wild. Some time later the Navajo came pounding up on his horse a little too near to our roadside supper for comfort. Chanting something at the top of his voice he galloped the poor horse around and around for several hours, keeping us awake.

After a night camping between two huge rocks sculpted by the wind and known as the Elephant's Feet we pressed on the next morning wishing the family good luck for the rest of their journey back to California. As we drove through the dusty settlement of Tonalea we saw our Navajo friend with a very sore head sitting in the back of an open pick-up truck with his horse, both looking much the worse for wear.

Of all the wonderful vistas we had on this trip the Grand Canyon was in a league by itself. From the cool green northern rim of the canyon we descended on foot 3,500 feet and 14 miles to the Colorado River, getting hotter all the time. We lit a large fire to ward off the coyotes and camped under the stars right beside the river, which, considering the size of the canyon, is remarkably small. The next afternoon we walked slowly back through a terrain decorated with various desert flowers and large yuccas. The last hour, dragging ourselves up a zigzag path to the canyon rim, was a major effort.

Another memorable episode occurred at a crossroads in the Cascades almost at the Canadian border in Washington State where we chatted to a farmer. Without any cue from us, he declared: 'This was a great country until it was ruined by that man Franklin Roosevelt.' We were stunned by such an opinion, which was so contrary to the collective judgement of most commentators and historians, not to mention the voters at four elections, that all we could do was suck in our breath and smile. There was no sign of 'ruin' either on him or indeed in that beautiful state.

Admittedly we were in a very benign mood. We had recently climbed the elegant Mount Shuksan (9,100 feet), which resembles the Matterhorn when seen from the right angle. This was a three-day affair with two nights under a primitive plastic tent at the base of the mountain at Lake Anne. Fortunately we had good weather as the climb proved to be a long day. Coming down we had to descend a convex snow slope, which was so steep we could not see the bottom for what seemed a long and anxious time. We were roped and properly equipped with crampons and ice axes but we had to move very slowly.

When we had first approached Shuksan we had encountered drenching rain, which obliterated the mountain from view. Reckoning that heavy snow on the upper slopes would prevent a climb for several days we made a temporary retreat 120 miles back to Seattle to stay with a new friend. Taking this young American, whom we had met on another mountain, at his word we stayed with him for a few days. He was an eighteen-year-old supermarket manager. With a group of friends he had rented a fancy house overlooking Puget Sound, which was built in a spiral with rooms at five half levels all the way up. It was a very beautiful house with good views of the Sound and the Olympic Peninsula. He came from Alaska and was as pleased as punch with his rapid progress in retail management.

At the end of our mountain adventures in the Cascades when, because of gale-force winds, we had failed to climb the highest mountain, Mount Rainier (14,400 feet), we turned east for the long drive home. Just beyond the little town of Huntington, Oregon, the car's timing mechanism burnt out so we had to be towed back. The mechanics were very obliging and worked late to put us back on the road. The next day we had reached the same spot when we 'threw a rod', a piston broke away inside the engine and thrust through the casing. It was the end for 'Old Paint', which we sold for $40, the price of its two new tyres. Luckily Huntington was on a Greyhound Bus route. Two and half days later we reached Champaign via Chicago.

Many things irritated us during our American stay, among them extravagance with words and corny commercialism, an over-insistence on getting down to the lowest common denominator, reaching the IQ of ordinary Joe or Josie to make them take notice or at least smile. 'Corn' of various kinds and relentless boosting of the banal made us flinch. One silly example of needless boasting is that many states put an advertisement on their car licence plates. Illinois, for instance, was 'The Land of Lincoln'; Wisconsin, 'Land of Lakes'; Michigan, 'Water Wonderland'; Alabama, 'The Heart of Dixie'; Nebraska, 'The Beef State', and so on. Most fatuous of all was Idaho whose licence plate proclaimed, 'Famous Potatoes'. I'm sure people drove miles to see those potatoes. When we chatted over supper about each day's events we often remarked on the latest irritating phenomenon or trait that had grated with us. Some evenings we would find ourselves trumping each other's revelation two or three times. We were having the time of our lives but our cultural teeth were frequently on edge.

Despite that enduring feeling we often found ourselves defending Illinois against criticism from the many Easterners on the campus. For them Champaign-Urbana was a hick town where nothing happened and nobody famous ever came through. We had heard a similar sort of criticism in Oxford by people who said they just had to go off to London, for the women or the theatre or just to get away from academia. Actually we found both universities bursting with life and our diaries always had more things to go to than we had time for. There was much less student drama and student politics in Illinois than in Oxford but, for instance, there was more music or at least more music that suited out middle-brow tastes. The political folk-singer Pete Seeger performed a couple of times, hitting just the right idealistic note for students with his songs of protest. Nor did national politicians shun the campus. Adlai Stevenson who had been Governor of Illinois gave a lively talk. Introduced as the putative Leader of the Opposition, although no such position exists in America (he had been defeated twice by Eisenhower), he quipped that the grand title was 'no substitute for office'. Another time we were actually introduced to one of the sitting senators for Illinois, Paul Douglas, and to Senator William Fulbright from Arkansas who both gave talks in the Students' Union. At that time we had not lived on the east coast and did not feel we were in a backwater.

Fulbright, then chairman of the Senate Foreign Relations Committee, was very much a Southerner on civil rights issues but otherwise a liberal and an internationalist. He had been a Rhodes Scholar at Oxford in the 1920s and, soon after becoming a senator, was instrumental in establishing the Fulbright scholarships. He was the only senator to oppose funding for Joe McCarthy's notorious red-hunting Subcommittee on Investigations when McCarthy was at the height of his influence. Later Fulbright opposed American support for the invasion of Cuba by anti-Castro Cubans and also the Vietnam War. His most prescient thought was as follows:

Power tends to confuse itself with virtue and a great nation is particularly susceptible to the idea that its power is a sign of God's favor, conferring upon it a special responsibility for other nations – to make them richer and happier and wiser, to remake them, that is, in its own shining image. Power confuses itself with virtue and tends also to take itself for omnipotence. Once imbued with the idea of a mission, a great nation easily assumes that it has the means as well as the duty to do God's work.

From *The Arrogance of Power*, 1966

Well before the end of the first year we knew our one-room efficiency apartment at 300 South Goodwin Avenue in Urbana would not be tolerable for a second year. Through a contact at the Institute we had the good fortune to rent a little blue house with a long front garden on West Church Street in Champaign, the other side of town. It had been an old carriage house for the much larger house next door. There was a fair-sized living room downstairs heated by an ancient gas heater, which depended on a fan blowing air through a red-hot cast-iron grill. Upstairs we had a study and a bedroom whose window looked straight into the squirrels' nest in the maple tree. The other welcome neighbours in the tree were two cardinal birds, a scarlet male and a fawn female. It was a very unusual house for modern America, quite small and within our budget. It was our very own dolls' house, which suited us perfectly. When we left it to go home we cried all the way down the road, partly for the house and partly because we realised it was the close of a very happy idyll.

During the second year Jennifer had a much better post as a research assistant in the Illinois Historical Survey. Her crucial skill was her expertise in French, which had been much improved by a summer in Brittany living with a French family. The state had first been colonised by the French canoeing down the great rivers from Canada. In the early eighteenth century they established a substantial town with a fort on an impressive bluff overlooking the Mississippi. One of Jennifer's tasks was to read and catalogue a collection of documents including wills and land grants written in Kaskaskia. Her job was made all the more pleasant by the director of the survey, Margaret Pease, who became a good friend.

To round off our American adventure we sent our trunks off by rail to join the *Mauretania* in New York while we took our last trip to New England, pausing at Niagara Falls on the way. For our second year in Champaign we had bought a 1948 Pontiac from another student for $100. It still had a badge inside to show that it had once been owned by a state agency, so despite a huge mileage we hoped it had once been properly maintained. We arranged to give the car to a friend in the same way that we had been given 'Old Paint' by Tom Farrar. Joe Litterer who was a professor of management at Illinois fortunately had other reasons to be in New York. He was glad to have the Pontiac even though it meant driving 800 miles home to Champaign.

Five years later when I gave a lecture in Illinois on behalf of the British Information Services I went out on a big family picnic with Joe and Marie Litterer. There were too many for one car so I drove the Pontiac while he drove his new Ford estate. By this time you couldn't get the Pontiac into first gear but that didn't matter too much as Illinois is very flat and you could start in second. The climax came on the way home from the picnic when the new car broke down! The old car came to the rescue, ferrying most of the party home.

The Litterers later moved to Amherst in Massachusetts and bought themselves a holiday house on an island in Maine opposite a village called Friendship. All around that part of Maine the settlements have names that evoke peace and upright living such as Liberty, Hope and Freedom. Their house, which had once belonged to the manufacturer of a popular soft drink called Moxie, was one of only three on an island two miles long. It had good views of the ocean to the east yet seemed very secluded because it was hidden from the mainland by a hill. I don't suppose the original settlers were ever completely self-sufficient but with the mainland out of sight it must have felt like it. In the summer of 1980 when I was first at the UN we visited the Litterers for a few delightful days of sailing, swimming and walking. Alas we were never able to go a second time.

10

Political and Economic Planning 1960–1962

While I was at the Institute of Labor & Industrial Relations in Illinois a director of the Eastern Gas Board paid a visit to deliver a short talk about labour matters in Britain. After the lecture he sounded me out to see if I would like to join his department. I suppose I had too much personal knowledge of the Tottenham Gas Company and my father's role there as a shop steward so I brushed it aside without serious consideration. At that stage I thought I would only find a satisfactory professional life as an academic.

On returning home in September 1960 I quickly found a post as a senior research officer at Political and Economic Planning (PEP), a small research organisation founded in 1931 when the economic depression demanded radical solutions. For me it seemed a good stepping-stone to a university lectureship once I had finished my BLitt thesis for Oxford. I was employed to embark on a three-year study entitled 'Trade Unions in a Changing Society' funded by the Leverhulme Trust. My colleague was Bernard Donoughue who had been a contemporary at Oxford and who had also been to an American university as a postgraduate. We were guided by a small group chaired by Lord Geoffrey Heyworth, a retired chairman of Unilever, the company behind the Leverhulme Trust. The guidance was outlined or hinted at during quarterly lunches in PEP where the wine was rather too good for my concentration. Actually the most useful member of this group was Ben Roberts, Professor of Industrial Relations at the London School of Economics.

The Director of PEP was Richard Bailey, a smooth-talking, silver-haired journalist who seemed to do more for his private clients than for PEP. Bernard and I never had rows with Bailey but in the second year we started to grumble to more senior colleagues about his absences and failure to provide any valuable stimulus. Fortunately we did get some useful support from the Director of Studies, John Madge, who was a much more conscientious manager. In the second year Dick Davies

141

joined the staff to take charge of finance, particularly the raising of funds from trusts and wealthy individuals. He had been a fund-raiser for the Labour Party and would relate many comical episodes and vignettes of various labour leaders. He was a great asset to the morale of this small organisation, which had about a dozen researchers working on three or four projects plus a few administrative staff.

The most important of these projects was a study of the European Common Market which was only three years old and still feeling its way. A Conservative government had declined to join the negotiations for the Treaty of Rome in 1956 but only four years later Harold Macmillan's government was considering applying for membership. Germany, though much more devastated by war than Britain, was making a very fast recovery and would soon outstrip us in gross domestic product. France, which was mauled as much psychologically as physically by the war, was also gaining ground perhaps through its trade preferences in the Common Market, perhaps also through a governmental policy called 'indicative planning', not the direction of industry as in the Soviet Union but by encouraging industrialists to create needed enterprises through subsidies, grants and tax concessions. PEP publications certainly helped to inform British policy makers and MPs and may have nudged Macmillan's government to apply to join the Common Market in 1962, only to be rebuffed by de Gaulle.

For our project I wrote a 40-page broadsheet entitled *Trade Union Membership* which analysed the current extent of union loyalty in Britain and attempted to project future growth. Among other things we envisaged a substantial increase in membership among lower paid local authority workers, a projection that turned out to be right. At the time the National Union of Public Employees (NUPE) was recruiting members in this sector at a faster rate than the much older General and Municipal Workers. On the morning of publication NUPE demanded 250 copies but at less than half price. We tried to negotiate a smaller discount but in the end unwisely rejected their offer and simply sold them half a dozen at full price. It would have been cleverer to distribute many more copies to a keen buyer than to bargain for a better price. We were not a commercial publisher. We lived on research grants from foundations and hardly ever covered the cost of publication. Dissemination of our ideas and proposals was our *raison d'être*, not balancing the books.

Looking back on the six years I spent studying and writing about labour relations in Oxford, Illinois and at PEP, I can see I was over-optimistic as to the future progress of the ordinary working man, the foot soldier of an advanced industrial society. Throughout the 1960s and 1970s the level of industrial conflict in Britain was high. The trade unions were strong with a large membership. From time to time they rose to peaks of influence which a sluggish economy could not sustain. Various governments, Labour and Conservative, attempted to contain their power and their aggression with 'prices and incomes policies', a National Economic Development Council and even industrial courts. Trade union leaders were given seats at the top table in all of these institutions, which did smooth out some of the difficulties and misunderstandings. They did not, however, solve the problem of sluggish growth and poor productivity, especially when compared to our industrial competitors in Europe and America.

One great plus for PEP was its office at 16 Queen Anne's Gate, one of the most beautiful streets in London and very convenient for me. Bernard and I shared a rather pleasant but cold garden room which looked out towards St James's Park. In the summer we often used to lunch in the park. On one occasion I met by chance a contemporary from University College who was working for a world-famous consulting engineer who also had offices in the street. My friend looked lovingly at the footbridge across the lake and drooled over its simplicity and beauty. The trouble with his job as a civil engineer, he said, was that he was always designing small parts of large, highly profitable projects, such as the foundations or the fire escape, but never could feel any pride in his particular contribution. That was not our problem at PEP. We contributed nearly 100 per cent of a small but useful exercise, which we hoped might get some attention.

The 1960s saw London take the first steps to control parking. Westminster Council proposed to introduce parking meters in its central area including Queen Anne's Gate. Bernard Donoughue and I understood the necessity for parking control but we felt ugly meters on four-foot poles would mar the beauty of this early eighteenth-century street. We suggested, instead, that there should be one or two ticket machines for the whole street where motorists would buy tickets to place in their windscreens. Such systems are now common all over the country. We canvassed all the offices in the street including the Architectural Press and the National Trust. The architectural journalists gave us much encouragement but the manager we met in the National Trust seemed to think more about parking his motor car than retaining the appearance of this civic gem. We sent our proposal to the city council but it made no progress. We should have lobbied the politicians as well as the council officers. All too soon a line of grey metal stumps grew out of the pavement topped with coin meters. It took the council about another 30 years to adopt our ticket system.

While at PEP I also wrote in my own time the first of half a dozen academic articles which have been published in journals such as *Political Quarterly* and *International Relations*. At its annual conference in Scarborough in 1960 the Labour Party voted to scrap Britain's nuclear weapons, a reversal of policy which seemed to suggest that it was unfit to govern the country. The party leader, Hugh Gaitskell, vowed 'to fight, fight and fight again for the party we love' in order to reverse this decision. After a year of hectic campaigning and no doubt arm-twisting, the conference at Blackpool the next year endorsed the Executive Committee's policy of multilateral disarmament and rejected unilateral disarmament. The left wing of the Labour Party and the unilateralists claimed that the platform was only sustained by the trade union block votes and that the 'progressive' members in the constituencies favoured the enlightened unilateralist policy. Whether they were winners or losers in the party battles, the Left always liked to claim the high moral ground and the support of the activists and canvassers as opposed to the moneybags of the large trade unions.

Philip Williams, who was a Fellow of Nuffield College in Oxford, doubted these claims so recruited me to see if we could penetrate the mysteries of the party's seemingly secret ballot. Many trade union leaders who wielded three quarters of the votes declared their views in advance but the remaining quarter was made up of constituency parties with only one or two thousand votes each. With some patient research, some good maths and fine logic we proved that the Left's claims were quite erroneous. A majority of constituency parties supported the official policy of multilateralism both at Scarborough in 1960 and Blackpool in 1961. Twenty-seven years later a PhD student contacted me to say he had examined our article closely and found it to be largely accurate. We were only wrong about the votes of one or two very small trade unions.

As a result of my article, the editor of *Political Quarterly*, Tom McKitterick, encouraged me to write more. My first proposal was to examine the unjust and corrupt political system in Northern Ireland. McKitterick, who was himself an Ulsterman, despaired of it ever being reformed and therefore could not bear to tackle it in the journal. At the time I did not particularly mind this rejection but in retrospect it was clearly a pity that I did not have a chance to do a little political muck-raking there. The Northern Ireland civil rights movement was already gearing up and the conflict began in 1969. By the by, all aspiring journalists should read *The Autobiography of Lincoln Steffens*, the patron saint of investigative journalism; one of whose chapters is headed 'Muck I Raked in Boston'.

Instead of Northern Ireland, I wrote about reform in America and Britain. I chronicled President Johnson's Civil Rights Act of 1964, Britain's first Race Relations Act of 1965 and the legalisation of abortion in 1967, something which I discuss at length in a later chapter. The American law, which banned racial discrimination in schools, jobs, housing and public places, was most notable for its passage through the Senate over a Southern filibuster lasting 54 days. Under Senate rules a minority with barely one third of the votes could block any bill just by talking night and day. Never before had senators been able to bring cloture to a civil rights measure. However, after much pressure from President Johnson and increased pressure from the public following the March on Washington the previous year, the cloture was achieved and the Senate passed the bill. The first British Race Relations Act took its cue and much of its inspiration from this American law and the American experience.

In the light of these articles McKitterick tried to appoint me as assistant editor for *Political Quarterly* with a view to succeeding him in a couple of years but this was blocked by Professor William Robson of LSE who was joint editor. Probably that was just as well because, although the title sounded grand, the job might have led me off in an entirely new direction and I would never have gone to the United Nations. In time McKitterick was replaced by Professor Bernard Crick, the biographer of George Orwell. In later years Crick became a champion of education for citizenship in schools so was often questioned in the media. He articulated the case methodically but always in such a mournful whine that I sometimes wondered if he really gave this admirable cause much advantage.

Besides the fun of writing these articles I also had one lucky spin-off. Just before I left for New York in 1980 to become the BBC's UN correspondent, the owners of *Political Quarterly* gave a party for contributors. On hearing where I was going one of the directors offered to put me in touch with a friend of his in New York who might help me find an apartment. His friend was a wealthy Irish-American who had made his money supplying American troops in Europe. By chance he was going to be away on business as I arrived but he offered to lend me his spacious apartment in walking distance of the UN for a couple of weeks while I got my feet under the table. It was a very welcome gesture as there was much to absorb at the UN without having to find an apartment at the same time. It was very much a case of 'the kindness of a stranger'.

11

Daughters

In the first three years after we returned from America we had two daughters, Alison in July 1961 and Juliet in February 1964. Ever since they have been an important part of our lives. In nurturing our children we did not follow any pundit's theory but simply applied common sense. My excuse for including them in my story is that while children they made us laugh and as adults they surpassed their parents' achievements. They can and should speak for themselves as adults but Jennifer and I are the keepers of the collective memory of their exploits and the delightful quality of their remarks as children.

Jennifer gave birth to Alison in King's College Hospital under the supervision of the Queen's own gynaecologist, Sir John Peel, acting as a National Health Service consultant. He actually saw her twice: on her first antenatal visit and when Alison was a few days old. The hospital's attitude to fathers seems very old-fashioned now; I was not allowed to be with Jennifer while she was in labour and certainly not allowed at the birth. So I first saw Alison when she was two and half hours old, a lovely small baby. In the next bed to Jennifer was a single mother with an obvious mental handicap. I could not help thinking that through no fault of its own her babe would start life with far poorer prospects than our Alison.

Soon after Jennifer became pregnant a second time the foetus threatened to appear very early. As a result Jennifer spent about three months in bed at home in order to avert a premature birth. Eventually, one week late after all, Juliet insisted on coming into the world before either the midwife or the doctor could arrive. For a few minutes it looked as though I would be the midwife but fortunately our doctor arrived in time to take over the final stages of the delivery. So, after a very anxious period lasting months, Juliet made a near perfect entry.

Using a little simple psychology Jennifer foresaw that Alison, now two and a half, might be a little miffed by a rival for her mummy's attention.

So on the day Juliet was born Alison was given a small baby doll which delighted her. So much so that when friends arrived to congratulate Jennifer and admire the new baby Alison danced to them as they entered the front door waving her doll. 'Look,' she said, 'we've got a new baby,' by which she meant her doll. I'm sure it's a benign trick that has been pulled many times. In this case it worked perfectly.

Just to illustrate the fun these two pretty daughters gave us I recall a number of anecdotes, some of which were so striking that I took an exact note of them at the time. For instance, when Alison was four and Juliet 18 months and still in her high chair we took in a stray black kitten. We named her Louisa and she stayed with us until she died eighteen years later. Jennifer took her in partly to help Juliet shed her fear of animals; she had already been nipped by a dog. Very soon Louisa produced several litters of kittens, provoking of course curiosity and providing the occasion for some gentle lessons in reproduction.

Alison: 'Where does the daddy cat keep his seed? And how does he put it in the lady cat? Is she asleep when he puts it in?'

Juliet: 'Is the daddy cat's seed all furry?'

On 15 September 1966, with the Rhodesia crisis nearly a year old a communiqué of the Commonwealth prime ministers was headlined in the papers, 'Ultimatum to Smith' and 'Wilson gives ultimatum to Smith', meaning the Rhodesian Front prime minister, Ian Smith. Jennifer and I were talking about it over breakfast when Alison, now aged five, interrupted.

'Why has Mr Wilson said that to Rhodesia?'

'Because,' I said, getting down to her level, 'they've been very naughty men.'

Quick as a flash Juliet, aged two, butts in: 'The ladies aren't naughty.'

A memorable piece of applied logic for a two-year-old and one that has made us laugh ever since.

Another gem of Juliet's logic came on our first family venture abroad in 1967 when she was three. We had embarked on the cross-Channel ferry at Dover and were all standing on the top deck looking at a very calm sea, when suddenly the boat lurched forward.

'Has it got wheels?' asked Juliet.

* * *

148

Luckily for everyone we made friends with a number of similar families near us in Dulwich. This meant that our daughters had many opportunities to play with similar age children out of school in the safe haven of our houses and gardens. Unlike my own childhood, they never played in the street simply because the motor traffic past our door made it unsafe. Fortunately we had sufficient space in these houses and gardens for up to half a dozen children to play or run together full tilt, if necessary. We had television but our children were never in thrall to its programmes. They spent far more time playing imaginative games either with their toys and dolls or with other children. So perhaps I ought to record a grateful thanks to the Armstrongs, the Bennetts, the Joneses, the Welchs, the Kings and the Eastwoods, both parents and children, who all helped our daughters to become competent and engaging social beings.

One day in the garden Jennifer overheard an earnest conversation:

Little John Welch: 'What do you want to be when you grow up? I'm going to be a fireman.

Alison: I'm going to be a bridesmaid.

John Welch (by now obviously acquiring some wisdom): 'I don't think you can be a bridesmaid ... all the time.'

'What do you want to be when you grow up?' I said to Juliet one day. 'A boy.' Another of Juliet's probing questions was, 'Why is the sky blue?' Indeed. A question that, like all parents since the beginning of time, we were unable to answer.

At the age of five Juliet was looking out of the bedroom window one dark morning when she suddenly announced, 'I can see China'; pause for smiles; 'I can,' she insisted. Pause for more smiles. 'I've got good eyes,' she continued, nodding her head and opening her eyes very wide.

One day while Jennifer was fixing the catch on her bra behind her back Juliet asked: 'How do you know where to do that up?'

Jennifer: 'I've got used to it.'

Juliet: 'How did you get used to it?'

Jennifer: 'Oh with lots of practice.'

Juliet: 'How did you know the first time?'

Touché.

Jennifer had two very characterful aunts, Lalla and Julie. Lalla Battensby had been a headmistress and been awarded a CBE for her services to education; Julie Ward, actually a 'wild' aunt rather than really being related, had taught English in girls' secondary schools. Both were very cultivated and agreeable company. We twice spent Christmas in their house in a little village in Dorset. On one of these visits Alison woke up very early on Christmas morning to open her toys on the end of her bed. But being only four she got in a muddle trying to open both her stocking and Juliet's and play with the toys in the dark. Suddenly she let out a cry of despair. When we looked in on a tearful Alison she exclaimed, 'Father Christmas left too much toys.' A few years later when Juliet had met these aunts several times, she announced, 'Aunties have skirts over their knees.' At the time younger women such as Jennifer wore short skirts well above the knee.

During a particularly hilarious breakfast Jennifer said with a smile: 'Quiet, Juliet, I can't get a word in edgeways.'
Juliet: 'How do you say a word edgeways?'

One evening Juliet, the rascal (now five and a half), got out of bed to come downstairs while we were watching the Chancellor of the Exchequer, Roy Jenkins, being interviewed on the BBC television programme *Panorama*.

'Who's that funny man?' said Juliet.
Me: 'He's the man who looks after our money.'
Juliet seemed quite satisfied with this answer and snuggled up on the sofa and took no more notice of Jenkins.
The next morning I picked up the letters from the doormat. They were all in buff envelopes, obviously bills.
'What are they about?' asked Juliet.
'They're all very dull,' I replied, 'all about money.'
Juliet: 'Are they from the man we saw last night?'

On a snowy day in November 1969 Juliet (now five and three-quarters) told us about a game she had been playing with her local chums. 'We went to the antique,' she said. We were blank. 'You know ... where Scott went.' Laughter.

Top left: K.H. aged 6.

Top right: Atop Ben Nevis 1945.

Bottom: K.H. & Eric atop the Ober Rothorn just after the Matterhorn 1947. *Photo: Hilary Longley-Cook.*

Top: Moretons Fives Team 1952.

Bottom: Harrow 2nd XV 1951.

Top left: Just married, 1958.

Top middle: Eric, Violet, Juliet, Alison, Jennifer, 1970.

Top Right: Eric with Alison, Epping Forest, 1962.

Bottom: Jennifer, Juliet, Alison, Keith, 1978.

Top left: On Helvellyn 1975. *Photo: Frank Palmer.*

Top right: North Face of the Bionnassay 1970.

Bottom: Atop Helvellyn interviewing Joss Naylor (nearest camera) on his record run 1975.
Photo: Bill Neate.

Top: UN Correspondents with the Secretary General, 1983. *UN photo, Yutaka Nagata.*

Bottom: Presenting *World Chronicle* (UNTV), 1983, with Ted Morello, Raghida Dergham, Michael Kallenbach. *UN photo.*

Top left: Tommy Koh. *UN photo.*

Top right: Jeane Kirkpatrick & Charles Lichenstein. *UN photo, Yutaka Nagata.*

Bottom: Olara Otunnu, President of the Security Council, 1981. *UN photo.*

Top left: For a US lecture tour 1965. *FCO photo.*

Top right: Professor Peter Huntingford.

Bottom: With Dick Walker (Rand Daily Mail) at Etosha Pan, Namibia 1983. *UN photo.*

Top left: Madeleine Simms 1967. *Photo: Angela Phillips.*

Top right: Douglas Stuart 1970. *BBC photo.*

Bottom: Sir Anthony Parsons with Javier Perez de Cuellar 1982. *UN photo.*

Juliet: 'John Gilgrass went home before the end of the game: so we said he'd died.' We must have told them earlier about Scott's last expedition to the Antarctic, which had clearly made a deep impression. As indeed it had made with me when Eric my father told me the same story, which had unfolded in reality when he was a ten-year-old. I don't suppose I ever used that story in such an imaginative way as Juliet and her chums.

In December 1970 (when Alison was nine and Juliet almost seven) Jennifer and I were chatting in the kitchen with Stephen Hargreaves, who was a master at Dulwich College. Alison and Juliet were playing at the table. I was telling Stephen about *The Twelve Parts of Derbyshire*, a 200-page poem written by Jennifer's father Edward Boaden Thomas, when up got Juliet and went out to come back to present Stephen with a copy. She couldn't read the title but she knew we were talking about her grandfather's book. Perhaps this is the place to record that Juliet took a long time to master reading. We think it may have been a function of being left-handed. Her early writing was well formed but back to front as if seen in a mirror. By the time she was eight her brain had made the correction so perhaps we need not have worried at all.

A few minutes later I was relating to Stephen the latest developments at the abortion charity of which I was then a director. The Board had just had a very droll dinner with an American psychologist who had invented a simple tube for use in early abortion which he named after himself. He had fists full of his invention, the Karman cannula, which he dished out like visiting cards. I was just explaining this gadget to Stephen when again Alison and Juliet went out on cue without a word from us to come back triumphantly waving these plastic tubes, which they must have picked up from my desk. Amidst laughter, Stephen remarked, 'What advanced kids you've got.'

One Sunday in January 1971 when we planned to go out to an exhibition Alison, aged nine, and Juliet, almost seven, suddenly came into the kitchen while we were eating breakfast. They were clutching well-made placards set on sticks which read: 'Children's Own Way Day'; and they chanted their self-styled slogan loudly. They didn't want to go out. They wanted to have a full day's hard play at home, thank you very much. Were we parents too organised, too anxious to show them this and that?

151

We laughed heartily and conceded the point. They had used their initiative and clearly copied tactics seen on television. As we felt they should certainly take part in domestic decision-making, on this occasion we were quite pleased to let them have their way. Actually for years and years they played together and with friends very well for hours at a time. From the age of six until about twelve Alison and Juliet's absolute favourite pastime together was to play with sets of paper dolls which they could dress in many different paper dresses and for which they could make up little stories to match.

As a footnote to their play I should say that Jennifer was very clever in steering them into new activities and new games. She sprang into action on the rare occasions one or other of them said she was bored. There are so many new things for a child to learn and to do that she had exactly the right touch to guide them in a new direction. Jennifer was also very skilled at defusing their quarrels and diverting them towards more productive play. I loved reading to them and playing with them but was never as effective at it as Jennifer. On one memorable occasion when I was writing a book I plainly failed. Juliet aged six came into my study to get my attention and ask me to join her in some kind of game. I tried to humour her but explained I really had to press on with the work. Her heartfelt response was: 'I hate books', and she ran off feeling that her daddy had let her down.

Both Alison and Juliet went to the local schools, Rosendale Infants and Primary, which were five minutes walk away, and then to Mary Datchelor Girls' Secondary School in Camberwell. Datchelor was a voluntary-aided school founded in 1877 on the initiative of the Charity Commissioners who later nudged the Clothworkers' Company into taking over as governors. It seemed to us extraordinarily well run except for sport where only girls already good at hockey and tennis got any attention. Too late I realised that our daughters received almost no basic instruction and little time actually playing the games; consequently they did not become proficient at either game. I did raise my concerns with the staff in charge of sports but should have pressed the matter more strongly. I should also have spent more time encouraging them to play sport and coaching them as far as my expertise extended in hockey and tennis.

The school was particularly strong in music with the mistress in charge having lots of drive and being very enthusiastic. Indeed the school ran on a six-day timetable, rotating over the five weekdays so that those breaking off from the regular timetable of lessons for individual music tuition did not miss the same class every week. For new girls this system took a little getting used to but actually it worked very well. Alison became a proficient flautist as well as learning the piano out of school. Juliet tried hard with the bassoon but never quite felt she would master it so gave up after three years. Jennifer was able to give both of them some help with their music, having reached a high standard at the piano as a girl.

Apart from sport, most of the other subjects must have been taught well, particularly languages. Juliet became very proficient in French and Alison in Russian. When she reached the sixth form Alison decided she would go to Oxford like her parents. It was normal at Datchelor for some girls to try for Oxbridge but only in the third year sixth. Together with one of her friends, Alison overcame staff resistance and insisted on taking Oxford entrance in two years, despite some shaking of grey heads. The girls were vindicated in that both gained entry; indeed Alison's friend Angela Maclean is now a professor of mathematics at Oxford and a Fellow of All Souls.

The 'Death of Datchelor' should be the title of a seminal education history. Here was a very good school that essentially closed its own doors because of obscure educational theology. The Inner London Education Authority (ILEA) was in overall charge of the school and paid most of the bills. Its policy was to dismantle the grammar schools, on the grounds that they were selective and elitist, and convert them to comprehensive schools, which would admit all secondary-age children. Bending to this political wind the headmistress, Enid Godwin, arranged that Datchelor should move to Sutton in outer London beyond ILEA control and remodel itself as a five-form entry comprehensive school for girls. However, as the time approached for this move, Sutton Council foresaw that it needed a smaller school than first envisaged. Instead of five-form entry it would need only three-form entry, say 80 children a year rather than 120.

It was upon this point of educational theology that an excellent school closed and its staff were dispersed. The school had celebrated its centenary only two years previously and Miss Godwin was only its fourth headmistress. Yet Godwin felt that three-form entry would not produce enough high-flying children to fill a good sixth form. Most girls even in the 1970s were still leaving grammar school at 16 and not trying to move on to higher education. The places in universities were not available, the aspiration among the parents was lacking and the motivation among the pupils was not there. Following the accepted educational calculations concerning the ratio of entry pupils to eventual sixth-formers Godwin may well have been right for a time but clearly is out of date now.

The parents of Datchelor girls protested loudly at several large meetings held at the school. They would have put up with the inconvenience of the move to Sutton about 30 minutes away by train but they objected to the school being closed. While the school in Camberwell was being run down it blighted many of their daughters' education. But Godwin was supported by her governors from the Clothworkers' Company who were probably glad to be rid of the expense and the responsibility. She insisted on closing the school.

Fortunately Alison had already moved on to Somerville College in Oxford before the school actually closed but Juliet, three years behind her, clearly had to move for her sixth form. Jennifer enquired of many local state schools but none would offer a course that would prepare her for Oxbridge. Instead we were obliged to transfer Juliet to Alleyn's, a private school subsidised by the Dulwich Estate, set up under Edward Alleyn's original seventeenth-century bequest. According to Juliet it was not as well run as Datchelor but it did prepare her well enough to get her into Somerville. Luckily Alleyn's was just converting from a boys-only school to a mixed school. It had taken its first girls in the sixth form only the year before Juliet entered otherwise she might have been forced to go much further afield. Actually moving to a mixed school at the age of 16 proved a great advantage for Juliet who, until that time, had been somewhat socially shy. Now, as a good-looking girl amidst 600 boys she thrived.

After being a parent for 50 years I am more than ever convinced that parents need their children as much as the other way round, a conclusion I have already set out in my chapter on Harrow. 'Don't miss it' would be my advice to all couples.

12

BBC Ten O'clock 1962–1965

By 1962 I had become dissatisfied with the research life although I did not quite know why. Seeing an advertisement for the post of producer on the BBC Home Service programme *Ten O'clock* I consulted Marilyn Evans who was leaving the post and who happened to be a friend of my PEP colleague Bernard Donoughue. Although I probably paid too little attention to her caveats about the management I felt it would be a good move. As we used to listen to the programme most evenings I certainly knew what it was about. After an interview with a BBC selection board I was offered the job but at the starting point on the producer payscale. As I was already being paid £200 more a year at PEP I negotiated myself two rungs up the pay ladder before I took up the job in December 1962.

Very soon I realised that the key attraction of journalism was the daily feeling of creation and achievement. We started each day at 11 a.m. with a clean sheet plus a news diary indicating some of the things that might happen. We finished the day by broadcasting a 20-minute current affairs programme which commented on some of the main news, filled in the background of certain stories and usually discussed some topic that was not in the headlines. It employed three simple techniques: an interview with a news maker or an expert, a discussion between two or three contributors and a straight comment from a journalist. Only occasionally in those days did we produce a short feature because we rarely had a reporter or extra producer who could devote the whole day to assembling a documentary package.

No matter what difficulties we encountered trying to find the right contributors, shepherding them into a studio and coping with technical problems, we always got the programme on the air. We always achieved a listenable, informative programme, sometimes with exceptional contributors. We went home about 11 p.m. feeling we had achieved something useful. Yet we rarely had to carry something on from one day to another.

For all my time in broadcasting the technical difficulties were always a major factor. Ideally a producer would ask a contributor to come into our studio at Broadcasting House and if that wasn't possible then we would suggest one of many other BBC studios around the country. In major cities like Manchester and Edinburgh these studios would be manned but in many places they were unattended. In a place like Cheltenham or Oxford, for instance, the contributor had to collect the key from a hotel or a town hall and then open the line connection to Broadcasting House by following a few instructions. It sounds simple but people often made mistakes or the studio had not been left in proper order by a previous user, so that the connection took time or even failed altogether. Later on in my career when I was a reporter and correspondent I ran up against the problems frequently faced by contributors in unattended studios. While reporting from Londonderry, Northern Ireland in 1972, for instance, I recorded an interview with the Irish prime minister, Jack Lynch, in County Donegal, just across the border in the Republic. All went well until I tried to play the interview back to London from the unattended studio in Londonderry. The interview played well on my tape recorder but the level as received in London was very low. After several attempts I was talked through the correct procedure over the phone by an engineer in Belfast who was familiar with the studio. But it still didn't work and we couldn't understand why. The next day when they sent an engineer to investigate he found the studio's own electrical system had developed a fault. The contents of the interview were reported by BBC news but the recording itself was never used.

Another frequent problem, particularly in transatlantic connections, was echo. The contributor at the far end would hear his voice coming back to him, delayed by half a second. Correspondents encountered it often and some learnt to talk right through it without the listener detecting that something was wrong. Several times when reporting from New York I overcame this recurrent irritation by simply taking off my earphones and broadcasting a straight piece without them. Outside contributors did not really have this option as invariably they were being questioned from London and had to keep their headphones on. Our studio managers and control engineers were well aware of these and other technical problems and most of the time overcame them, but as a producer one could never be sure that the technical link-up would achieve acceptable broadcast quality.

During most of my 30 years in broadcasting we used specially booked high quality telephone lines; ordinary phone connections were usually dire, were often interspersed with electronic timing pips and were generally unlistenable when broadcast. Only very rarely did we attempt to use them. Overcoming these technical difficulties added to the excitement and the sense of achievement each day.

When I arrived on the fourth floor of Broadcasting House (BH to cognoscenti) the *Ten O'clock Programme* was well established and worked to a smooth routine. The editor was a dour but efficient Anglo-Indian named Stephen Bonarjee. The programme was more lively and more spontaneous than its predecessors but after five years had got into too much of a routine. There were set ways of tackling subjects and there were favoured speakers plus others whom we were instructed to avoid. There was even a list of experienced broadcasters and their subjects that was given to all producers. We sometimes referred to this list as our 'Repertory Company'. It was a reliable system but somewhat unadventurous and one that led to several conflicts with Bonarjee who did not like to take the risk of putting on an untried speaker.

On the plus side Bonarjee really was the editor every day – unlike many BBC people who had the title 'Editor' but who delegated this most important task to underlings while they concentrated on internal politics, such as lobbying for a bigger budget or more programme time or fending off critics, especially critics from the political parties. However, the obverse of Bonarjee's close attention was that producers had too little scope for innovation. One of my favourite colleagues, Dennis Bleakley, called Bonarjee 'our nose wiper' because he attempted to supervise each producer too closely. He wasn't much of a broadcaster himself so in my view he did not listen very closely to what was actually said or how it was delivered. He was far too sensitive to minor criticism from higher management and from the great and the good, such as MPs or the political parties; he was also much opposed to any of his producers making the occasional broadcast, even just doing an interview. One result of this attitude, common among BBC managers at that time, was that it rather belittled the expertise and talent of his own staff.

I soon made it one of my daily objectives to push on to the line-up at least one unfamiliar subject not tackled at all by the news department or even mentioned in the news diary. Another was to bring to the microphone new contributors who really had expertise relevant to the subject under discussion, rather than MPs or journalists listed in the 'Rep Company'. Of course producers who took care with their choice of speakers could make themselves a lot of extra work. Sometimes you would have to make more than a dozen phone calls to find the right expert who could also perform that night from wherever he or she was. The nearer it got to programme time the more anxious everyone became, especially Bonarjee. Just occasionally it got very close before we finally booked a speaker but in a four or five item programme you always had the option of expanding the existing items to fill the 20-minute space. Most subjects could bear to be examined for more than the three to four minutes we would normally allot them.

After I had been at *Ten O'clock* a few months we took over the *Today* programme, which then ran two editions after the seven o'clock and eight o'clock News. Previously it had been run more as light 'infotainment' than as a news programme. It was presented by an ex-announcer, Jack de Manio, whose genial incompetence appealed to much of our audience. It was said that the Programme Presentation Department had parked him there so that he couldn't ever read the ordinary News again and because it meant getting up very early, which would, in due course, induce him to leave. He was very pleasant to work with and he lasted in the end another seven years on *Today* but he was not a sharp current affairs broadcaster who could conduct a serious interview.

Although Bonarjee had manoeuvred in order to bring *Today* into his mini empire he did little to change its nature in the two years I worked on it and he left it distinctly underpowered. One producer gathered material and made bookings during the previous day, handing over to the studio producer in the early evening. The second producer wrote the script for De Manio and edited all the tapes. Very little was done live as we assumed, wrongly, that ministers, MPs, managing directors and other VIPs would not want to come to a studio so early. The studio producer usually went to bed well after midnight in The Langham across the road from Broadcasting House. The Langham was the shabby former Edwardian hotel with a royal connection and somewhat dubious reputation that the BBC used for offices, the BBC club and a large library. It has since been sold and reopened as a luxury hotel. The studio producer got up about 5 a.m. to put the programme on the air on his own!

For me, the two most stylish contributors to *Today* were Tim Matthews and Bernard Mayes. Tim was a very droll freelance broadcaster who could make the most humdrum subject sound hilarious and as such was the perfect foil for Jack de Manio. I think he must have made a good living from broadcasting because he owned a Rolls-Royce. Pride in this car induced him to overplay his hand in a clever but all too obvious manner. At the height of the Cold War he dreamed up a scheme of taking his Rolls to Russia (you can see the attraction of the alliteration at once) with Jack de Manio, claiming that Soviet controls were being eased. On the way Matthews sent back daily reports to *Today*, usually featuring some backchat with de Manio. On one occasion Jack kept interrupting their chat by asking, 'Tim? Is the engine on?' just to emphasise of course how silent the Rolls-Royce engine really was. Were they subsidised by the makers? Almost certainly to some degree. Later Tim moved on to Esso to make films but I have often wondered whether a BBC editor had taken him to task for blatant advertising. Incidentally, they never got into the Soviet Union.

Bernard Mayes was an Englishman who had established himself as a well-known broadcaster on public and university radio in California. To mark his transition, he emphasised the second syllable of his first name in the American way rather than giving equal weight to both syllables. Listen to an American talking about George Bernard Shaw and you will see what I mean. 'BerNARD' had a strong, laid-back voice and a keen eye for the bizarre in a state that provided him with plenty of material. For *Today* he used to send two- or three-minute vignettes by air freight, usually four or five at a time, about once a month. His pieces were rarely tied to a hard news story so were ideal for air freight, which gave us good broadcast quality at low cost.

Many years later, in 1978, we made an hour's feature together about the Reverend Jim Jones and the mass suicide he had inflicted on his flock in Guyana. Jones, who was white but claimed Cherokee descent, had set up his own People's Temple in San Francisco, which attracted a large, black, middle-aged congregation. In the best traditions of self-made hell-fire preachers in the mould of Elmer Gantry, Jones was manipulative yet was totally unhinged. His high moral pose went hand in hand with sadistic practices. He preached interracial love, which had a magnetic appeal for poor blacks and a few guilt-ridden young whites. His own family, his flock in California and his Guyana community were all genuinely interracial but this aura concealed a hideous reality.

At his peak in the 1970s Jones claimed 9,000 followers and for a time he was courted by politicians and celebrities, such as the Mayor of San Francisco and the Lieutenant Governor of California, as someone who could lead the black underclass to a better life. He was even appointed Chairman of the city's Housing Corporation. Yet within two years he fell from grace. Thinking himself persecuted, he led his flock off first to a new church in a rural part of northern California and then to an unpromising stretch of Guyana they called Jonestown where they attempted to be self-sufficient. In fact they lived on welfare and other remittances from the home state. Under pressure from worried relatives still back in California Jones's paranoia became acute but his charisma and his bullying held his simple-minded flock together for a few months. Fearing capture by American agents after some of his followers had murdered a visiting congressman who was very suspicious of Jones's true nature, Jones persuaded almost all his followers to take cyanide and even to poison their own small children. He described it as 'revolutionary suicide'. Only a handful of the 'settlers' survived. Nine hundred and thirteen people died, the largest mass suicide in modern times.

Soon after the story broke in Guyana our New York correspondent, Paul Reynolds, went off to Guyana while I flew to San Francisco. In a fortnight I tracked down a number of members of his church who had not gone to Guyana. To those who had lived for years in thrall to Jones he was a man of infinite resource, of consummate cunning, all-seeing eyes and endless stamina. It was apparent that even his ghost could still make people fear for their lives. They were very reluctant to talk. One woman told me, 'Of course, I didn't believe him when he said he was God,' but she said it without much conviction. Despite the graphic pictures of all the bodies laid out at Jonestown some people still feared his revenge might strike them somehow and somewhere. Not only blacks were affected in this way. A white middle-class journalist who had once been a friend and confidante of Jones in northern California claimed she and her son had received threats from some of Jones's former enforcers. She confessed she was scared of being a victim, so scared she was quite incoherent in a tape-recorded interview.

The most compelling single clue to the tragedy that I came across was a speech Jim Jones made on the approach to the Golden Gate Bridge in April 1977, only three months before he decamped to Guyana. The occasion was a public meeting to support suicide prevention barriers for the bridge, which alas is a popular spot for self-destruction. Jones turned up with busloads of supporters to make a key speech, the main thrust of which was that society had to bear 'collective responsibility'. 'Suicide,' he claimed, 'is a symptom of an uncaring society.' 'We are all sinners' is a common theme among religious cults. It was also evidence that by 1978 Jones had been thinking about suicide for some time. Jones also related that just before the event his twelve-year-old son had asked him, 'Maybe it would cause people to care if I jumped off the bridge while you were speaking?' Those present were never certain if the story was true or whether Jones had made up this obscene thought just to draw attention to himself.

By good fortune I met a reporter on the *San Francisco Chronicle* who had recorded this speech on behalf of his wife, the public relations officer for the suicide barrier committee. Joel Pimsleur realised he had a hot property and it took a week of phone calls before I could even hear it to determine if it was useful. During that week Pimsleur's office had been ransacked, tapes and a recorder had been stolen, but not the Jones tape, perhaps because it was on a cassette labelled 'Menachem Begin'. The quality was not perfect but it was usable. Remarkably it had no wind noise and little distortion. I bought a copy for $50, which I thought a reasonable price for a historical document – one of the last sane speeches of a self-destructive madman. I used part of the speech in the programme *The People's Temple* and it should be in the BBC archives even now.

Getting the programme back to London was a saga in itself. When we had mixed my interviews with Bernard's narration to make an hour-long programme I took the two large reels – at the high quality speed of 15 inches per second, usually used only for music – out to the airport some miles to the south of San Francisco. In the Trans World Airways air freight office it was handled briskly and I thought efficiently by a smart, experienced employee. I felt sure it would reach Broadcasting House in plenty of time for them to listen to the programme before being broadcast. But two days later I had a frantic call from my editor, Alastair Osborne, to say that it had not arrived and could I send a backup. I rehired the studio, no doubt at great expense, and we rerecorded the whole programme. In retrospect we felt we should have recorded a backup first time round but then I had never had such unreliable delivery by an airline before. Once again I packed up the two large reels and drove out to the air freight office. This time a young man was on duty who handled the whole thing in a manner I felt was just too casual. By now the time left before the broadcast was awfully short. It would only reach BH 5,000 miles away in time if everything went perfectly. I had no faith in this second attempt but contrary to my gloomy forebodings the second tape arrived on time and was broadcast on schedule. Moral: don't judge by appearances, though whether or not it was an error by the first dispatcher that caused the tape's delay I shall never know.

* * *

161

From the point of view of the producer, doing a stint on *Today* had its attractions because the overnight producer was in overall charge without our 'nosewiper' looking over his shoulder. One morning in 1964 Jack de Manio announced just before eight o'clock that he felt too ill to present the next edition. He had had a heavy night drinking. On the spur of the moment I presented the programme, which wasn't too daunting as I had written the script. This hiccup to what was a national institution prompted a call from the *Evening Standard* and a small paragraph on the front page. Stephen Bonarjee did not approve but could not say what else I could have done at such short notice. I suspect it was one of several incidents that made him feel he did not really want me in his team.

The funniest item I ever put on the air was spawned by the quater-centenary in April 1964 of Shakespeare's birth. The Shakespeare Memorial Theatre at Stratford-on-Avon had the brilliant idea of inviting everyone with the name of Shakespeare to a party. Among the 50 or so who turned up were some rural characters with Warwickshire accents that should have been copied by all actors playing yokels in any of Shakespeare's plays. One of our reporters from Birmingham recorded some priceless interviews with people who had never seen let alone read a Shakespeare play yet they chatted away in vintage Anne Hathaway. I kept a copy of this little feature which I used for many years when giving the occasional lecture about feature production to the BBC Training Department. Alas, the tape was lost when I was posted to New York in 1978.

Being on the *Today* rota meant a producer did five overnight sessions in a fortnight which on the face of it looked like a lot of time off. In practice though I found that one spent all the next day recovering from a five o'clock start. Sometimes the lack of sleep could still be felt the following day. I remember thinking on several beautiful summer mornings as I walked home along the chestnut avenue that leads to our house, as other people hastened to work, that night work was not living. When *Today* was later changed into a mainstream current affairs programme rivalling *The World at One* I was glad I was no longer part of that team. Overnight work is no way to live.

For our evening programme the BBC laid on quite a nice cold supper for staff and contributors. In part this was used as an inducement to persuade an MP or some other eminent speaker to come to BH to broadcast live. It was always laid out for us by the BBC butler dressed in black jacket and striped trousers – I suppose it was the gear he wore when serving meals to the governors at their meetings. He was efficient and agreeable but, alas, proved too friendly with a woman on the staff, for which he was sacked. There may have been justification for his dismissal but this reminded us of a tale told of the first director general, John Reith. Some time in the 1930s one of the well-known announcers got divorced. There was debate at the highest level as to whether or not he should be sacked, but in the end sanity and tolerance prevailed. However, Reith is supposed to have said that the offender could no longer read the religious 'Epilogue'. Much later it emerged that Reith, while professing high moral principles at the BBC, was actually pursuing young women himself.

From our point of view the cold supper table often engendered lively discussion with some of our interesting contributors. Of these I only remember the two occasions when speakers were indiscreet. When government ministers came to BH they were usually accompanied by a civil servant – to brief them if need be on the subject under discussion and to maintain liaison with their office should it be necessary. On one occasion in 1965 Michael Stewart, then foreign secretary, came to explain government policy on something, probably Rhodesia. While he was out of the room taking a phone call, the Head of the Foreign Office News Department, Michael Hadow, casually rubbished his boss as being 'second rate'. I was rather shocked that a civil servant should make such remarks about someone he was supposed to be advising. Very soon afterwards Hadow was appointed ambassador to Israel. Years later when he died, one of his colleagues described him in his obituary as 'a self-confident not to say brash operator'. As a broadcaster Stewart certainly wasn't second rate. Harold Wilson moved him to another ministry after a time but brought him back to the Foreign and Commonwealth Office (FCO) later.

Although the staffing on *Today* was too thin the working rota on *Ten O'clock* left some time free for other work. Terry Boston, who later became a Labour MP, encouraged me to make proposals for the Third Programme which any producer in Talks & Current Affairs could do. The 'Third', which was run by the novelist Howard Newby, was heavily weighted towards the arts, though it still broadcast some current affairs programmes. Newby held very civilised monthly meetings to discuss offers from producers at which the dominant voice was the poet, George Macbeth, and one of the more energetic contributors was Philip French who had been chairman of the Film Society and an editor of *Isis* while

I was at Oxford. I produced only a few talks for the Third, but two of them now seem prescient.

By the summer of 1963 the campaign to bring about Negro equality in the United States was near boiling point. Freedom rides, sit-ins, stand-ins and wait-ins were commonplace in the South, led by young blacks who could no longer wait for the American dream to reach them. I was familiar with all this from living in Illinois, a northern state, which still practised *de facto* segregation – there was still a wrong side of the tracks in the university town of Urbana-Champaign. Now I had the opportunity to broadcast two first-hand accounts by activists seeking to change things. One of them was a personable black American named Haywood Burns who wrote a long, thoughtful talk on the leadership and tactics of the non-violent protesters. He also quoted the Negro poet, Langston Hughes, who asked: 'What happens to a dream deferred?' Does it dry up, fester or does it explode? By 1963 a crisis was clearly growing which really did explode in 1968 when Martin Luther King was murdered. Black anger spilled out in vast riots which destroyed whole swathes of Detroit, Washington and other cities. Haywood Burns was still in his twenties and I expected him to become a leading black politician but perhaps he found the academic life more agreeable.

The other talk on the same subject was given by one of my professors at the University of Illinois. Personal contact is very important in broadcast journalism because you want to be sure that your speaker can talk in a listenable manner. On his way back from a sabbatical in Singapore Bill Ellison Chalmers gave a 20-minute talk on the first steps taken in Urbana to integrate blacks in housing, schooling and jobs. His main conclusion was that the official committee had to be pushed by unofficial citizen pressure and by a determination by the blacks to take direct action themselves. Without challenge from the blacks, progress was likely to be minimal.

Another of the talks I produced for the Third illustrated the BBC's attitude to its producers at the time. Nudged by one of the BBC's governors, Newby suggested to me that I should devise a programme with Clark Clifford who was visiting London. Clifford was a lofty example, quite common in America, of the all-purpose lawyer who is appointed to responsible posts by presidents of both political parties. He served four presidents in high positions including that of Secretary of Defense under Johnson. In short order I briefed myself about this man's experience and ideas, persuaded him to come to the studio and recorded a 30-minute interview. Then, however, I was instructed to edit the interview so that it should sound like a straight talk. No senior editor listened to the interview to decide whether it was good or bad; the principle was that producers should not put themselves on the air. After a great deal of painstaking editing with razor blade and sticky tape it worked, but only just.

Thirty years later this seemingly impeccable public servant was caught up in the financial scandal of the collapse of BCCI bank. Clifford was chairman of First American Bankshares, a subsidiary of BCCI, but claimed he knew nothing of its illegal activities. He was investigated by the district attorney and named by a congressional committee as a suspect. To a reporter, he said: 'I have a choice of either seeming stupid or venal.' His reputation was definitely sullied but he died soon afterwards aged 91 without being indicted.

Attlee

In January 1963 very soon after I joined the BBC, the *Ten O'clock* programme arranged to interview the former prime minister, Lord Attlee, on his eightieth birthday. As I had a lot to learn about broadcasting I decided to go along with the producer to see how these things were done. The sound engineer's car was already full so I borrowed a small bug-shaped Morris Minor from a friend. When I arrived at my friend's flat in Marylebone early in the morning he asked if the trip was still on as he had heard on the radio news a fragment saying Lord and Lady Attlee were going to have lunch in London at 1 p.m. While in the evening a grand dinner was going to be held in Attlee's honour in the House of Lords. It looked, therefore, as if our interview at Attlee's house at Great Missenden might be called off.

I phoned the office at Broadcasting House to discuss it with the producer, Denis Bleakley, but had to wait 25 minutes before he called me back. When Denis returned the call he was surprised by my report about the lunch in London because his appointment with Attlee was mid-morning. Without checking, he decided to drive off as planned. Just as well because the news report turned out to be garbled.

The weather was exceptionally cold and the roads covered with packed snow. At 35 miles an hour my little light car slipped gently from side to side – simple manoeuvres, especially overtaking, were quite perilous. Nevertheless, with little traffic on the roads I made good progress. Just before Great Missenden I gave someone a lift in the hope of getting precise directions to Attlee's house. He got out in the centre of the town after giving me some indication as to where it was. He felt some proprietary interest in local notables because, he said, 'We lost the Earl of Buckinghamshire the other day.' He was obviously preparing himself for other noble deaths.

Helped by another local, I missed the house and arrived late during the middle of the interview. I pushed open the front door and barged into the kitchen only to find Lady Attlee quietly washing up. The interview by Honor Balfour of *Time* was straightforward, although Attlee did need a little prompting. He still had a slight speech defect brought about by a stroke a year earlier.

After the interview while Denis and Honor were still cooing the congratulations and the radio engineer was packing up we all drank Attlee's health in champagne. Lady Attlee then announced that they intended to catch a train in 15 minutes and asked if anyone could give them a lift to the station. That's where I made myself useful at last. If they didn't mind a small car I would be glad to take them to the station. To my surprise there was no counter bid from my colleagues so Lady Attlee accepted.

Everyone then left the house which producer, interviewer, engineer and three press photographers had virtually taken over for the morning. As the photographers prepared to take a last photo on departure for London Lord Attlee did something characteristic but hardly photogenic. Clad in wellington boots he clambered down some icy steps to his garden with his case in one hand and three empty milk bottles in the other. Carefully he put the bottles out for the milkman.

We then left rather too hurriedly for an 80-year-old who had some trouble easing himself into my small car. On the way to the station Lady Attlee hinted that they wouldn't mind going all the way to London by car. So I offered again. I now felt I had scooped my colleagues for I had the Attlees to myself for the next hour and a half but I also had a considerable responsibility. I had to be very careful not to injure a fragile national treasure.

As we drove towards London Lady Attlee, sitting in the back seat, did most of the talking. She chatted about her dogs and her neighbours and it became pretty clear that she ran her house much like any other aged, middle-class housewife. She had a very pronounced middle-class accent and talked of things being 'frightfully expensive' and 'awfully dreary!' in a rather standard fashion of the time. She was very pleased to tell me that she had recently won some premium bonds in a raffle organised by a local women's club.

166

She was considerably younger than her husband and still seemed energetic for her age. She was not, however, either intellectual or political. In fact when I asked her in jest if she regretted not being prime minister herself she poured out her scorn of politics and announced, quite baldly, that she was a Conservative – 'always have been, always will be'.

During most of this conversation Lord Attlee sunk his chin into his neck and fell into a seemingly comatose silence. He brightened up a little, however, when she related to me how she came to marry him. She had gone on holiday in Italy with her brother and Attlee who were friends. The holiday lasted five weeks. 'Quite a long time to get to know a person, don't you think?' 'Still, he didn't make love to me before we were married.' Interpret that as you will; I could hardly probe it further.

As we approached London I began to prod Attlee very gently. I was conscious of the fact that he had already endured one interview that morning from my organisation and would have to give more interviews later in the day. Therefore I kept out of politics. Instead I got him to talk about his days at Oxford by telling him that I also went to University College. This started him off on a long trail of fond reminiscence. He was very proud of his contemporaries at Univ who apparently were kings of the sports fields and masters of the Examination Schools. When he was up at the turn of the century, Univ won the rugby cup and was Head of the River – the latter was quite out of the question in my day when we had a long wrangle in the Junior Common Room about the enormous cost of the boat club. However, after naming three or four of his contemporaries who took first-class honours, he chuckled as he said, 'They never came to anything much – no judgement, you know, these people who are too clever, no judgement. I myself got a Second. What did you get?' It was the one time in my life that I thought myself fortunate not to have a First.

Lady Attlee quickly took up this point on which they had long agreed: 'No judgement.' 'No judgement' they kept nattering to themselves as we bumped over the ice.

As we came nearer to the Great Western Hotel at Paddington station she thanked me for the ride and asked me to join them for lunch. It was not an important lunch as we had been led to believe but just for the two of them and now me. After we had unloaded the car I tried to move it up a few feet to a parking place but it wouldn't start. Somewhat out of keeping with the splendour of the surroundings I hopped out of the car and pushed it to a parking bay.

On entering the hotel Lord Attlee was plagued by photographers and though obviously tired he had to endure their 'one more' and 'just one more, please sir' until we were all heartily sick of them. The Attlees then had little appetite for lunch during which Lady Attlee began to treat her husband like a small boy, telling him what he could eat and drink and that he should go for a rest immediately afterwards. Unfortunately for Lord Attlee she was firmer in speech than in execution for after lunch she allowed the press photographers to take charge of him once again.

Two interesting facts emerged during the lunch. They had lunched in the hotel only once before. On the day of their election victory in 1945 they had been the guests of Lord Portal, then chairman of the Great Western Railway and a member of Churchill's government. The grand dinner announced to the world by the BBC as if it was being given by the Lords was actually being given by Lady Attlee. She explained that the invitations couldn't show her as the hostess because of protocol, but that she had thought of the idea, had done all the organising, had drawn up the guest list and finally, a point she underlined, she would have to pay for it. The contrast with Churchill's really grand eightieth birthday (which had taken place eight years earlier) was immediately apparent. No Westminster Hall, no public subscription for a huge portrait, no grateful nation treatment at all. It was somehow in character for this unassuming man who entitled his autobiography *As it Happened.* Nye Bevan commented that it was a good title because 'he never did anything – things happened to him'.

At the time I felt the Lords were rather thoughtless not to have laid on an official dinner. When Lady Attlee said, 'I don't know how we are going to pay for it,' her husband reassured her by remembering some American cheques that had just arrived for lecture fees or book royalties. I left after lunch feeling I had had a very intriguing day. The *Evening Standard* reported that 'the Attlees lunched quietly with a friend'.

A couple of months after this episode I was sent on a training course for new broadcasters during which we all had to compile our own magazine programme. For one item I recorded a report from the top of the Post Office Tower in London. The structure had reached its full height of 580 feet but there was no floor, just the open girders like the spokes of a wheel. When finished a year later it would have a revolving restaurant on the top so I tried to describe the view that the diners might enjoy. Bestride a couple of open girders I could look down almost

500 feet to the equipment block at the base. My minder from the Post Office was a little anxious about my safety but fortunately a good head for heights enabled me to keep my balance and record my report on a hefty hand-held tape recorder at the same time. It was a fine day so I could see the hills 20 miles to the north and south of London. In my enthusiasm for this prospect I said I could see the North and South Downs. Actually to the north are the Chilterns and to the south, the North Downs! When the programme was played back to the training course no one noticed but I winced, knowing I had made a silly mistake. On the other hand they did all ask how I'd managed not to mention the exposure. Sadly the Post Office Tower only functioned as a restaurant for a few years because it had to be closed after being bombed by the IRA.

Rookes v. Barnard

Towards the end of 1964 Tony van den Bergh enlisted me to produce a documentary on a famous labour case known as Rookes versus Barnard. Tony was a larger than life freelance broadcaster who had prospered while Lawrence Gilliam ran the Features Department but who was now finding commissions difficult to get. Tony looked like every theatre director's idea of Sir Toby Belch, bearded, rotund, loud-voiced and just a little disreputable. He had been a boxer and a boxing commentator. He had worked for a cigar company, Four Square, and had run their publishing offshoot with the same name. He was enterprising, sometimes hard-working and a devoted patron of the bar. He also edited a monthly magazine called *The Foreman*, which was where he got the idea for a programme on Rookes and Barnard. As this case had been running since long before I left the trade union study at PEP I felt I had enough expertise to produce the programme.

Douglas Rookes was a draughtsman working for British Overseas Airways at Heathrow where the company had agreed, in return for a no-strike clause, that the Draughtsmen's Shop would be 100 per cent union members. When Rookes left the union and refused to rejoin his mates threatened to strike. After much to-ing and fro-ing BOAC dismissed him. Instead of suing the company Rookes brought an action for damages against three union officials because they had brought about his dismissal. For the previous 50 years the trade unions had thought they were immune from such an action but the courts now thought otherwise.

169

Rookes won the case with 'exemplary and aggravated damages' in the High Court. This was overturned on appeal, but taking his case to the Lords, Rookes won a unanimous decision in his favour, nine years after leaving the union.

The trade union movement was up in arms because it undermined their whole right to strike. Harold Wilson's government promised an inquiry and a new law to make clear a union's immunity in such a situation. Unfortunately, in making our programme we couldn't interview any of the named principals because the Lords dismissed the exemplary damages and that issue was therefore still *sub judice*. But we did mount a thorough examination of the issues in law and industrial relations with contributions from BOAC, the British Employers Confederation, the General Secretary of the TUC, the leader of the Draughtsmen's Union, plus academic labour lawyers.

A few days after it was broadcast the *Ten O'clock* team mounted a pilot for the first BBC phone-in programme, something that was then common in America but unknown here. Douglas Rookes used this opportunity to complain that our programme had not interviewed him. He wasn't very rude but he frightened Bonarjee who was always alarmed lest the BBC be taken to court. As a direct consequence, he called me in to suggest that as I had spent much of my time on this programme without telling him I might like to go to Documentaries instead. In part he did not like anyone working on programmes outside his control, though theoretically we were encouraged to do so. By this time I was fed up with working for such a man who was so frightened of authority or of outside criticism. So I agreed to the transfer which turned out well.

13

BBC Documentaries 1965–1969

Stephen Bonarjee did not like my independent attitude and therefore engineered my move to Documentaries. Actually I was not reluctant to go because I had begun to feel somewhat frustrated by the limited scope of being a producer under Bonarjee. For the next four years I had a much freer hand choosing the subjects for programmes after some discussion with the head of the department and then producing, writing and editing them entirely unsupervised and to my own standards. Besides the urgent political stories, such as Rhodesia and Czechoslovakia, I also chose to tackle a new range of social subjects such as adoption, divorce, abortion, hard drugs, juries and the honours system. For me the most valuable part was having the space in which to learn how to write a 2,000-word script in a couple of days. Having both the freedom and the discipline of the deadline did wonders for my writing skills. It was a vital step along the road to becoming a well-rounded journalist, someone who can tackle any subject and produce a text from the available material proportionate to the time available.

The Documentaries Department was headed by D.G. Bridson who had been a pioneer of this type of programme from the 1930s. I say 'headed' the department because he did not wish to 'run' the programmes as such. He devoted himself to making his own programmes, usually in long series, and left the other producers in his department much of a free hand. I joined the department just as it was gearing up to produce a weekly half-hour documentary entitled *Focus* – a useful title that enabled us to tackle virtually any subject in some depth. I think the idea came from Alan Burgess, another veteran producer who had worked in the old Features Department under Laurence Gilliam. Alan was certainly the senior producer of our team and inveigled the well-known broadcaster Edgar Lustgarten to be the old-style presenter. He was 'old-style' because the whole script was written for him by a producer. He just applied his rich voice to enhance the meaning and attract an audience.

He had been broadcasting and making films for many years, mostly about crime stories of various kinds. Personally, he was small and somewhat gnarled but quite professional to work with.

My other colleagues for a few months were two BBC trainees, David Elstein and Jeremy Nicklin. Elstein, who was extremely bright, should have gone on to become Director General of the BBC but was lured away to the commercial sector and was the first Controller of Channel 5. Nicklin, on the other hand, made a silly mistake while reporting for a *Focus on Housing* programme which I produced. He described some run-down houses in Hull as 'back to back' when in fact there were no such houses in the city, as the town clerk wrote to tell us in no uncertain terms. Nicklin had been to university in Hull and should have known better. Anyway this error was included in his final report at the end of his probationary period as a trainee. Whether or not that was crucial I do not know but BBC management pushed him out or indicated that he might as well leave. By that time he had already shown his general competence during a trip to Paris with me to make a programme about the presidential election in which Francois Mitterand was the chief challenger to Charles de Gaulle. I felt that the Corporation was now losing a talented individual but my opinion was not sought. Jeremy went off to work in the French advertising industry, not too reluctantly as he had a French girlfriend.

Very soon after we began *Focus* we made a programme about the newly declared independent Rhodesia. Alan Burgess had been there several times so wrote the historical background while I went off to Rhodesia to collect material about the condition of a country that faced international condemnation. I had interviews with, among others, the Governor General (then in limbo) and Malcolm Smith, the editor of the *Rhodesia Herald*. He was known to be under pressure from Ian Smith's regime so I was asked by George Camacho, the head of Talks & Current Affairs in Radio, to establish discreetly whether he was going to crack. In fact his morale seemed fine but he was eventually forced out of office for resisting censorship. By printing the front page of the newspaper with the censored stories blacked out he mocked the government's claims that all was quite normal.

At that time many Rhodesians were still cocky that they could maintain their independence. The possibility of economic sanctions having any bite was regarded as a joke. In a whites-only club in Salisbury someone fingered me to a Special Branch policeman who took me aside to interrogate me for a few minutes. Luckily the correspondent for Associated

Press was also there – a jolly Englishman who told me his nickname was 'GoodEvans, all one word'. Evans vouched for me with the policeman but not before he had filed a report to his HQ.

With a hired car I was able to drive all over the country on the 'tramways' – roads built with just two strips of tarmac with grass in between giving a single lane for traffic. Quite a few drivers seemed to enjoy playing chicken, that is driving as fast as they could towards the approaching vehicle in the hope that the other would flinch and bump off to the side of the road. To ensure I returned to tell the tale I bumped off the road most of the time. In the north I stayed with a prosperous farmer named Black and his talkative wife. My hosts were very affable. They organised a large late-night dance party for their African workers during which the dancers slaked their thirst by drinking straight from buckets of beer. I suppose the Blacks were trying to show me that their African workers were not yet ready for self-government. By chance it was the night of the 1966 British election in which Harold Wilson's government was returned to power. The Blacks stayed up most of the night listening to the results on the BBC World Service hoping for a change of government and a change of heart towards an independent Rhodesia.

At their farm I also interviewed their articulate African manager in his own well-appointed grass hut. Mrs Black wanted to muscle in on that interview but I kept her out, saying her presence would alter the whole character of the exchange. How could he be relaxed and frank in his opinion of the new regime if the owner's wife was there too? The farm manager was very moderate in his views but he certainly did not want white rule to continue. Yet somehow his employers were under the illusion that their manager loved them and wanted white rule to go on as before.

In the south of the country I went to Bulawayo, the second city, where I talked to a former mayor who was also the mother of someone I had met in London. In the circumstances she was remarkably upbeat. She strongly disapproved of the colony declaring unilateral independence but thought it wouldn't last long. Nevertheless, as her husband had just retired they soon moved to South Africa. I also interviewed the Anglican Bishop of Mashonaland, Cecil Alderson, who gave a well-reasoned view of the political change. This was such a good interview in itself that after a small excerpt had been used in the *Focus* programme I was able to persuade the new Controller of Radio 4, Gerald Mansell, to run a 20-minute version as a stand-alone programme. I was at last getting on the air with official encouragement! About 30 years later, when I was giving a short talk at Greenwich University about being a correspondent, one of the audience made a surprising intervention. He was a collector of old photographs. He had acquired from a junk shop several volumes of family photos belonging to the bishop who had died in office aged 67 only two years after I had met him. Why, we both wondered, had these volumes been jettisoned and how did they turn up in Britain? It remains a mystery.

On my last night in the country I was invited to dinner at a private house in Salisbury with about a dozen white Rhodesians. The whole table discussed the political situation in Rhodesia and Britain throughout the meal and I was subjected to a stream of questions. Finally someone turned to me to ask: 'Is it true that the BBC is run entirely by intellectuals?' The word was emphasised to make it rhyme with reptiles! 'Unfortunately not,' I replied. 'Some are boneheads like everywhere else.' No one pressed the point.

When I returned to Salisbury, Ronnie Robson, our resident correspondent, told me that the BBC had just been expelled 'bag and baggage' and all its personnel had been declared *'persona non grata'*. Robson at first thought it was because of my encounter with the plain-clothes policeman but it turned out that Bush House had aroused the ire of the Smith government. Some months previously the BBC's Africa Service had installed a special transmitter in Francistown, Bechuanaland, just over the border from Rhodesia, to give better reception to its broadcasts. The actual incident that provoked our expulsion was a little competition. The BBC's French Service to Africa invited listeners to write a letter telling Ian Smith and Dr Hendrik Verwoerd, Prime Minister of South Africa, why they should change their policies. Clearly the Rhodesian authorities were a little too sensitive. They insisted the BBC had to go and for several years it had to rely on a Rhodesian stringer.

In the aftermath of the Second World War Britain concentrated on rebuilding the houses and factories destroyed by German bombing. It was not until the 1960s that it began to invest in new infrastructure such as motorways, oil and gas wells in the North Sea and universities. The discovery first of gas and then oil in the North Sea promised to give a great boost to our sluggish economy. One year I persuaded the American company Philips to take me out by tug to one of their drilling rigs some 40 miles off Lowestoft. I roamed about the huge rig even climbing the tower, describing what I saw and interviewing whomever I liked. Before the Piper Alpha disaster in 1988 the North Sea oil industry was almost entirely good news.

Drilling in the seabed miles from shore is a particularly tough job, carrying all the time the inherent risk of disaster. While I was on the rig they were replacing the drill bit, pulling up hundreds of feet of pipe for hour after hour. Each length is gripped by the turn-table in the floor, then unscrewed at high speed before being lifted by a crane into a stack guided by gloved hands. Each move contains the danger of a heavy length of pipe flying off into one of the 'roustabouts' or of someone stepping accidentally on to the table while it revolves at speed. As the pipe comes out of the hole mud flies all around, splattering the roustabouts and their foreman every time. I watched as these operations went on relentlessly in a strong wind full of sleet. They were paid what seemed very high wages and no wonder. In contrast I also went into the cabin where they analysed the mud core for its geological content as it is spewed out of the inside of the drill pipe. On this rig the two geologists were French and described themselves as 'mudloggeurs', a nice piece of franglais. Their cabin was stifling and their work looked very boring. On this particular exploration drill they had had no results up until then.

For this *Focus on the North Sea* programme I went out in a small support vessel but ten years later I flew out a hundred miles from Aberdeen in a helicopter. In the interval the oil had begun to flow in large quantities and promised to make Britain an oil-rich country. The cue for the later programme was the death of a number of divers while working on the seabed. The water was much deeper in this area than off East Anglia and the dangers of getting the bends or of suffering from other hazards were high. Again, the divers were getting very well paid but we couldn't help noticing that their young boss who kept his feet dry and took none of the risks was doing very much better.

My very first trip in a helicopter had been made across Dartmoor in 1968. I was making a documentary with an easygoing freelance named Leigh Crutchley who had a deep, rich voice. Our cue was an agitation by a few MPs for the Ministry of Defence to release some of the land commandeered for gunnery ranges during the war. At Tyneham on the Isle of Purbeck the Royal Armoured Corps still used the whole village, taken over in 1942. On Dartmoor a much larger area, used intermittently for artillery practice, was inherently dangerous to the public, not only during the firing but also because of unexploded shells. The conservationists added their voice by claiming that the gunners destroyed ancient barrows and other archaeological remains.

A brigadier who arrived by helicopter gave us a briefing in the middle of the moor as to the amount and frequency of the shelling and of the safety precautions. He stressed that gunnery was a precision business and that they took great care to keep within the boundaries of the range shown on the map. He ended by pointing to an unremarkable stone barely sticking out of the ground, which he said they had apparently damaged. We would never have noticed without it being pointed out. To our ill-informed eyes it was just another stone. No matter, they were showing how careful they were and how responsible they felt towards preserving an ancient building block.

When the final interview was finished the brigadier suddenly announced that he was going on by car but that we could go wherever we wanted in the helicopter. As we had collected all the material we needed it was too good an offer to miss. Newton Abbot station, I said, and we zoomed across the moor at high speed. It is a delightful way to travel if you can stand the engine noise. But then the claim of expert army precision unravelled. As we reached the main line on the eastern edge of the moor the pilot asked, 'Where's the station?' It seemed an odd question for a pilot to ask a passenger. I had never been there before but grabbed my one-inch-to-the-mile Ordnance Survey map to direct him. Under my direction the pilot landed in a field beside the station yard. It shattered my faith in military map reading. And needless to say we pointed out in our programme that the army's claims not to shoot outside the designated areas should not be taken at face value.

In the summer of 1968 Geoffrey Bridson embarked on a ten-part series on the United States for the Third Programme. It covered historical, cultural and economic aspects as well as political but it proved a little too ambitious for one person, so at the instigation of Anthony Moncrieff I was commissioned to produce two programmes on the presidential election campaign. As a result I was present on Michigan Avenue in Chicago when the police charged into a crowd demonstrating outside the Conrad Hilton Hotel, the Democratic Party's headquarters. In fact I was actually on a street corner interviewing someone when the police patrol of some 30 men surged past me on to the avenue and into the crowd, batons waving. As the crowd fled in all directions I was one of several people who were pushed through the ground-floor window of the hotel, fortunately without injury. Forty years later a short excerpt of my report describing this deplorable and chaotic scene was replayed in a series on *1968 – Year of Revolutions*.

At the end of that overwrought week in Chicago at which Hubert Humphrey was nominated to be the Democratic presidential candidate I produced a 45-minute discussion for the Third Programme before flying off to Colorado for three weeks in the Rockies. On my return I compiled a documentary on the election campaign, visiting St Louis and Detroit before finishing up in Washington and New York. Willard's Hotel in Washington, which was empty awaiting demolition, had been acquired by the Republicans as their temporary headquarters. It was there that one of Nixon's right-hand men earnestly explained that the world had not realised that Richard Milhous Nixon was one of its great intellectuals. I expressed scepticism about such a claim but in fairness used it in my programme when I returned to London. By the time Nixon was forced from office six years later he had shown himself to be more crook than clever.

Although the British media, including the BBC, gives an inordinate amount of attention to American affairs, we journalists rarely point out that the two-party battle is often repetitive and we never mention other parties or other candidates. At the beginning of the century the Socialist, Eugene Debs, had garnered millions of votes in five presidential elections. Even in 1948, as a second red scare began to grip the United States, the former vice-president, Henry Wallace, standing as a Progressive, gained over a million votes, almost as many as the Dixiecrat, Strom Thurmond, who carried four states. For a novel angle on the 1968 election, therefore, I went to see the Socialist Party candidate for vice-president who was an academic with an office in Dupont Circle in the centre of Washington. Quite properly, he underlined some of the domestic deficiencies in the record of the major parties: low wages for a substantial section of the labour force (women more than men, but white as well as black); no health insurance for anyone not in regular employment; and labour laws which still favoured the employer in practice, especially in conservative states. None of these issues were tackled by either Humphrey or Nixon.

By the time the interview was finished it was about 7 p.m. on a lovely sunny evening. As I had borrowed a Volkswagen Beetle I offered to drive the interviewee to his home in the north-west quadrant of the city. Driving along New Hampshire Avenue the windscreen was suddenly shattered by a bottle. We stopped the car but failed to identify the culprit from among a group of idle men standing on the pavement. 'We should report it,' said my passenger, 'but it's not worth it. Nothing will happen.' It seemed a bleak verdict on the social mores of the capital city where the politicians constantly claim 'it's a republic of laws, not of men'. I drove on peering through a windscreen with a hole in the middle and the rest like a spider's web of cracks.

One of the hazards of travelling a lot in foreign parts is that often you drive on unknown roads in cars with which you are unfamiliar. Driving on the tramline roads in Rhodesia was one good example and an episode in Italy was very nearly for me a bad example.

In 1967 I was driving south from Naples to a small town called Battipaglia along the spectacular coast road above Salerno. The road is well engineered with many tunnels. As I entered the first tunnel, which curved sharply to the left, I switched on my lights only to find they didn't work. So I suddenly hit the pitch dark at 60 miles an hour. Luckily there was no other traffic on my side of the road. And for some time I simply guessed the angle of the curve and slowed right down until some sunlight appeared from the other end. Then at last I could steer along the curb. When I emerged I had to negotiate several more tunnels at slow speed before I could find a garage to repair the lights. Unwisely I had taken it for granted that everything was working. I was more cautious after that episode.

Just after New Year, 1966, I produced a programme entitled *Focus on the Honours System*, which then was shrouded in mystery and to some extent still is. At the beginning of my enquiries no fewer than two ex-prime ministers, five retired top civil servants and three general secretaries of civil service trade unions all declined to record an interview about how the recipients were nominated and the selections made. Most of the civil service people found the issue embarrassing and best left unrevealed to the public. This attempt to close ranks simply spurred me on until I did find a knighted ex-permanent secretary to a government department, an ennobled ex-chief whip, a party leader who was a privy councillor, plus several MPs and academics. During the previous 13 years of Conservative government 'Political Honours' had been shovelled out to about half of all Tory MPs. Altogether the Conservative administrations from 1951 to 1964 conferred on their supporters in Parliament 2 earldoms, 19 viscountcies, 32 baronies, 40 baronetcies and 84 knighthoods, not to mention many lesser gongs to active party members outside Parliament. Lord Redmayne, the ex-chief whip, defended the practice by saying it had always been part of the Party machine for all governments, implying it was a necessary lubricant of political power.

Harold Wilson came into office in 1964 promising to sweep away this practice yet Redmayne pointed out that in its first two years Labour had matched the Tory average for honours and had actually created twice as many Life Peers. Some changes have been made since but under Blair's government we had the 'Cash for Peerages' scandal in which the voracious appetite of political parties for funds still engendered clandestine practice no better than the worst in Lloyd George's day. Honours systems, like bonus systems, are inherently open to favouritism and corruption. They are used in part by governments and other elite groups in our society to exert control over subordinates and to suppress criticism from the lower ranks. We would do better without them.

Historians now look back on the 1960s as a time of significant social advance. They point to the fact that Roy Jenkins was Home Secretary while the laws on divorce, abortion and homosexuality were all liberalised. While Jenkins supported these measures I feel he has been given too much credit as he did not initiate them. They began as private members' bills for which the government simply allowed sufficient time to get them through into law. No doubt the Home Office could have killed these bills if it had wanted to but instead it smoothed the path in their passage through Parliament. The bold, hard work that went into devising these reforms and pushing them through Parliament against strong, sometimes bitter opposition was undertaken by a few MPs and their determined extra-parliamentary supporters.

I found that this kind of social issue made gripping radio because people would bare their agony or their dilemma. One young woman sobbed as she related that she could not bear to divorce her husband who had left her for another; he had put his heart into fitting their flat with a stylish array of shelves and bookcases, which reminded her every day of her lost life. An unmarried professional woman described the agony of giving up her child, which had been fathered by a foreign diplomat. When she asked for my help I could do little else than refer her to a social service NGO, which I realised was probably too little and too late. A journalist needs a certain detachment in dealing with his contacts, just like a doctor or lawyer dealing with their patients or clients, in order to retain objectivity and to be able to move on to the next subject. I still feel, however, that in some way I let them down. The work of a journalist is a picaresque ramble, picking up stories and people for short periods and then moving on to the next. In most cases each of these documentary programmes left me better informed but the one topic that also changed my own life was abortion, something I describe at length in the next chapter.

14

Abortion

'Autobiography is an unrivalled vehicle for telling the truth about other people.'

Philip Guedalla

How my interest was aroused:

The doctor at the big hospital told me all the things that could be wrong with this baby – [as a result of German measles during pregnancy] – it may be blind or deaf or be deformed or I may not carry it to full nine months or it may die after it was born … and then said, 'But I can't do anything about it; you'll just have to hope for the best.'

Mrs Jones, *Focus on Abortion*, BBC Home Service
(15th February, 1966)

Mrs Jones was a very moving contributor to a radio documentary I produced on the cue of Lord Silkin's Abortion Bill. The programme was a sober examination of attitudes to unwanted pregnancy and a discussion of possible solutions including Silkin's proposals. The most vivid parts of the programme were personal accounts of how women dealt with unwanted pregnancies while in law most abortions were still illegal. The interview with Mrs Jones (not her real name) was done in Manchester so I never met her myself; nevertheless, her story was so powerful it turned me into a supporter of abortion reform.

In the event, the outcome of her pregnancy was appalling. Months after the child was born it slowly emerged that he was blind, deaf and had a heart murmur. Two and a half years later when the interview was conducted he could not even sit up or feed himself. A professor in Leeds told her bleakly that he would never grow up like her other children and she should not expect him to reach his teens.

181

From then on I took more interest in the subject. A year later I produced another programme while David Steel's Abortion Bill was fighting its way through the Commons, being careful of course to maintain BBC impartiality. Soon after the Act was passed in 1967 I wrote an article with Madeleine Simms for *Political Quarterly* on 'How the Abortion Lobby Worked',[1] which was the embryo of our book *Abortion Law Reformed.*[2] Madeline had been General Secretary of the Abortion Law Reform Association and was one of the team who briefed parliamentarians as Steel's bill ran the gauntlet of the Commons and the Lords. In 1971 a few months before the publication of our book I was invited to join the Management Committee of the Pregnancy Advisory Service (PAS), which helped women to get terminations in the private sector if they could not get one in the Health Service. The Abortion Law, which had come into force in April 1968, unlocked a demand among British women which the Health Service was not fulfilling. In fact the Health Service has never been able to meet the demand for abortion. Successive governments have defended the law and slowly increased the medical staff and facilities but none has endeavoured to make it a universal option for all British resident women comparable with the universal maternity services.

By the time I had developed from an informed commentator into an activist I had a clear view of the subject. The basis of my position was and is that motherhood should be voluntary. A society that banned abortion stood for compulsory motherhood which was not only cruel for the women but often disastrous for their unwanted children. Now that society had the means to terminate early pregnancy safely without danger to the woman's health it was sensible on medical and social grounds to permit it. At the Pregnancy Advisory Service we never advocated abortion for its own sake or as a desirable method of birth control. Most of us had families and children and thrived on the experience. We simply thought that all pregnant women should have a choice. Our position was summed up neatly in an advertisement devised by our information officer, Helene Graham, for display on the London Underground. 'If you're happy to be pregnant fine. If not, why not consult Pregnancy Advisory Service?' In the mid-1970s a national campaign emerged entitled 'A Woman's Right to Choose' – whatever her reasons and regardless of whether she could pay for it herself.

Some people soon began to describe our policy as 'Abortion on Demand', which had logic but for me was too aggressive and impractical. For one thing almost everyone, including the most ardent feminists, agreed that a foetus should not be terminated after it was viable. But mostly I objected to the pressure on doctors implied in 'abortion on demand'. They were entitled to object to abortion just as much as women were entitled to ask for it. They were not automatons forced to carry out abortions just because they were paid by the Health Service. In our view an ethical doctor who objects on principle should refer a pregnant woman to a more sympathetic colleague. Unfortunately many doctors, especially those with reactionary religious beliefs, did not follow this course but obstructed their patients' wishes in various ways. When abortion turned out to be safer than childbirth such obstruction could itself be seen as illegal. The very first clause of the 1967 Act stated that a doctor may terminate a pregnancy if he and another doctor consider:

> that the continuance of the pregnancy would involve risk to the life of the pregnant woman or of injury to the physical or mental health of the pregnant woman or any existing children of her family greater than if the pregnancy were terminated.[3]

In practice, therefore, there were no contraindications for termination up to the viability of the child.

For centuries women with unwanted pregnancies had been suppliants whispering their requests furtively on the margins of medical practice or worse still in the so-called 'backstreets' to practitioners without training, safe facilities or medical backup. Now abortion was legal for a range of medical, psychological and social reasons if they were vouchsafed by two doctors. The law had been changed but when the Act came into force in 1968 neither the personnel nor the facilities existed to cope with demand. The Health Service, though national, made no preparations while many nurses and doctors were still positively hostile to the idea of abortion despite the change in the law. A private medical abortion sector did exist, run by a few doctors in private practice, but their capacity was limited. Moreover, their prices were very high – nothing less than £100 and often much more – thus providing a brake to expansion in that sector and discriminating against poorer women.

The core mission of PAS was to create an agency where women could find a sympathetic hearing, be examined by two ethical doctors, be referred to a gynaecological surgeon and be operated on in a licensed theatre with full medical backup and all at an affordable price. We supplied the links which turned all these individual factors into an organisation. Our most important innovation near the start, was that we recruited and trained a corps of laywomen counsellors who received the patients and advised them of their options and what we could provide. The patient was then examined by two of our sessional general practitioners. If the pregnancy was confirmed and met the requirements of the law the doctors usually, but not always, authorised the termination. Once the abortion had been agreed the counsellor booked the patient a bed, told her how to reach the surgeon and, if she was hard up, provided a loan or a grant so she could pay. In the early days willing surgeons and nursing home beds were in short supply. It often took many phone calls to find a suitable place.

When I joined the Management Committee of PAS, the number of patients was growing rapidly. It was clear we needed something more certain than ad hoc arrangements with a dozen or so sympathetic private practitioners. Some of these gentlemen and their clinics had received unfavourable coverage in the press. In fact, for most of the 1970s the popular press ran scare stories inspired by the religious opponents of abortion, such as the Society for the Protection of Unborn Children (SPUC); stories about safety, about psychological damage to the woman's health, about termination causing sterility, about over-charging, about foetuses discarded into waste baskets or thrown into furnaces while still crying. All of these stories except with regard to high prices were distorted or exaggerated.

At PAS we realised we had to safeguard our own reputation by establishing an arrangement with a clinic where the facilities and the staff were beyond reproach and where the charges would be reasonable. Soon after I joined the committee two young businessmen with interests in nursing homes made us an offer we could not refuse. Trevor Heathcote and Michael Reynolds had owned a nursing home in Birmingham where they had collaborated with a notable abortion pioneer, Martin Cole. They now offered to put a newly acquired nursing home (Fairfield) in Buckhurst Hill, East London, at our disposal. We could send all our patients there to have their terminations carried out at an agreed fixed price. We secured a three to two majority on the board of directors, chose the medical director and participated in the appointment of the matron. Moreover, the profits from the enterprise were to be evenly split so that we would be able to build up our funds to help poor women.

The day-to-day running of the nursing home (staff, supplies, transport, accounts) were all handled by Michael Reynolds, who was an accountant by training. Our chief safeguard was that the PAS treasurer, Alan Golding, a practising accountant, was also a member of the Fairfield board. He ensured that the accounts were properly compiled and that we received our share of the profits. After some discussion and an inspection of the nursing home we accepted this arrangement, which ran pretty smoothly for more than eight years. The initial distrust of Heathcote and Reynolds simply because they were entrepreneurs turned out to be quite unjustified. I was one of the three unpaid PAS directors of Fairfield throughout this period.

The deal meant that we had the advantages of strategic control without the risks and burdens of ownership. In any case, at that time we could not raise the capital to purchase a London nursing home. The rebate on each patient meant that we had a revolving fund with which to help women who could not pay the standard fee.

Of course the arrangement also gave the owners assured bed occupancy, a good profit and the protection of our ethical practice and charitable status. We had critics from within PAS and from others in the non-profit abortion sector but very little from elsewhere. Although some civil servants at the Department of Health periodically gave PAS a hard time for the most extraordinary non-medical reasons, they did not harass Fairfield. In part, this may have been because our first medical director was Dorothea Kerslake, a retired consultant gynaecologist from Newcastle. She had practised a liberal abortion policy in her NHS hospital for years prior to the 1967 Act and was fireproof against administrative criticism. Her medical record was very good and her standing with her peers at the Royal College of Obstetricians and Gynaecologists was excellent.

While Fairfield was being remodelled for our use (it was already a licensed nursing home) I proposed that we should rename it after the first chairman of the Abortion Law Reform Association (ALRA). Janet Chance had founded ALRA in 1935 with two other stalwart, fearless women, Stella Browne and Alice Jenkins. Mrs Chance was a good-looking, outspoken woman with great personal magnetism and a capacity for inspiring devotion from her associates. She also had advanced views about sex expressed in a rather anguished manner in her book *The Cost of English Morals*, published in 1931. She had claimed that conventional English morality led to dire results, denounced the 'spinster-minded of both sexes' and called on all women to demand the same rights of sexual enjoyment that men had always taken for granted. She had also founded a pioneer advisory organisation named the Sex Education Centre where she discovered a high incidence of attempted abortion among the clients, the key fact that led her to the need for abortion law reform. To me she seemed the perfect exemplar for our cause and a suitable name for our nursing home.

I canvassed this idea at a PAS management committee meeting where it received general approval but then at the next meeting there were second thoughts. Faint hearts thought we might be leading with our chin, not that Mrs Chance was a notorious name to conjure with. During the war she had broadcast a series of folksy talks for the BBC called *Talking it Over With Ma Rattigan*. It's true that in her later life she had had serious mental problems, finally committing suicide in 1953. But no one on our committee knew that. Nevertheless, some of my colleagues said we didn't want to go around telling people that our clinic was in the abortion business. Alan Golding ridiculed my proposition because 'Chance' was a dodgy name. 'There will be jokes about it,' he said. 'Take a chance and end up at the Chancy nursing home,' cracked Elizabeth Mitchell. I tried to shame my critics by saying they had no sense of history, no feeling that we ought to honour one of our most distinguished pioneers. A decision had to be taken so I was outmanoeuvred and outvoted. It was about the only time that I disagreed with Alan Golding with whom I worked in great harmony for the next nine years.

In its first decade the course of PAS was influenced most by Peter Diggory, Malcolm Potts, Alan Golding and Peter Huntingford. Diggory was a young, bearded, ebullient consultant gynaecologist who had pursued a permissive abortion practice prior to the change in the law in 1967. In the early years he kept telling us that abortion as then practised was a fairly simple and safe procedure and that new techniques were being developed which would improve it still further. He could talk enthusiastically about serious medical matters with a light touch and with a smile on his face. His 'can do' attitude put new energy into our efforts.

Unlike some prominent gynaecologists who opposed reform and contended it was a difficult operation, which should be restricted to consultants, Diggory spoke from the experience of over a thousand safe operations. At the time it looked as if the majority of the Royal College of Obstetricians and Gynaecologists was opposed to reforming the law. By publishing his results and taking an active part in the political struggle Diggory risked his reputation with his senior colleagues. During the difficult passage of the Reform Act through Parliament Diggory had been medical adviser to the bill's sponsor, David Steel MP.

Malcolm Potts was a very bright young doctor who had recently completed his medical education in Cambridge. Taking advice from Peter Diggory, he became the Medical Secretary of the International Planned Parenthood

186

Federation (IPPF), thereby acquiring an interest in abortion because at that time it was one of the most common methods of birth control worldwide. He toured the member organisations of the IPPF, urging them to adopt the latest techniques and bringing back first-hand reports of good innovative practice, which he brought to our attention. He was not a gynaecologist and never did abortions himself but his medical qualifications allowed him to make a proper assessment of technique and safety. In his day job he was a radical medical administrator while for us at PAS he was a constant source of new ideas. For a couple of years in the 1970s he was also our chairman.

The first chairman of PAS was Alan Golding who was a partner in a medium-size accountancy firm. Golding had been treasurer of the Abortion Law Reform Association in the 1960s. Following the example of Dr Martin Cole who set up the Birmingham Pregnancy Advisory Service, Alan Golding was one of the prime movers in the establishment of the Pregnancy Advisory Service in London in 1968. In contrast to Diggory and Potts he had a deadpan manner which often brought management committee meetings back to earth and practical policy. As one might expect he had a nimble way with figures, producing instant lucid answers to frequent questions about the cost and the price of our services. He was one of the sheet anchors of the organisation throughout the 1970s who bestrode the Advisory Service and the Fairfield Nursing Home, keeping them both in step and on course.

Professor Peter Huntingford was a consultant gynaecologist who at one time had been outspoken against reform but later changed to the opposite tack. In part he was influenced by David Paintin, a junior colleague at St Mary's Hospital who was a firm supporter of a woman's right to choose. Huntingford had been the youngest professor at St Mary's in his speciality – perinatal medicine – when appointed in 1965. By the time he joined the PAS management committee in the mid-1970s he had already set up a Day Care Abortion service in Tower Hamlets. Doctors who operated inside the NHS always had more freedom to experiment with new ideas and provide new services because their activities were not tainted with a suspicion of private profit. Like Diggory he could urge the Department of Health to accept new practice at PAS because he could show that it worked.

Once Huntingford had embraced the idea that abortion should be allowed in law he became a formidable advocate who spoke with the authority of direct operational experience. He became the most quoted advocate of abortion from among the senior ranks of the medical profession ready to occupy exposed positions. In 1980, for example, he asserted in a television programme that many women were only being granted an abortion on the condition they had sterilisation at the same time. 'Sterilisation simultaneous with abortion should be banned,' he declared. Although many feminists cheered such remarks some of us in the pro-abortion camp thought they were sometimes too provocative or too absolute.

Despite such unsubtle or perhaps rash assertions Huntingford had none of the natural self-confidence of Diggory or Potts and often agonised before making a decision. I was particularly struck by his deep-set eyes surrounded by dark bags, which made him look as if every word was uttered more in sorrow than in anger. We invited Huntingford to be our chairman in 1976, in succession to Malcolm Potts. In this role Huntingford robustly defended PAS practice against the petty and sometimes ignorant demands of the Department of Health and Social Security. He had the stature, experience and conviction necessary to protect our position against an opportunist press and a host of critics whose religious ideology made them impervious both to the facts and to reasoned argument.

Although we were dealing with a very emotional subject our committee and our staff maintained a cool, detached approach. Our service helped thousands of women every year to cope with a personal crisis and almost every week it brought on tears or some other emotional response from one or two of our patients during the course of consultation. There were also a few dramatic episodes at management level, the most notable being the attempted amalgamation with the British Pregnancy Advisory Service (BPAS) in 1972 and the resignation of a newly appointed Director in 1977.

The Attempted Amalgamation 1972–73

By the summer of 1972 PAS was handling about 12,500 patients a year, most of whom had their abortions at the Fairfield Nursing Home with which we had a contract which was mutually satisfactory. We were, however, always trying to improve our service, reduce its cost to the patient and look ahead. Dealing with Fairfield was dabbling with private medicine, which most of our management committee disapproved of in principle. We hoped that eventually the National Health Service would cope with the demand so that any woman, anywhere in the country, could get a free abortion within the law. Our medical advisers, Peter Diggory and Malcolm Potts, were also pressing the Ministry officials about moving to simpler methods than the conventional dilatation and curettage, methods that would be safer, quicker and cheaper. Above all, patients would not need to stay overnight in the nursing home which was an important point for any woman wishing to be discreet.

Peter Diggory had been pioneering these methods in his own hospital and had published a medical research paper on the first thousand cases, showing that for early cases these methods were an improvement. Similar methods had also been pioneered in America where cost was an even bigger factor in the abortion equation. Malcolm Potts introduced us to a laid-back Californian psychologist named Harvey Karman who had invented a simple piece of equipment known as the Karman Cannula. This was an opaque plastic tube about a quarter inch in diameter with a slightly sharp but soft probe, which could be pushed into the uterus, if necessary without anaesthetic. His medical colleagues used the cannula, sometimes in an ordinary doctor's office, to remove the contents of the uterus by suction, a technique known as vacuum aspiration and actually invented in Eastern Europe.

It was in an atmosphere of modest success plus hopeful signs of radical change, both technical and administrative, that we looked over our shoulder at the other abortion charity centred on Birmingham. The British Pregnancy Advisory Service had also started in 1968 but had grown much faster, seemingly with much greater financial success. They had been able to buy four properties suitable for nursing homes, two of which were coming into operation. Our management committee thought that we would be able to provide a better and cheaper service if we combined with BPAS. In particular we felt we could virtually eliminate the expensive private abortions still provided by individual surgeons in private practice.

The BPAS chairman was Francois Lafitte, Professor of Social Administration at Birmingham University. He was the stepson of Havelock Ellis, a pioneer of birth control and of scientific research on human sexual practice. Lafitte had been a *Times* leader writer during the war and had worked among the movers and shakers of post-war Britain. He had a high regard for his own opinion and totally dominated his colleagues on the trust which nominally controlled BPAS. In practice he took all the strategic decisions, closely assisted by the competent manager of the organisation's counselling service, Nan Smith.

From the very first exchange with our chairman at the time, Ruth Pomeranz, Lafitte was very pushy, pressing us to change our name to London PAS.[4] He felt upstaged by our name, and insisted on calling us LPAS both in speech and in the minutes. He had changed their original name from Birmingham Pregnancy Advisory Service to British Pregnancy Advisory Service to give it wider appeal. His early proposal, which for a time we favoured, was aimed at having one charity abortion service for the whole country. The tentative plan was very prescriptive and centralised – a national, non-profit, private abortion service. Like many an entrepreneur, Lafitte did not like competition.

One reason for Birmingham's interest in amalgamation or at least close cooperation was that it had over-expanded its facilities and needed us to take up the slack, particularly at its new clinic in Brighton, known as Wistons. At the time BPAS was ferrying patients 200 miles from the Midlands to Brighton by minibus, which we thought bad practice, especially as many of the patients had already come from Ireland. They were also anxious to stop our business partners, Trevor Heathcote and Michael Reynolds, expanding to other parts of the country.

There followed four 'summit meetings' between the two committees, two in Birmingham and two in London at which Lafitte tried to impress us with the strength of his organisation, stop us expanding and absorb us into his unified abortion referral service. He was very well organised with briefs and accounts and snowed us under with an avalanche of paper. 'Can we agree...', said his Background Note prior to the first summit in December 1972, '... neither organisation will undertake fresh developments ... without prior consultation? Can we agree to cooperate on price with the aim of progressively cutting the cost to patients, including foreign women?' He also wanted us to cut payments to doctors, nurses, counsellors and privately owned clinics. 'Can we agree on "Total domination of the private abortion sector?"'[5]

Francois Lafitte, not unexpectedly, was chairman of the first summit held in our subsidiary office in Fitzroy Square. Besides pressing us to commit ourselves to the above proposals he also claimed that before the end of the following year BPAS would have six nursing homes with a capacity of 60 to 70,000 a year. By late 1974, he claimed the cost of an abortion would be down to £35 from £55. They had already offered us ten beds a day at Wistons in Brighton and said grandly they would take all our patients from October 1973. We would be required to charge only £5 for the preliminary consultations in London while they took £46 for the operation.[6] Our staff had already objected to their insistence that women would have to spend two nights in their nursing home while the management committee saw that the £5 fee would mean we would make no profit at all and therefore have no money to top up our loans and grants for indigent women. We agreed only to send those patients to Wistons who could not be accommodated at Fairfield and after some discussion they climbed down on fees and on the two nights requirement.

At this and every subsequent summit Lafitte tried to convince us to wriggle out of our contract with Fairfield or at least to abandon our hope of either buying or renting Fairfield in order to run it entirely to our design. In fact we had agreed a new seven-year contract with Fairfield months before the first contact with BPAS. The asking price for Fairfield (£250,000) was, he asserted, too high as they had just acquired a property at Fawkham in Kent, which he said would be more convenient for patients than Fairfield, which was in Buckhurst Hill.[7] We never saw Fawkham but like most of his claims and most of his projected figures this one was overblown. We dismissed his idea that it would be more convenient for our patients and staff as a remark made by someone who knew little about travel in the London area. Buckhurst Hill was on the Underground while Fawkham was 25 miles by train from Victoria station.

Lafitte also produced their Trust Deed and revealed that the members only met four times a year. Between times it was run by the chairman and the staff director: indeed none of the other members of the trust who came to various summits made any impact on us whatsoever. This was very much a one-man band. He offered us two places out of ten on their Trust, leaving all their current members in place.[8] It was clear he intended a takeover rather than an amalgamation.

The minutes for these summits were prepared by one chairman and then sent to the other chairman for amendment and approval. In a letter to our chairman, Leah Harvey, after the first summit, Lafitte wrote: 'There was one passage you wanted deleted I have left in. It reported something which I said and I remember saying it; so I saw no reason to take it out.'[9] For me that encapsulated his whole attitude. Several times we found his minutes claimed we had agreed certain of his proposals when in fact we had done no such thing.

From then on the summits essentially made no progress. We went over the same ground several times. While he criticised our use of Fairfield we criticised Fawkham which we said was particularly unsuited to foreign women who needed a nursing home in London. At one point Lafitte boasted that they had 'bought bargains' rather than property in the right place. He wanted us to commit ourselves to use Fawkham before we had seen it or before it was even in operation.[10] He was always emphasising cost while we felt convenience and quality of service were equally important.

In February 1973 Lafitte, forever bombarding us with paper, produced a statement of the aims of BPAS entitled 'The Eight Articles', which he hoped we would subscribe to. Malcolm Potts disparagingly described them at the second summit as 'statements of religion'. Among other things they talked about 'deliberate frugality' with regards to cost, 'long-term self-liquidation' when the Health Service could cope and a 'rigid attitude to the high rewards demanded by doctors and other staff.[11]

BPAS had more resources than us and more staff available to produce the thoughts of Chairman Lafitte. Certainly we were inefficient in fulfilling our commitments to produce comparable documents, such as our accounts, but in part we also dragged our feet because we did not like the atmosphere of these summits. Three months after the fourth such meeting Lafitte wrote a long and distinctly tetchy letter to Malcolm Potts, now our chairman, which finished off any further progress. It began with 'Dear Potts,' which set the tone. He accused Malcolm of being 'exceptionally gullible' over a plan by a private doctor to market pregnancy-testing kits at £3 a time. 'BPAS already did pregnancy testing without charge,' he wrote. Malcolm had commended this proposal by an enterprising GP because he felt providing such a service was desirable regardless of who actually did it. 'There will be no more joint meetings,' thundered Lafitte, 'until we know what the purpose is to be and have been persuaded that our time will not be wasted.'[12]

That was the end of the negotiations to amalgamate, though we did send a small number of patients to Wistons in Brighton who could not be accommodated at Fairfield until our business partners opened their second nursing home in London called Leigham which mopped up most of our surplus. The whole episode taught me how difficult is the process of negotiation, something I bore in mind when, as the BBC's UN correspondent, I often reported on the lack of progress in various international negotiations involving many parties and much more important issues. More than 20 years later, long after Lafitte had left the chair and all our original members had left our management committee, PAS did join forces with the British Pregnancy Advisory Service.

The Resignation of the Director

The most bizarre episode in the early history of PAS was the resignation of a newly appointed director ten days after she took up her post. On her first day in the office she demanded that the Board dismiss her deputy and promptly left never to return. To my surprise the majority of the Board supported her action and insisted on compensating her with a handsome sum. Then with a dramatic flourish, punctuated with a sudden outburst of expletives, this majority of middle-class, responsible citizens marched out in solidarity with the director, leaving the organisation in the hands of the three-member minority. It was an intriguing example of how a voluntary organisation can fall apart despite good intentions, liberal instincts and the professional caution of its activists.

Myra Gainsly, our second director, retired in April 1977 after five years of rapid growth and progress. After advertising the post, weeding the applications and interviewing a shortlist in a systematic manner the management committee (as it was still called) appointed a late but well-known applicant, Dilys Cossey. Seeing that the new director would not be able to overlap with her predecessor, the management committee, at the instigation of Madeleine Simms, created a new post of deputy director to cover the hiatus and run day-to-day operations. They appointed a reliable and hard-working member of staff, Doreen Lloyd.

Dilys Cossey was 41, married without children but with two very dependent elderly parents. She had been Secretary of the Abortion Law Reform Association in the run-up to the Reform Act of 1967 and then General Secretary of the Birth Control Campaign. She had also been secretary of one of the new Community Health Councils in South London. I was not at the selection committee but thought on the basis of her curriculum vitae that she would be suitable.

About a month before she was due to start, Dilys Cossey went into the office in Margaret Street near Oxford Circus to prepare herself for taking over. She decided that she would occupy the same small office used by her predecessor on the fourth floor and she asked Doreen Lloyd to move up from the basement to an adjoining office so that 'we can work closely together, as Director and Deputy Director must'.[13]

Over the next two or three weeks Ms Lloyd, who was older and more experienced than her new boss, resisted this move. She explained that she would share a desk in the adjoining Admin office but would retain her main desk in the basement where she could talk to staff privately when she exercised her function as the Personnel Officer. She also pointed out that she would have to share the office adjoining the Director's because of a shortage of space and that it contained a couch for those patients who fainted during the initial consultation, something that happened quite often, and was therefore unsuitable as her only office. In any case, she said, the building was quite small and she could easily come to the Director's office as necessary.

Without waiting to see if such an arrangement could work to her satisfaction, as it had worked in the past, Ms Cossey kept insisting on her point of view, thus generating a full-blown row before she even took up her post. On the 8 August 1977 when she arrived on her first day she came equipped with a letter to Doreen Lloyd in the form of an ultimatum: move your office next to mine or face dismissal by the Board. 'I am therefore giving you formal warning that you have 24 hours in which to establish your office in the next room to mine... If you have not made these arrangements by 9.30 a.m. tomorrow, I shall have no choice but to refer the matter to the Board.'[14] Thereupon she walked down through the office handing out copies of her ultimatum to the staff she had never met, even going on to our other office in Fitzroy Square. She had left PAS never to return.

Responding by letter, Doreen Lloyd tried to reason with her, pointing out that Ms Cossey's demand meant that three other members of staff would also have to move. She also questioned whether the close contact demanded by Ms Cossey was actually necessary because of their different roles. When appointing the new Director the Board had made it clear that her primary function was to find a new building which ideally would have space for our entire operation – consulting rooms for patients, doctors and counsellors, and a medical unit, which would be able to handle some 300 abortions a week. Meanwhile the function of the Deputy Director would be to keep the existing system functioning smoothly until the transition to a new building and a new system could take place.

Doreen Lloyd reminded her that the Board no longer wanted to be involved in the internal issues which should be sorted out by the staff themselves while the Board would stick solely to policy issues. She also wrong-footed Ms Cossey by pointing out that under the Procedural Agreement only recently agreed with the trade union 'the next step in the disputes procedure is a meeting between you, me and the Shop Steward'.[15]

The day after she left, Dilys Cossey followed through on her threat: 'I note that you still refuse to do as I ask on office arrangements for yourself, and I am therefore putting the matter before the Board. I am recommending that you should be dismissed on the grounds of (1) insubordination and (2) general evidence of a refusal to work with me as Director in a sensible and cooperative manner... I have also told the Board that I shall not attend the office until this matter is resolved.'[16]

At the same time Dilys Cossey fired off a four-page memorandum to each Board member justifying her actions. To me it was plain she wished to have her own way by dictat, throwing her weight around even before she had taken up the post. She complained that 'there are no sanctions I can apply when she refuses to do what I ask, because the contract of employment is with the Board'; consequently she was 'recommending her dismissal'. Most disturbing of all, she recognised the possibility of a protest strike by the staff but dismissed it as 'a small price to pay to resolve a major internal problem ... if the staff were irresponsible enough to go on unofficial strike, it would be no bad thing to bring this out into the open. If dismissed Doreen Lloyd would possibly take the matter to an industrial tribunal, but she would almost certainly lose'.[17]

This memorandum showed she was quite unsuitable to be our Director. She had no idea how to manage people except by 'sanctions', no understanding of how damaging a strike could be to staff/management relations, no appreciation that while we were closed many of our patients would be unable to find alternative help and, most crass of all, no realisation that PAS could lose a case before an industrial tribunal which might cost us thousands of pounds. To contemplate such an outcome, even with a much stronger case, would have been a reckless decision for a charity that had few reserves.

Once she had left, Dilys Cossey tried to contact Board members by phone only to find most of them on holiday, including myself. However, a message got through to me in my capacity as Vice-Chairman, before the Chairman had been able to respond. When she explained her complaint to me and demanded we dismiss Doreen Lloyd I declined to do so. I had not seen her memorandum and I could not understand why she thought office arrangements so important. I advised her to return to the job and make the best of things until the return of the Board.

I also advised Doreen Lloyd to carry on as usual. It seemed highly unlikely that Ms Lloyd was being unreasonable or doing anything contrary to the best interests of the organisation. Her manner was well suited to dealing with patients and she had a five-year record of solid achievement at PAS. To dismiss her summarily would have been a gross injustice and a disservice to the organisation. In addition, it would have caused uproar among the staff and possibly a strike. In contrast, Dilys Cossey was an unknown quantity who clearly had not made a good start.

A day or two later the Chairman was able to phone Dilys Cossey and declined to call an emergency meeting of the Board to discuss her case as some members were still on holiday. Meanwhile Dilys Cossey had received support from one or two Board members who were close friends. Nevertheless, eleven days after her initial appearance in the office and before the issue had been tested at the Board she lost confidence in her position and resigned with a thousand word 'first and final report'.

It was an absurd document, which purported to tell us how we should run an organisation already seven years old. Besides going over the familiar ground, she made pointed attacks on both the Chairman and myself for not suspending Doreen Lloyd 'in order to make it possible for me to start work at PAS' and for 'not arranging a Board meeting'. On her last page she was reduced to whining: 'I have suffered greatly from these events.' She told a sob story about how in order to take up the job at PAS she had had to reorganise her domestic arrangements for her sick mother and her housebound father and had persuaded her husband to change his usual routine. She said she had spent 'the best part of £200 on this, taken from very meagre savings and we now have additional outgoings that cannot be met from my husband's income'. She also claimed she had withdrawn her application for another job and had lost three months in which she could have been looking for a job: 'some sort of compensation from PAS would not be out of place'.[18]

The crunch came at the Board meeting on 19th September 1977 in Alan Golding's accountancy office in Great Portland Street 200 yards from the PAS office. Fearing that he had lost the confidence of some members of the Board, Peter Huntingford asked the members a week before the meeting if he should stand aside from the chair while we discussed this issue, saying that if he were defeated he would resign. He also sent a four-page memorandum to the Board in which he rejected all Dilys Cossey's arguments. His key phrase was: 'the Director was not appointed to dictate to the Board or its Chairman.'[19] I urged him strongly to take the chair, saying that Cossey clearly hadn't the temperament or expertise for the job: 'Had the accommodation problem been solved I am certain she would have touched off other crises not only with the staff but with outside bodies such as the Department of Health. As a Board we made a bad mistake in appointing her and we are lucky to have escaped with only a few bruises.'[20]

In the event, we had a full house of seven directors with Huntingford in the chair. Four of the members (Leah Harvey, Elizabeth Mitchell, Malcolm Potts and Madeleine Simms) quickly made it clear they supported Dilys Cossey and deplored the Chairman's action in not backing her up. By that time, however, even they realised it was too late to reinstate her. She had sent a final letter of self-justification and complaint that the Board had not supported her against an insubordinate deputy.

The Chairman had already authorised payment of her salary until the end of August but that was not enough for her four supporters. The central wrangle at this meeting was therefore over her claim for compensation. Someone proposed an *ex gratia* payment free of tax of £1,200, thus multiplying her claim by six. Peter Huntingford, Alan Golding and myself all saw her resignation as a self-inflicted injury, which merited no payment beyond that required in the employment contract (which she had not kept because she did not give us notice of resignation). Certainly I was even more annoyed by their proposal than by her claim. At the time it would have paid for 200 counselling sessions and it proved to be very galling to the staff who were on much lower pay scales. We were outvoted four to three but all three of us insisted that our dissent be recorded in the minutes.[21]

Despite a heated discussion, the Board remained sufficiently cool to confirm Doreen Lloyd as Acting Director for the time being and to resolve to appoint a new director in due course. I was, however, mistaken in my prediction that we would suffer only a few bruises. At the close, Leah Harvey, one of the longest serving members, resigned expressing the view (not recorded in the official minutes) that PAS should be wound up and the assets handed to BPAS.[22] Mitchell, Simms and Potts also said they would resign as soon as a replacement could be found who could give us a quorum.

As she left, Elizabeth Mitchell (Lady Elizabeth Mitchell no less) swept out of the room letting forth a torrent of vulgar abuse directed at the three men who formed the minority. Her attitude if not her words were endorsed by Harvey and Simms, which left me wide-eyed and speechless. During the seven previous years these three women had not uttered a vulgar word nor even raised their voices. Now it seemed to me they resented our action, our votes, our views and our sex. The whole episode would have made the basis for a good 'Aga saga' about the liberal professional classes.

Voluntary organisations are often unstable and not infrequently break apart from internal dissension. A comparable event occurred in the National Gypsy Education Council (NGEC) in 1973. The chairman,

Lady Bridget Plowden, also vice-chairman of the BBC and a quintessential member of the great and the good, was reduced to tears while chairing her own AGM. ' I think you are all perfectly beastly,' she said, 'I've had enough of this fucking committee.' After which the meeting broke up in pandemonium. A year later just before the next AGM Lady Plowden and her group on the NGEC forced through a motion freezing all the assets in the hands of the trustees before resigning.[23]

Fortunately the resignation of the PAS Director and four of the Board members proved to be no more than a hiccup in its history. None of the staff supported Dilys Cossey: indeed many of them had not even met her because she came and went on the same day. The Admin Team was already overseeing all the day-to-day procedures and they strongly supported their chairman, Doreen Lloyd. A new member, Barbara Chandler, was appointed to the Board six weeks later by which time Elizabeth Mitchell and Madeleine Simms had formally resigned while Malcolm Potts resigned soon after. The organisation moved smoothly on to the real business in hand such as submitting a report to the Department of Health on our first year of day care abortions and renewing the search for new premises in which we could install our own medical staff and operating theatre. In the three months after the convulsion on the Board, PAS helped more patients than in the equivalent period the year before.

One general lesson that strikes me now is how difficult it is to make a managerial appointment. Dilys Cossey was well informed about abortion and had experience working in related organisations but it turned out that she lacked basic managerial and political skill, could not see the wood for the trees and did not know she had made a silly decision even as she resigned from such a good post. She cut off the branch on which she was standing and then demanded PAS pay for the saw.

Our colleagues on the Board were taken in by her self-serving letter. They paid her a large sum in compensation for falling on her sword, a sum that directly reduced PAS's ability to help poorer women with grants or loans. I felt that they also gave away some of the charity's assets just to soothe an old friend.[24]

I left the PAS Board at the end of 1979 when I was appointed BBC United Nations Correspondent in New York. It proved to be the end of my career as an activist in the cause. When I returned to London five years later I was always too busy as a freelance broadcaster to devote any time to voluntary work, although I continued to be a member of the Reform Association.

In retrospect I have wondered whether my association with such a radical and controversial movement came at a price? In all my job interviews in this period and beyond I cited my articles and book on the subject and stated that I was an unpaid member of this abortion charity. No one ever commented on this part of my c.v. during a job interview even to ask if its demands interfered with my job as a radio producer and editor. On one curious occasion a member of the Board of Management, rang me at home to ask how he could get an abortion for his au pair. I referred him to PAS and quite properly never heard the outcome. I regret to say that this helpful advice was not reciprocated when I could have done with his support some years later.

Ordeal by Media

The most threatening moment came in August 1971 when Peter Birkett wrote an article about PAS for the *Sunday Telegraph*.[25] At that time I was notionally in charge of relations with the press, though we had made no attempt to engage their interest. Birkett whom I had met in Northern Ireland had been tipped off by Martin Mears, an anti-abortion solicitor in Lowestoft who was secretary of a small organisation called LIFE – Save the Unborn Child. Mears had previously sent a letter to the BBC complaining that I was acting for PAS yet was a BBC employee, implying that I worked for PAS from Broadcasting House. He demanded that I be sacked.

The BBC's Solicitor, Mr Jennings, informed me confidentially about this letter, remarking that it might well be defamatory. After I had explained my unpaid position at PAS he agreed that I could use my own time to advance any legal cause and that the BBC would not seek to censure or to stop me. Soon afterwards Birkett's article appeared stretching over three columns in the middle of the front page. (A threat of a strike at the BBC only made page 3.) Birkett's report stated correctly that he had phoned me at the BBC. I had explained to him what service we provided and how it was all approved and licensed by the Department of Health but he did not report that. I did not say or imply that I could get anyone an abortion or that patients rang me at the BBC in order to fix an appointment. It was so much routine information that I thought nothing more about the interview.

Quite by chance the day before publication we left as a family for a camping and climbing holiday in Norway. It proved to be one of the most fortunate exits I ever made and one I recommend to those who feel 'hounded by the press'. While we climbed the highest mountain in

Norway in deep snow, crossed glaciers and walked along Peer Gynt's ride I never gave PAS a thought.

While I was away, Birkett's piece provoked a brief frenzy in the national newspapers. It was yet another way to attack two of their favourite Aunt Sallys – the BBC and those who provided abortions. The next day the *Daily Mirror* wrote a fictitious story, headlined at the top of page 7, 'Want an Abortion – Ring the BBC'. It alleged that my BBC phone number had been given to women asking about abortion (which was false) and reported Mears' demand that the BBC dismiss me. Its last paragraph speculated unfavourably about the outcome: 'It seems almost certain he will be told he must dissociate himself from the service and the clinic and that he must not use a BBC phone for anything other than BBC business.'[26]

Over the next week most of the national papers picked up the story. 'BBC to investigate charges of bias in favour of abortion' said a *Daily Mail* headline. It said 'three leading anti-abortion organisations' had complained to the Chairman and Director General of the BBC, Lord Hill and Sir Charles Curran, and would write to the Prime Minister, Edward Heath, and the leader of the Opposition, Harold Wilson, asking them to back a watchdog committee for radio and television.[27] One of those organisations was named as 'Sanctity of Unborn Life' or SOUL for short. It turned out to be an evangelical Protestant anti-abortion group which had only just been launched. It had already attacked the Secretary of State for Health, Sir Keith Joseph, for 'selling out to the pro-abortion lobby and the medical media' and criticised his Chief Medical Officer, Sir George Godber, for commending Newcastle upon Tyne for 'having (in 1969) the highest rate of Health Service abortions in the country'.[28] Later it emerged that my phone number at the BBC had been given to both LIFE and SOUL by Phyllis Bowman of the Society for the Protection of Unborn Children. Our opponents – with confusingly similar names – were clearly networking hard.

The press scrum also besieged our house in Dulwich in order to embroider their story still further. Finding us away, they knocked on our neighbour's door and for some days would not believe her when she said she had no idea where I was nor knew anything about my work for a non-profit abortion referral agency. By Wednesday, the BBC's Director General, Charles Curran, made a statement to the press roundly defending my interest and my conduct at the BBC. According to a terse report by the *Daily Mirror* entitled 'BBC Producer Cleared' Curran 'ruled that Mr Hindell's activities did not affect his programmes'.[29] The *Daily*

Telegraph, no friend of abortion, quoted Curran at greater length. In a letter to LIFE he wrote that 'Keith Hindell would not be prevented from taking calls concerning the clinic's work' but that the BBC 'expects staff to use office phones sparingly'. The article went on to report 'Mr Curran says he's satisfied Mr Hindell's private activity has not in any way affected the programme content of *The World Tonight*.[30]

Newspapers have a poor reputation for following through to the end of a story especially when their initial article trumpeting a scandal turns out to have been a damp squib. Somewhat to my surprise therefore the next issue of the *Sunday Telegraph* neutralised almost all traces of their initial innuendoes. On 8th August a three-paragraph story on page 4 headed 'BBC Man's Dual Role' also quoted Charles Curran at some length. Curran was satisfied that Mr Hindell 'had not let his spare time activity as an official of PAS and an abortion clinic interfere with the content of his programme'.[31]

By the time I returned, blissfully ignorant of the whole affair, media interest had subsided and had moved on to other things. The BBC Solicitor had himself answered questions about me and had made the point that my activity for PAS was voluntary work in my own time, as he had agreed earlier. Certainly he handed me a file of newspaper cuttings from seven national newspapers all of which angled or mangled the story to the taste of their own editors and from some of which the uninformed bystander might have concluded that I was misusing the BBC's time and phones. 'You've probably got an action here if you seek the advice of a libel lawyer,' Jennings said cheerfully.

When I read all these cuttings I found most of them to be straightforward with the exception of the *Daily Mirror* piece which made me laugh rather than get angry. Curran had clearly defended me robustly. *The Guardian*, the *Daily Mail*, the *Daily Telegraph* and the *Catholic Herald* all quoted his statement in some form or another, with minor errors but without distortion.

Several of my colleagues rang me to sympathise with me over my nasty experience, but as I had been in Norway the missiles had all failed to hit the target. A lawyer with whom I often travelled to work remarked upon the case but immediately said, 'Don't for heaven's sake ask me to try litigation.' I followed his advice. Generally speaking journalists should not sue each other because we all make mistakes and one man's mild observation or reasonable surmise can easily be another's outrage. The BBC it seems saw off Martin Mears because he never bothered me again.

On returning to Broadcasting House, however, I did feel a slight touch of the mistral. A studio manager whom I knew well asked me in the lift how much money I was making from abortion. When I said 'None at all', she gave me a knowing look and said, 'Well if you aren't making money out of it, what's the point?' I wonder how many other people at the BBC took a similar view?

In this memoir I have highlighted the people with whom I was closely associated and the events which I saw first-hand. I must, however, set my remarks in the context of the organisation as a whole. By the end of 1979 PAS was a large team embracing surgeons, general practitioners, nurses, counsellors, receptionists and paramedics who supervised such things as pregnancy tests, and of course administrators. In all about a hundred people played a part on a full-time or regular part-time basis. We had two offices in central London (one exclusively for foreign women) and our own nursing home in Richmond. By the middle of the 1970s the staff had taken over the running of the organisation through an elected Administrative Team. The Management Committee of volunteer activists who had brought PAS into existence had been transformed into the Board of Directors who oversaw broad strategy and had ultimate legal responsibility.

The hard work and dedication of all these people is vividly chronicled in a slim volume entitled *Out of the Backstreets* compiled by our information officer, Helene Graham, which was published in 1989 by PAS to mark 21 years of the organisation. In the offices, consulting rooms, the nursing homes and the operating theatres the watchword was always 'the best interests of the patient' and of women in general. The staff worked hard to meet individual needs, to respond with compassion and efficiency to the desperation felt by so many of the patients, and to learn the lessons when appointments went wrong or where the service delivered fell short of our standards. Once the Admin Team got into its stride there was continuous feedback and a constant search for improvement and innovation. They were dealing with individuals yet improving the system for all patients.

While all this professional work was being carried out in Margaret Street, Fitzroy Square, the Fairfield Nursing Home and the Leigham Nursing Home in Streatham there was constant sniping by the critics, and frequent sniping by the media, not so much against PAS in particular as against legal abortion services in general. Certain officials at the DHSS, which was unable to provide a universal abortion service in the same way that they provided universal maternity services, seemed inclined to obstruct our progress and foot-fault some of our most routine affairs. On our flank, undoubtedly influenced by the press and the anti-abortion lobby, even London Underground and the advertising industry were 'agin us'.

When we first started to advertise our service in the mid-1970s London Underground rejected our adverts because we used the word 'abortion' – a medical operation undergone legally by over a hundred thousand women a year! This was circumvented in time by variations on that advert mentioned earlier – 'If you are Happy you are Pregnant, Fine. If Not Consult PAS'. The Post Office did not even permit us to use this slogan in their Yellow Pages until August 1978, ten years after the Reform Act. London Underground was only slightly ahead of this attitude when it conceded the word 'abortion' in our adverts in May of the same year. In view of the prevailing low standard of taste in the advertising industry and the many dubious products and services they publicised, a conspiracy theorist might wonder if there were not secret cells of 'Opus Dei' or some other reactionary sect located as gatekeepers in London Transport and the Post Office.

At the end of 1979 PAS produced a series of papers in response to John Corrie's private member's anti-abortion bill which was going through Parliament. Among other things the bill proposed that referral agencies, such as ourselves, should not be allowed to be linked to nursing homes where the abortions were carried out. If passed it would have sent us back to 1970 before we agreed a contract with Fairfield and would have meant we would have had to dispose of our new Rosslyn Nursing Home in Richmond. It posed a major threat to the charitable abortion sector which coped with a third of all demand.

In our papers we summed up our achievement in statistics. We had treated 120,000 women since the start 11 years earlier. Thirteen thousand of them had been resident abroad, mainly in Ireland, Spain and Italy. 'London – The Abortion Capital of Europe' screamed the tabloids all too often. We winced because they were often followed by nit-picking inquiries from the DHSS sleuths. In retrospect, however, we should have been proud of the description – we were providing a reliable service for much of Western Europe.

Not all of our clients had had abortions because some proved not to be pregnant while a significant number changed their minds between being approved for an operation and the appointment at the nursing home. At the same time we had disbursed some £450,000 in loans and grants to those women who could not afford the fees, some ten to twelve per cent of the total. (See an excellent paper by Helene Graham dated December 1979 and an earlier one 'Facts About PAS 27/4/79'.) Our all-in price at the end of 1979 was £90, very similar to BPAS, which had boasted about how it was going to slash prices. Because of accelerating inflation at the end of the 1970s our prices were actually cheaper in real terms than when we began our link to Fairfield in 1971.

We had also pioneered Day Care Abortion with the approval, some would say despite the officious intrusion, of the DHSS which supervised no other operation in the private sector with anything like the assiduousness that it devoted to abortion. Despite a successful, incident-free trial in the mid-1970s PAS did not get permanent approval for Day Care until January 1979.

Altogether it was a tremendous achievement, which preserved the health or the sanity of thousands of women, as well as safeguarding many existing families and marriages by warding off unwanted children. No doubt it also served sometimes as default birth control for the lazy, the feckless and the ignorant as well as conserving the figures of some young women frightened of acquiring a maternal spread. During the whole of this period we had only one casualty when a patient suffered a sickle-cell crisis. This incident was very regrettable and we took even greater care to obviate this condition thereafter but it did show in statistical terms how much safer the operation was than childbirth. It was a negative event but its very rarity proved our contention all along: abortion is a very safe operation.

Notes

[1] Keith Hindell & Madeleine Simms, 'How the Abortion Lobby Worked', *Political Quarterly*, No. 3 (July–September 1968)
[2] Keith Hindell and Madeleine Simms, *Abortion Law Reformed* (Peter Owen, 1971)
[3] Abortion Act (1967), Clause I–(1) (a)
[4] Minutes of meeting at BPAS between the Trustees & Mrs Ruth Pomeranz
[5] Francois Lafitte, Background Note (2.12.72), points 4(a), 4(b) & 4(a)1
[6] Minutes of First Summit BPAS and PAS (19.12.72)
[7] Ibid.
[8] Ibid.
[9] Francois Lafitte to Leah Harvey, Letter (1.1.73)
[10] Minutes of Second Summit (22.1.73)
[11] A note on the aims of BPAS (February 1973)
[12] Lafitte to Malcolm Potts, Letter (28.6.73)

13 Dilys Cossey (DC) to Doreen Lloyd (DL), Letter (8.8.77)
14 Ibid.
15 DL to DC, Letter (8.8.77)
16 DC to DL, Letter (9.8.77)
17 DC to PAS Board, Memorandum (9.8.77)
18 DC to Peter Huntingford (PH), Letter (19.8.77)
19 Confidential Memorandum PH to PAS, Board (13.9.77)
20 Keith Hindell to PH, Letter (14.9.77)
21 Confidential minutes of special meeting of PAS Board (19.9.77)
22 See a handwritten draft of the minutes, probably written by Elizabeth Mitchell who was Secretary until the end of that meeting
23 See a colourful account by Thomas Acton, then secretary of the National Gypsy Education Council – Thomas Acton, *New Society* (21.11.74)
24 She later became chairman of the Family Planning Association
25 *Sunday Telegraph*, 1.8.71
26 *Daily Mirror*, 2.8.71
27 *Daily Mail*, 2.8.71, p.9
28 *Catholic Herald*, 30.7.71, p.2
29 *Daily Mirror*, 5.8.71, p.13
30 *Daily Telegraph*, 5.8.71, p.3
31 *Sunday Telegraph*, 8.8.71, p.4

15

The World Tonight 1970–1979

Towards the end of the 1960s BBC Radio responded to popular and commercial pressure by expanding to four national networks, abandoning the old names for four colourless digits, namely Radios 1, 2, 3 and 4. The Home Service became the speech network, Radio 4. A couple of years later News and Current Affairs was reorganised into three 'Sequences' in which the news bulletins and the current affairs comment and discussion programmes were moulded together. 'Sequence editors' were appointed with higher salaries and larger budgets. In the run-up to this change Brian Bliss who had been the editor of *Radio Newsreel* recruited me from Documentaries as a senior producer for the Evening Sequence. In January 1970 a new team took over the *Ten O'clock Programme* from Stephen Bonarjee who was edged out sideways into a new mini empire. In April we began the two new programmes of the Evening Sequence, *Newsdesk* at 7 p.m. and *The World Tonight* at 10 p.m. Both programmes were presented by former star correspondents, *Newsdesk* by Gerald Priestland and *The World Tonight* by Douglas Stuart, both of whom had been Washington correspondents for the BBC. Little did we dream that *The World Tonight* would last for more than 40 years.

Douglas Stuart gave more thought and time to preparing his interviews for the programme than any other presenter I worked with in 17 years as a producer and editor. With the help of producers he always worked out his questions carefully in advance. Unlike some of today's presenters he did not lecture the audience or presume to tell the interviewee the answer he was expecting. Once the interview had begun he really did ask crisp questions. If we were interviewing some office holder who we thought might be evasive we would devise a sequence of questions anticipating that if he said X in answer to the first question Stuart would ask Y in response and so on. On the air, therefore, he was thorough if not totally spontaneous. Even if the interviewee did not respond fluently or cogently or honestly the listener was to some extent still informed by the questions.

However, he was sometimes difficult to work with as he lost his cool occasionally when something went wrong, such as when a line connecting us to a distant studio was delayed or gave dreadful quality. Not that he was the only one of us who became too snappy from time to time. In addition, Stuart never mastered the use of the portable tape recorder, which is the most important tool of the radio reporter outside the studio. Consequently he had to have a producer with him if we went out of the office to interview someone. One of my colleagues went with him to Germany to interview Albert Speer, Hitler's architect and later Armaments Minister, when he published his memoirs on coming out of prison. Driving on the autobahn, Stuart nearly got them both killed by taking a wrong turn and then panicking. Nevertheless, they came back with a good sustained interview for the programme, in part because he was very knowledgeable about Germany.

Gerry Priestland presented *Newsdesk* which was intended to replace the somewhat portentous *Radio Newsreel* with a brisker and more informal round-up of the news in short packages of two minutes each. I had worked with Gerry several times in Washington during my earlier visits. He was easier to work with than Stuart, although he did seem even then to be tiring of news. Later he became of his own volition the BBC's Religious Affairs correspondent but that was in the 1980s after I had left the department.

Brian Bliss, our boss until the mid-1970s, had a completely different style from Bonarjee whom in effect he replaced. He was a 'hands off' editor who rarely attended the morning conference at which the editor of the day planned the programme with two or three producers. He also made very few suggestions as to items or speaker: having chosen his team of producers, he was largely content to sit in his room and monitor output or, it should be said, gossip with a curious cast of much younger girlfriends. Apart from the early days he hardly ever stayed in the evening to see the programme broadcast, let alone guide the editor of the day. It was a refreshing change to be given almost a free hand.

At the start, three senior producers – Greville Havenhand, Tom Read and myself – edited one or other of the two programmes from start to finish each day. Most weeks we worked a four-day week. When editing the programme we worked from 11 a.m. until after the end of the programme at 10.30 p.m. and later on at 10.45 p.m. On the other two days we helped with programmes as necessary from 11 a.m. until about 6.30 p.m. It was a very agreeable timetable (very similar to that at *Ten O'clock*), which enabled me to write two books in my free time. An MP we had on the programme once related that by chance he had opened a desk in the BBC's World Service at Bush House to find the draft of someone's book. When the producer he was with nodded without surprise, the MP, who may have been a trifle anti-BBC, said, 'I bet you are all doing it.' Thereupon he opened another desk to find yet another draft book confirming all his worst suspicions about BBC overstaffing. For the record, I never wrote any of my books or articles at the BBC, only at home on my days off.

To begin with, producers on *The World Tonight* didn't broadcast personally, as with *Ten O'clock* in Bonarjee's day. After a time, however, things began to loosen up. I began to do interviews for the programme, particularly if we needed to go to the interviewee. Towards the end I also made quite a number of short features of three to six minutes in length or 'packages' as they were called in our jargon. One I remember was about the growing popularity of country cottages in the late 1970s. I went round a number of cottages in Essex with an estate agent. Some cottages were charming, some were very plain and uninteresting, all of them seemed overpriced. I tried to convey some of my lack of enthusiasm for the idea of a weekend place by remarking at the end that I would be going off to my own version, a little blue tent in the Lake District. Not so long after that Jennifer decided that she wanted something to show for all the hard work she put in as a schoolteacher. While I was climbing in the Pyrenees she found an old cottage in a superb mountain location, which we have enjoyed ever since.

Another memorable feature concerned the farmer and fell runner, Joss Naylor. In 1975 he tried to set a new record for the Bob Graham Round in the Lake District. In 1932 Graham had set a standard for endurance fell running by reaching 42 peaks over 2000 feet and covering 75 miles in 24 hours. Graham's record was impressive but by the 1970s it had already been broken several times by various runners including Naylor. Now he set out to try to improve his achievement in the course of which he would climb 37,000 feet in 24 hours. On a beautiful clear midsummer morning Naylor started on his epic run just outside Keswick, shirtless and in running shoes. I got up very early to see him off and then, with judicious use of a car, caught up with him two or three times during the course of his run to see how he was doing. He was not a stylish athlete. Uphill he hunched forward, bending much more than his companions. Downhill he splayed his feet, bounding down in an effective if ungainly manner. Mid-morning I met him on the summit of Helvellyn, one of the Lake District's noted three thousanders. The top is a long broad plateau, flat enough for one of the early aviators to land a plane. Carrying my tape recorder, I ran alongside him for about 300 yards, snatching a short interview. 'Poor man,' said Jennifer in reproof at my media pushiness, but Naylor in fact cracked a joke which came out well on the air.

Naylor was 39, lean and wiry. On each leg of the run he was accompanied night and day by two other runners who usually ran either beside him or just behind. They were not pacemakers – he was only racing against himself and the mountains. The next morning just before six Naylor reached the summit of his seventy-second peak, completing his course of 105 miles with plenty of time and energy in reserve. It was a prodigious feat, the equivalent of running four marathons end to end. Was it the 'Run of the century'? I took the material back to our local studio at Radio Carlisle and edited it into a feature, which was 'piped' down the line for *Newsdesk* later that evening. A few weeks later Naylor accepted a post at the Sellafield nuclear plant, no doubt for sound career reasons. It was a coup for the Atomic Energy Authority to employ the fittest man in Cumbria and perhaps all Britain, in part to dispel popular myths about the health hazards at such a plant.

As time went on at *The World Tonight* I did more reporting despite an undercurrent from the News Department that only their reporters assigned to our programme should be heard on the air. On one occasion this antagonism burst out while I was producing a 30-minute profile of Max Beloff, the first Vice-Chancellor of the new private university at Buckingham. We had very little time to prepare and needed to gather material in two places far apart, one of which was Buckingham. I proposed that Michael Vestey the reporter, should go to Buckingham to get the key interviews including one with Beloff. In the meantime I would zoom off in another direction to get the views of less important fry who would also feature in the package. Vestey was incensed by this proposal, thinking he should do all the interviews as well as voicing the narration. When I insisted on grounds of practicality he walked out, refusing to take part. Brian Bliss, the editor, said '*tant pis*', so I went ahead and, by cutting some corners, made the entire profile myself.

On the surface the BBC has editorial independence but that is only maintained in the face of pressure exerted from many quarters behind the scenes. Most of the time editors, producers and reporters are not aware of it because most of the pressure is applied higher up the chain. The BBC has a small staff to field complaints from the public or from outside organisations but the pressure that counts is usually applied by someone of substance, such as an MP or a business leader, to a senior boss such as a network controller, the director of the service, or to the director general. Pressure and complaints are weighed as much by who they come from as by their substance.

When Harold Wilson was marking his first ten years as Leader of the Labour Party in 1973 Brian Bliss asked me to do a profile. As normal with such a programme I talked to critics as well as supporters and to politicians from other parties besides Labour. Just before I went to interview Wilson himself some of his henchmen started to tell me whom I should interview and whom I should drop. The name that scared them was the left-wing journalist Paul Foot who had just brought out a lively and critical book on Wilson. They tried to imply that if we persisted with Foot we would not get the interview with the Leader. After a number of phone calls Wilson's staff backed down. However, in view of the tense situation, Brian Bliss came with me to the Leader of the Opposition's room in the Commons to provide support if needed. Wilson of course was more than capable of answering his critics, including Foot, so the interview went well and the profile was broadcast on *The World Tonight*. Not all BBC bosses would have supported a member of staff against a 'big beast' as Brian Bliss did.

After a few years the travel budget for the programme was increased so we could make reports overseas. As a result I made programmes with Douglas Stuart in Israel and South Africa. We went to Israel five years after the Yom Kippur War and just before the initiation of the peace talks with Egypt in 1978. The Israelis were in a confident mood. Everyone we asked readily gave us an interview except the Prime Minister. It was only after Douglas charmed his wife during an interview that Menachem Begin agreed to see us. He was one of those people who always look ill. He was slight, balding, with transparent skin and a hoarse voice. He saw himself as the heir to the Jewish leader, Ze'ev Jabotinski, for whom he had worked in Poland and whom he still quoted frequently. Like thousands of other Israelis he had been through hell on his way to the promised land. In his case he had served a year in a Soviet gulag, only being released with many other prisoners to join the Free Polish Army because of pressure from the British government in the middle of the war. When he reached the British mandate in Palestine he repaid his rescuers by becoming leader of the terrorist organisation, Irgun Zvai Leumi, which murdered several hundred British soldiers and hastened Britain's departure.

Once Israel became a state in 1948 Begin became a right of centre politician opposing the Israeli Labour Party, which dominated politics for the next 25 years. When we talked to him he had only been Prime Minister for a year. He expounded his version of the notion of 'Eretz Israel', the land of Israel as defined in the old Jewish books. The whole of Judea and Samaria, he kept saying, were Israel's by right – a much larger area than that defined by the UN at partition. He gave us no hint that behind the scenes he was negotiating with Sadat, preparing to ask him to Jerusalem and even gearing himself up to return Sinai to Egypt in return for peace.

Besides Begin, we met many veterans of the Jewish post-war exodus from Europe to Palestine and ex-members of the various militant organisations. Most agreeable of all was Ezer Weizman who was then a Cabinet minister. Unlike Begin he had fought in the RAF during the war and still peppered his conversation with RAF slang such as 'it was a good show' and 'bang on, old boy'. In the 1948 war to establish the State of Israel he had flown second-hand Spitfires against the Arab air forces. In the 1990s he was elected to the largely ceremonial office of president but, like quite a few other Israeli politicians, was caught breaking the foreign currency rules and had to resign. A sorry end to a great and colourful career.

Throughout my time in News and Current Affairs, South Africa was a running story which we returned to frequently. In my last year on *The World Tonight* Douglas Stuart and I went to South Africa for a couple of weeks, bringing back some very good material from the black township of Soweto outside Johannesburg where the uprising had occurred in 1976. Besides covering the current situation with regard to Apartheid, we also reported on the supposed contribution the South African Navy could make to western defence, as claimed by Pretoria and by its apologists in Britain and America. We visited the naval base at Simonstown, east of Capetown near the Cape of Good Hope. In the event of a global East-West conflict such a naval base would have been valuable but it did seem to us that the actual strength of the South African Navy was unimpressive whatever was listed in *Jane's Fighting Ships*.

An Internal Convulsion

In the mid-1970s Ian McIntyre brought on an internal convulsion soon after he was appointed Controller of Radio 4. He was an excellent broadcaster himself and tried to make some radical changes to the network, which he thought was too dominated by News and Current Affairs. He felt that the Sequences thought they 'owned' their air time and were not subject to changes initiated by the Controller. He had a prolonged battle with the *Today* programme in which he returned it to something near its original format by splitting it into two editions. Unfortunately he mistakenly assigned the programme time in the middle to the Presentation Department, which produced a truly dire effort called *Up to the Hour*. It had no real character and contained too many trails for other programmes, which is the regular currency of Presentation. The resistance from *Today* and other parts of News was fierce. The Managing Director of Radio, Ian Trethowan, and others in the top echelon were much more attuned to news than to culture so soon the schedule reverted to its previous pattern as McIntyre was bundled out of Radio 4 into the quieter waters of Radio 3.

As *The World Tonight* was the most serious of the Current Affairs programmes we were not pressed to change, perhaps because McIntyre had occasionally presented it himself. However, *Newsdesk* was dropped in the main because it was felt there really was too much news and current affairs in the early evening. In response to McIntyre's call for new ideas we started a daily 30-minute programme called *The World in Focus*, devoted exclusively to foreign affairs. I argued strongly against the title because so many others also claimed to embrace the world. In a memo to the Controller of Radio 4 I listed more than a dozen programmes that used this word in their titles. I was congratulated for my research but still overruled. Despite the title the programme served a very useful purpose, enabling us to widen our coverage to corners we normally left untouched.

I thought it somewhat regrettable that McIntyre was forced out as he was a great improvement on some of his predecessors who had largely been colourless if not supine in the face of News. At the time *Today* was edited by an ex-tabloid journalist, Mike Chaney, whose aggressive, downmarket approach grated with McIntyre. His other *bête noire* was William Hardcastle, an ex-editor of the *Daily Mail* who presented both *The World at One* and *PM* for many years. Hardcastle had a somewhat bilious view of competing programmes, which bordered on contempt,

and a similar attitude towards some of his own colleagues. He seemed
to draw most of his stories from his old paper. In fact one day our
deputy editor, Vincent Duggleby, showed that every item in *The World
at One* had been drawn from *The Daily Mail.* Hardcastle hadn't lasted
long as editor of the *Mail* and some thought he lasted too long in
current affairs broadcasting.

One of McIntyre's welcome innovations was to bring producers from
all departments together to discuss the current issues of broadcasting.
Drama, sport, light entertainment, religion, outside broadcasts, music
and current affairs producers worked hard within their own little capsules
but rarely met their counterparts except in the canteen or the bar.
McIntyre's sessions in the rather grand 'Council Chamber' at Broadcasting
House were intended to broaden our minds and introduce the corps of
producers to each other. Alas, the idea of cross-fertilisation was derided
as a waste of time by McIntyre's critics and seemed to die when he
moved on.

From a personal point of view, the best break I received at *The World
Tonight* came in October 1973 while I was covering the Conservative
Party Conference in Brighton when Ted Heath was still Prime Minister.
While there I was phoned by Brian Bliss who asked if I would be willing
to go to New York for six months as the Current Affairs producer. It
was an opportunity too good to miss. From January to July 1974 I had
an incredibly busy time arranging coverage of the unfolding drama of
Watergate for all the current affairs programmes. Day after day I would
find American correspondents, congressmen and academics to explain
and discuss the latest development. Gradually Nixon and his aides,
Haldeman and Ehrlichman, had the ground snatched from under their
feet. More and more details of their nefarious and illegal activities and
their cover-up slowly emerged to be latched on to by a self-righteous
Congress and a hungry media. So much so that when Nixon finally
resigned after the Judiciary Committee of the House voted for his
impeachment, I felt that the BBC had contributed to his downfall by
telling the world about his misdeeds.

As it happened I was climbing in a remote part of British Columbia
when the end came. After a very enjoyable fortnight in which we did
some new routes we left by helicopter and then drove back across the
Rockies to Lake Louise. *En route* we stopped at a wayside restaurant
where I spotted a newspaper on a stand outside. The headline said
'Nixon About To Resign?' As I picked it up a genuine cowboy came
out of the door so I asked him 'Well, did he?' 'Say, buddy, where have

you been?' was the reply. Clearly I was a newsman completely out of touch.

This exhilarating experience in New York and Washington in 1974 was invaluable. Four years later when Alastair Osborne was editor of the Evening Sequence the New York producer job fell vacant in the middle of someone's assignment. Because of my familiarity with the set-up I was sent out almost overnight to fill this vacancy for another four months from October 1978 to January 1979. The period wasn't so exciting but it covered some of the declining months of the Carter presidency when he began to lose confidence in himself. The economy was stagnant yet inflation proceeded apace. The price of gold soared and the retail gold market in New York, jammed with customers selling their old jewellery at fancy prices, provided colourful material for several programme items sent to London. Later on in 1979 Carter called on his whole Cabinet to resign yet did not seem to realise that he was simply demonstrating he had made bad choices in the first place. Carter claimed there was a 'crisis of confidence in America', which, translated, meant his ratings in the opinion polls had sunk very low. In our system there could have been a change of government but with a fixed-term system such a sensible readjustment to circumstances doesn't happen.

Not that the Carter presidency should be written off as an unmitigated failure as so many Republicans maintained. Among other things his diplomatic skill brought about the Camp David Agreement in 1978, which led ultimately to the peace treaty between Egypt and Israel, bringing an end to 30 years of conflict. Another wise move was American withdrawal from the Panama Canal Zone, also denounced by candidate Ronald Reagan and the Republicans in the 1980 election but never reversed.

During this second session as New York Current Affairs producer the most striking event was the so-called 'Jonestown' mass suicide, which I have described in Chapter 12. I was also a witness to a minor but intriguing affair in the art world. In January 1979 I recorded an interview with Nelson Rockefeller who had been Governor of New York State and Vice-President under Gerald Ford. Rockefeller decided to turn his large collection of modern art into a commercial money-spinner by selling copies. The Nelson Rockefeller Collection, Inc. sells licensed reproductions of more than a hundred paintings and sculptures. Some people who owned other copies of bronzes also held by Rockefeller, such as my friend Fred Morgan, editor of the *Hudson Review*, were not exactly pleased. They felt that with duplication their fairly rare pieces cast originally as 'limited editions', would become all too common and therefore devalued. Less restrained critics described the Collection as 'overpriced knock-offs'. Rockefeller responded in his charming, wide-eyed way, which had won him New York State and had nearly won him the Republican nomination for president, that he was only motivated by a desire to share with others the joy of living with these beautiful objects. Good reproductions, he maintained, would not devalue the originals but enhance interest. A brazen excuse for a commercial endeavour, in which catalogues had been sent out to thousands of potential customers. The business continues to this day. This venture, however, was probably the penultimate time Rockefeller made the news. A week or so later he died of a heart attack in bed with his research assistant who never explained publicly what had happened. It was a somewhat undignified end to an energetic and glamorous life, which achieved early lift-off into high orbit thanks to the fortune founded by his grandfather John D. Rockefeller.

One pleasant feature of the producer's job in New York was that I rarely had to work at weekends. New York may be one of the biggest metropolitan areas in the world but you can still escape its summer heat with an hour's bus ride to the wild hills of New York or New Jersey, to a landscape so studded with rock that it's never been farmed. One Sunday when the mountain laurel was turning pink and the water lilies were opening yellow I walked to Terrace Pond, a small lake set in a fold of rose-coloured rock three miles from the road and 1,300 feet up. When I arrived just after noon I shared its splendours with a solitary nude bather at the far end.

After my swim, as I watched gypsy moths gobbling oak leaves and blue dragon-flies coupling with intent, I reflected on this idyllic spot. There are hundreds like it in America but how long can they resist, not the hungry developers but the well-meaning state? I had barely finished my lunch when half a dozen teenagers arrived to go straight in with the dash and shouts of their kind. Scarcely had they come up from the first dive when two park rangers appeared wielding the long arm of New Jersey law. When the Pond was on private land the owner had allowed bathing without fuss. But then the State had acquired it for the public good, no less. Alas, soon afterwards someone had drowned in this deep pond. A rescue had been mounted – scuba divers, helicopters, all the apparatus of the caring state. Laws were then invoked and it became forbidden to camp, light fires or swim at Terrace Pond and too many notices told you so. Fires, and perhaps camping, one could understand, but swimming? If there was one place on earth where the instinct to swim overwhelms one, this is it.

The rangers were really quite human, enforcing these fatuous rules. 'Come on out, young lady,' they called, ruining the girl's beautiful dip.

'Come on out. Where's your ID card?'

'I don't know.'

'You don't know, huh!' said the forceful one.

'In the car I guess.'

'Right, you're gonna come back to the car park to show me.'

At that moment, splosh! A boy fooling about with a Frisbee slipped off his perch – intentionally – and fell down the rock into the inviting water.

'Right! You! Out! You heard what I said to the others. Where's your ID? We'll be taking you all back to the car park now.' That meant a 30-minute walk back to the bottom of a steep hill. The boys and the girl complied, sullenly, when the rangers persisted. They were doing a bad job really well, explaining why the rule had been imposed and where else they could go to swim, hire canoes and rowing boats, all under supervision. They were model law enforcement officers.

Of course New Jersey is not the only over-anxious state. Similar restrictions can be found in American national parks where you need permits to climb mountains or even walk certain trails. It's supposed to be for your own safety but it's actually to save them trouble. It's a common attitude among outdoor bureaucrats in Britain too.

But thank goodness Big Brother couldn't see everything. The rangers failed to spot the nude swimmer at the other end, and half an hour after they had left with their charges another batch of teenagers skipped down the rocks bowling an inflated rubber tube to frolic in the pond. What was clearly needed, I thought, to intimidate the bureaucrats was a mass swim-in with 500 bathers, preferably nude. That might just have got them to see the absurdity of their over-anxious concern.

Ireland

Over the decade of the 1970s I went to Ireland sporadically as a producer and reporter. Usually it was for a short stint in the rota of personnel who kept the news and views flowing from Northern Ireland into the BBC news room in London. As a producer I did several two-week

sessions in Belfast and as a reporter I spent a number of weeks in both
Belfast and Londonderry.

The government and the pundits never chose to call it civil war but
that's what it was. Northern Ireland was polarised between Republicans
and Loyalists, between Catholics and Protestants. Both sides had their
horrible terrorist groups who waged war against the state and each other,
in the course of which they were helped by many of their own unarmed
supporters, if not directly then indirectly by not fingering activists to
the authorities. Of course there were innocent bystanders but actually
far fewer of them were really spotless than met the eye. Each 'tribe'
supported its own in much the same way as the Sunni and Shiah
populations supported their own during the Iraqi Civil War of 2003 to
2010, which was also officially termed an insurgency.

Innocence is a much abused term in such situations. Loyalist and Protestant
citizens had long supported an unfair system which discriminated against
Irish Nationalists and Catholics. Some would say this had happened since
time immemorial and certainly since the Protestant plantations of the
seventeenth century. Ever since partition in 1921 Protestant majorities had
maintained their dominance in everything through what might be called
'democratic means'. No significant opposition to this gross distortion of
democracy emerged among Protestants over the half century before 1969.
Nor indeed did any Westminster government grasp this nettle as they should
have done. In the Second World War we were fighting for democracy and
a fair, non-discriminatory society, knowing that Northern Ireland was
anything but fair and just in the treatment of its Catholic citizens. After
the war Westminster governments turned a blind eye to the situation until
it blew up in their faces. Conservative governments did nothing, in part
because the Unionist Party of Northern Ireland was a useful political ally,
sending a substantial bloc of MPs to Westminster. Labour governments did
nothing because they thought they had more important things to deal with.
In the event the civil war from 1969 to 1998 cost more than 3,000 lives
besides the billions it has cost the taxpayer. When the IRA blew up the
Grand Hotel in Brighton in 1984 it nearly took the lives of the Prime
Minister and many of her Cabinet. If that bomb had succeeded the retribution
that would have been meted out by Englishmen against the Irish in Britain
might have been awful and indiscriminate. Similarly, when the IRA fired
mortar bombs into the garden of Number 10 Downing Street in 1991
while the Prime Minister, John Major, was meeting Cabinet members, three
people suffered minor injuries but the knock-on effects might have been
even worse than after Brighton.

Over all these time periods the Catholics and later Nationalists did little to reassure the Protestants in Ireland that their demands were reasonable and would be achieved peacefully. From long before the formation of Northern Ireland violent anti-British, anti-Protestant groups seemed to want to destroy or at least expel the Protestant community. Once partition had taken place in 1922 the Irish Republican Army conducted sporadic violent campaigns, not only to destroy the provincial government at Stormont and kill its uniformed officers but also to replace the Republic in Dublin. So much so that the Dublin government often convicted and imprisoned IRA members just as enthusiastically as did Stormont. Under threat from the IRA the Northern Ireland government compromised its own democratic legitimacy by perpetuating discrimination against Catholics in all fields of government and civil society.

As a journalist in Northern Ireland I found little to admire in the provincial government or in the citizenry who sustained it. The BBC only organised intense coverage when the violence became extreme – the violence perpetrated by both sides, not just the IRA. Reporters and producers were sent from the mainland because the local staff could not meet the demands from London. Day after day we reported bombs, sniping against the army, the killing of Royal Ulster Constabulary officers and assassinations of supposedly militant leaders. The political reporting was done against this dire backdrop. The IRA threatened the very existence of the United Kingdom and the lives of a million citizens. The Loyalist terrorists also besmirched the reputation of the UK as a peaceful, democratic country where political problems could be worked out rationally. The conflict was not brought to an end until the Good Friday Agreement of 1998, and one still cannot be sure that this compromise to share power will endure or actually resolve the problems of such a divided community.

A few incidents in which I was involved stick in the memory. One evening in 1972 the newly formed Ulster Defence Association (UDA), avowedly non-violent, mounted a huge demonstration in Belfast. The Northern Irish Protestants are fond of marching; it's been their favourite way of demonstrating their numbers, their discipline and their power. On this occasion they mustered hundreds of men in some narrow streets running down to the Springfield Road in an attempt to create a Protestant 'no go area' with barricades and checkpoints to exclude possible IRA bombers. The UDA leaders claimed the residents had demanded UDA protection. The UDA members, dressed in olive-green anoraks, bush hats and even a few tin hats and gasmasks, were armed with pick handles, stones and bottles and they far outnumbered the troops deployed to stop them establishing a permanent defendable zone.

I was able to get alongside the UDA ranks while this ugly stand-off continued for three hours. Before the days of mobile phones I knocked on a door at random and asked to use the phone. No problem, said the family who appeared to ignore the whole incident, though there was a lot of shouting outside. I stood with an open door reporting to the Belfast news room just what was happening for some time. The UDA's demands were referred up the chain of command all the way to the Home Secretary, William Whitelaw. It was very tense but in the end the UDA withdrew their phalanxes without gaining their main demands. The confrontation dissolved.

A day or two later I went to a Co-op grocery shop which had just been raided by four gunmen. The raid was bungled because the men spent too long in the shop. After they had taken all the money from the till they continued to scoop up cigarettes and meat. Acting on a 999 call, units of the King's and Royal Welch Regiments surrounded the shop before the gunmen had finished. A police detective who went into the shop was seized at gunpoint as a hostage. His captor tried to escape with him. The other three fired five shots at a second detective who went to his colleague's aid. A bullet went through his jacket but missed his body.

Outside, the army used a loudhailer to induce the gunmen to surrender. Inside, both employees and customers implored the young men to go quietly as they couldn't escape. For a while the raiders also held two women as hostages and threatened to make a break with them. A young woman shop assistant named Philomena, whom I interviewed afterwards, showed considerable nerve and courage, acting as an intermediary between the police and the gunmen, undoubtedly helping to dampen their initial desire to go out in a blaze of gunfire. In the end it was a canister of CS gas fired into the shop that persuaded the men to come out with their hands held high and their eyes full of tears. No one was hurt, though two of the shop assistants were violently sick from the gas. This was a rare incident, in which the gunmen were caught in the act but which ended without bloodshed. Too often the terrorists had the initiative and did exactly what they planned. Four hotels, for example, in which I stayed at one time or another in Belfast and Londonderry were bombed, three of them destroyed. The newly built Europa Hotel in Belfast, which was the main watering hole for the media, was bombed several times despite heavy security on the doors. The hotel continued to operate after repairs but the damage was very visible and the feeling that it could happen again was always there for the next 20 years.

Once the IRA had learnt how to make bombs from sugar and agricultural fertiliser they used them frequently; at the height of their insurgency they deployed more than 70 bombs a week. Sometimes they gave a warning to avoid casualties – thereby showing their honourable intentions (as they saw it) – and sometimes bombs went off without warning or without a warning being correctly received and understood by the police. One day I spent a tense hour watching at a safe distance a bomb disposal officer dismantle a bomb on the steps of a public building. We were about a hundred yards away watching this man fiddle with this lethal device, all the time expecting that the next second would be his last. In this case he was successful but over the years quite a few of his colleagues were killed. So many in fact that the army devised various clever methods of turning the bomb into a controlled and relatively harmless explosion; small armoured vehicles were developed that could 'de-fang' a bomb by remote control so that whatever happened no one was injured.

Along the south-western outskirts of Belfast a number of post-war estates had been built which were exclusively Catholic. Lenadoon out beyond the then notorious Andersonstown was an area reckoned by the local media to be controlled by the IRA. After a shooting was reported to the Belfast news room I drove out to make an eyewitness report. In the middle of this estate was a large sports field or open space sloping uphill for 200 yards. Around this pleasant green area was a quadrangle of council houses and some low-rise flats. As I arrived two soldiers came under fire from the top of the hill and dived behind a low wall about two feet high where they were pinned down. As with the bomb disposal officer I felt that at any minute I would see them killed. Again I imposed myself upon a local family, using their telephone to report this violent incident. My tape recorder picked up the sniper fire as it hit the wall just in front of the soldiers. After a long, tense wait the army brought up an armoured car behind which the soldiers were able to make a relatively safe escape. The sound of the sniper fire was later used to embellish my report sent back to London.

Besides reporting many more incidents than I have mentioned I also recorded interviews with Ian Paisley soon after he became an MP, Brian Faulkner when he was Home Affairs Minister at Stormont and Martin

McGuinness when he was a 21-year-old commander of the Provisional IRA in Derry. That last encounter was soon after the split between the Official IRA who this time did not join the fighting and the newly formed Provisional IRA who thought they could destroy the Ulster government and its link with London. McGuinness was very cocky at the time, referring disparagingly to the Official IRA as the 'stickies'. After being convicted of carrying explosives and ammunition he served a term in prison but years later became a 'born again' peacemaker in alliance with Gerry Adams. Today McGuinness is a Deputy First Minister of Northern Ireland.

The emergence of McGuinness as a political leader and office holder in the current regime illustrates the impracticality of a common demand for 'peace with justice'. The IRA killed approximately 1,800 people in the 30-year campaign from 1969 to 1997. Most of their attacks were against the army and police but even so their operations murdered about 700 civilians and injured thousands more. They executed, it is thought, 63 people on their own side, accusing them of being 'informers', and carried out cruel punishments, such as knee-capping, on many more. A similar indictment can be compiled against the Protestant terrorists and gangsters, such as the Ulster Volunteer Force, although the total number they killed and injured was smaller.

Thousands of IRA Volunteers were caught, convicted and imprisoned at Long Kesh (Maze Prison) but all were released after 1998 under an amnesty, which was part of the Good Friday Agreement. This amnesty was the price of peace but by no stretch of legal argument could the thousands of victims be said to have received justice. Realistically peace is more urgent than justice, less nebulous and more attainable. In recent years we have seen the emergence of UN international tribunals, which have tried and convicted some of the worst criminals in the Balkan wars of the 1990s and in Rwanda and Sierra Leone. Such retribution is welcome, though it only reaches a small fraction of the guilty. Some international lawyers claim that such courts will deter political leaders in the future lest they meet the same fate as Slobodan Miloševic and Radovan Karadžic. Unhappily I feel this is wishful thinking. In Western Europe and the United States, for instance, there has been a functioning criminal law for hundreds of years yet it appears to have little deterrent effect on ordinary criminals. Can we really expect an International Criminal Court to deter political and religious extremists?

* * *

The last act in this awful Irish fratricidal story as far as I was concerned was the destruction of the Baltic Exchange in London in 1992. At the time I was working for a BBC World Service programme called *Seven Seas*. I had several times been into the Exchange Hall, which was an elegant Edwardian building in St Mary Axe in the City. Ships were still being chartered for cargo by ship brokers bidding and bargaining with each other in a manner that had been going on for some 250 years. The electronic age had not quite arrived.

The IRA set off a truck load of fertiliser mixture causing a massive explosion which killed three people. It shattered the entrance and the inside of the main hall. The day after I was driving across London on the way to see my mother when on the spur of the moment I thought I would see the damage. Police had cordoned off the front of the building but as I was strolling round the back a door opened and a policeman beckoned two or three people inside. They wanted to reach their offices but I quickly tagged along and was let in without question let alone scrutiny. We were warned that the main hall was too dangerous for us to enter but after a while I found I was able to walk all over it, crunching on glass at every step. It was a sad end to an elegant building. It was eventually dismantled in 1998 and replaced by the Swiss Re building, colloquially known as the 'gherkin'.

I was a duty editor on *The World Tonight* for ten years, leading a small team to produce upwards of 800 programmes. This was essentially a desk-bound job, thinking up ideas, assigning tasks, finding and briefing speakers, fixing technical facilities such as studios and the lease line, and finally putting the programme on the air. It provided a reliable comment on the day's news for several hundred thousand listeners a day. This was our primary task yet it is my individual contributions to the department's output that I remember most vividly. Getting out of the office to make a feature was regarded by everyone as a 'perk' especially if it meant foreign travel.

One 'Bunbury' that I particularly enjoyed was a two-week visit to the Salzburg Seminar in Austria. The BBC made a practice of sending staff to this excellent institution, which had been started by three students in 1947 as an offshoot from the Harvard Food Relief Campaign. They thought that the students of Europe needed help to make an intellectual recovery just as much as a physical one. Most of Europe had been in the grip of Fascism for more than ten years. With

American confidence, ingenuity and funds the Schloss Leopoldskron was acquired from the widow of the Austrian playwright Max Reinhardt. Initially just a summer vacation course, it was soon expanded to a year round programme of two-week seminars. The subjects began with American law but slowly broadened out to embrace any topic of global concern. On my session we studied nuclear proliferation under the guidance of three men who had worked on the Manhattan Project, four ambassadors, two directors of international energy agencies and the chief American policymaker on non-proliferation. As now, the nub of the problem was how to promote civil nuclear power without enabling more states to build nuclear weapons. It was serious, heavyweight study and it was very stimulating, especially as it was held amid the splendours of the prince bishop's eighteenth-century schloss set on the outskirts of Salzburg with its own beautiful reflecting lake. To regard it simply as a 'perk' was certainly to do it an injustice.

I enjoyed myself so much that I went back nine years later to make a programme to mark the fortieth anniversary of the seminar. Two of the founders were present still very spry. By that time some students and a few staff were also being drawn from behind the Iron Curtain, even from the Soviet Union. As from the beginning the faculty gave their services without pay. American topics, particularly American law, remained the most popular. It was and still is a benign example of American cultural expansion very similar in spirit to the many colleges Britain has planted around the world. For those dull souls unmoved by the intellectual discourse or the baroque décor of the palace there is always the view of the Alps across the lake. The seminar flourishes still as the Salzburg Global Seminar.

16

Plays

'A man writes much better than he lives.'
Samuel Johnson

Towards the end of the 1960s some of the subjects I dealt with in documentaries prompted me to think they might make good dramas. Over the next 20 years I wrote a number of radio dramas and five stage plays. Nine months before I went to be the New York producer in January 1974 the likely impeachment of Richard Nixon prompted me to write a radio play about the only previous president to face such a trial. President Andrew Johnson, who came to the White House in 1865 after Lincoln was murdered, all too soon fell out with the Republican majority in Congress by vetoing their plans for radical reconstruction of the South. Under the constitution a president can only be impeached for 'high crimes and misdemeanours'. Outraged by Johnson's criticism the radical Republicans tried to frame a case against him on the grounds that he had dismissed his Secretary of State for War in order to take over the army but the evidence produced in the Senate was flimsy; in fact some of it was plain laughable. A genial old general and a memorable country bumpkin were unconvincing witnesses. Nevertheless, Johnson only survived the impeachment by one vote, which of course made the climax very dramatic. The special conceit of my play, *The Trial of Andrew Johnson*, was that I cast it in the form of a 'live transmission' from the Senate by two journalists as if radio had existed in 1868. This deliberate anachronism was designed to give the listener some feel of what an impeachment of Nixon might be like. Some years later celebrity trials in the USA, such as that of the footballer O.J. Simpson, were reported and discussed in much the same way as I had envisaged.

This 45-minute radio play was not only broadcast by Radio 4 but also in translation by stations in The Netherlands and Yugoslavia. A German station turned it down because they did not like my use of the

225

journalists and wanted the story played absolutely straight. My feeling was that much of the original proceedings were tedious and therefore unusable in a play and that even the more lively witnesses had little substance to add to the case. The essence of the drama was a president on trial who was very nearly convicted.

Such was the topicality of the play that I had quite a lot of correspondence with another half dozen radio stations in Europe and America, though they all had their own particular reasons for turning it down. But one of these rejections ought definitely to be recalled as it encapsulated some vintage BBC practice. Despite Radio 4 having broadcast the play the BBC External Service rejected it because 'it would constitute the sort of comment it is not our place to make in this form'. The External Service, now the World Service, was financed by the Foreign Office although the BBC was supposed to have total editorial control. Clearly the editor of Drama still touched her forelock to our ally even if the story was a century old! I thought this so odd that I protested to Gerard Mansell, Managing Director of the External Service. Why should a service so geared to current affairs turn down an historical drama with such a strong contemporary interest? 'I have considered her [Mrs Barbara Halpern] arguments carefully,' he replied, 'and do not feel this is a case where a Managing Director should have the temerity to overrule an experienced editor.'

When I went to New York in January 1974 the question of impeachment was a popular topic engendering much speculation about whether the House of Representatives would embark on it and if it could succeed. It also became a theme for comedy shows, cartoons and wry newspaper columns. One weekend some wags put on what they described as 'An Impeachment Fair' with all kinds of gimmicks putting the knife into 'Tricky Dicky'. I had a little fun making a short radio feature with these people who ridiculed their president with smiles on their faces but were in deadly earnest. The only item I remember was 'Impeachment Ice-Cream', which somehow wrapped Nixon's face around genuine peach ice-cream. As the facts of Nixon's crooked conduct in office tumbled out over the next six months it became clear that he had committed 'high crimes and misdemeanours', which would properly justify an impeachment. Once the House Judiciary Committee recommended impeachment Nixon quit. A pardon from his successor, Gerald Ford, prevented any further prosecution.

The 1970s was a time of political turbulence in Britain with eight different administrations being formed within the decade. One issue that eventually triggered a change of government in Westminster was the future of Scotland within the United Kingdom. On *The World Tonight* we discussed the pros and cons of home rule many times and Douglas Stuart and I made a special feature about it from Scotland. As a result the historian in me went back to the winding up of the Scottish Parliament in 1707. At that time antagonism between the two countries with the same Queen ran high but both had sound reasons for union. The English Parliament wanted to bind Scotland to the Hanoverian succession in order to keep out the autocratic and Catholic Stuarts. The Scots were in dire economic straits and welcomed the offer from Westminster to pay off their debts.

My radio play broadcast in January 1977, entitled *An End to an Auld Sang*, dramatised the political events and anti-Union riots in the run-up to the so-called 'adjournment' of the Parliament in March 1707. I cast Daniel Defoe as my narrator because he was an English agent in Scotland at the time and wrote a partisan account of the events later. The opposition to the Treaty of Union tried to hold out for a federal union in which the Scottish Parliament would at least have home rule. They were outmanoeuvred by the Queen's Commissioner, the Duke of Queensberry, who with a combination of argument and patronage secured a two to one majority in favour. As the Parliament was adjourned for the last time the Lord Chancellor for Scotland, Earl Seafield, remarked, 'Now there's an end to an auld sang.' The play was enlivened with some popular songs of the period of which the most pointed was 'A Parcel of Rogues in a Nation', the lilt of which is with me still.

Throughout the 1970s I was heavily involved in helping to promote women's rights to abortion. As I have laid out in Chapter 14 I wrote a history of the reform movement entitled *Abortion Law Reformed* with Madeleine Simms and became a director of the charity Pregnancy Advisory Service. Out of this experience I slowly developed an idea for a slightly surreal play. It envisaged a pregnant woman rehearsing the arguments for and against abortion while under anaesthetic during a termination. In her mind the debate takes place in a children's playground where she is confronted by her beautiful twin embryos. The boy opts for life while the girl backs up her mother's decision for the termination. In the middle of this sometimes fierce argument the father turns up to plead for the twins to have life. He is welcomed as an ally by the boy but castigated by the embryonic daughter for not using a contraceptive and told he ought now to have a vasectomy. To which his response is 'Ouch!' Just as the woman is beginning to weaken, two sperms appear, with male and female chromosomes, XX and XY, to provide a bizarre diversion. At one point the woman plays affectionately with her putative children using an old nursery rhyme that my mother had sung to me as a child. Bouncing the children on her knee one at a time she sings:

> Under the water, under the sea
> Catching fishes for my tea

Whereupon she raises them high up into the air and then lowers them to the ground as she poses the question, 'Dead or Alive?' The girl opts for 'Dead!'

From the rhyme I took the title for my play: *Catching Fishes For My Tea*. In September 1978 it was produced with great zest and imagination by the local amateur theatre in Norwood. The producer John Anderson then took it with the same cast to a drama festival at the Royal Flemish Theatre in Brussels and finally to the Young Vic where he set up a splendid climbing frame and a sandpit on the stage. Once again I offer my thanks to Anderson and his excellent cast who really entered into the spirit of the play. A couple of years later while I was at the UN my daughter Alison produced the play at the Oxford Playhouse while she was secretary of the university dramatic society known as OUDS.

17

Four Years in the Peace Palace

By 1980 the United Nations had grown from 51 member states into an almost universal body. The words of the Charter had been fleshed out into a living institution, which had assumed a competence over many international questions. It had identified many of those global problems itself through debate and enquiry and had established agencies to advise member states on how to cope with them. As a result the variety of subjects dealt with in my news reports was very diverse. Such diversity presents difficulties for the single reporter working on his own, especially without support from a library or a news index system. The UN itself had the handsome Dag Hammarskjöld Library but it was not geared to supplying instant information with indexed, dated newspaper cuttings such as is maintained by the BBC at home and other major news organisations. A lot of back history had to be carried in one's head.

In four and a half years at the United Nations I wrote more than 3,000 separate stories and did about 200 interviews. In reviewing my output at the UN the first thing that strikes me is the sheer number of different subjects that I covered not just about the UN but about events in the United States. During the first year, for instance, I wrote 650 pieces for the BBC, Canadian Broadcasting and National Public Radio of which four-fifths concerned the UN: what the UN bodies decided; what UN agencies were doing, reporting and asking for; what ambassadors were saying in the Security Council and the General Assembly; what lesser diplomats were saying in the corridors and what visiting critics and non-governmental organisations were demanding should be done. That by the way is an easy way to get reported: saying something striking at a place where there are always plenty of correspondents eager to write something new, eager to earn an extra fee and sometimes bored with routine UN work.

Interspersed among my UN work I responded to frequent requests from BBC news desks and programmes in London for reports and interviews concerning striking or querky happenings in the United States. About half of these were written at weekends when the UN generally did not function. With my colleagues in Washington and New York, I shared the cover at weekends. As the BBC's New York correspondent was often travelling, in practice I worked six days a week for almost the whole time. At times of crisis the UN Security Council itself met at weekends so I had to be there, but normally I tried to be the BBC duty correspondent on Saturday when I could fit my shopping and my laundry in between writing and broadcasting one or two stories from home. Sunday I tried to preserve for walking among the hills and lakes of upstate New York and western New Jersey.

The United Nations should be seen first and foremost as a forum for discussion, for airing views, reporting dire events and attempting to devise solutions. This role as a permanent conference ready to discuss anything is extremely important. Sharing the difficulties and disasters in one's own country with other diplomats is itself a soothing and constructive process. It is far more efficient than the old bilateral diplomatic system which existed for centuries until the creation of the League of Nations. The small countries in particular benefit from having a single place where they are certain of a hearing, if only from the media, where they can readily ascertain whether they have support for their plight or their view, and where some kind of solution or mitigation can be devised at least on paper.

The Peace Palace is part of the UN system but it's actually the headquarters of the International Court of Justice in The Hague rather than in New York. I have given this chapter its somewhat ironic title because that is what UN headquarters aspires to be. While I was there, however, the continuing Cold War between East and West prevented any solutions to the major political problems – such as Palestine, Afghanistan, Kashmir, Kampuchea, Namibia and East Timor. The Security Council was too frequently only a debating chamber rather than a body that could assess threats to peace and security, negotiate a broad-based solution and enforce it, which was the original conception. Yet under the surface the ice was melting, though it was not apparent until after I had left New York. The deadlock was made absolutely clear whenever one of the permanent members of the Council cast their veto from time to time. During my time at the UN the United States vetoed 17 draft resolutions, Britain vetoed 5, and the Soviet Union and France 4 each.

In one extraordinary session on 30th April 1981 France, the United

Kingdom and the United States each vetoed four African resolutions which would have imposed oil and other sanctions on South Africa because of its operations in Angola and in order to force compliance over Namibia. An arms embargo against South Africa had already been in place since 1977 but these draft resolutions would have extended sanctions to several other spheres.

With the end of the Cold War the use of the veto declined dramatically except by the United States, which continued to prevent the Council reaching decisions critical of its own aggressive actions, such as in Panama and Nicaragua, and likewise blocked resolutions in order to protect Israel from sanctions and strong criticism.

The odd one out among the permanent members was China, which seemed to deal with the UN at arm's length. Their diplomats did not play a significant part in the counsels of the organisation, and sometimes abstained or pretended to be absent from the Security Council by devising a procedure of their own described as 'non-participation'. The Charter says that a majority decision must include 'the concurring votes of the permanent members'. With China in a semi-detached mood for some years, the Council quite sensibly turned a blind eye to the requirements of Article 27. This tactic, or fudge as journalists called it, was also used at least once by Britain. In January 1980 during the transition process in Rhodesia the Council voted by fourteen to zero that Britain should ensure the immediate withdrawal of South African forces and that it should confine the Rhodesian forces to bases. The British ambassador, Sir Anthony Parsons, explained patiently that Britain had already done both things. He couldn't vote 'No' because that would have been a veto. Nor could he vote 'Yes' because that would have implied he accepted the Council's criticism and rebuke. So in order to let the Council make a decision he announced Britain 'had not participated'. Embarrassed smiles all round.

The very existence of the veto casts a shadow over all the deliberations of the Security Council. Whatever the issue the 15 members always ask themselves 'Will the draft resolution attract a veto?' Great ingenuity of diplomatic language is often employed in order to accommodate one or other of the permanent members. All political assemblies need to compromise to maximise support but the existence of the veto puts diplomats into emollient mode before they put pen to paper. Many points are omitted from draft resolutions simply because one of the permanent members might ... just might ... veto. So the veto power carried by the five permanent members of the Council creates an enduring

Caudine Forks under which countries and their diplomats must duck or sometimes crawl in order to produce a document with any prospect of success.

In exculpation of the veto one should say that extreme positions, such as UN enforcement action under Chapter VII of the Charter or comprehensive sanctions or expulsion from the UN, are usually non-starters. Most important of all the veto means that the UN Security Council cannot wage war against one of the permanent members which, as they all had atomic weapons, is just as well, unfair, unjust though that may be. It also means, however, that while a debate to examine the conduct of one of the big five can be initiated in the Security Council in practice the Council cannot censure any of them in a resolution. Proposals have been made that the permanent members should limit their use of the veto to enforcement action but most of them are resolutely against such a self-denying measure. They are all ready to assert that the conduct of other member states is a threat to peace and security and call upon them in presidential statements and Council resolutions to desist but they will not allow the Council to make similar pronouncements about themselves. There are many factors that inhibit clear thinking and firm action at the United Nations but the veto is the most important one.

One other effect of the Cold War was that the Soviet Union still had a small army of client states who followed its line on most issues, especially if it was contrary to the views of the United States. For its part Washington's client states in Latin America who had played a significant supporting role in the early years of the organisation were drifting away. Argentina and Chile were still in the fold but some of the others were strongly influenced by Cuba and resented American domination of the hemisphere.

This phenomenon was most obvious in the voting patterns in the General Assembly, which the State Department analysed in minute detail every year. But it was probably more important in the Security Council where the developing nations had some cohesion through the Non-Aligned Movement. Some western commentators write of the 'non-aligned veto' because they can sometimes organise enough members on the Council to prevent a resolution reaching a majority. Frankly I think this absurd special pleading. If seven non-permanent members of the Council cast negative votes on some issue they are simply following normal democratic practice or freely expressing their point of view. To equate such a happening, which usually takes a great deal of organisation, with the casting of one vote by a permanent member is to distort the language and misrepresent the procedures of the Council.

The General Assembly in which all states are represented and have one vote embraces the best and too often the worst of the United Nations idea. Viewed over its 66-year history it is a great forum for raising new issues and floating new ideas around the world. Concepts such as the equality of women and rights for individuals have challenged entrenched patterns of social and political behaviour which are as old as humanity itself. By embracing these progressive ideas the United Nations has embarked on an ambitious course to change the behaviour of *homo sapiens*. Similarly, the General Assembly has been the forum where the new notions of climate change and environmental conservation have been discussed and given enormous impetus towards the furthest corners of the earth.

Where the General Assembly and indeed most parts of the UN have been weak is in implementation, converting the striking ideals and sonorous phrases into practical action. In 1981 the Assembly had more than 150 members (now 193) and was one of the most cumbersome parliamentary bodies in the world. Born in the era of the steamship, it met regularly for only three months a year. Although some sessions were invariably held in the next year these were only seen as clean-up sessions dealing with business left over from the main Assembly. Every year its agenda was clogged with items that were virtually identical to the previous year. Most of them were nodded through without a vote in the last two weeks before the Christmas recess. Consequently many of them were frankly worthless.

On the plus side it is useful that every single country, no matter how small, has the opportunity to address the whole Assembly and many more occasions to express its point of view in committee or in some negotiating conference preparing the draft of a new treaty such as that dealing with the Law of the Sea. Without such an assembly the world would be run only by the big blocs. During the Cold War that meant the West, the East, the Non-Aligned Movement and to a lesser extent the Organisation of African Unity, the Association of Southeast Asian Nations, the Organisation of American States, the Islamic Conference and the Arab League. Nowadays it means the Group of 8, the European Union, perhaps the World Trade Organisation and always, of course, the United States acting unilaterally whenever it wants to.

In practice the Assembly's decisions on controversial political matters were mostly decided by the developing countries acting together either as the Non-Aligned Movement or with their economic hats on as the Group of 77 (actually over a hundred) in alliance with the Eastern Bloc. Almost every year there were heated disputes about the budget because 90 per cent was paid for by some 20 rich countries while the other 130 paid very little but had the votes to insist on expensive projects and lavish conferences. Just as I left, these disputes became so bitter that the United States withheld a substantial proportion of its dues in order to get its own way and later to reduce its annual contributions.

However, on issues where there was no obvious South/North divide such as the use of outer space, or any new problem that required innovation, it was the large and the middle-sized states that could field a strong team of diplomats and technical experts who were able to draft the resolutions and guide the committees towards sensible solutions. From September to December there is a great deal of activity. If an enterprising or determined country wishes to make an impact it needs at least a dozen diplomats attending committees and preparing draft resolutions and amendments to be hammered out in committees or corridors. At the same time an active mission tries to play a part in its own groups, be they geographical, political, economic, linguistic, religious, ethnic or cultural.

Peace-loving people look to the secretary-general of the UN for leadership towards a better world. Dag Hammarskjöld gave real leadership mainly because he stood up for small nations against bullying by the USSR and the USA. More recently Kofi Annan gave a lead in a less dramatic way by pushing the member states towards reform of the organisation against their inclinations. But neither of these two able international civil servants can be said to have dominated the UN. A secretary-general even in his second term has to remain the servant of the organisation, carrying out the decisions of its organs such as the General Assembly, the Security Council and the Economic and Social Council. A secretary-general makes lots of speeches, written it should be emphasised by speech writers, but mostly these are pretty bland, usually no more than gentle hints as to what might improve the running of the organisation. Moreover, a secretary-general can only rarely make jokes lest they be misunderstood and trample on some sacred cow.

All but one of the secretaries-general have been diplomats or civil servants, which is just as well because their main task is to navigate through rough political waters, not to create waves themselves. In the 1980s first Kurt

Waldheim and then Javier Pérez de Cuéllar held sway on the thirty-eighth floor. Both were diplomats by training, though Waldheim had dipped into politics by running for the presidency of Austria before he was elected Secretary-General in 1971. At the time the media thought him a competent though somewhat timid operator. Behind closed doors he was often a slave driver to his staff. He was uneasy dealing with the media, something I noticed even before I took the correspondent's job in January 1980. The previous November I made a short reconnaissance trip to the UN. Iranian students had just taken over the American embassy in Tehran so I was commissioned to get an interview for my Radio 4 programme *The World Tonight*. We wanted to know if and when the UN would respond to a flagrant breach of international law on the protection of diplomats. Somehow I persuaded him to come to one of the UN's studios in the basement but during the interview he threatened to walk out because he thought I was pressing him too hard. One of the rules I subscribe to for politicians and public officials is 'never walk out of an interview once begun'. The media will only embarrass you by playing over and over the questions you wouldn't or couldn't answer, as happened with Henry Kissinger on the BBC TV programme *Newsnight* in the 1990s.

Over the next two years Waldheim rarely faced the press corps beyond his annual *tour d'horizon* press conference prior to each General Assembly. In one short session at the noon briefing for UN correspondents on the American hostages in Tehran he was plainly uncomfortable and hurried out before the questions were finished or the usual half hour had passed. Some of my colleagues were particularly scornful of him, calling him the head waiter – he was tall and he dressed very soberly. What we did not know was his astonishing ability to cover up some of his real war service for 40 years, and no one could have foreseen his ability to ride out that storm to become the elected president of his country. However you judge his honesty about his war service, clearly he had very considerable political appeal to his own countrymen.

Waldheim undoubtedly was very conscientious and perhaps worked too hard. According to Andrei Gromyko who was Soviet foreign minister throughout the 1980s Waldheim once went to sleep during an opera of *War & Peace* in Moscow. Gromyko nudged him to wake him up saying 'the French are invading'. As Waldheim woke up he asked, 'Where? Lebanon?' Clearly he still thought he was in the Security Council rather than at the opera.

* * *

235

In the 1980s the lively or forceful personalities at the UN who caught most media attention were: Diego Cordovez, an Under Secretary-General who got landed with Cyprus and Afghanistan; and Brian Urquhart, the Under Secretary-General for Political Affairs who was in charge of 'Peacekeeping' and was the most influential member of the secretariat. Sir Robert Jackson who had been an abrasive but effective international civil servant for years was almost at the end of his career. He had written a seminal report in 1970 known as 'The Capacity Study', which was really about the incapacity of the UN to deliver aid and development largely because the autonomous UN agencies were inefficient and failed to cooperate even when faced with dire emergencies. The UN system, he said, was actually a 'non-system' beyond the control of governments and incapable of controlling itself. The study had made waves but did not lead to much improvement. By 1979 Jackson was in charge of famine relief for Kampuchea. In the one interview that he gave me he brushed off any criticism of the relief efforts with bluster so I suspect if I had known him better I would have taken a dim view of his overbearing manner.

Diego Cordovez was an urbane, plump, outgoing, cigar-smoking Ecuadorian diplomat with something of a reputation as a ladies' man who was brought into the UN by Waldheim and handed a couple of impossible problems – Cyprus and Afghanistan. My colleagues in the BBC Eastern Service who knew much more about Afghanistan than me thought he was conning the world that some progress was being made when none was apparent. In fact despite appearances Cordovez was fulfilling a useful role. He conducted endless negotiations in Geneva and elsewhere in which he shuttled between the delegations from Pakistan and Afghanistan in what are known as proximity talks. The two sides never met for face-to-face negotiations but Cordovez went back and forth between them, latterly when they were actually in adjoining rooms in Geneva. He does not claim to have got the Soviets out of Afghanistan and recognises that they left for their own reasons. However, his seven years of sporadic diplomacy in which he also visited Moscow, Kabul and Islamabad many times, certainly eased them out a little sooner by helping them to retire with a semblance of dignity.

This was a good example of how persistence with the diplomatic course rather than with more forceful options can sometimes bear fruit. The UN is an institution that does not die whereas the politicians and even the terrorists it has to deal with are mortal. Sometimes a change of leadership can alter the whole atmosphere of a negotiation and open up possibilities not dreamt of earlier. When Cordovez took the Afghanistan brief he had no idea that Mikhail Gorbachev would soon take the leadership of the Soviet Union and introduce the revolution of *perestroika*. Cordovez should be given much credit for taking on what seemed a hopeless task and bringing it to a successful conclusion despite many rebuffs. I would commend this episode to all students of diplomatic history, especially to would-be diplomats.[1]

Brian Urquhart was the absolute opposite of Cordovez. Cool, dry and terse where Cordovez was flamboyant, Urquhart had grown up in a family that was active in the League of Nations Union and which believed strongly in the mission of the UN to save the world from the scourge of war. He had been recruited to the organisation in 1946 by Gladwyn Jebb, the Acting Secretary-General in charge of the first General Assembly in London and had worked his way up through the professional ranks to the most important job to which an international civil servant could then aspire. On a day-to-day basis his department looked after the main political problems such as Palestine, Namibia and Kampuchea, and also maintained the peacekeeping missions in the field. He had helped Ralph Bunche invent the very first peacekeeping mission in Sinai after the Suez War of 1956, the United Nations Emergency Force.[2] An American ambassador, William vanden Heuvel, described Urquhart as 'one of the movers and shakers' at the UN, although most of his influence was exerted discreetly behind the scenes. In the 1980s he certainly had the ear and the confidence of both Kurt Waldheim and Javier Perez de Cuellar.

In what he announced was his last Security Council appearance in March 1982 Sir Anthony Parsons, then British Permanent Representative, was paid a flowery tribute by the Spanish ambassador who assumed he was going to be Britain's next ambassador in Washington. 'I think,' said Sir Anthony, 'the excitement and interest involved in that will in fact outweigh my longing for the more vegetative life of retirement which I have desired now for over 40 years [laughter]'[3] He was about to retire at the age of 60 as required by the rules of the Foreign and Commonwealth Office (FCO), yet congratulatory letters and flip remarks from colleagues all seemed to point to him being appointed to Washington when Nico Henderson also retired later that summer. Two days later Argentina invaded the Falkland Islands and both men worked absolutely flat out for the next three months and both worked well beyond retirement. In the event Parsons was not appointed to Washington but later became a foreign policy adviser to the Prime Minister. Margaret Thatcher had a low opinion of most of her colleagues and civil service advisers and was particularly scornful of diplomats because they strove to resolve issues rather than win them. Consequently she interrupted them frequently. On one occasion in the late 1980s she interrupted Parsons who responded with an effective and memorable riposte. 'If you would just let me finish, Prime Minister, you might find you actually agree with me.' He figures prominently in my chapter on the Falklands.

Iran

My first year was dominated by the American hostage crisis rather than Afghanistan, which was actually a much more serious problem. The hostage crisis matched two unequal protagonists and therefore seemed soluble. As now, the Iranians always played their hand without restraint as if they could vanquish the 'Great Satan'. During 1980–81 Iran was nominally run by President Banisadr and dealings with the UN were conducted by the American educated foreign minister, Sadegh Ghotbzadeh, who was later convicted on trumped up charges and executed as a spy! Their ambassador in New York made it all too clear that the government could not touch the revolutionary students holding the American diplomats in their mission, let alone influence the *ex-cathedra* pronouncements of the Ayatollah Khomeini. Waldheim and the UN Commission of Inquiry had a frustrating time therefore trying to find someone who was really responsible and reliable who could actually deliver. Both Waldheim and the Commission suffered the humiliation of travelling to Tehran but not even being allowed to see the American hostages to assess their condition, let alone negotiate for their release. Waldheim himself was nearly mobbed by threatening crowds while being taken to a cemetery for victims of the Shah.

The facts of this incident are still unclear to this day. In a report broadcast in January 1981 soon after the hostages were eventually let go ABC television accused Waldheim of panicking and of having to be whisked out by helicopter. It also accused him of giving too much away during his unsuccessful negotiations with the Iranians. This report did Waldheim's reputation much damage in America notwithstanding that the US Administration, its ambassador in the UN and former President Carter all came to his defence. Waldheim denounced the report as 'libellous ... totally unfounded and unjustified'. However, it attracted worldwide attention in part because it was prepared by Pierre Salinger, President Kennedy's former Press Secretary. Carter, in his ham-fisted way, vitiated his support for Waldheim by also congratulating Salinger on his story.

For months the Iranians pressed the UN Commission to publish its report which they naively expected would be a damning indictment of American support for the Shah. Waldheim's only bargaining chip was to maintain that the report could only be published when the hostages were released. In 1980 after the hostages had already been held for 129 days Waldheim let down his austere diplomatic guard enough to say 'I have never tried so hard to achieve a solution of such a delicate problem.' At the same time the UN was being heavily pressured by the Americans who were hinting that if the UN did not achieve a breakthrough quickly much worse would follow. On 23rd April 1980 Waldheim made some prescient comments: 'political pressure on both sides sets limits to patience'. Washington's patience plainly ran out two days later when it launched the abortive rescue mission.

From then on negotiations continued without any sign of progress until just before Reagan assumed office nine months later. Before the abortive helicopter mission the Americans had shown extreme impatience for the methods of the UN. Their number two in New York, William vanden Heuvel, even vented his spleen on the Non-Aligned Movement, which he claimed had done nothing to help the hostage crisis and had not even put it on its agenda. 'Is there not a single member prepared to demand that the Non-Aligned go on record as insisting that Iran release the hostages?' After the failed airborne rescue the US had no alternative but to revert to a negotiated solution with the help of the UN. President Jimmy Carter, a born-again Christian who during his 1976 election campaign had espoused peaceful methods, in the event turned out to be no more trustworthy than his Iranian adversaries.

The failed helicopter rescue set off some stringent criticism in the American media. Some asserted that it was a bold attempt to emulate the Israeli rescue of hostages taken by the PLO at Kampala airport in Uganda. This sense of incompetence was underlined when 16 people were rescued from the Iranian embassy in London in May 1980 ten days after the American failure in Iran. The east coast newspapers at least were full of praise for the SAS and the British police.

When the bodies of the American servicemen were brought back from the Iranian desert to the United States I committed a *faux pas* occasioned by being dumped with a story at the last moment. Clive Small, our Washington correspondent, phoned me minutes before the service at Arlington National Cemetery was due to take place with President Carter in attendance. Would I cover as for some reason he could not? I should follow it on television, he said. The result was I tuned in late to watch the last part of the ceremony and filed the usual straightforward broadcast with appropriate solemn intonation. Unfortunately I said the servicemen were being buried at Arlington whereas in fact it was only a memorial service. No one noticed or if they did they never told me. Before the days of email one's minor errors as a broadcaster were rarely drawn to one's attention. Thirty years later it emerged that I wasn't the only one to make a mistake as to who was buried at Arlington. In 2010 the Inspector-General of the US Army reported that the dysfunctional management of the national cemetery had left many graves mis-marked, unmarked and even empty.

Only a week or so later William vanden Heuvel showed his colleagues how to rise above an insult and an assault with textbook diplomatic sangfroid. Just as he was entering the Security Council chamber together with the Russian ambassador, Oleg Troyanovsky, two young American Maoists emptied red paint all over them. Troyanovsky's face was completely covered in paint while vanden Heuvel's suit was ruined. Two oriental Americans were expressing their contempt for Washington, Moscow and Peking alike. One of them had interrupted Deng Xiaoping's visit to the White House the previous year. In the chamber they were quickly apprehended and handed over to the FBI because attacking a diplomat is a federal offence. It was recognised as a bad lapse in security because they could have, in the days before metal detectors were installed, been carrying weapons. Nevertheless, the two ambassadors managed to smile throughout and went off down the hall arm in arm beaming all the way. The session was suspended for 45 minutes.[4]

In September 1980, just as the General Assembly was getting underway, Iraq invaded Iran, thus initiating one of the bloodiest conflicts of recent times. Within a day or two the president of the Security Council issued an anaemic statement appealing for the two sides 'to desist from armed activity'. In the manner of the UN, the Council could not bring itself to use the word 'ceasefire' because that implied the armies should stop in their positions, which then favoured Iraq. No matter that Iraqi tanks had already destroyed much of the city of Khorramshahr. Was it that the Council felt powerless or had no confidence in its own ability to persuade the parties to see sense? More likely it was because four of the veto powers had a strong interest in Iraq prevailing. France and Russia were Saddam Hussein's main armourers while the United States and to a lesser extent Britain were still sore about being ousted from positions of influence in Iran in 1979 and 1950 respectively.

Once again the Iranian diplomats and political leaders came to the UN claiming to be the victims, this time with more justification than over the hostages where they had been the aggressor. Generally speaking it's the weaker party in a dispute or a conflict that shouts loudest at the UN that its territory or its rights have been violated. Diplomatically, the Iraqis easily outpointed Iran by smartly sending Ismat Kittani to the UN as their lead spokesman. He was a very smooth Kurd who had been Iraq's UN ambassador and head of Waldheim's private office. The Iranians, showing naivety rather than good sense, declared they would not talk about the war while Iraq remained on their territory, thereby losing the first round in the competition to influence the media.

A few days later the Iranian government sent Shams Ardakani as their special envoy to deal solely with the war. During a bizarre appearance before the press corps he called the Iraqis 'Fascists' and likened Saddam Hussein to Hitler. Ardakani portrayed his country as the entirely innocent victim, rejecting the Iraqi accusations of violations of the border and attempts to subvert Iraq's Shiah majority. He also claimed they had plenty of spares for their American-built planes and weapons because they had been stockpiled under the Shah. A month later the Prime Minister, Mohamed Ali Rajai, appeared at the UN. He was a kind of Iranian redneck. The former foreign minister, Ghotbzadeh, had said that his performance as minister of education showed he was unfit to be prime minister. Like the Iranian diplomats in the mission Rajai wore a heavy dark suit and a white shirt buttoned at the collar but without a tie, giving an appearance of scruffiness. This affectation of Iranian scorn for western dress and society is continued to this day. Rajai was a small, unshaven mathematics teacher who spoke only in Farsi, yet the diplomatic corps crowded into the chamber to hear him denounce Iraq as a puppet of Washington and claim that American surveillance planes (AWACs) from bases in Saudi Arabia were supplying Iraq with intelligence. That might have been true.

Opening the subsequent news conference he announced that he would not answer any questions about the American hostages. Whereupon the correspondents all groaned and got up to leave. Sensibly Mr Rajai changed his mind but continued to play the victim. He said he had some sympathy for the American hostages as he had been imprisoned and tortured himself by the Shah's regime. He claimed that he had had a fingernail pulled out and had been beaten on the soles of his feet, whereupon he took off his shoe and sock to show us a bruise on the ball of his foot. He would not acknowledge that Iran was facing a deadly opponent or that it needed armaments from 'The Great Satan' to keep its planes in the air.

The war went on for another eight years with both sides suffering huge losses and neither side achieving any gains. It was one of three gigantic errors made by Saddam Hussein – the others being the invasion of Kuwait in 1990 and his decision not to withdraw in the face of the UN-authorised military response the next year. Although it was a full-scale war to rate with Vietnam and Korea, the Security Council did not exert itself to bring it to an end until late in the day while the General Assembly never debated the war at all. Despite the best efforts of their special representatives – Olof Palme and Diego Cordovez – neither Waldheim nor Perez de Cuellar was able to mediate a ceasefire between Iran and Iraq or even negotiate safe passage for the hundred ships trapped in the Shatt al-Arab waterway. Some observers considered this a failure of United Nations diplomacy or lack of forcefulness on the part of the Security Council. In my view it was more the pride, obstinacy and plain stupidity of the two sides that prolonged the war years after it had reached a stalemate. Iraq pleaded with the Security Council to impose a peace but Iran would not accept the Council's plan embodied in Resolution 598 of 1987 until it was itself exhausted.

The United Nations Press Corps

The UN press corps was a very mixed bag. The pillars were the correspondents of the major news agencies and broadcasters such as Reuters, Associated Press, United Press International, Agence France-Presse, TASS and the BBC, plus Canadian Broadcasting Corporation, Deutsche Welle, the American networks CBS, NBC, ABC and the Voice of America. All these news organisations had permanent correspondents who covered the UN systematically and diligently. In addition, a few of the world's notable newspapers such as *The Times* and the *New York Times* had permanent correspondents. There were also over 200 journalists who were accredited to the UN, most of whom merely came in for particular events and stories of special interest to their organisations.

When the Secretary-General's press secretary, Francois Giuliani, gave his daily briefing at noon he could rely on a minimum of 20 correspondents being present with all the main organisations represented. When there was big news in the making such as a meeting of the Security Council to formulate urgent action concerning violent conflict or war then the number of correspondents would double or even quadruple. Some of these more spasmodic attenders had offices within the UN building but were not often seen on the UN beat.

The UN had a liberal policy of assigning offices on the press floor rent free. It was an inducement to post a correspondent to the UN permanently and ensured a far wider coverage for UN news. However, once an office was assigned the UN had no control over the news traffic from that office so that many journalists used their free office to cover general American news as well (as indeed we did at the BBC). For some correspondents American news had much greater priority than the UN so occasionally the UN held an audit to establish that at least some of each correspondent's output was about the UN and was in fact being used by the journalist's parent organisation which vouched for his (or her) credentials.

By and large I'm sure the UN gained a great deal of coverage by this somewhat generous system. Office rents have always been high in New York – even an organisation as well endowed as the BBC dropped its staff correspondent in the 1970s and almost abandoned its UN office simply because it saw other priorities for its money. However, the UN's relaxed policy also attracted the dubious, the marginal and the incompetent, some of whom tried to make up for their own deficiencies by parading an exaggerated loyalty to the UN. After one extraordinary news conference in which correspondents had given a UN official a close grilling, one of these 'hangers-on' attacked those of us who had asked the difficult questions. He shouted at Michael Littlejohns of Reuters and myself exclaiming that we were completely out of order. We laughed as did most of our colleagues but it did raise the question as to who these curious people were and whether their organisations really existed. It provoked some kind of verification exercise by the UN Press Office, which concluded that the man in question, Alexander Gabriel, plus one of his acolytes/friends/runners really did report UN news to a genuine organisation.

Not many correspondents were convinced by the UN's judgement as Gabriel's accreditation was with Transradio News Agency which had gone out of business in 1951! By the 1980s Gabriel was a wizened little man who attended regularly but said very little. He was obviously having a hard time making ends meet. Once upon a time he had worked as a genuine journalist but by now, though he could not stay away from the place, he was just going through the motions. UNCA did not want to run an exclusive club, though it would have liked to exclude the incompetent, the flatterers, and especially the nincompoop who lived in the building because he had no apartment to go to. If the paper whose label he carried, the *Daily Gleaner* in Jamaica, really used some of his output I shudder to think of the outcome and cannot believe that it did the UN much good. Without the inane reports from this individual the *Gleaner* would have relied on a reputable wire service and been much better served.

At one time the reporters were so numerous at the UN that they could support their own bar but this had been discontinued before I arrived as initial interest and, let it be said, hopes for the UN had subsided during the political stalemate induced by the Cold War. By 1980 the greatest surge in press interest came at the beginning of each year's General Assembly when presidents, prime ministers and foreign ministers came to speak to the world from the podium. Consequently at this time there was an influx of political and diplomatic correspondents who were simply following their men around the globe to report their every remark. The SG's annual news conference just prior to the Assembly was always held in the largest conference room to accommodate the 200 or so journalists, although most of them left New York as soon as their news-maker had given his address or finished his bilateral consultations. Few non-resident journalists worked at the UN right through the three months to Christmas in which the Assembly did most of its business.

During the rest of the year the briefings and news conferences were held in a much smaller room in the press section. By tradition these were formally opened by the President of the Correspondents' Association UNCA who stated how long the conference would last before asking the first question. The most effective president of UNCA in my time was the correspondent of the Associated Press of Pakistan, Iftikhar Ali, who was always genial and very well informed. The biggest thorn in the UN's flesh was Michael Littlejohns of Reuters who from the same seat in the back row would lob devastating questions at the UN spokesmen and women. He had been there for decades, time to know his subject and perfect his technique.

Another irritant for the UN establishment was the *New York Times* correspondent Bernard Nossiter. His brief, he told me, was to be much more sceptical and adversarial than his predecessor, Kathleen Teltsch. Towards the end of her long stint at the UN Teltsch had been seen as still starry-eyed about the achievements of the UN whereas her editors had backed round to a decidedly hostile quarter. Nossiter had a young assistant who did all the routine legwork so that he was free to nose out stories that embarrassed the UN. He had several mini-scoops, which in that delightful American phrase 'left the rest of us for dead', though they were more to do with personnel than with unexpected shifts in policy or the allegiances of member states. If you took the view that reporting the UN straight didn't matter much because the implementation of its resolutions was poor then you could admire Nossiter's reports which made the front page. But if you were a single-handed correspondent, as most of us were, then you hadn't the time for such sidebars. The deliberations, decisions and actions of the member states and of the Secretariat were more than enough to report to one's home country. Unfortunately anything published in the *New York Times* about the UN got a lot more attention than articles published elsewhere. It was our local newspaper and everyone read it.

In one particular instance Nossiter certainly brought about a change in UN policy. He discovered in May 1981 that the UN had secretly financed a quarterly newspaper supplement in order to promote the proposed New International Economic Order (NIEO). The supplement was inserted into 14 leading newspapers including *Le Monde, La Stampa, Asahi Shimbun* and the *Indian Express.* The papers themselves colluded with this deception by appointing a paid coordinator and an editorial board, which met in various cities, all expenses paid, to decide themes and approve articles. In return the papers received over $400,000 between them, officially to cover the cost of the newsprint. Most of the articles were written by genuine journalists but each paper was required to run in each supplement three articles prepared by UN agencies. When the UN itself quoted from the supplement to prove its own virtue or efficacy the cosy but hidden circle was complete.

The NIEO proposed a massive transfer of wealth, technology and expertise from the developed to the developing world. In 1981 it was still being negotiated in a series of multilateral conferences in which all member states could take part. The Reagan administration was strongly against it but most governments in the developed world were sympathetic to its objectives if not to all the details. If the UN officials had been open about the supplement from the start the actual views expressed would not have been so objectionable. Initially the money was donated by a Japanese shipbuilding magnate but this was not revealed to member states until published in detail in the *New York Times*. It was only when the Japanese money ran out after three years and UN officials were trying to solicit more at a conference in Geneva that the truth emerged.

When that happened the Under Secretary-General for Press and Information, Yasushi Akashi, saw nothing unethical in the arrangement. 'It helped correct,' he said, 'the current imbalance in the flow of information' about the economic issues dividing the rich and poor nations. It took two or three noon sessions in the press room with Michael Littlejohns (rather than Nossiter) raking the spokesman, Francois Giuliani, with well-informed and embarrassing questions before someone in the Secretariat saw they had to throw in the towel and stop subsidising the supplement. It was a good instance of a free press providing a corrective to an ill-judged and dishonest policy, although it should be said that too many well-regarded newspapers had played a leading role in this deception and had not lived up to their principles. The negotiations for the NIEO ran into the ground the following year.

Another extraordinary character among our colleagues was Louis Halasz who filed reams of material for *Time*. He was a Hungarian who larded his private conversation with foul words and filthy stories. He had a wonderful deep voice but was so prolix that he had to be avoided or one would never get back to one's work. When Waldheim left the UN he hired Louis to ghost his memoirs. They were friends of a similar age and background but made a contrasting pair of central Europeans – one cool, taciturn and efficient; the other garrulous, amusing and raffish. I wonder if their collaboration was harmonious or stormy?

The UN is a forum for governments to meet, discuss, negotiate and sometimes reach decisions. It's also a convenient place for dissident or alternative groups to air their grievances, not in the General Assembly, only occasionally in the conference rooms but more often as guests of the Correspondents' Association. With the help of a sympathetic correspondent a group could call a news conference which might attract anything from five to fifty reporters, depending on the issue. In the 1980s movements such as POLISARIO (Western Sahara) and FREITILIN (East Timor) or Puerto Rican nationalists or the internal parties in

Namibia all made their pitch this way. Other much less militant organisations such as the Sami people of Northern Norway or advocates of a universal peace day would also get a hearing. How much coverage they got really depended on timing. If they struck lucky and arrived on a slack news day a dozen or so correspondents would attend out of sheer curiosity, some of whom would file stories especially if they were freelance. Most of these groups were given a polite hearing but some were badly mauled whenever correspondents realised the spokesmen before them were concealing the real axes they had come to grind.

A good example of this concerned Ralph Schoenman, a maverick American peace revolutionary who had been Bertrand Russell's secretary. In the aftermath of the massacre at Shatila in Lebanon in 1982 Schoenman tried to pass himself off at the UN as an eyewitness. He held a session in the UNCA room more than a week after the event. Twelve years earlier he had been sacked for misusing Russell's Peace Foundation. Although Russell liked Schoenman and gave him much credit for various initiatives he eventually repudiated him in a 17-page private memorandum for being unreliable, bad-mannered, self-important and dishonest with the funds.[5]

In his presentation to UN correspondents Schoenman brought no new evidence but simply his opinion. He accused the Israelis of carrying out the massacre when in fact it had been their Christian Lebanese allies. Journalists are keen to listen to people who can challenge those in authority with first-hand evidence but they are impatient with the opinion of just another writer like themselves. If his evidence and views were cogent, we asked, why didn't he publish them himself? After about 15 minutes his bias was so acute that many of us left the room. We had better things to do than listen to a rant. I doubt that Schoenman got much coverage.

In a place like the UN journalists are often pressed to report propaganda, sometimes junk and even lies. They can be neutral and simply report everything deadpan; they can also indicate their scepticism by saying, for example, 'the Illyrian ambassador claimed or asserted or alleged that such and such happened'. Sometimes the objective, impartial reporter can match one quote from one source with rebuttal from another. A broadcaster can also convey a little more by the tone of voice in which he says 'claimed' or 'asserted' and so on.

Many inflated claims were made at the UN which I reported in reasonably anaemic tones because they were the views or the demands of governments. BBC News is a hungry monster with many mouths consuming different diets simultaneously. What might be of no interest to the world at large might be relished by one of the regional or language services. Another way to deal with such episodes was to report the main thrust but omit the more lurid or absurd persiflage. Rarely did one go to a news conference and report nothing.

When we were faced with an unreliable spokesman or we recognised dodgy information we tended to ask even more searching questions and to persist until we got some kind of answer. On one occasion when the former UN Commissioner for Namibia, Sean McBride, made a series of demands for action against western companies who were mining uranium in Namibia I indicated through my questioning that he was out of touch with reality. The Contact Group of Britain, France, West Germany and the United States all needed 'yellowcake' for civilian and military use, and in the Cold War they were certainly not going to give it up. In any case South Africa was one of their major trading partners. Legal action against the companies would have been pointless while these governments bought their products.

After McBride's unimpressive news conference his partisans came back to my office on the other side of the building to remonstrate with me. How dare I ask such questions of Sean McBride was their attitude, as if he were God Almighty. Didn't I realise that my comments were those of 'the fascist BBC'. One could only laugh as these minders or partisans simply reinforced my view that their champion was indeed disregarded by the main diplomatic players. It was only later that I discovered McBride came from an IRA family and had himself been Chief of Staff in the 1930s. After a few years as a politician in the Irish Dáil he transformed himself into a peacenik so successfully that he was awarded both the Nobel Peace Prize and the Lenin Peace Prize. The prestige from the first I feel might have been clouded by the reputation of the second.

Some of the more remarkable episodes played out on the fringes of the UN in this way concerned the nature of the new revolutionary government in Iran. During 1980 and 1981 a trickle of reports indicated that the regime was intensifying its persecution and even execution of many of its opponents. The revolution was eating its own children. In July 1981 a large group of Muslim students held a hunger strike around the base of the Ralph Bunche memorial opposite the UN, claiming that more than 50 children under the age of 15 had been executed after brief trials. Four months later a former Iranian envoy to the UN, Dr Mansur Farhang, gave an informal briefing to UNCA members. At the height of the hostage crisis the previous year he had vigorously defended

Ayatollah Khomeini. Now he described him as 'the most hated figure in Iranian history'. The Ayatollah and his followers were conducting 'an unimaginable reign of terror' and all in the name of Islam, though plainly at odds, he said, with Shiite tradition. It was only 18 months previously that Farhang had lambasted correspondents for not understanding the Iranian revolution and not sympathising with the seizure of the hostages. Now he described the Ayatollah as an irrational, treacherous, religious fascist. A month later a group of Americans formed a Committee for the Defense of Human Rights in Iran chaired by former ambassador William vanden Heuvel. They claimed that 3,350 people had been executed since the onset of the revolution.

Confronted by such figures, the journalist distant from the scene can only report them as being claimed by a particular organisation or individual. As I never had any complaint about these statistics either from the Iranian embassy or from colleagues in the BBC's Eastern Service in Bush House I assume they were true enough. Four years later Iranian students held a huge demonstration outside the UN also beside the Ralph Bunche memorial. By then they claimed the Khomeini regime had executed 30,000 people and held 100,000 political prisoners. A month or so later the National Council of Resistance of Iran (a well-financed organisation operating inside Iran as rebels and outside as a pressure group) published a list of the 1,185 people whom they accused of being torturers. Meanwhile the students' society compiled a gruesome account of the various tortures used by the regime, which they claimed were worse than those used by the Shah's henchmen. Again I reported these claims and again my reports were never challenged. That does not make them true but it leaves me with a great distaste for this regime and scepticism as to what might now, in 2012, be achieved by diplomacy. The prolonged diplomatic efforts to dissuade Iran from enriching uranium and thus give itself the potential to produce nuclear weapons have been admirable but whatever the outcome I doubt that the Iranians will ever abide by such agreements.

The UN Charter is an uplifting document full of ideals and aspirations yet practical in its definition of the organisation's main institutions. It is, incidentally, shorter than the American Constitution and far shorter than that ponderous, unreadable document known as the proposed European Constitution, which failed at the first fence in 2005. However, all observers at the UN should constantly remind themselves that all resolutions, votes and decisions at the UN are political. The axe of national advantage can always be heard being ground to a sharp edge somewhere in the background. Nevertheless, some decisions by its deliberative bodies are so counter to the very notion of a United Nations 'determined to end the scourge of war' or to 'reaffirm faith in fundamental human rights' that one wonders how ambassadors could articulate some of the actions their governments require of them.

Two examples come to mind which were unusual in themselves and particularly egregious. The first was the repeated support, year after year, for Democratic Kampuchea as a legitimate member state with a vote in the Assembly, which I discuss later. The second was the election of Ismat Kittani as President of the General Assembly in 1981.

Kittani was a smooth but stocky Kurd who was well known around the UN both as an Ambassador for Iraq and as a senior member of the Secretariat. Yet a year after his country invaded Iran and embarked on a bloody eight-year war he was elected as President of the General Assembly. This invasion was not only a flagrant violation of all those lovely principles but had drawn direct condemnation from much of the western and Non-Aligned world. He campaigned hard in the spring and summer of 1981 and was supported by the Arab and Soviet blocs and by many of the Non-Aligned states. After one candidate was eliminated on the first ballot Kittani and his opponent, Khwaja Mohammed Kaiser of Bangladesh, tied with 73 votes each.

This was the first contested election for president for 19 years. The usual practice is for the regional groups to take it in turn to make one nomination who is then elected by the Assembly without opposition. Why, we asked, were the Arabs so crass as to nominate a candidate from such a country as Iraq? And why, we asked the other states, were they so supine as not to kill this candidacy stone dead by indicating they would not work with the spokesman for such a country? When on the second ballot the vote was tied a rule was applied for the first time. The two names were put in a hat and Kittani's name came out. He may well have been more adroit at conference management than Kaiser but that was no excuse for voting for him. There were plenty of other competent Arab diplomats who would have done the job just as well as Kittani. And what can one say about the IQ of the six ambassadors who spoiled their ballots, any one of whom could actually have decided the result? Who can tell? Despite all the voting that goes on at the UN, perhaps some of them were not completely *au fait* with the basics of democracy?

* * *

250

Reviewing my despatches from the UN 25 years later I am also struck by the number of stories that report only the beginning. Interesting, I say to myself now, but what on earth was the result? One such story was the arrest, trial and imprisonment of Alicia Wesolowska, a staff member of the UN Development Programme (UNDP). She had fallen out with the communist government of Poland and had resisted a demand that she return home. *En route* to a new UNDP posting in Mongolia in August 1979, she was arrested while unwisely visiting Poland to see friends and family. Six months later the UN Staff Union protested about the arrest and asked for the UN to take her case to the International Court of Justice. It was not a very sensible request because the World Court does not deal with individual or criminal cases, though it might have heard arguments about infringement of the UN's diplomatic privileges. A few months later she was convicted of spying for NATO and sentenced by a closed court to seven years' imprisonment.[6] The official Polish report said she had confessed. What, I wonder, was the real story?

The UN Secretary-General protested about her arrest and the fact that for years no UN official was allowed to see her but the Polish authorities refused to budge. During her second year in Rakowiecka prison in Warsaw she twice went on a hunger strike, such was the extent of her despair. Twice she was forcibly fed for many days through a tube thrust down her throat. In January 1981 the Staff Union conducted a symbolic one-day fast at the UN. It even enlisted the novelist Graham Greene who from his home at Antibes cabled the Polish government asking that her human rights be restored. He also urged Waldheim to make a forthright public intervention, which Waldheim was very reluctant to do, thinking that only discreet diplomacy had a chance of helping her.[7] Over the next three years both Waldheim and Perez de Cuellar raised her case with Warsaw. Perez de Cuellar even told the Staff Union he would not visit Poland unless the government promised her release. Eventually the Polish government released her in February 1984 after four and a half years in gaol while the Secretary-General was visiting Warsaw. Clearly there had been a confidential deal. Under pressure from the UN, Jaruzelski's government grudgingly allowed her to take a job in the Warsaw office of the UN Economic Commission for Europe but even then she was still denied her civil rights for a further five years and was not allowed to leave Poland. In effect the Polish government was playing cat and mouse with her.

* * *

Wesolowksa was not the first among UN staff to have her privileges as an international civil servant trampled on by governments. When the Staff Union held a meeting in December 1979 to protest at the detention of seven of their members in five different countries the Soviet Union demanded that members of the 'so-called union' be punished for 'grossly slanderous attacks on member states'. Just before Wesolowska's release the Staff Union calculated that eleven countries were holding UN staff under arrest contrary to international law.[8] In 1983 there had been another egregious case in which the Secretariat held steady for a time but ended up abandoning its principles and bowing to Soviet pressure. Alexander Yakimetz, a Russian with eleven years' satisfactory service at the UN, claimed asylum in the United States when he was recalled to Moscow before the end of his contract. Once granted asylum he tried to return to his UN job but was forbidden to enter the building by the Secretary-General pending a review. The Assistant Secretary-General for Programme Planning and Coordination challenged this decision pointing out that Yakimetz had just had special training on planning and budgeting which would be wasted if his position was not confirmed. While suspended, Yakimetz was even promoted to a higher staff grade. Citing all the proper staff regulations, he asked for his contract to be renewed, strongly supported by his departmental chief, but this was overruled by Personnel and upheld by the Secretary-General. Finally the case ground into the UN's Administrative Tribunal, which six months later rejected his appeal by two to one, the votes being strictly along Cold War lines. The United Nations was denying its own principles of employment on merit proclaimed in Article 100 of the Charter, which also said that staff 'shall not seek or receive instructions from any government'.

Talking to the press after the judgment Yakimetz confirmed some of the worst accusations made against the UN and the USSR by a previous and more prominent defector, Arkady Shevchenko. Yakimetz said that the USSR required its citizens seconded to the UN to act as spies and that he did not lift a finger without the Soviet mission knowing about it. That probably applied equally to UN employees seconded from the Soviet satellites but one has to ask: did it also apply to UN civil servants from quite a few other countries as well? I don't know the answer but I suspect covert control of members of the Secretariat was and still is more common than is acknowledged by the UN itself. Certainly in the McCarthy era the Americans vetted all their citizens who applied to be UN employees.

* * *

Another 'unfinished' story was a UNICEF project to raise money for handicapped children by launching a worldwide children's song competition. In the first year it attracted a million entries. The winner who came from the Philippines had written her song originally in tagalog. It was set to music by the British popular singer Roger Whittaker, who had used the same formula on BBC Radio 2, and it was first performed in Radio City in New York in September 1980. The 13-year-old songwriter confessed that she really wanted to be a 'detective'. The hope was that it would raise millions for UNICEF but did it? And what became of the writer? Or indeed of the song competition? At the UN I never heard another word about it.

One story, which started fairly well in 1980 but has finished beyond the predictions of the most gloomy Cassandra, was Rhodesia. Fourteen years of white-ruled independence had just been brought to an end through negotiations at Lancaster House. A British viceroy, Lord Soames, had held the ring for a few months before elections handed the new state of Zimbabwe over to the dominant black party, the Zimbabwe African National Union (ZANU). When Zimbabwe was officially welcomed as the one hundred and fifty-third member state of the UN in September 1980 the new prime minister, Robert Mugabe, came to New York.

At his first and only press conference he revealed a little of what was to come in the latter part of his term in office. In fact two issues were touched on that both came to the fore in the early years of this century – the nationalisation of property and the treatment of white farmers.

I've rarely been to a press conference that began on time let alone early. This one ended ten minutes before it was due to begin. Mr Mugabe with an entourage of 27 was greeted by the American ambassador to the UN, Donald McHenry. In his opening remarks Mugabe tried to allay suspicion in the United States of his Marxist credentials. He said that Zimbabwe was a 'very safe place to invest ... there's no nationalisation process under way and we don't intend to nationalise any interests'. Before he had left Salisbury (not yet renamed Harare) Mugabe had been instrumental in securing bail for Edgar Tekere, the Secretary-General of ZANU and a Cabinet minister, who was charged with murdering a white farmer. Seated on the floor amid a scrum of correspondents I asked Mugabe why he hadn't suspended Mr Tekere from his Cabinet. From the tone of his reply the question touched a nerve. Tekere was not a convict and was innocent until proved guilty, said Mugabe, and with that he terminated the conference before most of the reporters had really tuned into his wavelength let alone been able to ask a question.

Perhaps this barely concealed contempt for the media is one reason for the rapid decline of his country? By the onset of the twenty-first century Mugabe's government and political party had created a hell in which no one, black or white, was safe. The bullying and murder of their mainly Ndebele opponents in Morgan Tsvangirai's party was appalling, far worse than colonial rule had ever been. At the same time mismanagement of the economy brought record inflation, exceeding 10,000 per cent per annum. The power-sharing deal, which was finally forced on Mugabe in 2008, has yet to resolve the political problems. Let's hope Mugabe himself gets his just deserts. So few corrupt and crazy leaders do.

One man at the UN that year whom Mugabe might have found to be a soulmate was Ieng Sary. As Deputy Prime Minister and Foreign Minister of Democratic Kampuchea he came to New York to ensure that his regime was still accepted as the legitimate government. Only in the UN, its critics might say, could an organisation that had murdered millions be seen as the lawful representative in the main representative assembly.[9] Only in the UN could such a man – very benign to look at – be allowed, nay encouraged, to sign documents, which he and his gang had flouted on principle and on a mass scale. Conservative critics had a point.

This was a good example of relying too much on the letter of international law, which some would have us do to the exclusion of common sense. The world knew that the Pol Pot regime had murdered millions; there was already plenty of eyewitness testimony and mountains of corpses and skeletons. There was no excuse for the United Nations to recognise by a majority of two to one the Khmer Rouge as the legitimate government. Their so-called legitimacy rested solely on brutal conquest in 1975 aided and abetted by China. The United States, Britain and most of the member states went along with this awful farce only because it was Vietnam that had ejected Pol Pot and installed its own puppet regime. For all its faults Vietnam had done the world a good turn. If it had not invaded Kampuchea Pol Pot, Ieng Sary and the rest of that mad, murderous crew could have still been there. The UN could have simply refused to recognise the credentials of either claimant and left an empty chair until such time as a properly constituted government had taken its place.

One reason was of course the dead hand of the Cold War which froze brains and attitudes in many capitals, East and West. Vietnam was strongly supported and supplied by the Soviet Union. During the General Assembly in 1980 the Association of Southeast Asian Nations sponsored a resolution that urged an international conference to negotiate the withdrawal of Vietnamese forces followed by UN supervised elections. The Soviet Union, also relying on the Charter rather than good sense, declared that this was intervention in the internal affairs of the People's Republic of Kampuchea, 'a state,' said Oleg Troyanovsky, that would 'one day be represented in the UN'. When retired ambassadors write their memoirs I wonder how often they blush at the words uttered on instruction from headquarters? 'Those who lost in Vietnam,' he said, 'are attempting to have their revenge,' and went on to accuse the United States of promoting the destabilisation of Indo-China, working hand in glove with Peking.[10] For his part Sir Anthony Parsons thought the vote in favour of Democratic Kampuchea – the most atrocious regime since Stalin – was a farce. After he had cast Britain's vote in favour he made what he called a 'blistering attack' on the regime. Then abandoning his diplomatic sang-froid he rushed out of the chamber to avoid the 'outstretched handshakes of the Pol Pot delegation'.

As if to underline the hypocrisy and sheer silliness of all sides the UN Secretariat arranged a little ceremony with the media on hand at which Ieng Sary signed three human rights instruments including the International Covenant on Civil and Political Rights. It was as if Hitler had sent Ribbentrop to sign the Convention on Genocide during the Second World War. Ieng Sary was eventually brought to trial in Cambodia in 2009, charged with war crimes and crimes against humanity. The case continues still.

The Reagan Administration

With the inauguration of Ronald Reagan as president in January 1981 we soon became very conscious of the incompetence of the new administration, at least with regard to issues and people at the UN. The Republican transition team had had more than two months to make appointments and to brief the new personnel as to the new direction of policy. Yet many times during that first year US officials at the UN would give a lame reply when asked about policy: 'That question is still under review.' The Reagan team were determined to be different from Carter but for a long time they did not know how and had no better guide than a hazy reference to the UN in the Republican Party platform.

At times the Administration's spokesmen tried to make a virtue out of their slow thinking. They were pleased, for instance, to hold up both the North–South Global Economic negotiations and the Law of the Sea negotiations. Eliot Abrams, a very green Assistant Secretary of State for International Organisations, made it obvious at the UN that he was only too pleased to throw a spanner into the UN works, saying he thought it had a 'salutary effect... It shows a force of mind and a belief in one's own position'.[11] Except that at the time he could not tell the media what his government's position was on the Law of the Sea.

Abrams went on to explain that the Administration's approach to foreign policy and diplomacy was one of crude carrot and stick, a policy of rewards for friends at the UN and punishments for enemies. 'I want to be able to tell an ambassador as he goes out to his post: "In the last five years ... this country has voted for us five times and against us a hundred times. Then you act on it."'[12] He also admitted, however, that some countries were too important for it to be applied strictly. He did not specify but it was obvious he had in mind large strategic countries such as India and Pakistan. Mr Abrams was a protégé of two hard-jawed cold warriors, Senators Daniel Moynihan and Henry Jackson, as well as being the son-in-law of the Editor of *Commentary*, Norman Podhoretz. Moynihan's book, *A Dangerous Place*, about his time as UN ambassador was obviously Abrams' bedside reading.

The new ambassador, Jeane Kirkpatrick, was more knowledgeable than Abrams but had little more experience in diplomacy. She was plucked from a throng of contenders for this plum post of ambassador with Cabinet status supposedly on the strength of her *Commentary* article 'Dictatorships & Double Standards', which was a sharp critique of Carter's foreign policy towards the Shah, General Somoza and other Latin American autocrats, whom she described as 'moderates'.[13] It was her view that traditional authoritarian governments were less repressive than revolutionary autocracies, were more susceptible to liberalisation and, above all, were more compatible with American interests. 'Because the miseries of traditional life are familiar,' wrote Mrs Kirkpatrick in 1979 while a professor at Georgetown University in Washington DC, 'they are bearable to ordinary people.' 'Such societies,' she went on, 'create no refugees, in contrast to revolutionary communist regimes, which create refugees by the million.' This was the era of the boat people fleeing both Vietnam and Cuba. But of course it entirely overlooked the millions of Latinos who had migrated to the United States from wretched right-wing Latin American regimes.

In view of all the horrors inflicted by juntas in Argentina, Chile, Honduras, Guatemala, Peru, Paraguay and Brazil, most of which were already well documented and plain to view, it was curious to speak up for 'traditional autocracies'. America had no urgent need for the support of General Pinochet in Chile or the military junta in Argentina. Nevertheless, the argument seemed to resonate well with President Reagan and was certainly influential in determining the administration's blinkered policy towards El Salvador and Nicaragua, which provided mini examples of the contrasting types of autocracy right there on America's doorstep. This analysis and the policies that flowed from it did not endear her to many nations at the UN, nor indeed to many Europeans. The BBC TV programme *Panorama* broadcast a fairly caustic profile of her which she greatly resented. Her press officer, Joel Blocker, came to my office to enquire what I knew about it – very little, I had not seen it – and to ask could I put pressure on London to repudiate it?

The article in *Commentary* was a well written manifesto for cold warriors containing some neat turns of phrase. She did, however, make an error of judgement that made her blush later. 'Although there is no known instance of a revolutionary socialist or Communist society being democratised right-wing autocracies do sometimes evolve into democracies.' Ten years later the Soviet Union, its European satellites and most of its Third World client states evolved into some form of democracy.

At her confirmation hearing before the Senate Foreign Relations Committee, Alan Cranston refused to accept her description of Carter's foreign policy as a failure. Did she reject the Camp David Agreement and the Egypt–Israel Peace Treaty? or the normalization of relations with China? or the Panama Canal Treaty? Well…, she muttered, the treaty had not been finalised when she wrote her article. So had it had bad results, pressed Cranston? Well … not so far, she admitted.[14]

In her opening statement she had unwisely boasted of 'first-hand knowledge of virtually every corner of the world' but two senators showed she was not so familiar with the business of the United Nations. Larry Pressler asked a series of questions to which she could give no answer. Did the US need a separate ambassador for the Law of the Sea negotiations? Or the Moon Treaty? Or Global Economic negotiations? Was Reagan going to advance nuclear disarmament with the Soviet Union? She had no answer. Edward Zorinsky drew attention to three human rights instruments, which were awaiting ratification by the Senate – 'Civil and Political Rights', 'Economic, Social and Cultural Rights', and the 'Elimination of Racial Discrimination'. She admitted she had not read any of them and then apologised for having to say, so many times, to these and other questions 'don't know', 'not sure', 'I'm going to study that', etc.[15]

Finally Joseph Biden, now the Vice-President, undercut her ridicule of the Carter Administration's record at the UN. He pointed out that the US had persuaded most developing countries to vote against the Soviet invasion of Afghanistan, to deny Cuba a seat in the Security Council and to stop the Vietnamese regime in Cambodia being recognised at the UN. In a written statement he warned that her more confrontational style might well vitiate these gains. The committee recommended her appointment by 16 votes to none but few reporters or commentators, if any, followed up her various lacunae.

Despite being exposed as being less than the master of her brief she scorned an induction proffered by the State Department and underlined her view by appointing three outsiders to key positions in the UN mission, rejecting candidates from the Foreign Service. Instead she took induction briefings only from the White House staff, in part because her instincts were political rather than institutional and in part because she realised the centre of power and decision making on foreign affairs would be on Pennsylvania Avenue rather than at Foggy Bottom. She also began with an acute aversion to the new Secretary of State, Alexander Haig, something which adversely affected her first 18 months at the UN. Two years after Haig had left office she let rip at him during a question and answer session with The Women's Forum in New York. 'I'm sure Alex Haig thought he was going to wipe me out in the first nine months in the job, and he didn't'.[16] That petty, unprofessional piece of revenge exposed the deep divisions in Reagan's Cabinet and was unbecoming for a serving ambassador.

She took almost two months to give her first half-hearted press conference at which she admitted the new administration was slow on the draw. I gave her a hard time as this near verbatim report makes clear.

She's nobody's pushover

It didn't take members of the United Nations press corps long to discover that Jeane Kirkpatrick is not a pushover, as indicated in these excerpts from her first press conference as UN ambassador.

Jeff Kamen, Independent Network News: "Well, my question to you is how will the spirit of the Reagan administration be manifested differently than the spirit of the Carter administration (toward Third World nations)?

Ambassador Kirkpatrick: "You were here. I wasn't. I think that the spirit with which we will approach our relations with all nations, large or small, is one of sincerely desiring to find common understanding and to pursue common goals."

Keith Hindell BBC: "...the review (of U.S. prior policies at the UN) of the Reagan team has been going on for four months. That seems like an awful lot of time ... how much longer should we expect it to go on?"

Ambassador Kirkpatrick: "Well, first of all, you count time a little differently than I do."

Hindell: "Starting Nov. 3."

Ambassador Kirkpatrick: "But we didn't have an administration in place ... you say four months. I say from Jan. 20, from Inauguration Day; most of us (Cabinet members) were confirmed shortly thereafter."

Hindell: "All (selecting staff, security clearances, etc.) are handled a lot quicker in other countries."

Ambassador Kirkpatrick: "So be it. But quicker doesn't necessarily mean better. Not many countries have been through the sort of election which we have just been through ... we did not simply change presidents, we really changed the government in a way we don't often do."[17]

Wisconsin State Journal

As the year went on the State Department and Kirkpatrick stumbled badly over several major issues which had been in the pipeline for years. Ten days before she came to New York the Secretary of State had sacked all the top officials in the team negotiating the Law of the Sea Treaty, one of them only learning of his fate by reading the newspaper en route to the UN. The team leader on Carter's watch, Eliot Richardson, who was still a consultant, called it a 'massacre'.[18] When a new Assistant Secretary of State for Oceans was appointed four days later he had neither a compass nor a crew, neither a policy nor a team of experts to help him. Five months later when the Law of the Sea negotiations were resumed the Administration was still without a policy on an issue of vital importance to its navy, its merchant marine, its commerce and its mining industry. The same lack of competence became evident again over South Africa in March and again in late April. At that time the US said it was not ready to negotiate over

Global Economic negotiations; yet everyone else was. Is this tardiness the price for having a written constitution that grinds slowly and a spoils system in which all the top people are sent packing every four or eight years? Or perhaps it's just the conceit that comes of being more powerful than the rest of the world put together?

During her first year Kirkpatrick had two public rows with Alexander Haig who was not exactly her chief yet was supposed to have overall responsibility for foreign policy. One incident concerned the Israeli destruction of the Iraqi nuclear plant Osirak in June 1981, the details of which I relate on pages 267–68. The other serious disagreement was over the Falkland Islands, which I deal with in the next chapter.

Mr Haig also kept putting his foot in it, most notably when he claimed to reporters in the White House that he was 'in charge' after Reagan had been shot and wounded on 30 March, 1981. That phrase attracted much adverse comment because according to the Constitution the succession moves first to the Vice-President and then to the Speaker of the House. Haig explained too late that all he meant was that he was in charge in the White House Operations Room in the absence of the President and Vice-President. For four days running American newspapers expressed deep distrust of this man perhaps because he had previously been chief of staff to President Nixon during the final months of Watergate. A commentator in the *New York Times* described his claim as a unique example of 'bad judgment, bad performance, bad timing and bad choice of words'. Later on Haig cited as current a nuclear strike doctrine that had been abandoned years before, only to be corrected somewhat tetchily in public by the Defense Secretary, Caspar Weinberger.

Mrs Kirkpatrick was a great deal more forceful than her predecessor, Donald McHenry, who was a career diplomat thrust into the post in 1979 when Andrew Young was dismissed by Carter for talking to the PLO – another glitch by this huge foreign policy machine. At the start Kirkpatrick was very academic. For instance, at an early press conference she responded to a sharp question as if to a student by saying, 'If you'd read my book you would know the answer to that question.' It was a pity that the questioner was not quick enough to respond with something like, 'And if you read my article tomorrow you'll know what I feel about your policy.' Despite having been a professor for years she did not, at the start, deliver her speeches in an appealing and comprehensible manner. Her style was involved, often oblique, almost pernickety and delivered in something close to a gabble. In her first UN debates she was easily eclipsed by other performers.

Over her four years at the UN Jeane Kirkpatrick certainly improved her style of public diplomacy. She learnt that the 'class' of diplomats, bureaucrats and journalists whom she had to address and persuade was not necessarily antipathetic to the American view just because it expressed scepticism or asked hard questions. By the time of the 1981 General Assembly debate on the Soviet occupation of Afghanistan she could hold the attention of most of the delegates. The Soviet invasion, she claimed, had had a shattering effect on the prospects for stability in South Asia and the Persian Gulf. It was a momentous event that shook the foundations of world order and marked a watershed in the post-war era. 'Nothing in the long history of Afghanistan resembled the destruction wreaked there since 1978,' which she compared to the invasion of Genghis Khan 700 years earlier. This was trenchant acceptable rhetoric at the time but now those words could so easily be applied to American action in both Afghanistan and Iraq.

Despite her embarrassing mistakes Jeane Kirkpatrick had a wide circle of support in the United States and Israel. She was showered with awards and had at least two academic positions named after her, one in Harvard and the other in Israel. Certainly her calibre was head and shoulders above most other members of Reagan's Cabinet, some of whom were abysmal. Towards the end of Reagan's first term she was often tipped for National Security Adviser to the President or even Secretary of State in the next term but that did not happen.

The Election of a new Secretary-General 1981

As the delegates to the General Assembly gathered in September 1981 they knew that one of their tasks was to choose a secretary-general to take office in the new year. Kurt Waldheim's second five-year term was drawing to a close but his ambition led him to think he was indispensable. For more than a year he had all too obviously been paying courtesy calls on capitals around the world to line up support. Before the Assembly opened he announced that strong expressions of confidence from member states had led him to think it would be his duty to accept another term. He could not have been relying on many African votes because the African group had already made it known that it thought it was its turn to nominate a secretary-general. The Foreign Minister of Tanzania, 39-year-old Salim Ahmed Salim, was their declared candidate. He was personable, experienced and competent but was *persona non grata* with

261

the United States because he had all too publicly show his delight at the discomfiture of the US when China was admitted to the UN in 1971. According to newspaper reports he had 'danced in the aisle' in the General Assembly hall. Salim's candidacy was strengthened by being endorsed by the Non-Aligned Movement, which at the time had 96 members, almost enough for the required two-thirds majority. It also had four elected members of the Security Council – Niger, Panama, Tunisia and Uganda.

Near the end of October 1981 the Security Council got down to the task of choosing in closed session its nominee to be placed before the Assembly. Under a curious procedure the 15 Council members could each vote in what was theoretically a secret ballot for both candidates Waldheim and Salim. Both got majority support – nine votes or more – but both were vetoed; ballot papers of 'Permanent Members' were a different colour. As the Soviet ambassador told us with a broad smile that he had not cast any vetoes we assumed that Waldheim had been blocked by China and Salim by the US. A day later the Council held two more votes in which Waldheim now scored eleven but Salim slipped below the threshold of nine, the minimum for a majority vote. Clearly not all the Non-Aligned members were supporting their man. On the other side the Europeans, Americans and Soviets all voted for a third term for Waldheim.

Although these votes were cast in the Security Council's private conference room media correspondents were able to glean most of the details by questioning ambassadors as they emerged. It was while Kirkpatrick was running the gauntlet of the correspondents that she gave the first indication that it might be the time to open the race to other candidates.[19] Salim was probably out of the race but China would not budge in its opposition to Waldheim. Before the process had begun China had announced it would only vote for a candidate from a developing country and it stuck to that resolve.

Eight further ballots in November failed to give a result, a majority vote without a veto. As the presidency changed at the beginning of December to Uganda, Kirkpatrick described the situation as 'complex paralysis'. No one anticipated that Olara Otunnu, who was only 32, would be the man to break this deadlock. On his third day as President he called the leading candidates to a consultation in which he persuaded both of them that they had little chance of success. Waldheim withdrew immediately and Salim five days later. It must have taken considerable nerve and ability for this young African to face down Africa's champion who supposedly had the backing of 51 states.

With the race thrown open seven new candidates put themselves forward, of which the best known were the former UN High Commissioner for Refugees, Saddrudin Aga Khan and the Secretary-General of the Commonwealth, Shridath Ramphal. Some of the others were known at UN headquarters but none had a name recognised by journalists on the foreign desk let alone the man in the street. One of the 'also-rans', Ambassador Radha Krishna Ramphul of Mauritius spawned an unkind diplomatic joke, something pretty rare at the UN. He had served 15 years or so at the UN during which he had occupied a number of important posts including President of the Security Council. When he failed to get any support some wag coined the phrase 'there's no fool like an old Phul'.

When the Council voted again only two candidates got a majority vote. Saddrudin scored well but was vetoed by the Soviet Union. On the other hand, Javier Perez de Cuellar, a senior Peruvian diplomat who had also been a UN Under Secretary-General, got ten positive votes without incurring a veto. Consequently the Council recommended him to the General Assembly which elected him by acclamation four days later.[20] He took the oath of office in English and made his first speech to the Assembly in Spanish, French and English. He was the first Latin American to hold the post.

Olara Otunnu had already emerged as a man to watch in May of 1981 when he managed to bring new impetus to one of the UN's perennial issues – the seemingly unsolvable riddle of Namibia. Over ten days of intermittent Security Council debate Otunnu kept the African group together in its demand for sanctions against South Africa. This ground had been covered many times before (and was still eight years away from a solution) yet he managed to make a good point with humour. Those opposed to sanctions had argued that they did not work. 'Well if sanctions do not work,' he said, 'why should three permanent members on this council cast the heavy weight of their votes against measures which would not work anyway?' (laughter and applause from diplomats in the chamber). It also struck a chord among those millions who felt frustrated by South Africa's endless stonewalling to prevent independence. The effectiveness of sanctions is an immensely complex argument in its own right.

Although he knew it would attract a triple veto, in his final speech insisting on sanctions Otunnu said that Africans had been patient to a fault over Namibia, to the point of absurdity. He reminded the three western permanent members that Namibia was the Council's unique responsibility: 'no amount of words, no amount of vetoes can shake away that responsibility'. Unlike most African UN diplomats at that time his speeches were agreeably free of nationalistic or Marxist claptrap. At the time Washington was embarking on a strategy of pushing for a deal whereby the African countries would persuade Cuba to withdraw its forces from Angola in return for American pressure to get South Africa to allow Namibia to go forward to independence.

Otunnu is an Acholi from north-east Uganda, the fourth of twelve children of an evangelical Christian preacher. As a student at Makerere University he had emerged as too prominent a critic of Idi Amin so fled first to Oxford and then to Harvard where some astute professor helped him into a New York law firm. From there he went back to Tanzania to take part in the Uganda Liberation Front, which when it had ousted Amin and formed an administration sent him back to New York as deputy ambassador. He was only 30 when promoted to be ambassador in 1980. His success at the UN helped him become Foreign Minister under Prime Minister Obote, although he didn't last long because Obote's regime was ejected by Museveni. Despite lacking patronage from Kampala he managed to carve out a place for himself in New York first as Director of the International Peace Academy and then as the Secretary-General's Special Representative for Children and Armed Conflict. After he left the UN his most startling move was to accuse in 2006 President Museveni's government of 'genocide' in northern Uganda. By 2011 he was leader of the Uganda People's Congress and was arrested while taking part in demonstrations against rising prices.

Another young and dynamic ambassador who punched way above his weight was Tommy Thang-Bee Koh from Singapore. He was a short, slight figure who wore large, thick-rimmed spectacles long after they had passed out of fashion. He represented a rare member state at the UN – a successful and prosperous developing country – and he was not afraid to criticise the political conduct of his peers. For instance, in October 1981 he made some eloquent and generous remarks after the assassination of President Anwar Sadat of Egypt when most of the Arabs sat silent. 'A man shows courage,' he told the General Assembly, 'when he pursues an unpopular course believing it to be right even though his friends desert, abuse and condemn him.'

Koh's most notable diplomatic triumph was to bring the Law of the

Sea (LOS) negotiations to a successful conclusion against all the odds. As the elected President of the third LOS Conference (1981–82) he conducted a very sophisticated and patient diplomatic exercise in which he broke up the 54 delegations into manageable small groups and cajoled them into reaching an agreement. He deliberately included the troublemakers and extremists (his words) in each of these groups and then slowly wore them down so that they accepted reasonable compromises.

The Group of 77 (which then numbered more than a hundred states) had the votes to dominate the conference but Koh persuaded them it was essential to reach all decisions by consensus otherwise the major countries would not participate. In fact the American delegation behaved in a short-sighted way by driving hard to achieve some of their priority objectives and then not ratifying the treaty. It's a common American tactic, repeated at the Kyoto Climate Change negotiations, which only a very strong country can carry out. The rest of the conference ends up accepting some provisions solely to appease the big bully or the dominant interest, provisions which then cripple the treaty for no good reason if that country does not in the end participate. Although it may meet the short-term political goals of the USA such conduct eats away at its reputation for honest diplomacy and fair dealing.

Tommy Koh was a strong supporter of the UN but had the confidence to be a frank critic of both the Security Council and the Secretariat. After leaving the UN in 1984 to be Singapore's ambassador in Washington he stated baldly that the Council was not realising the central goals expressed in the Charter, namely the peaceful settlement of disputes and the maintenance of peace and security. He also pointed to the routine corruption of the ideals of the Charter by leading member states, which impeded the work of the Secretariat and delayed reform. The communist countries would not allow their citizens to become independent international civil servants, instead insisting they could only be seconded for a few years, and moreover, siphoning off much of their salaries. For their part, some western countries, such as West Germany, paid generous supplements to their nationals serving at the UN, thereby distorting the agreed international salary structure. In addition, virtually all member states lobbied the Secretary-General hard, often with contingent monetary inducements such as funds for UNICEF, in order to get their nationals appointed to posts on the staff. Tommy Koh was one of few UN figures who stood out for recruitment and promotion only on merit.

When UN finance became a major issue in the late 1980s Koh called for the 'junkets and needless conferences' to be cut, citing the Economic and Social Council in particular for moving every year to Geneva for its summer session at great expense. At the same time he criticised the Reagan administration for withholding its assessed contributions and the American Congress for deciding to reduce the US contributions permanently in order to bring about change at the UN. What, he asked at the Heritage Foundation in Washington, is your real intention: 'to reform the UN or to emasculate it?' Unfortunately quite a few in this conservative think-tank and in Reagan's White House wanted to emasculate the UN.

Tommy Koh was frank more often than not but like all diplomats sometimes he had to defend the indefensible. At the end of a UN Conference on Kampuchea in 1981, two and a half years after Vietnam had ejected Pol Pot's regime, Koh was spokesman for the Association of Southeast Asian Nations. To explain their continued support for so-called Democratic Kampuchea and to conceal his own blushes Koh told an amusing story. When Machiavelli, a suspected atheist, was dying, said Koh, a cardinal called on him to renounce the devil. For hours he refused but finally in a weak voice he croaked: 'Now is not the time to make enemies.' It wasn't much of a joke but it was told well.

During the General Assembly journalists would be showered with invitations to parties by the various delegations, especially the Arab delegations, some of whose receptions were incredibly lavish. Because my most regular outlet for placing stories was the midnight news on the BBC World Service, most evenings I worked until its deadline New York time, which was 7 p.m. Often I worked much later, fulfilling requests from regional services such as the Arabic Service or the Far Eastern Service. One year when the resolutions were piling up near the end of a General Assembly I found myself throwing into the bin half a dozen invitations which I had not been able to attend. Probably that was a good thing for my health and waistline but I may well have missed a good contact or some useful information. At least three times I arrived at one of these diplomatic receptions after almost everyone else had come and gone, the most memorable being a party for Olof Palme, then an ex-prime minister of Sweden. Palme had been recruited by Waldheim to mediate in the horrible Iraq–Iran war in which hundreds of thousands of young men were killed, bringing no gain whatsoever to either side. To embark on this war was actually Saddam Hussein's greatest crime among many. So, one evening, after a long day, I mistook the time on an invitation to meet Palme at the residence of the Swedish ambassador, a long way up town on the west side. Despite being, as I thought, rather late I felt I ought to go.

The Swedes like all the Scandinavians were strong supporters of the UN and often a source of good information. I actually arrived well after the closing time stated on the invitation to find only two people remaining, the ambassador whom I had met before and Palme. They were just sitting down to eat a scratch meal amid the debris of the party. I apologised for being late and began to withdraw but no, they insisted I join them for supper, mostly of bread and cheese and wine. Unlike the Arab receptions this had obviously been a modest affair but probably all the better for that. Palme was an enlightened charmer so it was an evening well spent. His murder in Stockholm in 1986, still unsolved, was a great loss to the international community as well as to Sweden.

One of the most serious events considered at the UN while I was there was the destruction by Israeli bombers of the nuclear plant known as Osirak in Iraq on 7th June, 1981. Israel asserted that the purpose of the reactor was to produce Hiroshima-type bombs, the technology having been acquired piecemeal from France and Italy. Israel claimed it destroyed the plant at that time because it would have become operational in a few months. It was a clear case of unprovoked aggression contrary to the Charter but strangely it was not contrary to international law. Iraq had remained 'at war' with Israel ever since 1948 through the three subsequent Arab–Israeli wars.

In the Security Council debate the Iraqi Foreign Minister, Sadoon Hamadi, demanded that the Council impose an arms embargo on Israel supposedly to stop American supplies of advanced aircraft used in the attack. He also demanded that Israel should open its nuclear installations to inspection by the International Atomic Energy Agency (IAEA) as Iraq had done already. Considering the severity of the attack the debate was low key. Hammadi scarcely raised his voice.

In a very protracted debate which went on for a week, the French ambassador assured the Council the reactor was an exact replica of two built in France. With such a plant, he said, neither the enrichment of uranium nor the production of plutonium was practical. There were much simpler ways of producing weapons grade uranium or plutonium; 'it would be absurd for a country which wanted a bomb to build a reactor of this type.' Both France and Britain rejected the Israeli claim of self-defence and said Israel ought to pay compensation.

Diplomats on the Council spent days trying to devise a resolution that would condemn Israel, demand that she submit her nuclear plants to IAEA inspection, pay reparation and impose an arms embargo, yet still be acceptable to the US. Much of the debate was an unfocused platform for shaming Israel. Although the US condemned the raid fairly promptly the administration took several days to refine its position and decide what it would accept in a Council resolution. In the middle of the week the White House even asked a congressional committee to determine if an American law on the sale of weapons to Israel had been broken. Even though America had no diplomatic relations with Iraq Mrs Kirkpatrick negotiated directly with Hammadi and staved off the imposition of sanctions. With the help of the Secretary-General, Hammadi and Kirkpatrick agreed a compromise. Kirkpatrick told a new recruit to her staff that she had 'negotiated' the word 'aggression' out of the resolution, contrary to the advice of the State Department lawyers.

In its resolution the Council then unanimously condemned the attack, recognised Iraq's right to set up nuclear plants for peaceful purposes, called on Israel to open its nuclear facilities to IAEA inspection and 'considered' that Iraq was entitled to redress. However, the Council did not use Chapter VII of the Charter to make its demands mandatory and Arab demands for an arms embargo against Israel were squeezed out under threat of a US veto. The *New York Times* reported that Haig felt Kirkpatrick had given too much away, a story that was officially denied. Correspondents often quote to each other the old adage, 'Never believe anything until it is officially denied.' Many a time this cynical view seemed all too true.

In recent years we have sometimes seemed poised on the brink of a similar pre-emptive strike against nuclear facilities in Iran. This is exactly the type of case the Security Council ought to be able to deal with, perhaps in the future *must* be able to deal with, if we are to avoid a nuclear strike or even a nuclear war. Yet there are so many impediments to action that it's almost impossible to think it would ever work or at least that it would ever work quickly enough to prevent a nuclear explosion. The only time the Charter mechanisms afforded to the Security Council actually worked was in the case of Iraq in 1991. On that occasion the seizure of one state by another was so clear cut it enabled all members of the Security Council except Yemen to see it had to be reversed, otherwise it was a threat to all sovereign states. The Arab states were divided on the matter, though what any of them hoped to gain from Iraq's annexation of Kuwait is difficult to see.

If Iraq had possessed in 1991 a credible nuclear weapon and a proven delivery system would the Security Council have acted as promptly and with as much firmness as it did? There are always plenty of governments that opt for inaction in almost all situations. This tendency would only be more in evidence if there was a risk of a nuclear explosion or of a cloud of radiation dust being sent up into the stratosphere. In the light of its twelve-year record of dealing with a recalcitrant Iraq after the Gulf War is it likely that the Council would have reached agreement on effective action against a nuclear Iraq in 1991? More likely, the international community would have been paralysed by its own fears and doubts. Only the United States, Israel and perhaps Britain would have had the resolve to act against a nuclear-armed Iraq in 1991. Today, confronted by an unsophisticated government in Tehran, fired up by Islam as well as by nationalism, it seems even more unlikely that the Charter mechanisms will be adequate once Iran has acquired long range nuclear-armed missiles.

Many strong supporters of the United Nations argue that in such circumstances the Security Council should take action short of war, such as trade sanctions and arms embargoes. These were the methods applied to Iraq after the first Gulf War in order to persuade her to dismantle and destroy an arsenal of weapons of mass destruction. This non-violent pressure was supplemented by rigorous air patrols, which in effect contained Saddam Hussein's expansionary ambitions and enabled the Kurdish region to achieve autonomy and a degree of prosperity. Firm and sometimes deadly though this military pressure was it did not induce Iraq to abandon its claim to Kuwait or even to give an honest account of the Kuwaitis it had taken prisoner.

Throughout the twelve years of economic sanctions there were constant complaints that they were too effective, that they made the Iraqis' lives miserable. Neither the Council nor the advocates of non-violent methods solved the dilemma of how to deal with a truculent autocrat who did not feel the pressure in his daily life and ignored the sufferings of his population, many of whom he openly despised.

Moreover, those who argue that no action should be taken without the authority of the UN could not explain away the Security Council's lack of authority when operating so-called 'mandatory sanctions' under Chapter VII of the Charter. Iraq took little notice of these resolutions and subverted sanctions as much as it could while many other nations connived at breaking those sanctions. Furthermore the UN's own humanitarian agencies such as the World Health Organisation and the United Nations Children's Fund undermined the morality of sanctions by asserting that their clients/patients in Iraq were suffering. At times they acted as a black propaganda unit for Saddam Hussein, churning out estimates as to the number of deaths attributable to sanctions. I often felt that if you added all their dire warnings together the whole population of Iraq should have died. Whatever the validity of their estimates they certainly undermined the resolve of the member states and thereby vitiated the contention that non-violent methods could contain and disarm this aggressive state.

The Council bent over backwards to respond to the criticisms made by humanitarian agencies by setting up the Oil-for-Food programme but that spawned corruption, which also undermined the UN's credibility. The international community had not the stomach to persist with firm sanctions while diluted sanctions mitigated by Oil-for-Food looked as if they might go on forever without achieving much. What would sanctions against Iran or North Korea achieve today?

For a time some experts attracted attention with their proposal of 'smart sanctions' – essentially measures that would only hurt the autocrats or thugs in power. They would, it was argued in the Security Council as it applied such measures to Zimbabwe, induce a more cooperative attitude in the leaders while leaving the population well fed and in good health. Smart sanctions turned out to be a mirage. They were clever but ineffective. Even in the most dire national economic circumstance autocrats and their henchmen live well. They are impervious to inflation, unemployment, shortages or any of the normal indices of national decline. Restricting their travel or their overseas bank balances are so many flea-bites. So far this is an unsolved problem for the UN – how to get compliance without going to war.

The question of how to deal with 'rogue' states that are nuclear-armed is also an unresolved dilemma that will haunt the UN for the rest of this century. It is true that some of the time the United States looks like the most untamed, unstable, unsophisticated, fundamentalist state of all. Sometimes the cry of 'double standards' directed towards America has merit. But the fact that the rest of the world is not strong enough to confront the US militarily is no reason not to have the means to deal with the lesser fry who in their own way could also endanger us all.

Although the second Gulf War initiated by America and Britain in 2003 occurred long after I left the UN I must offer a view as to the UN's role. The justification for the war was based on faulty intelligence that Iraq still had an arsenal of weapons of mass destruction, plus the rockets for long-range delivery. The CIA and MI6 should both lower their heads in shame for getting their assessments so wrong. But unfortunately the UN's two inspection regimes both had a role in perpetuating the idea that these weapons still existed in Iraq. The UN commission, UNSCOM, verified the destruction of many weapons in the period 1991 to 1998 but its Australian chairman, Richard Butler, was convinced many weapons and substantial supplies for making more weapons still existed when his organisation withdrew from Iraq. The successor organisation, the UN Monitoring, Verification and Inspection Commission (UNMOVIC), headed by Hans Blix, did not find any substantial evidence in its fairly short period of operation, but even it could not give the Iraqi regime a clean bill of health.

All of this misinformation from the military intelligence services and the lack of definite information from the UN inspectorates was compounded by continual obstruction by Iraqi officials and the crowds/goons they hired to intimidate the UN inspectors over many years. Saddam Hussein made another of his crass mistakes by not allowing the UN inspectors to verify the complete elimination of his weapons of mass destruction and long-range rockets early on. It probably would have saved him from the invasion of 2003. No doubt he and his officials thought they were being cunning in hiding weapons, factories and materials or pretending to hide them from the inspectors, when in fact it brought on their own destruction.

The invasion of Iraq in 2003 was a very bad mistake, which caused a huge amount of unnecessary death and destruction. However, over the previous twelve years the UN had not itself provided a solution to an aggressive Iraq threatening its neighbours and exercising a tyrannical government at home. The Security Council did not agree to the invasion, which was clearly the right decision, but nor could it agree on and promote an effective alternative policy. The containment of Iraq had been provided by American and British planes patrolling the 'no-fly zones', something that was reasonably effective but was not directly authorised by the UN Security Council. When forceful action is taken despite a lack of endorsement by the Council that action may be illegal but it also may be very effective and beneficial, as it was over Kosovo and the Tanzanian invasion of Uganda to topple Idi Amin. If the Council is to prove more effective it has to devise new methods of achieving results and a new resolve to find solutions to crises. In the face of an aggressive or manic nuclear-armed state a deadlock in the Council could prove catastrophic for us all.

Whenever I found a likely respondent who could talk in reasonable English about an important topic I would try to get an interview. There is a deplorable habit common among broadcasters in recent years of talking about 'an exclusive interview'. Not only is this boasting about what is a routine broadcasting exercise but a proper interview is by its nature a one-to-one affair. In the public arena such as outside the Security Council chamber correspondents would crowd round diplomats as they emerged to ask about the state of play or press for a comment. The broadcasting correspondents would always run their tape recorders but would rarely in those circumstances recover more than two or three lines of usable response and even that would be accompanied by ambient chatter not conducive to good listening. For a sustained interview with a news-maker in which one could not only seek information but also test or challenge some of the answers I found that the best results were generally achieved in my own small studio.

Besides interviews with the leading diplomats such as Waldheim, Parsons, Koh and Kirkpatrick, I also interviewed a very mixed bag: Luiz Inacio Lula da Silva, then a Brazilian labour leader but later President; the Argentine General Roberto Viola, who was just about to become President; an elderly crown prince of Saudi Arabia posing as Foreign Minister; and, most strange of all, the Puerto Rican nationalist, Oscar Collazo, who in 1950 had tried to assassinate President Truman at Blair House in Washington. He killed a guard and wounded two others in what we nowadays would call a suicide mission. Badly wounded in a short gunfight Collazo was sentenced to death, a sentence that Truman commuted to life. After 29 years in prison he was let out by President Carter. Independence for Puerto Rico looked a lost cause in 1981 even though supported by the UN De-colonisation Committee, but I see that in 2012 Puerto Ricans will decide in a referendum whether they want statehood or independence.

None of the four last mentioned impressed me as being especially charismatic or competent or even honest. One other particularly odd interview was with the head of the UN Volunteers, Hikmat Nabulsi, who was a Syrian. The UN Volunteers recruited experienced people who were willing, out of idealism or the lure of adventure, to practise their skill or expertise for a couple of years in a developing country. They received modest expenses but no pay. As it had just passed the one thousand mark two years ahead of its target date it was a minor success story.

I arranged the interview through Nabulsi's office a day or two before, stressing that I wanted it for the BBC Arabic Service. I explained I would ask the questions in English but would like him to reply in Arabic so with editing he could be broadcast directly. When he arrived he claimed he knew nothing about giving his answers in Arabic and roundly upbraided his American woman assistant who protested that she had warned him. To me he said he could not talk in Arabic because he would have to use too many technical terms, which he only knew in English. My colleagues in the Arabic Service suspected that the real reason was that he was ashamed of his poor classical Arabic. The result unhappily was that we did the interview entirely in English and because of that it was never used.

At the end of my time at the UN I wrote a valedictory piece for the programme *From Our Own Correspondent*. While I was there the UN did not manage to solve a single violent conflict. It came close with Namibia but that took another five years to complete. It always seemed to have a reasonable chance with Cyprus but Turkish troops still occupy the eastern end of a divided island. It seemed in 1984 to have only an outside chance of resolving the Soviet occupation of Afghanistan but in fact it played an essential role in easing the evacuation of the Red Army, although that did not lead to internal peace. Generally the prospects were bleak. Iran and Iraq continued to bomb and fire rockets at each other's cities and Cambodia was still occupied by Vietnam. Nicaragua was fighting for its survival with Contra invaders armed and supplied by the United States. India and Pakistan confronted each other in Kashmir and still do 60 years after Britain left the subcontinent. Palestine was and is still grinding on though Israel had been one of the UN's first creations.

Some of these seemingly intractable conflicts have since been resolved in part because of the collapse of communism and the emergence for a time of a more cooperative attitude in Moscow. However, the UN's prestige in conflict resolution has not increased despite the end of the Cold War. Its peacekeeping deployments have greatly increased but they are often ineffective as peacekeepers unless the local combatants cooperate, as has happened in the eastern Congo where the UN's largest force has been operating for some years without being able to stabilise the situation. In many ways the prospects for the global security system are still bleak. The best thing the UN can do is never to give up on a problem. Instead it must constantly remind the belligerents, be they states or dissident internal groups, that peace is a far better condition than war and that the UN is always ready to help them achieve it.

Notes

Some of the following references (also in Chapters 18 and 19) are to my dispatches from the UN to the BBC. They were all numbered with the prefix N for News and are currently retained by the author. They should also be available in the BBC's archives.

[1] Diego Cordovez & Selig Harrison, *Out of Afghanistan – the Inside Story of the Soviet Withdrawal*, Oxford University Press (1995)
[2] Brian Urquhart, *A Life in Peace & War*, London, Weidenfeld & Nicolson (1987), pp.133–139
[3] My dispatch to *The Economist* (30.3.82)
[4] My BBC dispatch, N152 (30.4.80)
[5] Bertrand Russell, Private memorandum concerning Ralph Schoenman, dictated 1969, published as an appendix to Ronald Clark, *The Life of Bertrand Russell*, London, Cape: Weidenfeld & Nicolson (1975), pp.640–657
[6] My N83 (7.3.80)
[7] My N6 (13.1.81)
[8] UN Staff Union press release (9.2.84)
[9] According to Ieng Sary the government of Democratic Kampuchea had been dissolved and replaced by a union of patriotic forces
[10] My N413 (17.10.80)
[11] My N187A (7.5.81)
[12] My N187A (7.5.81)
[13] Jeane Kirkpatrick, 'Dictatorships & Double Standards', *Commentary* (November 1979)
[14] *Nomination of Jeane Kirkpatrick. Hearing Before the Committee on Foreign Relations*, US Senate, US Government Printing Office (15.1.81), pp.81–84
[15] Ibid., pp.88–91
[16] Jeane Kirkpatrick, *Legitimacy & Force*, Vol 2, New Brunswick, NJ, Oxford Transaction (1988), pp.216–219
[17] *Wisconsin State Journal* (16.3.81)
[18] My N102 (9.3.81)
[19] My N486 (30.10.81)
[20] My N596 (11.12.81)

18

The Falklands – A Classic Problem for Diplomacy

The Falklands dispute ought to be part of every basic course on diplomacy. Such a simple dispute between two states involving very few people and with very modest economic resources at stake could surely have been solved without resort to force? For 16 years the Foreign Office had held intermittent talks with Argentina intended to improve commerce between the Islands and the mainland of South America. The Falkland Islands were seen as an unwanted dependency, a hangover of Empire. If some form of words could change their status into something like the Channel Islands *vis-á-vis* the UK then it would surely benefit all sides. Almost the first contact I had with the British mission to the United Nations in January 1980 concerned a postponed session of the ongoing talks at a low diplomatic level. So much so that there was no news and I did not file a story.

The difficulty was not really the facts of the Islands and their small, isolated population. What prevented a peaceful change of status and relationships was the huge cultural and political gap between the main protagonists. Argentina had never been stable politically. Certainly liberal democracy had never been entrenched there or indeed anywhere in Latin America. It could be fairly labelled a failed political democracy and often a failed state. From the early 1970s its domestic conflicts were so bitter that a military junta was able to seize power and to employ brutal methods to maintain itself. Thousands of people suspected of being opposed to the regime just 'disappeared', most of whom were never heard of again.

Foolishly and irresponsibly, various British governments had largely turned a blind eye to this development. They continued to negotiate with this repressive regime in part because Argentina was a major trading partner but also because they chose to look the other way. Mrs Thatcher's government certainly had a 'touch of the Kirkpatricks' – an ability to reason that as the junta was anti-communist, it couldn't be too bad.[1]

The exact numbers of 'disappearances' were not known but it was obvious Argentina was now ruled by a vile government that ignored the rule of law and brushed aside basic human rights. Such a regime could not be trusted with the lives of 1,800 British citizens. We should have broken off all talks concerning a change of status for the Islands. We could not have concluded an agreement with a junta that Alexander Haig described as 'just a bunch of thugs'.

The seizure of the Islands by Argentina on 1 April, 1982 should have only confirmed this view. Initially it was prudent of Britain to engage in diplomacy, at least until its task force arrived in the South Atlantic. Without its own forces to match those of Argentina the diplomats could not have hoped to achieve anything in those circumstances. However, President Galtieri and his fellows in the junta made two basic miscalculations: first that Britain would not attempt to eject them from the Islands; and second, that when the task force was marshalled in the South Atlantic, Britain would not be strong enough to defeat the Argentine forces.

The first mistake was a poor assessment of the psychological mettle of the Thatcher government and the willingness of the British people to back a vigorous response. More serious was the simple military miscalculation that the Argentine forces would be strong enough to hold off the task force. Britain's strength was no secret; anyone could find it laid out in *Jane's Fighting Ships* and other military manuals. Only the Argentine Air Force posed a real challenge because it had far more planes based within range on the mainland than we could deploy from carriers in the South Atlantic. In addition, they had a few air-to-ship Exocet missiles which proved deadly when they struck the target. If they had made a better calculation of the military balance they could have waited until many more Exocets had been delivered from France. Deliveries of Exocets were actually suspended during the conflict so that the Argentine Air Force essentially ran out of them and could not have made more spectacular strikes even if they had wanted to.

In contrast to their highly proficient pilots, their navy in effect retired to base after the sinking of the cruiser *Belgrano* while their occupying army showed little initiative and no eagerness to engage. If they had made a proper assessment of the military balance after the invasion they still might have been able to conclude a negotiated settlement that would have left the UN administering the Islands.

At the United Nations I witnessed the diplomatic campaign at close hand. Hours before the invasion the issue was raised in the Security Council.[2] In due course the diplomatic baton was picked up first by the American Secretary of State, Alexander Haig, and then by the new Secretary-General, Javier Perez de Cuellar. Because the Argentine government did not settle at the UN this part of the story has been somewhat neglected by journalists and historians. In fact it was a textbook demonstration of mediation by an experienced diplomat.

Despite the clumsy and somewhat pointless landing on South Georgia by an Argentine salvage company two weeks before, the Argentine government took London by surprise in dispatching an invasion force. Not until a few hours before the troops went ashore did Whitehall accept that Argentina was intent on occupying and annexing the Islands. In the early evening of April 1st Britain asked the Security Council to consider the Argentine threat and insisted on an urgent meeting as the next day might be too late. Despite the lack of definite information Sir Anthony Parsons persuaded the President of the Security Council to issue a statement calling on both sides to exercise restraint. That same evening President Reagan phoned President Galtieri asking him not to go ahead with an invasion. The next day, however, the Argentine ambassador at the UN announced that his country had 'recovered the Malvinas'.[3]

Two days later after some very astute diplomatic lobbying Parsons persuaded the Council to pass Resolution 502 by a vote of ten to one with four abstentions.[4] Only Panama voted against. The Resolution called for an end to all hostilities, the withdrawal of Argentine forces and resumed negotiations over the future of the Islands. This proved to be the basis on which we built our case throughout the whole affair. Our affront at the invasion was thereby blessed by the Council and enabled us to describe our action to regain the Islands as 'self-defence', which is provided for under the Charter. It was the peak of our support at the UN. Despite being a clear case of unprovoked aggression on the part of Argentina the UN would never have taken firm action on our behalf. In fact at that time it had only once supported its own decisions by force and only twice with sanctions.

At this point the United States stepped in with an offer of mediation. It did not want its controversial policy of fostering good relations with unpleasant regimes in Latin America to be blown away in a war with its closest ally. My wife and I had already planned a holiday in the Caribbean. As soon as Alexander Haig picked up the diplomatic baton I reasoned that nothing substantial would be decided at the UN for some time so it was 'safe' to go off to St Thomas in the American Virgin Islands. Our timing proved to be perfect. A week later I came back to the most intense period of work in my whole life. I filed 200 news stories and interviews in 83 days on this subject alone besides covering other topics such as the Israeli invasion of Lebanon.

Haig went round the triangle of Buenos Aires–London–Washington twice without finding much willingness to compromise on either side. Although he was an ex-general himself he found little to admire in the Argentine leadership. On his return he let it be known that his visits to Buenos Aires had been a waste of time and that the Junta 'were a bunch of thugs with no one in charge'.[5] He negotiated with Galtieri and the Foreign Minister, Nicanor Costa Méndez, but found their authority was undercut by the other members of the junta who themselves would not or could not decide anything without consulting the corps commanders in the armed forces. On the same day that Haig returned to Washington Costa Mendez arrived in the US declaring that Argentina's sovereignty was 'non-negotiable'.

After the British submarine *Conqueror* sank the cruiser *Belgrano* on 2 May the Argentine ambassador, Eduardo Roca, denounced Haig's role as 'a deception intended to allow the British fleet to reach the Islands'. 'In its support, collusion and direct participation with Britain,' said Roca, 'the United States was guilty of an unspeakable strategy to bend the will of a free people and to steal its territory.' Some diplomats will say anything to please their masters although it was a bad error to impugn a government that was still anxious to be Argentina's friend. Perhaps he was under strain. In an interview five days earlier he told me he had been ambassador for only a month yet it felt like a hundred years.[7] He was replaced soon after as Argentina's negotiator at the UN by the Deputy Foreign Minister, Enrique Ros.

With Haig retired from the diplomatic field, the UN Secretary-General initiated a diplomatic process known as 'good offices'. For the next two weeks he explored the possibilities of negotiation and possible compromise with the ambassadors of the two countries while the British task force was steaming into a position from which it could recover the Islands. Day after day Perez de Cuellar called in Sir Anthony Parsons and Enrique Ros for separate talks. As they went into the UN headquarters they ran the gauntlet of reporters, fending off their impatient questions as best they could. Parsons had a knack of conveying seriousness of purpose without being too solemn. He knew that the press corps would have to write or broadcast something so he did his best to give us a morsel to chew on and a sound bite to quote. Enrique Ros was not so accomplished at this game but then he must have known he had the weaker hand.

Rarely did Ros say anything memorable and sometimes he simply kept his mouth shut shaking his head in despair.

After he had left office Perez de Cuellar described this system known as proximity talks as a 'cumbersome diplomatic technique'. After days of listening he dangled some ideas before the protagonists in the form of an *aide-mémoire*. It proposed that both sides should withdraw their forces by an agreed date followed by negotiations on the substantive issues with a target date for completion. It was also envisaged though not spelt out that the UN would have a role as interim administrator of the Islands. It was a reasonable start but unfortunately the *Belgrano* was sunk the same day with great loss of life. The Argentines were too mortified to assess the advantages of this simple scheme coolly and rationally.

For a time there were two or even three peace mediators churning around similar components in a diplomatic kaleidoscope – the Peruvian president, Belaúnde Terry, Alexander Haig (still active even after the US had declared for Britain) and the UN Secretary-General. They all tried to establish an agreed timetable for a ceasefire and withdrawal of forces. They attempted to determine the nature of an interim administration. Would it be led by the UN, with or without the direct involvement of Britain and Argentina? Would the wishes of the Islanders be 'paramount' or merely 'taken into account'? In addition, the mediators all sought to set a second timetable for the resumption of negotiations on the future status of the Islands after a ceasefire was implemented. Late in the day the Secretary-General encouraged the principals to decide how much of a role the Islanders would play in the interim administration and whether or not the few Argentine residents would be represented on the Executive and Legislative Councils.

Even though the Falklands problem was not complicated, the range of issues was significant, giving both sides plenty of scope to gain some advantage. Curiously it was the stronger power and the eventual victor who twice accepted a peace plan that would have conceded to Argentina some advance without retribution for the invasion. But three times the junta overplayed its hand and rejected both the Peruvian plan and the ideas put forward by Perez de Cuellar and his crisis team.

The day after the destroyer *Sheffield* was sunk by a missile Britain accepted the so-called Peruvian plan, which incidentally, Perez de Cuellar says had largely been drafted by Haig. Then a few days later when the task force was still marshalling and at the same time attempting to neutralise the Argentine Air Force, Perez de Cuellar got the British to agree that a UN administrator would assume all the functions of a British governor.

The Thatcher government was accused by critics both in Britain and abroad of being belligerent but actually it was much less bellicose and more ready to compromise than its opponents in Buenos Aires. It was not until two months after the invasion and a month after serious fighting had begun that Britain shrugged off calls for a ceasefire. Two weeks before the end just as the tide of war turned in Britain's favour the Security Council called on the Secretary-General to try once again to negotiate a ceasefire in the following seven days. 'What can I do in seven days?' asked a somewhat exasperated Perez de Cuellar. As he left the Council chamber that day Costa Mendez told a crowd of reporters that the resolution was 'barely acceptable' but that Argentina 'would tolerate it'. Almost in tears, he said, 'War is so cruel. Great Britain is showing a complete lack of proportion.'[8] There followed another six days of feverish proximity talks which Parsons dubbed 'mission impossible', as it proved to be.

As British forces closed in on Port Stanley opinion at the UN veered sharply towards Argentina. The UN loves a loser; its thinking is geared towards succouring victims and righting wrongs. Now that Britain was no longer the victim its original supporters in Resolution 505 melted away, four members of the Council veering right round with the change in the wind. Although the Security Council has a judicial function – its decisions form part of international law – it is first and foremost a political body. Ten days before the Argentine surrender it voted nine to two in favour of an immediate ceasefire and the implementation of the two original resolutions, 502 and 505, which Argentina had ignored for ten weeks. This was unacceptable to Britain because it did not set a timetable for Argentine withdrawal and would have left its forces in place in some parts of the Islands.

Parsons had announced in advance that Britain would veto such a resolution so his vote against was no surprise. Nor indeed was the American vote against unexpected, but a few minutes later Mrs Kirkpatrick shamefacedly said that she would like to change her vote 'if that's possible?' It was too late and in any case would have made no difference to the outcome as the resolution had already been killed by the British veto. By her totally unnecessary intervention she unnerved her closest ally yet got no credit from the Latin Americans whether they were democrats or autocrats. She explained that her government had instructed her to state, for the record, that it actually wanted her to abstain. Mrs Kirkpatrick told reporters: 'My instructions came too late.'[9]

This episode, reminiscent of a similar turn-about made by the Carter administration, was revealing. It showed the relative impotence of the UN ambassador despite being of Cabinet rank, and it was also a reminder that size and technical competence is not always an advantage. The American administration is so huge it creates its own internal tensions and bottlenecks, too often resulting in poor decisions, or slow decisions which sometimes amount to the same thing. In this case Mrs Kirkpatrick claimed that it was all a matter of communications. Although Britain had made its position clear on this resolution for the previous three days she claimed she only heard on the afternoon of the vote that Britain was not interested in exploring other amendments. Her instructions to veto, she told reporters, were then confirmed by high-ranking State Department officials though they did not reach Haig who was in Paris. The final instructions to abstain came without explanation too late and were followed by further orders to state in public how she should have voted. 'Throughout,' said Mrs Kirkpatrick, 'I acted on instructions from my government.'[10] But who was 'my government'? Was it the State Department or Haig or the White House?

In his book, *Caveat: Realism, Reagan & Foreign Policy*, Haig ruefully states that his efforts in the Falklands 'ultimately cost me my job'.[11] He says he admired Mrs Kirkpatrick and on most policy issues agreed with her except on the Falklands where their views were 'unreconcilable' (sic); 'each of us believed the other's position was contrary to the best interests of the United States'. On this issue as on several others the White House was countermanding its own Secretary of State.

A day or two later Kirkpatrick pleaded *mea culpa* in a speech which was almost self-flagellation. Talking to a friendly audience at the American Heritage Foundation in Washington she said that in the previous 18 months she had become 'deeply impressed with American incapacities at the United Nations ... our inability to find reliable allies, to make persuasive arguments, to put together winning combinations'. In the General Assembly where she claimed much of the voting was by blocs 'we are a country without a party', unlike the British who had cultivated reliable voting alliances through the Commonwealth. She then described the British ambassador, Sir Anthony Parsons, as an 'enormously skilful diplomat'; watching him during the Falklands crisis had been 'tremendously impressive'.[12] Although some delegations might not have been so fulsome about Parsons few would have denied that he had presented Britain's case, day after day, for over two months, with an effective mixture of cogent argument, appropriate restraint and much good humour.

Kirkpatrick went on to assert that American administrations had not understood that the UN was a political arena and had changed the ambassadors and the Assistant Secretaries of State for International Organizations far too frequently; on average they only stayed 18 months. 'By not learning the rules, the players, the game, we have often behaved like a bunch of amateurs in the United Nations.' When she reprinted this speech six years later she actually entitled it 'Learning the Game'. Perhaps this speech was just another way of getting back at Haig for making her look a fool? For a while she was in a benign mood. Although she was not normally an admirer of the UN she had already commended the Secretary-General, Javier Perez de Cuellar, for his mediation efforts even though they were unsuccessful: 'The UN's record in dealing with this conflict is commendable... We can be proud of it; proud especially of the Secretary-General.' Five months later she described Perez de Cuellar as 'a man of great intelligence and high integrity: he is an unusually fair, reasonable and decent man'. Mark you, she was hardly a reliable judge of character. In 1986 she publicly admired the personal qualities of Jonas Savimbi, the leader of UNITA in Angola, describing him as 'a man of courage, intelligence, strength and sophistication'; this is the same man who essentially prolonged the civil war for 20 years because successive peace agreements never placed him in power in Luanda.

With the breakdown of diplomacy the issue therefore was decided entirely by force of arms. The mediators had been unable to bridge a gap which the two countries had been arguing about for years, in the case of Argentina for over a century. The UN system for the peaceful resolution of disputes had failed either to prevent war or bring about even a ceasefire let alone a settlement. The powers existed in the Charter that would have enabled the international community to stop this war occurring and to eject Argentina from the Falkland Islands, yet the UN lacked the will and probably the capacity to act in such a forceful way. The Security Council as the instrument of the international community had failed to exert itself as in many other previous crises. In some crises of course a forceful intervention might have risked nuclear war between the great powers but not in this case. The Soviet Union abstained on those original resolutions which called on Argentina to withdraw. The Islands had no strategic significance and Britain would not have used its nuclear weapons to retain them.

Was it therefore a failure by the mediators, particularly by the UN Secretary-General? There were criticisms of both the methods and the style of Haig and Perez de Cuellar but personally I think they are misplaced. Argentina and Britain had the responsibility to settle but for various reasons one or other of them rejected all the compromise plans because they did not like the substance, not because they were offended by the means or the personality of the mediator.

After the first round of UN mediation, which lasted 15 days in May, sometimes including two meetings a day with each side, many regarded the process as a failure of the UN but Sir Anthony Parsons saw it differently. 'It was not a failure by the Secretary-General,' he said, 'he did as skilfully and as diligently as any man could have done.'[13] That was the verdict of one professional diplomat upon the conduct of another. Although Parsons was too clever a man to have upbraided the Secretary-General because he had to deal with him every day on many matters besides the Falklands, he would not have offered such praise if it was unmerited. Our ambassador came out of the crisis with his reputation greatly enhanced but curiously he did not discuss the Falklands in his analysis of the Security Council, *From Cold War to Hot Peace*, published 13 years later when he had retired to academia.

I have devoted a whole chapter to the Falklands War in part because I worked harder in this three-month period than I ever did in the rest of my life.

I must add one interesting personal footnote to this story. In the middle of the Falklands campaign there was a sudden lull during which I was asked to fly up to Canada to record a live interview on a breakfast radio programme. With the agreement of my colleague Clive Small I zoomed off to LaGuardia airport carrying just my briefcase. Only when I reached the security check did I remember my passport. No matter, said the official, and waved me through on the strength of my UN identity card. Amazingly it was just as easy leaving Canada and re-entering the US. It wouldn't happen nowadays without a great deal of fuss.

Notes

[1] See Jeane Kirkpatrick, 'Dictatorships & Double Standards', *Commentary*, (November 1979), and my article 'Madam Ambassador: An Appraisal of Jeane Kirkpatrick as US Permanent Representative to the United Nations 1981–1985', *Passport: Newsletter of the Society for Historians of American Foreign Relations*, 39: 3 (January 2009)
[2] My N168–171 (1.4.82)
[3] My N178 (2.4.82)
[4] My N191 (3.4.82)
[5] My N224 (26.4.82)
[6] My N265 (6.5.82)

[7] My N245 (1.5.82)

[8] My N372 (26.5.82)

[9] My N494 (3.6.82) & N405 (4.6.82)

[10] My N406 (4.6.82)

[11] Alexander Haig, *Caveat: Realism, Reagan & Foreign Policy*, Macmillan, New York (1984), p.269

[12] Jeane Kirkpatrick, *Legitimacy & Force*, Vol I, New Brunswick, NJ, Oxford: Transaction (1988), pp.215–220

[13] My N343 (20.5.82)

19

South Africa and Namibia

For about 50 years the white South African policy of apartheid was on the UN's agenda. From the early 1960s when the ex-colonial African states flooded into the UN, apartheid was often the most emotional question before both the General Assembly and the Security Council. The newly independent African states demanded boycotts and sanctions for weapons, trade, culture and sport. They also tried to expel South Africa from the organisation and did induce the South African diplomats to leave the Assembly. The three western permanent members of the Security Council blocked outright expulsion as they were entitled to do under the rules. So while I was there the South African ambassador still attended the Council whenever his country was on the agenda and sometimes spoke to explain and defend his country's position.

As a result, Britain, France and America were accused of hiding behind the Charter in order to protect their trade with South Africa and Namibia. To some extent this was true. Together with West Germany they also tried to use their diplomatic and business contacts to put constant low level pressure on the regime. Apartheid was brutal but it was a domestic policy, which under Article 2.7 of the Charter was exempt from UN scrutiny and interference. The Security Council could only intervene if South Africa posed a threat to international peace and security. That said, South Africa did make itself vulnerable because of its military intervention in the Angolan civil war, which went on for years. African states urged the Council to use force to expel South Africa both from Angola and from Namibia, which it had originally acquired as a League of Nations mandate. The African states were incapable of doing this for themselves. They wanted the western states to do the tough work for them but they got no takers. Embargoes on arms sales to South Africa was as far as the leading western nations would go. Black South African nationalists had to do their own fighting.

At the end of August 1983 when I was at home on leave in Wales I was sent forthwith to accompany the Secretary-General on a trip to South Africa and Namibia. I was told at the same time that the BBC's domestic News Department would no longer fund the UN office and the UN correspondent from April 1984, as it was pressed for cash. Instead Bush House News would manage and pay for the office, but then after four months I would have to vacate the UN correspondent's job so that another correspondent could be appointed. In effect I was being allowed one more year in the job.

The Secretary-General's trip had actually been agreed with South Africa after I had left New York for the summer but his office had got in touch with London while I was away to ask whether the BBC would like to send someone with him. I realised at once that though Bush House would be keen to have my reports from South Africa they had given me the trip as something of a sop for my impending redundancy. I left the next day without going back to London to collect my gear.

The journey to South Africa was unusually interesting. It began with a short low level flight from Birmingham to Heathrow on a fine afternoon. How wonderful and informative flying must have been in its first 50 years before the days of jets climbing to high altitudes. From about 5,000 feet it's like looking down on a geographer's plane table with all the details of houses and gardens, woods and fields, hills and valleys clearly laid out below.

From Heathrow I went on to the Ritz Hotel in Madrid which then was the epitome of restrained luxury and good taste. My colleague Douglas Stuart described the correspondent's life as that of a 'gilded vagabond'. This proved to be a perfect example. This was my most gilded moment. Alas, I arrived after midnight and left at 7 a.m. the next morning with coffee and croissant being my only taste of the hotel's five-star menu.

At Madrid airport the Secretary-General's small party boarded the Spanish royal plane along with half a dozen correspondents. The plane had been lent through the influence of the Secretary-General's Executive Assistant, Emilio de Olivares, a personable Peruvian who had been to military college with King Carlos. It was a DC6 which by then was an obsolescent model and showed its age. However, it contained a private office and sleeping quarters in the front of the plane, which made it ideal for this trip. The rest of us, staff and journalists, had to sleep in our seats during a couple of overnight flights.

The first stop was the Cape Verde Islands where we landed at a magnificent new airport built and paid for by South Africa as a quid pro quo for letting South African Airways planes refuel there *en route* to Europe and the United States. Of course such cooperation flouted not only a host of UN General Assembly resolutions, which demanded total sanctions, but also the declared policy of the Organisation of African Unity. Such double standards – to coin a phrase – with regard to measures against South Africa in the apartheid era were not uncommon among African states. On the one hand they demanded boycotts, embargoes and comprehensive sanctions but on the other they pleaded for exemptions for neighbouring states for whom South Africa was a major trading partner. The African leaders wanted the western nations to impose the sanctions and abide by them at some cost to their trade while getting special measures for themselves.

Cape Verde was then suffering from a 15-year drought and though it was near the end of the 'rainy' season it had had no rain at all that year. The Islands produced less than a fifth of the food needed and were reliant almost entirely on aid from the UN and other outside sources. While the aircraft refuelled the Secretary-General had a short conference with the President in the airport lounge to discuss further assistance. But not before we had been treated to a few rousing numbers played by a local band while we all stood on a rather tatty red carpet. The diplomatic protocol that has grown up around the arrival and departure of heads of state and heads of government wastes a huge amount of time and effort. It no longer oils the wheels of diplomacy but simply slows the process down. Waldheim was a stickler for such things but Perez de Cuellar simply endured them.

From there we had a long flight to Cape Town, arriving late in the evening. We stayed in the Lord Nelson Hotel, which has a splendid position looking down upon the city and where I had stayed five years before while making reports with Douglas Stuart for *The World Tonight*. Perez de Cuellar went to South Africa in order to give another push for Namibian independence. South Africa had agreed in principle to allow a UN supervised referendum in Namibia but insisted that it would not be implemented until Cuba withdrew its forces from Angola. Perez de Cuellar had two days of talks in Cape Town with Pik Botha, the ebullient Foreign Minister, but made little progress.

To be a successful or even a contented diplomat you have to take a long view and not sniff at small advances, so small much of the time that journalists often characterise them as failures. On this trip the Secretary-General could only nibble at the problem. The UN's transition plan for moving Namibia to independence had been agreed in outline some years before. It decreed that South Africa and the South West Africa People's Organisation (SWAPO) would both confine their troops to base during the run-up to the UN-supervised election, which would give birth to the new independent state. Despite saying that these would be the usual 'free and fair elections', the UN General Assembly had long before declared that SWAPO was the sole representative of the Namibian people. Consequently when Perez de Cuellar went to Namibia he met representatives from most of the other political parties but could not negotiate with them. Equally frustrating for him was that he could not negotiate about the Cuban troops who were defending the Angolan government against rebels armed and supplied by South Africa. The Pretoria government had made this its key sticking point. It claimed that the Cubans ought to leave before the UN transition plan was implemented because otherwise the Cubans might install SWAPO in power regardless of the true result of the poll. The real reason was that both Cuba and SWAPO spelled communism to the conservative South Africans. So the only concrete result of these talks, which advanced the independence process a fraction, was that South Africa withdrew its objection to Finnish troops being part of the UN peacekeeping force which would hold the ring during the period prior to the elections. Only when the Cuban economy began to crumble and some South African leaders were inching towards dismantling apartheid some six years later was the UN able to bring about an independent Namibia after more than 20 years of guerrilla war.

After the talks in Cape Town the Secretary-General was taken to the northern border of Namibia in an executive jet by some high-ranking South African civil servants in order to impress upon him that South Africa had everything under control. His staff and the media had to follow in the belly of a C130 transport plane, sitting on the floor amid piles of supplies. The flight from Windhoek took several hours as Namibia is a huge country, 800 miles from south to north. On arrival at Ruacana we were ferried to a hydroelectric power station on the Cunene River overlooking the border. All was quiet, not a man could be seen inside Angola. Yielding to the UN seemed many years away.

After less than an hour we jumped back into the planes to fly 200 miles back south again to the Etosha Pan game park where we were put up in a hotel overlooking a large water-hole. At dusk you could watch the elephants, kudus and occasionally lions drink their fill as you sat on the veranda of the hotel sipping gin and tonic. Unfortunately I did not see much of this wildlife because I had to send an interview

and a story back to London. By the time I had the report and the tape
ready the telephone office was closed. But someone kindly told me,
'Don't worry, after hours you can climb in a back window.' Which
indeed I did and found to my surprise that I could turn on the equipment
and make it work. I quickly got through to an operator but mistakenly
asked for London only to be put through to East London on the Indian
Ocean. I tried again and eventually was put through to *The World
Tonight*. Using the makeshift crocodile clips to feed the tape and to
boost my voice I was able to send my report and the interview with a
South African MP. Only to be told by the producer at the other end
when I had finished that they had moved on to another story. As there
was still more than an hour to go before programme time I felt they
had panicked too soon. Sadly, some of my colleagues preferred to go
for a speaker from the 'rep company' rather than wait a little longer for
an original report from the back of beyond.

The next morning we flew back to the capital, Windhoek, for the
Secretary-General's news conference with the local media. At the end of
this session the SG's spokesman, Francois Giuliani, announced that our
bus would leave in half an hour. As on several previous occasions the
bus had actually left very late I did not hurry to be exactly on time
but alas I chose the wrong day. Finding that the bus had gone I hailed
a taxi and gave the instruction, 'to the airport', only to be answered by,
'Which one?' I had not realised there were two, one was the Windhoek
city airport and the other 30 kilometres away, was the international
airport. We had landed twice at the city airport but I guessed that we
would depart from the international. It was a very risky guess. I knew
if I was wrong I would be stranded in Namibia and quite unable to
follow the UN party to Angola as there were no diplomatic relations
between the two countries and no commercial flights.

No sooner had I chanced my arm than the taxi driver announced
that he was out of petrol and drove off in the opposite direction to a
filling station. All this time I was fretting that the UN plane would
leave without me. Once the tank was filled we set out westwards through
the scrub in the hope that we would arrive in time at the right place.
On the way over a mountain pass we caught up with a large oil tanker.
On a twisting narrow road we could not overtake for what seemed an
age. Eventually when in sight of the airport I could see the UN plane
still on the runway. We drove straight on to the airfield without going

through the terminal or any passport control. I paid off the taxi driver with a good tip and then walked slowly across the airport with my case just to make the point that their hurry-up deadline was all too spurious.

As he had just been negotiating with the arch enemy of black Africa the SG now had to report progress to Angola. At Luanda airport he was greeted by a large crowd obviously drummed up by the governing party. Perez de Cuellar was often underrated but he certainly rose to this occasion with an off-the-cuff speech in Portuguese amid the hurly-burly of the demonstration. A huge banner proclaimed that the struggle for independence would continue and that victory was certain. The SG nodded in its direction by saying, 'My struggle is also for peace and my victory is also certain.' A rare moment when he sounded more like a politician than a diplomat.

After that he and his staff were whisked off in one direction while the media were sent to a hotel on the water's edge beside the harbour. No sooner had we reached our rooms than we were recalled and sent by bus to a government guest house 20 miles away outside Luanda. In the evening the UN party was given a grand dinner in a large hall with many locals in attendance. The entertainment seemed to be a version of tribal dancing corrupted with excruciating music, inappropriate dress and vulgar gestures, probably taken from western television. The main dish was some very tough goat which the next day on the plane to Geneva made most of us ill. Instead of flying on straightaway I stayed in Geneva a couple of days and then stopped in London for almost a week in order to regain control over my stomach.

As a result I missed all the drama at the Security Council over the shooting down by Soviet fighter planes of the Korean airliner, flight 007, over the Kamchatka peninsula in Siberia. The crew and 270 passengers were all killed. The Soviet Union showed itself at its worst by defending the indefensible. Its pilots shot down the unarmed commercial airliner after consultation with their commanders on the ground. Its diplomats claimed in the Security Council that the plane was violating Soviet airspace on a spying mission. As I have mentioned before, diplomats sometimes repeat the most blatant lies on behalf of their governments.

This incident not only provoked stern criticism of the Soviet regime throughout the West but also unleashed a burst of anti-communism and anti-UN feelings among the right-wing and redneck sections of America. A few days later in the same month, September 1983, during a meeting of the Committee on Relations with the Host Country, the Soviet spokesmen said that if the US continued to harass delegates as it had with Libya it was time the UN moved out of New York. Responding to this somewhat truculent proposal Charles Lichenstein, then Kirkpatrick's deputy, declared in jocular fashion that if that happened he would be the first down on the dock to wave them off.

This undiplomatic remark played well with the xenophobic sections of the American media but brought sarcastic comments about America's underlying contemptuous attitude to the UN from certain diplomatic delegations in New York. In addition, 24 Democratic congressmen signed a statement saying that by showing 'outright hostility to the goals of the United Nations' Lichenstein had proved himself 'unfit to represent the United States'. They called for his immediate resignation and for the Secretary of State, George Shultz, to retract these remarks. President Reagan, however, seemed to express hearty approval of Lichenstein. He said the US was not asking anyone to go but if they chose to go then 'goodbye'. When Kirkpatrick was questioned about this she declined to comment directly. Instead she said a proposal to hold split sessions of the General Assembly – six months in the Soviet Union and six months in the USA – was an academic suggestion that should be thought about. The six months in the Soviet Union would give delegates the opportunity to see two different ways of life. It was a telling remark leaving her attitude to Lichenstein's remarks just a trifle ambiguous. Lichenstein's scornful phrase got an enormous amount of favourable coverage in the US but actually proved to be his swansong at the UN. A few months later he resigned to take up a post with the Heritage Foundation in Washington.

20

Americana

It may surprise some people outside the media that most of the named BBC correspondents around the world are not employees of the BBC but freelance contributors. The UN correspondent had originally been a senior staff post but some years before I was appointed it was downgraded. During the time of my predecessor, Brian Saxton, some narrow-minded BBC foreign editor decided to close the UN office. It was only with the help of Charles Wheeler, already a veteran foreign correspondent, that Saxton was allowed to keep it open as the UN correspondent but only on a freelance basis. Wheeler said that the BBC 'would be mad' to close such a source of news particularly relevant to its World Service, which then broadcast in English and 35 other languages.

When Brian Saxton left the post in 1979 it was advertised internally as a 'Freelance Contract Post'. The so-called 'contract' gave a minimum guarantee of £6,000 a year, which was half my London staff salary and would have represented penury in New York. It was only by generating a large volume of stories that one could survive in New York at all. In fact most of the BBC's foreign contributors based around the world are still 'contracted' in this way as piece-workers. They are paid a fixed sum for each voice or text piece that is used or commissioned. They are paid for quantity rather than quality. They churn out as many 'updates' on stories as they can, especially nowadays when the BBC has so many more outlets such as Radio 5 Live, and the BBC News Channel and the BBC website which function 24 hours a day.

While I was at the UN the BBC had four staff correspondents in Washington and New York covering television and radio. They all had fine apartments, drew generous expenses alongside their salaries and, compared to me, lived like princes. Some were anxious about 'their' territory and did not like me filing any non-UN news. However, such was the appetite in London for American news there were usually some gaps for me to fill, especially when I covered at weekends. Querky reports for Radio 2 News lasting all of 40 seconds were a particularly fruitful source of revenue. I estimate that about one fifth of my BBC income came from non-UN stories gleaned from the Associated Press wire service, the CBS all-news station, National Public Radio and the New York and Washington newspapers. The most dramatic story of all – the attempted assassination of President Reagan in 1981 – occurred for all to see live on television.

From 2.25 p.m. until nine o'clock in the evening the nation's television stations were locked on to the story, broadcasting without interruption from adverts. The coverage was so professional on the three major networks and on the new Cable News Network that it looked almost rehearsed. For six hours they stayed on the facts and of course on the astonishing video recordings of the event itself.

Thirty seconds of video shot by three cameramen were shown over and over again until we all finally understood this chilling event. It must be said that until the White House announced that the President had been shot, no observer either on the scene or back in the studio had guessed it. The pictures, close though they were, did not at first show a president struck. What they did show were the grisly agonies of the three other men who were much more badly wounded than Reagan.

Through it all the reporters and presenters were so matter of fact about the whole thing, urgent but not excited; relentless, flat-voiced, emotionless; some would say professional and objective. There was no interpretation – just a little speculation about the President's injuries but no seeking after a motive; there was almost an unspoken assumption that it must be another madman. How different from 1963 when America was surprised and insisted for months and then years that there must be some sinister power or at least some conspiracy behind that dreadful deed in Dallas. One man couldn't have done it, they had asserted, over and over again.

It seemed that night that no matter how much sympathy there was for Reagan the question of eliminating handguns from American society was now aimed straight at him; a question that he could no longer brush off with a homily about how they do it in California. Commentators had already recalled him rejecting gun control when John Lennon was murdered in New York by a deranged fan the previous year. Millions, I thought, would want to see what Reagan would say now that he was himself a victim. When he recovered, I speculated, and stood once again in the verbal firing line, when the pleasantries were over, wouldn't that be the first real question? A question that surely he could not dodge any longer. But he and Congress and the American people have done just that with continuing dire consequences.

One story which really stirred my creative juices was the resurgence or persistence of 'creationism' as an acceptable orthodoxy. In March 1981, Arkansas – the buckle of the Bible belt – enacted a law that required biology teachers to give as much time to teaching creationism as to teaching evolution. 'Creationists' dismiss evolution as simply a theory without proof, and claim that their belief deserves equal treatment. The Creation Research Society required its 'scientists' to affirm that 'all basic living things, including man, were made by direct creative Acts of God during creation week, as described in Genesis'. This extraordinary campaign by 'creationists' to belittle and denigrate evolution had already been going on for a century when this law was enacted in Arkansas. That year similar bills were introduced into state legislatures in ten other states and the idea was being pressed in scores of school boards all over the country, a movement that continues to this day.

This Arkansas law of 1981 was sponsored by a 36-year-old insurance man, Senator James Holstead, who told me he was a fundamental Christian who believed in God the Creator. At school and university he had studied biology and chemistry and then believed the theory of evolution. Five years before his bill, however, he came to feel he 'needed a relationship with God' and consequently rejected evolution completely.

But as Holstead's example shows, a scientific education does not necessarily convince those who understand it. In a country where space exploration and genetic engineering seem to deny the existence of a supernatural creator millions of 'educated' people reject the scientific explanation for the origin of the human race.

My four and a half minute broadcast in *From Our Own Correspondent* was actually put on display at the Walker Museum in Liverpool as part of an exhibition featuring Charles Darwin and evolution. Twenty-five years later Christian fundamentalists seem to have more influence in the United States than ever while in Britain religion gets more attention than for many years. In Tony Blair we had the most overtly Christian prime minister since Gladstone. In the name of good community relations we are constantly urged by political leaders to 'respect' the various religions practised by our multi-ethnic population. I find that very difficult. I have no wish to upbraid or insult such groups but I cannot respect their reliance on ancient texts. Belief in the supernatural is quite simply the negation of the intellect.

In those days before mobile phones, satellite phones, email and computers, communicating with London was a constant headache. Because the BBC had immense traffic across the Atlantic it leased a line 24 hours a day. The competition from all the other correspondents and producers to get on the lease line was intense. The only sure time was the morning conference call at 9 a.m. New York time (2 p.m. London time) when each of the correspondents and producers could tell London about the likely news of the day and receive requests or commissions for specific stories or interviews. Most of us took the conference call at home. That was particularly apposite in my case because the UN never really stirred before 11 a.m.

The lease line must have saved money but operating it in the 1980s was often a pain. During office hours it was controlled by the staff in the BBC's New York studio in the Rockefeller Center who were very accommodating but often over-worked. In the evening when correspondents had to use it without the help of engineers it took a long dialling ritual just to connect to the lease line only to find, all too often, that it had an echo. As you broadcast a report to London you could hear your voice bouncing back about half a second later, which was most disconcerting. You could just blast away pretending to ignore it but actually you often lost concentration and then fluffed your lines. Sometimes I simply took my headphones off but that meant that London could not tell me in mid-flow about noise on the line or some other technical hitch. The limitations of the lease line meant that the television correspondents and producers used the normal phones most of the time, greatly adding to the expense. That option was not available to a radio freelance correspondent who had either to wait his turn or in the off hours struggle with the hazards of what now seems primitive technology.

Another hazard was not having an engineer or studio manager to hand who could service and repair one's equipment, such as microphones, and advise on operating equipment, such as tape recorders. When I took up the post in 1980 I was given a new cassette recorder but never told that it would not take metal tape cassettes. One day in my ignorance I put one of the metal (as opposed to plastic) cassettes in my machine only to find the recording of an important interview unusable and yet not understanding why. As I didn't understand the reason I made the same mistake again, which caused great chagrin until one of my UN media colleagues spotted the problem. Although occasionally one of the engineers was able to come over from the BBC New York office, most of the time I was a one-man operation.

As well as a two-room office, I had a soundproof broadcasting cubicle stuffed with equipment with a window on to the Security Council chamber from which I could usually see the faces of the Soviet, British and American ambassadors who sat next to each other. It might be described as an international political eyrie from which one could observe and listen without being overlooked oneself. At an earlier stage no doubt my predecessors had described the scene and broadcast the proceedings live. But by 1980 UN news was rarely thought so compelling that it had to be live. In addition, a closed-circuit television system was installed just as I arrived so all reporters could observe Security Council and General Assembly proceedings without leaving their own offices. Consequently, I did much of my work in the office from the closed-circuit TV and only went into the cubicle to cut a piece of actuality of a debate or to broadcast a dispatch to London.

Actually the BBC office at the UN was just about the best media office in the building. From a second-floor vantage point it overlooked the East River where one could find an interesting diversion whenever one lost concentration, such as while reading a dense UN report. Long lines of barges were always being towed or pushed past my window and on most days an ocean-going vessel would also steam past. More exciting were the seaplanes and helicopters that operated from two bases about half a mile further downstream towards the Brooklyn Bridge. The seaplanes were used for flying out to the far end of Long Island where many New Yorkers either had beach houses or teamed up with a group to rent a room or even just a bed in one of the fashionable towns such as the Hamptons. Joining a summer co-op was a quintessential New York experience, which I should have sampled but never got round to. At the time the price for a summer season seemed very high.

New York is regarded by many people around the world as an exciting eldorado. Its central site on Manhattan Island surrounded by two great rivers and protected by a fine harbour takes a lot of beating. The skyscrapers are but a dramatic way of emphasising the wealth that the city creates and attracts. The eight million people form a critical mass, which supports many cultural assets such as superb museums, libraries, many movie houses and plenty of theatres with all kinds of repertoire, including opera, ballet and modern dance. For the visitor it's the ideal place with a very wide choice of entertainment. The locals are generally very thrusting, innovative and diverse. But live there a while as I did for nearly six years and you notice the cracks in this façade.

I lived in an old apartment block on West 176th street near to the George Washington Bridge, which overlooked a small, neglected park. Most of the other residents were either Cuban exiles or immigrants from the Dominican Republic. It certainly wasn't smart or very secure. There was no concierge and the residents hired an armed security guard for each evening shift until midnight to stand in the hall and look tough. One night as I was returning late from the UN in a taxi, my driver stopped suddenly in front of a neighbouring block as a man rushed out chased by a naked woman screaming 'Rape! Rape!' We leapt out of the taxi and chased the man for a block but he escaped into the Subway station. On returning to the apartment block we found the woman still screaming abuse but by this time someone had given her a blanket. Within minutes the police arrived with a suspect and asked us to identify him. As neither of us had seen his face for more than a few seconds on a dark night we both said we could not be sure if he was the same man who had fled from the woman. For the police it was all in a night's work. I never heard an end to this story.

From this apartment I used to travel to the UN on a fast but decrepit Subway train in which one day a young man sitting too close to me asked, 'Ever been shot?' His accent was so thick that for few seconds I couldn't understand him and perhaps he couldn't understand me. Once I saw the ominous bulge in his pocket I moved off smartly to the other end of the carriage. At the next station he and his partner in the attempted shakedown jumped out and raced up the stairs.

The New York Subway must have been the only metropolitan underground that had 'sleeping cars' – in every train in this dilapidated system you could find a carriage without lights and another where only half the doors would open. Inside, the walls, seats, windows and maps were all covered with spray-painted graffiti while the floors were often awash with beer cans and litter. The stations were no better – most looked like a cross between a gaol and a catacomb. Iron bars fenced off redundant corridors, water dripped from the roof, rust and dirt were found everywhere. The air was putrid because there was little ventilation and virtually no lavatories. Down between the lines were piles of rubbish not to mention the fearless rats who knew a good home when they saw one. The air-conditioning worked in only a fraction of the carriages, making them intolerable in the summer heat and humidity.

The Subway was like this for years until a driver was killed in a crash after passing two red signals. It then emerged that trains were running without proper lights and horns because the city was broke and the state government would not increase the subsidy. Maintenance was deferred on outmoded equipment. But all this neglect resulted from what many thought a virtue: the fares were cheap, insanely, politically cheap, covering only half the cost of operating the system and leaving nothing to provide for capital replacement and investment. A system that doesn't pay for itself is at the mercy of politicians who never use it, of taxpayers who won't pay for it and the many voters who live way beyond its reach. In 1981 after the accident the politicians in Albany and City Hall did increase the subsidy and both the Subway and the rackety buses were slowly improved. Public transport in many American cities was then a cautionary tale on how not to manage and finance it.

Collectively New York was a very wealthy city, yet that description could all too easily be refined to what J.K. Galbraith famously called 'Private affluence and public squalor'. In the 1970s and 80s the city government was near to bankrupt and many public facilities besides the Subway, such as roads, parks and public housing, were a disgrace. Much of the Westside highway, for instance, had fallen into such disrepair that it was closed. Recently, I'm glad to say this highway has been turned into a popular public park. Nor was it just a failure of government or politics in that citizens did not pay enough tax. Great areas of the Bronx and Harlem had just been abandoned by private landlords unable to manage their property. Block upon block stood empty with boarded-up windows and battered-in doors occupied only by down-and-outs and vermin. Of course there were many well-appointed apartment blocks for most levels of income plus millions of pleasant suburban homes in the outer boroughs, Westchester County and across the Hudson in New Jersey. New York has an economic system that provides a good living for most of the urban masses but leaves far too many high and dry without income, housing or even food. There is a 'Third World' right in New York. No wonder that it was then a far more violent and noisy city than London.

When I began at the UN in 1980 I went to a local social services office to obtain a social security number so I could work for Canadian Broadcasting and National Public Radio. After waiting in a queue for some time I was seen by a weary young woman who before I could speak opened up with, 'So what do you want? Food stamps?' I don't think I looked on my beam ends. I was certainly wearing a jacket and tie! I laughed and declined the offer. More than five per cent of New Yorkers claim food stamps mainly because they are unemployed or, despite minimum wage laws, actually get very small pay packets. It's a long-running blot on the American system and way of life.

The BBC contract required me to give a good service of news from the UN but one of the BBC bosses thought that he owned me just as if I were a staff correspondent. In May 1980 I was asked to drop everything and wing off to Miami to cover some hideous black riots. On that day I was just completing a 20-minute profile of Waldheim for the Evening Sequence, which was to be broadcast the next day. I explained that I was willing to go to Miami but News in London had to square it with the editor of Evening Current Affairs because he would have had to postpone the Waldheim profile. As no one came back to me I went ahead with the Waldheim programme and someone else covered Miami.

Many months later when I was back in London on leave a boss known as 'snake lips' completely lost his rag over this incident. He accused me of not responding to the news room's direction and threatened to terminate my contract. I explained about the Waldheim programme taking priority and that if Miami was so important they should have persuaded Evening Current Affairs and Radio 4 to postpone their programme. But he didn't listen and continued to shout at me as if I was one of his minions. Managers are all too rarely called to account for such bullying behaviour.

Apart from him, the other desk editors I dealt with daily both at Broadcasting House and Bush House were a pleasure to work with. None of them gave me 'instructions' but only made requests to cover particular stories for particular outlets such as Radio Newsreel or the Eastern Service.

21

Peru

In April 1984 I went with the Secretary-General's party to Panama and
Peru. It was the first time he had returned to his own country since
being appointed two years previously so he and his staff were entertained
in style. He was greeted on the tarmac by President Belaúnde and by a
large military parade consisting of units from all the Peruvian armed
services. He was given Peru's highest honour and the keys to the city of
Lima. During his stay he was fêted by Fernando Schwalb Lopez-Aldana,
who was both Prime Minister and Foreign Minister, at a fine eighteenth-
century palace cum office called the Torre Tagle. His main UN appointment
was to open a session of the UN Economic Commission for Latin
America, which was particularly apposite at that time because the continent
was in the middle of a huge debt crisis and Peru's position was one of
the worst. The International Monetary Fund had earlier advised Peru to
make deep cuts in public spending – a policy which the Prime Minister
accepted but which the President rejected. While President and Prime
Minister were all smiles, entertaining the Secretary-General, they were
at the same time trying to solve a Cabinet crisis, which ended with the
Prime Minister's resignation. It takes considerable sangfroid to be able
to be cordial on the surface while getting to grips with dire political
and economic circumstances.

Besides sovereign debt, which 25 years later we have come to know
too much about ourselves, the other issue gripping Peru also has a
contemporary ring. Peru was under attack from a Maoist terrorist group
called the Sendero Luminoso or the Shining Path who perpetrated many
gruesome crimes. Many Peruvians had called for the return of the death
penalty as a punishment and a deterrent. Only the week before the UN
party had arrived three ordinary criminals had tried to bargain their way
out of gaol by taking hostages and murdering three of them. So although
Perez de Cuellar was the guest of honour and domestic crime was not
technically within the UN's responsibility he did not equivocate when

asked the tough question at a news conference. As a lawyer he said he was fundamentally opposed to the death penalty because justice could not be infallible. With any judgment there was always a margin of error. However, he totally repudiated terrorism even when carried out for sincere reasons. It was a violation of human rights and a cancer on society but that still did not persuade him. Despite the worldwide resurgence of terrorism he declared he remained totally opposed to the death penalty for any crime. UN officials are rarely so forthright.

Following up on that personal affirmation the Secretary-General also talked about a little known aspect of his work which revealed his own priorities. Asked about the UN's own record on human rights he said he dealt with difficult individual cases about once a fortnight. When a case was complicated or when a country would not cooperate with the UN High Commissioner on Human Rights then he tried to intervene himself, usually quietly without any public announcement. His last success only a few weeks previously had been the release of the Polish UN employee Alicia Wesolowska after five years in gaol, a case I have discussed in detail in Chapter 17.

We had travelled to Peru by Eastern Airlines, which was once a profitable airline but now, like many other famous names, such as Trans World Airlines and Pan American, is no more. On the leg from Panama City to Lima, Michael Stopford, one of the SG's speech writers, soft-talked the airline into upgrading the UN team to first class, including the journalists. BBC correspondents in Washington said they always insisted on going first class but no one ever suggested the UN correspondent should be that grand. And frankly I'm not sorry. The food and wine on this three-hour flight were absolutely superb, so much so that I felt it would be fatal to travel like this on a regular basis. The effect on one's weight and metabolism would not be benign let alone on one's ability to think straight and broadcast coherently. My feeling is that top people who live and travel in such luxury are giving themselves a handicap. They do not function as well as they could do when more sober and less well fed. In the 1990s when Dr Michael Irwin, Medical Director of the World Bank in Washington, pointed out that first-class travel was unnecessary and a waste of money the international civil servants rounded on him as if he had betrayed their class. They declared they were important people and they needed the space and quiet in which to work, which was only provided in the first-class seats. In effect they elbowed him out of the job. But he was right on both economic and health grounds.

In Lima we stayed in a large four-star hotel where again I was too busy covering stories and filing reports to have anything but the briefest of meals in the coffee shop. Just as well not only for my waistline but also for my bill. Inflation was running so strongly at the time that the hotel's price lists were upgraded each evening to account for it. While the main facilities looked grand the communications left much to be desired. In my room the phone line was clipped under the bed so I could not fit my 'alligator clips', which we used to plug the tape recorder into the telephone in order to boost the sound level and get a wider range of tone. I could only speak therefore directly into the phone, which in those days before universal satellites, meant very poor reception in London. As much of my material concerning the Economic Conference was of prime interest to the BBC's Latin American services who would have to translate my voice reports anyway I hoped I could send much of it by telex instead. In New York I could give my typed reports to a telex operator who retyped them instantly better than my original. But alas in this hotel the telex room was no more than a broom cupboard with an overworked telex operator with piles of stuff to send before mine. He pointed to another machine for me to use. I tried my best but I fear the end result in London was well below par. I had never worked on a telex machine directly before and I found it had all sorts of quirks and systems of its own that I could not figure out. My copy therefore was littered with mistakes which I could not correct and I suspect whoever handled it in London must have cursed me, if it was used at all. In retrospect I should have offered the operator an 'incentive' to send mine first but I hadn't worked long enough in the country to know if that would be an acceptable practice. Contact with London was a headache throughout my stay.

Following this trip to Lima with the Secretary-General in April 1984 Jennifer and I felt that now was the ideal time to have a last fling in South America. So when I finished at the UN in August we spent three weeks in Peru. At the time America and Peru were having a prolonged row over landing rights. There were no direct flights between the two countries so we had to change planes in the Cayman Islands *en route*. On the return journey we ran into gross overbooking by three airlines. Returning from Cuzco to Lima we found the Fawcett Airlines plane overbooked three days running and only got seats in the end after flashing my UN correspondent's identity card. A couple of days later it happened again in Lima where our carrier, Fawcett to New York, was full and we had to wait all day for two spare seats on Aeroperu. This time we had to change planes in Jamaica. As a result of these delays we had very little time to pack up my flat in New York. For the last leg back to London we were again delayed by airline inefficiency. This time the People's Airline, which then was a big business although it's since been gobbled by another, couldn't produce the seats for which we had booked. Luckily we were guided over to another plane for London though in the process someone stole some excellent Peruvian pisco sour from our luggage trolley. Nowadays airlines are obliged to compensate you for such overbooking but not then.

At the beginning of our holiday in Peru we went to the Explorers' Club in Lima for information and spotted a slogan pinned to the wall: 'Go there before it's all paved over.' It seemed a good omen for an Andean trip. As we left the club the city was plunged into darkness by a power failure. The only light came from the headlights of cars stuck in traffic jams. Just walking along the uneven pavements was hazardous by day as well as night as there were many potholes where cast-iron manhole covers had been stolen. At the same time there had been a bomb near the American embassy which added to the confusion. It was probably the work of the Sendero Luminoso who were still gaining in strength. Somehow we stumbled our way back to our hotel.

After a few days in Lima we drove in a little car to the mountain town of Huaraz where we found a well-run hotel managed by a Swiss couple. We then drove further into the mountains hoping to find somewhere to camp. Beyond Huaraz the roads were more like river beds, full of rocks and potholes. Coming back towards Huaraz we had to drive so slowly down the steep road that three small boys jumped on our back fender and hitched a lift clutching the roof rack. At our speed it seemed quite harmless and for them a lot of fun. The back window was so covered in dust we were not aware of them for some minutes. After they had dismounted one of our tyres burst a little further on just outside a hamlet. Almost at once some teenage boys dashed up to change the wheel for us in no time at all. They had clearly done it before. As a way of thanking them we gave them a lift, inside the car, a few miles miles down to a village and it was smiles all round.

Through the hotel we arranged a five-day trek in the Andes which went over a pass to a remote valley. We were accompanied by an *arriero*, a muleteer who took care of our packs and tent and cooked our food. Each day we would start out first with our light day-sacks while he was still packing up the tents but before lunch his mules would trot past us so that he reached the end of the day's trek long before us. Near the start he bought a chicken from a farmer which he tied alive to the saddle of a mule to be consumed a day later. Unfortunately this same chicken made me very ill, rather spoiling the climb up to the 15,000-foot pass surrounded by spectacular 20,000-foot peaks. That third night of the trek we camped in a hamlet so isolated that we felt we had really reached that mythical place, 'the back of beyond'. Next morning turning back west we were confronted by a wide dirt road snaking its way over the crest of the Andes. It had obviously been built recently by the military to take large trucks and even tanks. It was yet to be 'paved over' but it probably is by now. How right the Explorers' Club had been.

The end of our Peruvian adventure also marked the end of my four and a half years at the UN. There were new adventures ahead, first as a freelance radio presenter and then as an academic lasting many years beyond normal retirement age. Instead of my career tailing off it ended on a high and happy note if not accompanied by the glamour of reporting on the United Nations. At the same time I used my experience in the 'Peace Palace' on the East River as an activist in the United Nations Association, becoming a member of the Board of Directors and the chairman of the London and South East region. So far this period has lasted 26 years and has been full of interest and new experiences. But they are beyond the scope of this book.

Coda

Douglas Hurd when Foreign Secretary in the 1990s described the media in a lecture as 'bestride the world wielding a searchlight', illuminating some things very intensely but ignoring many other events. In this book I have tried to shine my torch of insight into some corners which have received little attention as well as giving a new angle on some familiar news stories which made global headlines.

The purpose of journalism is to report, explain and criticise, all of which are essential to the functioning of a modern state with a mass citizenry. It's the primary way of conveying information and gaining the citizens' compliance, in authoritarian as much as in democratic states. The practice of journalism in its various forms is usually interesting, often exciting, frequently fun and sometimes influential. But it essentially feeds off those who govern, or manage, or manufacture, or develop new ideas. In my view it is certainly much easier than government or diplomacy. Forming policy and implementing it is much more difficult than anything attempted by journalists. From time to time journalists and broadcasters aspire to expose politicians and to bring about the resignations of supposed failures or alleged crooks. Trenchant and necessary though these critics or accusers may be, do not be fooled into thinking that they ought to be running the government or managing the company or even coaching the team. Running the country, responding to a plethora of pressures and foreseeing future snags is altogether much more difficult. Journalists should not be deferential and should feel able to ask any question of anyone in authority but equally they should not be arrogant or overbearing or imply that exercising power is a simple matter.

When my father died in 1974 all sorts of questions came to mind that I should have asked before it was too late. I know almost nothing about the character of Eric's father and mother and what the atmosphere was like in his home. Most important of all I don't know why his

307

parents did not ensure he continued his education beyond the age of thirteen. I could have asked his siblings but it's too late now.

I suspect that many people have similar feelings and questions when relatives or close friends die. I trust that with this book I have anticipated some of the questions which my children or grandchildren might be curious about. I hope also that I have chronicled a reasonably interesting and productive life which may correct or balance the popular accounts of how English people lived in the twentieth century.

Jennifer and Keith Hindell lived entirely without recreational drugs, pop music, any interest in celebrities, very little television viewing, never went to a pub just to drink, never went to a religious service except for weddings and funerals, took moderately strenuous exercise until infirmity prevented it, cooked their own meals and never had takeaways. They did use computers and email but even in the twenty-first century they found little use for a mobile phone or the various exotic applications that go with it and no time for the social networks such as Facebook and Twitter. I suppose you could describe us as 'digitally sub-normal'. Yet I'm sure many other people lived in similar ways and that the advertisers', statisticians' and sociologists' profiles of 'normal' English life are therefore often misleading. Historians and novelists beware!

Index

309

Barton Stacey 96
Batchelor, Teddy 23, 24
Battensby, Lalla 150
Battle of Britain 26, 27–8
BCCI bank collapse 165
Beamish, Andrew 53
beard, at Oxford 115
Beau Site hotel, Zermatt 77
Beauchamp, Joan, anthology, *Poems of Revolt* 13
Bede, *Ecclesiastical History of the English People* 109
Begin, Menachem 211–12
Belaunde 301
Belgrano, sinking 276, 278, 279
Belloc, Hilaire, 'The Rebel' 13–14
Beloff, Max 210
Ben MacDhui 82
Beowulf 114
Berwyns 95
Bevan, Aneurin 72, 168
Biden, Joseph 258
Biner, Peter (Matterhorn guide) 78–80
Bionnassay 91
Birkett, Peter 199–200
Birmingham Pregnancy Advisory Service *see* British Pregnancy Advisory Service (BPAS)
Black Watch 100
Blair, Tony 295
   government, 'Cash for Peerages' scandal 179
Blaven 83
Bleakley, Dennis 157, 165, 166
Bliss, Brian 207, 208, 210, 211, 214
Blix, Hans 271
Blocker, Joel 257
Bluebird racing cars 5
boarding schools, verdict on 67–9
Bob Graham Round 209
Bonarjee, Stephen 157–8, 162, 170, 171, 207, 209
Boston, Terry 163
Botha, Pik 287
Bowlby, Nell 41, 64–5
Bowlby, Oliver 41, 45, 50, 61, 64–5
Bowman, Phyllis 200
Braintree, evacuation to 22–3
Bricklayers Arms, Edmonton 15
Bridson, Geoffrey 171, 176
Britain, UN veto usage 230–1
British Broadcasting Corporation (BBC)

Bush House News 286
Documentaries 1965–1969 171–80
editorial independence 210–11, 226
   Focus 171–5
   Focus on Abortion 181
   Focus on Housing 172
   Focus on the Honours System 178–9
   Focus on the North Sea 174–5
Home Service 30–1
   Ten O'clock 155–9, 163–70
   The World at One 162
   Today programme 158–9, 162
objectives 2
reorganisations 207, 213–14
technical issues 155–7, 296–7
Third Programme 163–4
   United States series 176–7
UN correspondent 145, 198, 229–74, 293–4
British Overseas Airways Corporation (BOAC)
   and *Rookes v. Barnard* 169–70
British Oxygen factory, Edmonton 6
British Pregnancy Advisory Service (BPAS) 187, 188–92
British Tigers in the Alps (documentary) 89–90
Brittain, RSM Ronald 96–7, 98
Broad Stand, Scafell 81
Brocklehurst, Geoffrey 47
Brown, Gordon, 'family values' 31
Browne, Stella 185
Bryant, Arthur, works 42
Bryant, Philip 'Pumph' 47, 61, 62
Bryant, Ted (KH's great-uncle) 126
Buchan, John 118
Buckingham University 210
Bullingdon Club 115
bullying, Harrow 49–50
Bunche, Ralph 237, 248
Burgess, Alan 171, 172
Burns, Haywood 164
Burns, Jock 101
Butler, Richard 271

Cader Idris 83
Cairngorms 82, 84
Camacho, George 172
Cameron, David, at Oxford 115
Camp David Agreement 1978 215, 257
Canadian Alpine Club 85
Cape Verde Islands 286–7

INDEX

Dauphiné 87–8
David & Harry, American students 117–18
Davies, Dick 141–2
Davies, W.H., poems 13
Davison, Ann, *By Gemini* ... 130
Davison, Frank 130
Day Care Abortion 187, 204
de Gaulle, Charles 172
de Manio, Jack 158–9, 162
Dean, Peter 90–2
Dean, Shirley 92
Debs, Eugene 177
Decatur (Illinois), field research 129
Deers, strike against 10–11
Defoe, Daniel 227
Deng Xiaoping 240
Department of Health and Social Security, and PAS 188, 203
Derber, Milton 129
  & Chalmers, *Plant Union-Management Relations* ... 130–1
Derbyshire Peak District, holidays 31
Dibona (guide) 87
Diggory, Peter 186, 188, 189
Dinky-Toy aeroplanes 24
disciplinary system, Harrow 41–2, 53–4, 59–61
dissident groups, and UNCA 246–7
Dom 90
Donoughue, Bernard 141, 155
Douglas, Paul 138
drama clubs, Oxford 113–14
Duffield, Gervase 57
Duggleby, Vincent 214
dyslexia, Eric Hindell and 9, 10

East St Louis (Illinois), field research 129–30
Eastern Airlines 302
Eastern Gas Board 141
Easy Troop 100–4
Ediswan lamp factory, Ponders End 6
Edmonton, lifestyle 14–15, 18–19, 21, 23–32
Education Act 1944 33, 39
Ehrlichman, John, Nixon's Chief Domestic Advisor 214
Eiger Nordwand 76
Elgol 83
Elinor (Army Yacht) 106–7
Ellis, Havelock 189
Elstein, David 172

Emery, John 86
Empire Windrush troopship 108
Enchanted Mountains, Pyrenees 93
Enfield, Borough 6, 19
Enfield Highway Co-operative Society 6
Epping Forest, walks in 12–13
Eton Fives
  Harrow 42, 44, 52–3
  Oxford 112
European Common Market 1960–2 142
evacuation organiser, Violet 16–17
Evans, Marilyn 155
Evening Standard 168
Everest 75
Exocet missiles 276
Explorers' Club, Lima 304

Fairfield nursing home (PAS) 184–6, 188–9, 191–2, 202
Faisal II King of Iraq 65
Falklands invasion 3, 237, 275–83
family holidays, climbing 81–4
  Chamonix 1939 80–1
  Zermatt 1947 76–80
Farhang, Dr Mansur 248–9
farming, Harrow school farm 57–8
Farrar, Tom 132, 134, 139
Faulkner, Brian 221
Faulks, Sebastian, *The Fatal Englishman* 113
Fawcett Airlines 303, 304
Fawkham clinic (BPAS) 191–2
field gunnery 95
first class travel 302
Fleming Committee, 1944 report 39, 68
Fletcher, Sir Frank 72
Focus on Abortion (BBC) 181
Focus on Housing (BBC) 172
Focus on the Honours System (BBC) 178–9
Focus on the North Sea (BBC) 174–5
folk dancing club, Illinois 132
food, Harrow 43
Foot, Paul 211
football
  childhood 25
  refereeing 103
Forbes, Muriel, and Harrow/ Middlesex cooperation 41, 70
Ford, Gerald 215, 226
Foreman, The 169
Forest School Camps 68–9
Fort William, holidays 31, 81
'Forty Years On' 48

312

Hindell, Eric Percival (KH's father) 6,
9–19, 30–1, 307–8
and education 9–10, 12, 17
and poetry 13–14, 36
and public libraries 12
and sports 26
climbing 76–84
dyslexia 9, 10
Home Guard 11–12
Mont Blanc 80
socialism 10–11, 17–18
trade union activity 10–11
Hindell family
lifestyle/holidays 14–16, 18–19, 30–1
origins 9
Hindell, Jennifer (née Thomas; KH's wife)
and climbing 83, 85, 87–9, 92–3,
122–3
and hitch-hiking 116
and Illinois Historical Survey 139
at Oxford 113–15
at Speech Research Laboratory (Il) 132
buys cottage 209
climbing honeymoon 122–3
daughters, birth/ childhood 147–54
mugged in 2000 2
wedding 121–2
Hindell, Juliet 114, 147–54
and climbing 83
Alleyn's School 154
Hindell, Keith
childhood
early life 1, 5–6, 16, 19
evacuation 22–3, 27–8
food 29–30
London blitz 27
sports/ games 22, 23–6
education
primary schools 21–30
Tottenham Grammar School 28–9,
33–7
Harrow 1, 39–73
modern history degree, Oxford
109–15, 121
postgraduate 121
Illinois assistantship 121, 125–40
family see under specific names
marriage see Hindell, Jennifer
works
Abortion Law Reformed 182, 227
journal articles 144–5
plays 225–8

An End to an Auld Sang 227
Catching Fishes For My Tea 227–8
The Trial of Andrew Johnson 225–6
Trade Union Membership 142
see also British Broadcasting
Corporation (BBC)
Hindell, Lily Jane (née Sanderson; KH's
paternal grandmother) 9
Hindell, Marjorie, (KH's aunt) 19
Hindell, Percival Nicholson (KH's paternal
grandfather) 9
Hindell, Raymond, (KH's uncle) 19
Hindell, Violet Ethel (née Hart; KH's
mother) 5, 6–7, 12, 15–19, 30–1
and education 17
evacuation organiser 16–17
Hiroshima bomb 31
hitch-hiking 116–21
HMS Conqueror (submarine) 278
HMS Sheffield (destroyer) 279
Holstead, Senator James 295
Home Guard, Eric Hindell and 11–12
homosexuality, Harrow and 68
Hong Kong
Japanese and 101–2, 105
posting 98, 99, 100–7
Hong Kong Regiment 103–4
honours system, Focus programme 178–9
Hornli ridge, Matterhorn 78–9
Hotel Sonne, Zermatt 76–7
house system
Harrow 41–4
Tottenham 33
Howard, Anthony 112
Hoyer-Millar, Garth 52
Hudson Review 215
Hughes, Langston 164
Humphrey, Hubert 177
Huntingford, Peter 186, 187–8, 196–7
Hurd, Douglas 307

Ieng Sary 254
Iftikhar Ali 244
Illini Readers 132
Illinois Historical Survey 139
Illinois University, assistantship 121, 125–40
Indian Express 245
individuals, uniqueness 2–3
Institute of Labor & Industrial Relations,
Urbana 121, 128–40
International Atomic Energy Agency (IAEA)
267